Legal, Ethical, and Technical Dilemmas in Military Artificial Intelligence

Bérénice Boutin · Taylor Kate Woodcock · Sadjad Soltanzadeh
Editors

Legal, Ethical, and Technical Dilemmas in Military Artificial Intelligence

ASSER PRESS

Springer

Editors
Bérénice Boutin
T.M.C. Asser Institute
The Hague, The Netherlands

Taylor Kate Woodcock
Research Department
T.M.C. Asser Institute
The Hague, The Netherlands

Sadjad Soltanzadeh
Department of Philosophy
University of Twente
Enschede, The Netherlands

ISBN 978-94-6265-758-8 ISBN 978-94-6265-759-5 (eBook)
https://doi.org/10.1007/978-94-6265-759-5

This work was supported by the T.M.C. Asser Instituut and the Dutch Research Council, Platform for Responsible Innovation.
This volume was developed in the context of the DILEMA Project on Designing International Law and Ethics into Military Artificial Intelligence, and was funded by the Dutch Research Council, Platform for Responsible Innovation (Nederlandse Organisatie voor Wetenschappelijk Onderzoek, Maatschappelijk Verantwoord Innoveren (NWO-MVI)).
Published by T.M.C. ASSER PRESS, The Hague, The Netherlands www.asserpress.nl
Produced and distributed for T.M.C. ASSER PRESS by Springer-Verlag Berlin Heidelberg

This T.M.C. ASSER PRESS imprint is published by the registered company Springer-Verlag GmbH, DE, part of Springer Nature.
The registered company address is: Heidelberger Platz 3, 14197 Berlin, Germany

Preface

This book emerges from the DILEMA project on Designing International Law and Ethics into Military Artificial Intelligence, which commenced in September 2020 and concluded in April 2025. The DILEMA project was made possible through a grant of over €600,000 awarded by the Dutch Research Council (NWO). The project was led by Principal Investigator Dr. Bérénice Boutin, Senior Researcher in International Law, and hosted at the T.M.C. Asser Instituut.

Over the years, the interdisciplinary research team comprised the following experts: Prof. Terry Gill, Emeritus Professor of Military Law; Prof. Tom van Engers, Professor of Legal Knowledge Management; Prof. Marten Zwanenburg, Professor of Military Law; Dr. Sadjad Soltanzadeh, Researcher in Ethics and Philosophy of Technology; Dr. Tomasz Zurek, Researcher in Computer Science; Dr. Magdalena Pacholska, Researcher in International Law and Marie Skłodowska-Curie Fellow; and Taylor Kate Woodcock and Klaudia Klonowska, both PhD Researchers in International Law. The close-knit interdisciplinary collaboration at the heart of DILEMA allowed us to advance our understanding of complex issues at the intersection of law, ethics, and technology.

The DILEMA project also worked in collaboration with project partners from academia (Geneva Graduate Institute (IHEID)), applied research (TNO), policy (Dutch Ministries of Defence and of Foreign Affairs, NATO Office of Legal Affairs), industry (Thales Nederland), civil society (PAX), think tanks (The Hague Centre for Strategic Studies (HCSS)), and professional organisations (International Society for Military Law and Law of War (ISMLLW)). This approach ensured that our research remained grounded in ongoing developments while also maintaining direct relevance to current policy needs.

The present book results in part from the DILEMA 2023 Conference organised on 12–13 October 2023. Bringing together over 80 participants and 25 speakers from more than ten countries, the conference covered broad and interdisciplinary topics around the risks, challenges, and opportunities of military AI. It offered a valuable forum for both junior and senior researchers to share their perspectives, as well as a momentous platform for building local and international connections across disciplines.

In this volume, six chapters were produced as a result of the DILEMA 2023 Conference, and six chapters were contributed by members of the DILEMA project team and DILEMA project partners. Together, they reflect a broad diversity of engagements on different aspects of the topic and from varied disciplines. As such, the volume offers a notable and valuable contribution to the ongoing scholarly and policy debates on military AI.

The Hague, The Netherlands
March 2025

Bérénice Boutin

Contents

Part III Technical Approaches

Part IV Governance and Accountability

Editors and Contributors

About the Editors

Bérénice Boutin is a Senior Researcher in International Law at the Asser Institute, University of Amsterdam (The Netherlands). She leads the DILEMA project on Designing International Law and Ethics into Military Artificial Intelligence, for which she secured a grant of over €600,000 from the Dutch Research Council (NWO). Her research explores the interplay between new technologies, such as artificial intelligence, and international law. This includes examining how international law shapes the governance and regulation of emerging technologies, as well as how these technologies challenge core notions and concepts of international law.

Taylor Kate Woodcock is a researcher in public international law at the Asser Institute, University of Amsterdam (The Netherlands). She researches international legal practices, human agency, and AI-enabled technologies. Her doctoral thesis, entitled *Human-Machine (Learning) Interactions: War and Law in the AI Era* and written as part of the DILEMA project, examines how the use of AI in military targeting operations can shape practices of legal reasoning and the exercise of human agency. Taylor has research experience in various fields of public international law, including international humanitarian law, international human rights law, international criminal law, and international arms control and disarmament law.

Sadjad Soltanzadeh is a Researcher in Philosophy of Technology at the University of Twente (The Netherlands). From 2020 to 2023, he was part of the DILEMA project, where his research explored the constituents of human autonomy, the limitations of autonomous systems, and the interaction between human and machine agency. In his book, *Problem-Solving Technologies: A User-Friendly Philosophy* (2022), Soltanzadeh has introduced the *activity realist* approach, which argues that the study of technical systems must be accompanied by the study of the human activities they are intended to support.

Contributors

Thomas Christian Bächle University of Bonn, Bonn, Germany;
Humboldt Institute for Internet and Society (HIIG), Berlin, Germany

Iris Cohen Thales Netherlands B.V., Delft, The Netherlands

Rianne Gouman Thales Netherlands B.V., Delft, The Netherlands

Elisabeth Hoffberger-Pippan Peace Research Institute Frankfurt (PRIF), Frankfurt, Germany

Klaudia Klonowska Sciences Po, Paris, France

Jonathan Kwik T.M.C. Asser Institute, Hague, The Netherlands;
University of Amsterdam, Amsterdam, The Netherlands

Sofie van der Maarel Faculty of Military Sciences, Netherlands Defence Academy, Breda, The Netherlands;
Centre for International Conflict Analysis and Management (CICAM), Radboud University Nijmegen, Nijmegen, The Netherlands

Tine Molendijk Faculty of Military Sciences, Netherlands Defence Academy, Breda, The Netherlands;
Centre for International Conflict Analysis and Management (CICAM), Radboud University Nijmegen, Nijmegen, The Netherlands

Gregor Pavlin Thales Netherlands B.V., Delft, The Netherlands

Lonneke Peperkamp Radboud University Nijmegen, Nijmegen, The Netherlands

Sofia Romansky The Hague Centre for Strategic Studies, The Hague, The Netherlands

Marcel Schliebs Oxford Internet Institute, University of Oxford, Oxford, UK

Marta Stroppa DIRPOLIS Institute, Sant'Anna School of Advanced Studies, Pisa, Italy

Tim Sweijs The Hague Centre for Strategic Studies, The Hague, The Netherlands

Tom van Engers Informatics Institute, University of Amsterdam, Amsterdam, The Netherlands

Vanessa Vohs Professorship for Security and Defence Policy, University of the Bundeswehr Munich, Neubiberg, Germany

Tomasz Zurek Informatics Institute, University of Amsterdam, Amsterdam, The Netherlands

Abbreviations

ACC	Autonomous Cyber Capabilities
AI	Artificial Intelligence
ALTAI	Assessment List for Trustworthy AI
API	Additional Protocol I
AR	Augmented Reality
AWS	Autonomous Weapons System
BCI	Brain-Computer Interface
C2	Command and Control
CDEM	Collateral Damage Estimation Methodology
CIL	Customary International Law
DARPA	Defence Advanced Research Projects Agency
DNN	Deep Neural Network
DSS	Decision-Support Systems
EU	European Union
GGE LAWS	Group of Governmental Experts on Lethal Autonomous Weapons Systems
GOSSRA	Generic Open Soldier System Reference Architecture
HAT	Human-Autonomy Teaming
HLEG AI	High-Level Expert Group on Artificial Intelligence
ICJ	International Court of Justice
ICL	International Criminal Law
IHL	International Humanitarian Law
iPRAW	international Panel on the Regulation of Autonomous Weapons
ISR	Intelligence, Surveillance, and Reconnaissance
LLM	Large Language Model
MHC	Meaningful Human Control
ML	Machine Learning
MUM-T	Manned-Unmanned Teaming
NATO	North Atlantic Treaty Organization
NCW	Network-Centric Warfare
OODA	Observe, Orient, Decide, and Act

PUR	Principle of Unnecessary Risk
UK	United Kingdom
UNGA	UN General Assembly
UNIDIR	United Nations Institute for Disarmament Research
US	United States

Part I
Theoretical and Conceptual Foundations

Chapter 1
The DILEMA Project: Bridging Disciplines to Address Military AI Challenges

Bérénice Boutin, Taylor Kate Woodcock and Sadjad Soltanzadeh

Contents

Abstract This introductory chapter sets the stage for the interdisciplinary exploration of military artificial intelligence (AI) conducted within the framework of the Designing International Law and Ethics into Military Artificial Intelligence (DILEMA) project as well as throughout this volume. It outlines the project's vision to address the legal, ethical, and operational challenges posed by the integration of AI into military contexts, including by broadening the debate on military applications of AI beyond autonomous weapons systems, moving from meaningful human control to human agency, and seeking to ensure legal compliance in the design and development of AI systems. Next, the chapter reviews the project's key achievements, including scholarly outputs, public engagement, and practical contributions

B. Boutin (✉) · T. K. Woodcock
T.M.C. Asser Instituut, The Hague, The Netherlands
e-mail: b.boutin@asser.nl

University of Amsterdam, Amsterdam, The Netherlands

T. K. Woodcock
e-mail: t.woodcock@asser.nl

S. Soltanzadeh
University of Twente, Enschede, The Netherlands
e-mail: s.soltanzadeh@utwente.nl

B. Boutin et al. (eds.), *Legal, Ethical, and Technical Dilemmas in Military Artificial Intelligence*, https://doi.org/10.1007/978-94-6265-759-5_1

to the debate on military AI governance. This volume builds on these achievements, bringing together twelve interdisciplinary perspectives on the promises and perils of military AI. These contributions explore the intersections of law, ethics, technology, and governance in shaping the future of military AI.

Keywords Artificial Intelligence · Machine Learning · Autonomous Weapons Systems · Decision-Support Systems · Interdisciplinarity · International Law · Philosophy of Technology · Computer Science

1.1 Introduction

Questions around the design and use of military applications of artificial intelligence (AI) have never been more urgent. For some time, global governance efforts have debated the legality and ethics of using AI-enabled and autonomous systems for military targeting. Concerns abound and opinions diverge on AI and the use of military force, including the mitigation of harm, enhancing military performance, safeguarding human judgment and agency, and ensuring safety and responsibility. The issues raised in these fraught and complex discussions indicate a need to consider the intersections of ethics, philosophy, law, international relations, computer science, and systems design, amongst others, requiring a truly interdisciplinary approach.

The DILEMA project on Designing International Law and Ethics into Military AI has, since 2020, sought to bridge these disciplinary divides and foster knowledge on how to understand and address AI in the military domain. Comprising team members from legal, philosophy, and computer science backgrounds, for four years this project conducted scholarship and expertise-driven activities, including the 2023 DILEMA conference, culminating in this very volume. This chapter introduces both the DILEMA project and the present book, which brings together twelve chapters that explore the promises and perils of military AI from the perspectives of law, ethics, governance, and technology.[1] The chapter first lays out the vision of the DILEMA Project in seeking to address the legal, ethical, and operational challenges posed by the development and use of military AI. It highlights three contributions of DILEMA in advancing debates, including broadening discussions to applications beyond autonomous weapons systems (AWS), moving from meaningful human control to human agency, and seeking to ensure legal compliance in the design and development of AI systems. Next, the chapter provides an overview of the key achievements of the project, namely scholarship, public engagement, and

[1] The conception of this volume, from the DILEMA project and conference through to the manuscript, was led by Bérénice Boutin, who also oversaw its overall management and provided substantive review for several chapters. Taylor Kate Woodcock was principally responsible for the substantive and editorial review, as well as coordinating the production of the manuscript, with the invaluable assistance of Cheya Took. Sadjad Soltanzadeh contributed to the substantive and editorial review of several chapters.

practical contributions to policy debates on military AI. Finally, the chapter introduces the twelve substantive chapters in this volume. These chapters broach issues surrounding military AI from a number of different perspectives, critically examining the legal, ethical, and operational implications of AI-driven warfare.

1.2 The Ideas and Vision Behind the DILEMA Project

1.2.1 Military Applications of AI, Beyond Autonomous Weapons Systems

In 2020, the DILEMA project sought to break new ground in the study of the role of artificial AI within the military domain. At the time, research and policy debates around military AI were dominated by a narrow focus on AWS. These discussions often centred on the red line between applications comprising fully autonomous systems and those requiring human oversight, emphasising the dangers of relinquishing life-and-death decisions to machines without direct human control.[2] While essential, exclusive focus on this lens was limited, overlooking broader and equally urgent implications of AI in military operations beyond AWS. The DILEMA project proposed that examination of the impact of AI in military operations can—and should—not be confined solely to questions of autonomy in weaponry.[3] Instead, the project examined a broader spectrum of AI applications integrated across various military functions, especially in areas of decision support and intelligence, where AI is purportedly used to assist, rather than replace, human judgement and agency.[4]

This pioneering perspective challenged the dominant narratives on military AI. The DILEMA project highlighted the crucial—if at times subtle—risks posed by ostensibly supportive AI applications. AI-driven decision-support systems (DSS), designed to assist humans in real-time combat or strategic planning, can inadvertently become *de facto* decision makers. As these systems become increasingly complex, fast, and adaptive, the once-clear boundary between human-controlled and machine-assisted decisions blurs. Particularly in high-stake, time-sensitive situations, human operators may defer to AI-driven recommendations without fully comprehending them or weighing alternatives. Known as automation bias, this tendency creates the risk that AI systems may undermine human decision making, despite formal oversight. The normativity of AI-driven DSS could exacerbate the erosion of genuine human judgement, compounding the risk that humans may become mere rubber stamps for machine-driven decisions.[5] DILEMA was among the first initiatives to

[2] Asaro 2013; Human Rights Watch and Harvard Law School 2015; Williams and Scharre 2015; Bhuta et al. 2016; ICRC 2016; Amoroso 2017; Ekelhof 2018b.

[3] A notable other initiative along these lines was: Lewis et al. 2016.

[4] DILEMA Research Proposal, p. 7. See: https://www.asser.nl/dilema/about-the-project/research-project for a summary.

[5] Ibid.

identify and interrogate this issue, emphasising the need for comprehensive analysis and oversight not only of autonomy in weapons, but of any AI system impacting military judgement and decision making.

1.2.2 From Meaningful Human Control to Human Agency

One of the core ideas of the DILEMA research proposal involves rethinking and refining the notion of 'meaningful human control' (MHC). While commonly used in academic and policy debates,[6] MHC remained relatively unclear and ambiguous. Existing discussions largely treated MHC as a binary criterion rather than a matter of degree, and located control primarily with the operators of AI systems. This failed to capture the nuanced relationship between humans and AI systems, particularly in situations where complex and adaptive AI systems are capable of making high-stakes decisions at speeds beyond human cognitive abilities. DILEMA challenged this dichotomy by seeking to reframe the debate around the notion of human agency. Rather than merely asking whether humans could intervene in AI-driven systems, the project emphasised the importance of understanding how AI could impact human decision making and agency at different levels. In exploring this paradigm, DILEMA sought to understand human agency not as a static state of control but as a dynamic process of interaction and interdependence between human operators and AI systems. The project thereby questioned whether human operators retained qualitative control over decisions and whether they understood the AI systems they operated. By focusing on human agency as an evolving, relational phenomenon, DILEMA sought to forge new ways to question and analyse the impact of military AI systems.[7]

1.2.3 Ensuring Legal Compliance in the Design and Development of AI Systems

Another innovative concept at the foundation of the DILEMA project was that of 'compliance by design'.[8] This principle emphasises that international law and ethical standards should be considered in the design and operational protocols of military AI systems. Taking the starting point that States have an obligation to ensure that their means and methods of warfare are able to comply with international law, DILEMA

---

[6] Amoroso and Tamburrini 2019; Crootof 2016; Ekelhof 2018a; Horowitz and Scharre 2015; Human Rights Watch and Harvard Law School 2016; Marauhn 2018; Schwarz 2021.

[7] DILEMA Research Proposal, pp. 8, 10. See n. 4 above.

[8] The initial title of the project as submitted to the NWO was 'Agency and Compliance by Design in Military AI Technologies'. Upon being awarded, it was decided to rename the project DILEMA to leverage the more impactful and memorable acronym.

posited that compliance is not merely a matter of prohibiting certain functions or responding to violations at the stage of deployment. Rather, it requires proactive engagement with the design and deployment of AI to ensure adherence to legal and ethical standards. This emphasises the importance of early-stage assessments and ongoing oversight to adapt to evolving capabilities and risks in AI systems. To this end, DILEMA aimed to explore and critically analyse how to promote ethical and lawful conduct resulting from human–machine interactions by assessing law and ethics as part of design and development processes, with the aim of promoting ethical and lawful conduct as an intrinsic part of the technology's functionality. This includes working on technical frameworks for compliance and certification, through which DILEMA sought to create actionable guidance for military stakeholders.[9]

1.2.4 Bridging International Law, Philosophy of Technology, and Computer Science

The DILEMA project team comprised researchers from the fields of international law,[10] philosophy of technology,[11] and computer science.[12] Such cross-disciplinary collaboration was especially innovative at a time when the fields of AI ethics and AI legal regulation were largely developing in isolation. Although debates on AI ethics and on the governance of AWS were both well underway, few projects attempted to bridge the two, let alone integrate technical insights from computer science into these discussions.

The close-knit interdisciplinary collaboration at the heart of DILEMA allowed us to advance our understanding of complex issues at the intersection of law, ethics, and technology. By bringing together researchers from international law, philosophy of technology, and computer science within the same research institute, the project created a uniquely conducive environment for collaboration. This co-location facilitated frequent informal exchanges and spontaneous discussions, which played a vital yet often underappreciated role in fostering mutual understanding and interdisciplinary integration. Unlike projects where researchers are dispersed across faculties and meet only periodically, this setup enabled a more seamless blending of insights and approaches. Each discipline brought unique and complementary strengths to the project. Philosophy of technology provided conceptual and theoretical foundations, enriching our understanding of technologies and their broader implications. Computer science offered technical expertise, clarifying how technologies operate, the trajectory of AI development, and distinctions between

[9] DILEMA Research Proposal, pp. 10–11. See n. 4 above.

[10] Bérénice Boutin, Taylor Kate Woodcock, Marten Zwanenburg, Klaudia Klonowska and Magdalena Pacholska. We also worked with Marta Bo and Jonathan Kwik, Associate Researchers in the DILEMA project.

[11] Sadjad Soltanzadeh.

[12] Tomasz Zurek and Tom van Engers.

different types of AI systems. Legal scholarship contributed in-depth knowledge of international law, including international humanitarian law (IHL) and responsibility frameworks, as well as critical perspectives on the role and foundations of international law in addressing emerging technologies. These exchanges ensured that the project's outputs were both theoretically robust and practically informed. Through this model of interdisciplinary engagement, the DILEMA project not only addressed key academic and practical challenges but also set a precedent for effective collaboration in addressing the governance of military AI.

While increasingly popular and sought after by research funders and universities, interdisciplinary collaboration is not without its frictions and challenges. First, as researchers from different disciplines approach the same topic through distinct lenses, they often relate only to their own frames of reference and vocabulary, struggling to understand each other and engage in meaningful discussions that can truly bridge disciplinary boundaries. At times this may even manifest through the use of the same vocabulary with distinct disciplinary meanings. One of the greatest challenges in fostering interdisciplinary collaboration is encouraging researchers to adopt a more open mindset, moving away from rigidly labelling concepts and questions as the exclusive domain of specific fields. Indeed, if researchers from a particular discipline view themselves as the primary authorities on certain topics or concepts, they tend to perceive contributions from other fields as insufficiently informed if not irrelevant, resulting in a lack of genuine engagement. In the experience of the DILEMA project, meaningful interdisciplinary collaboration requires sustained, open minded, and in-depth dialogue,[13] rather than sporadic meetings where researchers from different disciplines merely present their perspectives without engaging substantively with one another. Second, despite the fact that research institutions ostensibly promote interdisciplinarity as a central priority, in practice many institutional hurdles continue to hinder effective implementation of interdisciplinary projects. For example, many leading academic journals still define their scope in a mono-disciplinary way, which can make the path to publishing interdisciplinary papers quite arduous. Similarly, institutional structures within universities remain deeply embedded in disciplinary silos delimited by each faculty, and researchers and projects have to adapt in order to fit within these institutional and administrative disciplinary boundaries.

The DILEMA project also worked in collaboration with project partners from academia (Geneva Graduate Institute (IHEID)), applied research (TNO), policy (Dutch Ministries of Defence and of Foreign Affairs, NATO Office of Legal Affairs), industry (Thales Nederland), civil society (PAX), think tanks (The Hague Centre for Strategic Studies (HCSS)), and professional associations (International Society for Military Law and Law of War (ISMLLW)). This approach ensured that our research remained grounded in ongoing developments while also maintaining direct relevance to current policy needs. The project was therefore able to produce insights that

[13] One of the ways in which DILEMA fostered and advanced interdisciplinarity was through regular reading group sessions, held approximately once a month, where researchers from the team discussed and engaged together with literature spanning diverse disciplines.

not only advanced theoretical understanding but also offered concrete guidance for policymakers and industry.

1.3 Achievements and Results of the DILEMA Project

1.3.1 Key Ideas and Main Scholarly Contributions

Building on its innovative vision, the DILEMA project resulted in a number of achievements and contributions towards debates on military AI. The project's research and publications collectively advance the field of military AI governance by addressing the ethical, legal, and operational challenges posed by AI systems. Through an interdisciplinary lens, the project explored critical themes such as responsibility, human oversight, regulatory innovation, and the broader implications of deploying AI in warfare.

The project critically examined how military AI disrupts traditional frameworks of international law, particularly through the mediation of human decision-making processes. The integration of AI systems complicates legal analysis by introducing layers of technological mediation that alter established notions of accountability. This challenge is particularly acute in contexts such as targeting, where decision-making responsibilities are increasingly distributed among human operators, developers, and AI systems. This distribution raises profound legal issues, as existing international law struggles to address the distributed and mediated nature of decision making in AI-enabled operations. Building on these insights, the project explored how the distributed and mediated dynamics of decision making in AI systems differ from understandings presupposed by traditional frameworks. Unlike conventional processes, AI-enabled decision making introduces complex interactions between humans and machines, where algorithms, data inputs, and design choices play a pivotal role in shaping outcomes. This collaborative process blurs the line between human and machine roles, making it challenging to pinpoint accountability or ensure compliance with legal norms. The project underscored the need to rethink the foundations of international legal frameworks to address these dynamics, ensuring that compliance and accountability mechanisms remain robust and effective in AI-mediated environments.

The project also emphasised the importance of the pre-deployment phase, highlighting the obligations of States and developers to ensure that AI technologies are designed in compliance with international legal norms. This responsibility extends beyond operational use to encompass acquisition, testing, and deployment, underlining that compliance cannot be relegated solely to end-users. Safeguards must be established at every stage of development and deployment to mitigate potential risks, providing a nuanced framework for understanding how AI shifts accountability dynamics in modern warfare.

As highlighted above, a significant contribution of the project lies in its critical engagement with the concept of MHC. While MHC has been a dominant framework for addressing AI governance, the project identified its limitations, particularly its prescriptive focus on direct human intervention. This approach often fails to capture the realities of human–machine interactions in military contexts. As an alternative, the project proposes human agency as a more flexible and adaptable framework for oversight and accountability. Human agency is conceptualised as the capacity of humans to exert meaningful influence over decision-making processes, even when mediated by algorithmic tools. Agency is framed not as direct control but as the degree to which humans can retain substantive decision-making power in environments shaped by AI systems, and impact the outcome of the operation of AI systems. This perspective highlights the need to understand the distinct normative impacts of military applications on AI for targeting practices and to implement safeguards to ensure that DSS do not erode human judgement by relegating operators to passive roles. The project recognised that human agency can be exercised through different channels. While human–machine interactions may result in a diminished degree of agency of operators, design and regulation provide two important channels for humans to exercise their agency at the pre-deployment stage.

The DILEMA project broadened the scope of regulatory debates by moving beyond a narrow focus on AWS to consider the diverse and wide-ranging applications of AI in military contexts. These applications include DSS, targeting systems, surveillance tools, and AI's potential role in all kinds of operational and strategic decision making. By framing AI as an integral component of military infrastructure rather than focusing on weapons, the project highlighted its pervasive influence and the wide-ranging challenges it presents. This broader perspective underscores the systemic impact of AI on military planning, intelligence, and operations, demanding regulatory approaches that address its diverse roles and applications. This idea, that the challenges and implications of AI in the military domain go beyond AWS, has since become more mainstream,[14] highlighting the role of the DILEMA project as a pivotal force in rethinking the relationship between humans and AI in warfare. Through its innovative approach, the DILEMA project contributed to a shift in international policy discourse towards a greater focus on military AI in the broadest sense,[15] as well as on critical issues surrounding the use of AI in military decision making.[16] At the time of drafting the project proposal and launching the project, such applications of AI in military decision making could be conceptually anticipated, yet remained speculative and largely theoretical. However, the focus on AI-driven DSS has since proved prescient, as in 2024 such technologies were widely deployed by

[14] Horowitz and Lin-Greenberg 2022; Grand-Clément 2023; Stewart and Hinds 2023; Rivera et al. 2024; Klaus 2024; Nadibaidze et al. 2024.

[15] See, e.g., the Dutch Ministry of Foreign Affairs initiative on Responsible Artificial Intelligence in the Military Domain (REAIM), with the first REAIM Summit taking place in The Hague in February 2023 (https://www.government.nl/ministries/ministry-of-foreign-affairs/activiteiten/reaim).

[16] See, e.g., ICRC and Geneva Academy 2024.

Israel in the Gaza conflict,[17] bringing to the forefront the critical legal and ethical implications of AI-enabled decision making in warfare.

A key innovation of the project lies in its emphasis on proactive regulation. It advocated for integrating legal and ethical safeguards during the stages of AI development and testing, ensuring alignment with international law and ethical principles before deployment. This proactive stance reduces reliance on post-deployment remedies, which are often insufficient to address the harm caused by AI systems. It also recognises the central role of human actors in the creation, implementation, and regulation of AI technologies, emphasising their responsibility in shaping systems that align with humanitarian and legal standards.

The project further explored computational modelling as a tool for embedding principles of IHL, such as proportionality and distinction, into AI systems. These models aim to translate legal concepts into operational parameters, enabling AI systems to assess compliance during deployment. For instance, computational models may assist human operators in balancing military advantage against civilian harm. While these approaches offer innovative pathways for enhancing compliance, the project critically reflected on their limitations. Legal principles often require contextual interpretation and human judgement, elements that computational systems may struggle to replicate. Over-reliance on predefined parameters poses significant risks, including the creation of a false sense of compliance. The project underscored the importance of viewing computational modelling as a supplementary tool rather than a standalone solution, reinforcing the need for human agency at every stage of AI development and deployment.

In sum, the DILEMA project provided a comprehensive and critical examination of the challenges posed by military AI. By addressing accountability, oversight, regulation, and the limitations of computational tools, the project offered a transformative contribution to the governance of AI-enabled military systems. Its emphasis on integrating legal, ethical, and human-centred approaches ensures a robust foundation for future research and policymaking in this critical field.

1.3.2 Publications

1.3.2.1 Journal Articles

The project resulted in eight peer-reviewed journal articles, each addressing critical and timely issues. Bérénice Boutin's article, '*The Interplay of International Obligations Connected to the Conduct of Others: Toward a Framework of Mutual Compliance Among States Engaged in Partnered Warfare*' (2020, International Law Studies), examines how international obligations apply in the context of partnered warfare, proposing a framework of mutual compliance among States to ensure adherence

[17] Abraham 2023; Abraham 2024; McKernan and Davies 2024.

to international norms.[18] Sadjad Soltanzadeh's work, '*Strictly Human: Limitations of Autonomous Systems*' (2022, Minds and Machines), delves into the epistemic and logical constraints of autonomous systems, arguing that their design must be informed by the activities they aim to support.[19] Magdalena Pacholska's contribution, '*Military Artificial Intelligence and the Principle of Distinction: A State Responsibility Perspective*' (2022, Israel Law Review), explores how AI-enabled technologies interact with IHL, particularly focusing on the principle of distinction and systemic gaps in State accountability.[20] In '*State Responsibility in Relation to Military Applications of Artificial Intelligence*' (2023, Leiden Journal of International Law), Bérénice Boutin provides a comprehensive analysis of how States may incur responsibility for violations of international law involving military AI. The article examines State responsibility for wrongful use, attribution of conduct, and the obligation to ensure compliance during the development or acquisition of AI technologies.[21] Tomasz Zurek, Jonathan Kwik, and Tom van Engers, in '*Model of a Military Autonomous Device Following International Humanitarian Law*' (2023, Ethics and Information Technology), propose a computational framework for ensuring that AI-driven military devices operate within the confines of IHL.[22] Taylor Kate Woodcock's article, '*Human/Machine(-Learning) Interactions, Human Agency, and the International Humanitarian Law Proportionality Standard*' (2024, Global Society), analyses how AI-enabled DSS in military targeting impact legal reasoning and human agency, highlighting their unsuitability for proportionality assessments.[23] In '*A Metaphysical Account of Agency for Technology Governance*' (2024, AI & Society), Sadjad Soltanzadeh redefines the notion of agency as 'impact', offering a nuanced understanding of human–machine interactions in terms of varying levels and degrees of agency. He argues that technology governance must take into account different channels of impact in the contexts of use, design, and regulation.[24] Tasniem Anwar and Klaudia Klonowska's article, '*The Techno-Legal Co-Production of Terrorist Suspects*' (2025, Law, Technology and Humans), examines how algorithmic listing technologies co-produce legal categories of terrorist suspects, revealing how fluid associations and socio-technical assemblages challenge traditional legal distinctions and undermine mechanisms of accountability.[25]

---

[18] Boutin 2020b.

[19] Soltanzadeh 2022.

[20] Pacholska 2022.

[21] Boutin 2023a.

[22] Zurek et al. 2023.

[23] Woodcock 2023b.

[24] Soltanzadeh 2025.

[25] Anwar and Klonowska 2025.

1.3.2.2 Book Chapters

The project also produced nine book chapters. Klaudia Klonowska's chapter, '*Article 36: Review of AI Decision-Support Systems and Other Emerging Technologies of Warfare*' (2021), examines the criteria for determining whether AI technologies should undergo legal review under IHL.[26] In '*Autonomy in the Context of Decision-Making Dilemmas*' (2021), Sadjad Soltanzadeh et al. argue that structured autonomy-supportive education is necessary for addressing decision-making dilemmas arising from conflicts between values, obligations, and strategic gains that can be made in adversarial contexts.[27] Magdalena Pacholska's chapter on '*Autonomous Weapons*' (2023) provides an accessible yet comprehensive overview of legal challenges posed by AWS, including responsibility gaps and regulatory debates.[28] In '*Aspects of Realizing (Meaningful) Human Control: A Legal Perspective*' (2024), Bérénice Boutin and Taylor Kate Woodcock delve into the evolving concept of MHC and its application in military AI. Emphasising the importance of clarifying and operationalising MHC, the chapter highlights the need for robust pre-deployment safeguards to address ethical and legal challenges while ensuring human oversight and accountability in military operations.[29] Another chapter by Pacholska, '*Many Hands in the Black Box: Artificial Intelligence and the Responsibility of International Organizations*' (2024), addresses the often-overlooked responsibility of international organisations for AI-enabled technologies, focusing on their potential privacy violations and other legal implications.[30]

As part of the present volume, four chapters were produced in addition to this introductory chapter. In '*Normative Reasoning and Military AI: DILEMA's Dilemmas*', Sadjad Soltanzadeh critically assesses the ethical and legal limits of encoding normative reasoning into military AI, arguing that delegating morally significant decisions to machines remains fundamentally problematic.[31] In '*Rhetoric and Regulation: The (Limits of) Human/AI Comparison in Legal Debates on Military AI*', Klaudia Klonowska and Taylor Kate Woodcock analyse how analogies between human and AI performance shape legal debates, arguing that as such analogies promote a reductive understanding of IHL, legal compliance should centre on the complexities of human–machine interactions.[32] In '*The Computational Representation of Rules of International Humanitarian Law in Military Autonomous Devices: Issues, Problems, and Controversies*', Tomasz Zurek and Tom van Engers propose a computational model for applying IHL in autonomous systems, combining legal reasoning with technical design to support compliant and auditable targeting decisions.[33] In

[26] Klonowska 2021.
[27] Soltanzadeh and Mooney 2021.
[28] Pacholska 2023.
[29] Boutin and Woodcock 2024.
[30] Pacholska 2024.
[31] Chapter 2 in this volume.
[32] Chapter 3 in this volume.
[33] Chapter 10 in this volume.

'*Between Negligence and Malfunction: How to Address Responsibility for AI Failures*', Bérénice Boutin explores how due diligence obligations apply to State use of AI, proposing a new framework for assigning responsibility across the blurred line between human error and system malfunction.[34]

1.3.2.3 Edited Book

The present edited volume, *Legal, Ethical, and Technical Dilemmas in Military Artificial Intelligence*, edited by Bérénice Boutin, Taylor Kate Woodcock and Sadjad Soltanzadeh, examines how the integration of AI is reshaping military operations, decision making, and accountability. It addresses legal, ethical, and sociopolitical challenges posed by military AI, and investigates how AI transforms core concepts such as agency, responsibility, and control. The book explores the interdisciplinary dilemmas of AI in the military domain, where algorithmic systems operate in time-sensitive, high-stake environments, and the boundary between human judgment and machine-driven decisions becomes increasingly blurred.

1.3.2.4 Doctoral Theses

Two doctoral theses by Taylor Kate Woodcock and Klaudia Klonowska provide in-depth explorations of critical aspects of military AI and constitute key outputs of the project.

In her thesis entitled *Human–Machine (Learning) Interactions: War and Law in the AI Era*, Taylor Kate Woodcock explores how machine learning (ML) reconfigures targeting law assessments in military operations. Adopting a practice-oriented approach to understanding interpretative and rhetorical practices of reasoning in which legal meaning is constructed, she emphasises the centrality of the exercise of human agency within these practices. Analysing the interactions that emerge when practitioners use ML-enabled DSS, Woodcock argues that these technologies exert normativity that influences the exercise of agency and affords targeting law assessments by framing information, reshaping the conditions of decision making, and prompting human bias. She concludes that the human–machine (learning) interactions resulting from the habitual and institutionalised use of ML systems can reshape the interpretation of IHL, recontextualising factual determinations, imbuing logics of quantification into interpretation, and reconfiguring legal categories. This demonstrates the need to deliberately resist the logics of ML and reinforce friction points for military practitioners to exercise agency in targeting law assessments.

Klaudia Klonowska's doctoral thesis, *Techno-Legal Tinkering in War: AI Decision-Support Systems and International Humanitarian Law*, examines how AI decision support systems reshape the concept of a "reasonable commander" in targeting decisions. Rather than asking how AI DSS comply with IHL, Klonowska

[34] Chapter 13 in this volume.

investigates how socio-techno-legal assemblages redefine what is permissible in warfare. With over 30 interviews with military professionals and engineers from the United States and the Netherlands, a significant contribution of Klonowska's thesis to legal scholarship is the granular engagement with the technical details of how AI decision support systems are developed and used. The thesis develops a concept of 'techno-legal tinkering', which highlights the iterative adjustments in both AI systems (e.g., updates, fixes) and legal interpretations (e.g., adapting norms to technical standards) that enable certain ways of warfighting. As a result of this interplay, Klonowska concludes, reasonableness in applying targeting law cannot meaningfully rest on the *exercise of judgement* but rather in the calibrated and justified *reliance* of military decision-makers on AI decision support systems.

1.3.2.5 Conference and Working Papers

DILEMA produced four conference and working papers led by Tomasz Zurek, which tackled foundational issues in military AI and computer science. The paper '*Computational Modelling of the Proportionality Analysis under International Humanitarian Law for Military Decision-Support Systems*' (2022) proposes a computational model for evaluating the proportionality of attacks in line with IHL.[35] In '*Designing International Humanitarian Law into Military Autonomous Devices*' (2022), the authors outline a hybrid framework integrating data-driven and knowledge-based approaches to ensure compliance with international norms.[36] The paper '*Towards a Formal Framework for Motivated Argumentation and the Roots of Conflict*' investigates how value-based reasoning affects decision making in conflict scenarios.[37] Finally, '*Can a Military Autonomous Device Follow International Humanitarian Law?*' presents a formal model and experimental verification of a system designed to ensure that military autonomous devices comply with the rules of international humanitarian law.[38]

1.3.2.6 Policy Papers and Reports

The project also produced six policy papers and reports aimed at bridging research with policymaking, which contributed to policy-oriented discussions on the regulation of military AI. The 2020 report, '*Addressing Gaps in the International Regulation of Warfare and Dual-Use Technologies*', commissioned by the Dutch Ministry

[35] Zurek et al. 2022b.

[36] Kwik et al. 2022.

[37] Zurek and Wyner 2022.

[38] Zurek et al. 2022a.

of Foreign Affairs, summarised the findings of an expert meeting on this topic.[39] It examined the regulatory challenges posed by emerging technologies such as armed drones, drone swarms, and weapons systems with varying degrees of autonomy in critical functions, focusing on their potential to cause significant harm. The report identified normative and interpretative gaps in international law and proposed areas where interpretative guidelines or new legal instruments could enhance governance. In 2021, Bérénice Boutin authored '*Legal Questions Related to the Use of Autonomous Weapon Systems*', a briefing paper commissioned by the Advisory Committee on Public International Law (CAVV). This document provided a detailed analysis of the terminology, state of debate, and challenges in operationalising legal concepts related to AWS. It also proposed regulatory options to address responsibility gaps and ensure compliance with international law.[40] In 2023, the project team issued the *DILEMA Statement on the Global Governance of Artificial Intelligence in the Military* (co-authored by Boutin, Klonowska, Pacholska, Soltanzadeh, Woodcock, and Zurek), which offered comprehensive recommendations for international policymakers. The statement addressed the complex challenges posed by the design, development, and deployment of military AI, building on the interdisciplinary research conducted by the DILEMA team.[41] The report '*Decision-Support Systems and Human–Machine Interaction*' (2023), drafted by Taylor Kate Woodcock, was based on a panel convened by DILEMA at the REAIM 2023 summit. It highlighted the erosion of human control in the context of DSS in military operations, exploring their implications for human agency, ethical decision making, and regulatory design.[42] The *DILEMA 2023 Conference Materials* compiled extended abstracts of presentations delivered at the DILEMA Conference organised in October 2023. This 86-page booklet offered a detailed overview of the latest interdisciplinary research on military AI, covering topics ranging from international law to ethical and technical challenges.[43] The policy brief '*Controlling Military Artificial Intelligence: Harnessing Rules of Engagement and Military Directives*' (2025)[44] presents findings from an expert workshop examining how existing military frameworks, particularly rules of engagement (ROE), can be adapted to regulate military AI, ultimately concluding that while traditional ROE may be insufficient, tailored directives provide a viable approach to ensuring compliance and operational control. Together, these policy papers and reports sought to bridge academic research with practical policymaking, addressing the pressing need for improved governance of military AI and related technologies.

[39] Expert Meeting on International Regulation of Warfare and Dual-Use Technologies, see: https://www.asser.nl/dilema/news-and-updates/expert-meeting-on-international-regulation-of-warfare-and-dual-use-technologies.

[40] Boutin 2021.

[41] Boutin et al. 2023.

[42] Woodcock 2023a.

[43] Boutin 2023b.

[44] Kwik et al. 2025.

1.3.2.7 Publications for the General Public

The DILEMA project also contributed to public discourse on military AI through a series of publications aimed at general audiences. These short articles and blog posts effectively translated complex academic discussions into accessible formats, engaging a broader audience. In '*Beyond AI Ethics: International Law and Human Rights for AI Accountability*' (2020), Bérénice Boutin highlights the importance of integrating international law and human rights frameworks into discussions about AI accountability, arguing that ethical guidelines alone are insufficient to address the complex challenges posed by AI in both civilian and military domains.[45] Taylor Kate Woodcock's '*Artificial Intelligence: Is the Answer More Law?*' (2021) explores whether the proliferation of AI technologies necessitates further legal regulation. Woodcock argues for a balanced approach, emphasising the need to understand how current legal frameworks relate to human agency and new technological realities before developing new legal standards for the regulation of military AI.[46] In '*Eclipsing Human Rights: Why the International Regulation of Military AI is not Limited to International Humanitarian Law*' (2021), Woodcock underscores the need for a broader regulatory perspective, arguing that military AI must be governed not only by IHL but also by human rights law, in order to address its far-reaching implications.[47] Marten Zwanenburg's '*Biometrics and International Humanitarian Law*' (2021) examines the intersection of biometric technologies and IHL, addressing how these technologies can both enhance and challenge compliance with humanitarian principles, particularly in military and security contexts.[48] Klaudia Klonowska contributed three thought-provoking pieces to the public discourse. In '*Shifting the Narrative: Not Weapons, but Technologies of Warfare*' (2022), she calls for a broader understanding of military AI as a technology of warfare rather than merely a weapon, encouraging a more nuanced regulatory approach.[49] In '*Designing for Reasonableness: The Algorithmic Mediation of Reasonableness in Targeting Decisions*' (2024), Klonowska examines how algorithmic systems mediate the concept of reasonableness in military targeting, highlighting the risks and limitations of relying on such systems for legal and ethical decision making.[50] Her piece '*AI-Based Targeting in Gaza: Surveying Expert Responses and Refining the Debate*' (2024) provides a timely analysis of AI-driven targeting in conflict zones, presenting expert opinions to deepen understanding and advance discussions on legal and operational implications of AI-driven targeting.[51] Together, these publications demonstrate the DILEMA project's commitment to fostering public understanding and critical engagement with the

---

[45] Boutin 2020a.
[46] Woodcock 2021a.
[47] Woodcock 2021b.
[48] Zwanenburg 2021.
[49] Klonowska 2022.
[50] Klonowska 2024b.
[51] Klonowska 2024a.

ethical and legal challenges posed by military AI technologies. Next to short articles, the DILEMA Project team members also intervened in the public conversation through newspaper interviews, podcast appearances, and other media contributions.[52] Through these various public-facing platforms, the project aimed to broaden the reach and impact of its research, connecting with both specialist and non-specialist audiences.

1.3.3 Events

The DILEMA project organised numerous academic events and outreach activities, including conferences, expert meetings and workshops, policy-oriented events, and public lectures.

1.3.3.1 Conferences

On 12–13 October 2023, the project organised the *DILEMA 2023 Conference*, a large international conference around the complex and interdisciplinary issues raised by military applications AI.[53] The DILEMA conference offered a broad platform to engage in an interdisciplinary dialogue around both theoretical and practical questions related to military AI, and featured some of the latest research insights from the fields of law, ethics, computer science, and other disciplines. The conference sought in particular to promote innovative perspectives that contribute to advancing the boundaries of research in the field of military AI. It convened over 80 participants and 25 speakers (from over ten countries), and featured keynote lectures by Prof. Noam Lubell and Prof. Elke Schwarz. It offered a valuable forum for both junior and senior researchers to share their perspectives, as well as a momentous platform for building local and international connections across disciplines. Half of the contributions to the present volume originated from presentations given at the conference.

DILEMA also co-organised two conferences, fostering interdisciplinary dialogue on critical issues in military affairs and international law. The conference *'Honest Errors? Combat Decision Autonomy 75 Years After the Hostage Case'* (4 June 2021), was organised in collaboration with the Centre for International and Operational Law of the Swedish Defence University, the VID Specialized University, and the Lieber Institute for Law & Land Warfare of the United States Military Academy at West Point. This conference brought together eminent historians, international lawyers, strategic thinkers, and military ethicists to examine the legacy of the Hostage

[52] See: https://www.asser.nl/dilema/research/media-appearances.

[53] See: https://www.asser.nl/dilema/news-and-updates/dilema-2023-conference.

Case and the 'no second-guessing' rule in modern combat decision-making.[54] Key discussions explored what constitutes reasonably available information for decision makers and how to assess honesty in decision making. The *5th Silent Leges Inter Arma Conference* (21–22 September 2022, Bruges), was organised by the Belgian Group of the International Society for Military Law and the Law of War (ISMLLW) with the support of the DILEMA project. This conference convened military practitioners and academics, and fostered robust exchanges on contemporary challenges in military law and policy. Two conference panels were convened by DILEMA: one on 'War Algorithms: Between Review and Implementation', and another on 'Reflections on the Human in International Humanitarian Law & Military Applications of AI'.[55]

1.3.3.2 Expert Meetings and Workshops

The DILEMA project convened a number of specialised expert meetings and workshops to address critical and underexplored issues in the field of military AI, engaging academics, practitioners, and policymakers. These events, a selection of which is outlined below, reflect the DILEMA project's commitment to advancing the governance of military AI through interdisciplinary dialogue and innovative approaches.

The expert roundtable '*Trading Emerging Technologies: Security and Human Rights Perspectives*' (15 September 2020), organised together with Utrecht University, reflected on the underlying narratives put forward when regulating the trade of advanced emerging technologies.[56] The expert meeting '*Addressing Gaps in the International Regulation of Warfare and Dual-Use Technologies*' (11 November 2020) explored the regulatory challenges posed by technologies such as drones, robotics, and AI-enabled systems. Participants identified gaps in international law, including normative and interpretative deficiencies, and discussed whether new instruments or guidelines are needed to address risks associated with State and non-State actors.[57] The expert meeting '*Recent Developments and Current Debates on Military Applications of Artificial Intelligence & International Law*' (8 December 2020) examined the broader applications of AI in military decision making, emphasising the limitations of focusing solely on AWS. Discussions highlighted the impact of DSS on human agency and the need to integrate ethical and legal perspectives into regulatory debates.[58] The workshop '*Critical Reflections on AI Ethics Principles and Societal Inputs for the Governance of Military AI*' (26 April 2023), co-organised with

[54] See: https://www.asser.nl/dilema/news-and-updates/conference-on-honest-errors-and-combat-decision-autonomy.

[55] See: https://www.asser.nl/dilema/news-and-updates/silent-leges-inter-arma-conference.

[56] See: https://www.asser.nl/education-events/events/?id=3127.

[57] See: https://www.asser.nl/dilema/news-and-updates/expert-meeting-on-international-regulation-of-warfare-and-dual-use-technologies.

[58] See: https://www.asser.nl/dilema/news-and-updates/expert-meeting-on-military-applications-of-ai-international-law.

the University of New South Wales, Canberra, addressed the value and limitations of ethics principles as non-binding governance tools. Participants discussed how societal input could inform these frameworks and their relationship with legal norms.[59] The expert meeting '*Distinction and Discrimination under IHL and Military Applications of AI*' (11 October 2023) focused on the application of IHL principles to AI-enabled targeting systems. Participants debated how AI complicates compliance with key rules, including those prohibiting indiscriminate attacks.[60] The workshop on '*Agent-Based Simulations of Disruptive Autonomous Devices: Relations, Norms, and Trust*' (15 October 2024) convened scholars from computer science to discuss how to implement dynamic trust relations in multi-agent systems. Finally, the workshop '*Rules of Engagement for Military AI*' (6–7 November 2024), co-organised with the ELSA Lab Defence project, examined the challenges of designing rules of engagement (ROE) for AI systems. Experts collaboratively considered the elements needed for effective ROE and identified risks requiring complementary governance approaches.[61]

1.3.3.3 Policy-Oriented Events

DILEMA organised a number of policy-oriented events with policymakers and experts to address the challenges of military AI, focusing on regulatory, ethical, and operational solutions. These events demonstrate the DILEMA project's focus on advancing practical governance solutions for military AI through interdisciplinary dialogue. The panel '*The Interface of Ethical and Legal Principles on (Military) AI: Towards Mutually Strengthening Frameworks*' (13 May 2022, Hague Conference on Responsible AI, The Hague) explored the relationship between non-binding AI ethics principles and legal frameworks. The session examined how ethical principles can complement or risk undermining existing legal obligations and discussed ways to align ethical and legal standards for responsible AI governance.[62] The breakout session '*Decision-Support Systems and Human–Machine Interaction*' (15 February 2023, REAIM Summit, The Hague) addressed the implications of AI-based DSS for human control and compliance with international law. Discussions highlighted the need for human-centred design and pre-deployment safeguards to mitigate risks of DSS replacing human decision making in military operations.[63] The roundtable '*International Governance of Military AI: The Way Forward*' (28 November 2023, The Hague) assessed global and regional initiatives, such as REAIM

[59] See: https://www.asser.nl/dilema/news-and-updates/workshop-ai-ethics-principles-and-societal-inputs.

[60] See: https://www.asser.nl/dilema/news-and-updates/expert-meeting-on-distinction-and-discrimination-under-ihl.

[61] See: https://www.asser.nl/dilema/news-and-updates/dilema-elsa-lab-workshop-on-rules-of-engagement-for-military-ai.

[62] See: https://www.thehagueconferenceonai.nl/128772/sessie1.

[63] See: https://reaim2023.org/events/decision-support-systems-and-human-machine-interaction.

and the Belén Communiqué, to advance international regulation of military AI. Participants discussed ways to achieve consensus on governance frameworks and explored the role of existing legal regimes in ensuring compliance during development and acquisition.[64] The panel '*Beyond the Black Box: Unpacking Explainability in Military AI*' (9 September 2024, REAIM Summit, Seoul) focused on explainability in military AI, addressing its operational, legal, and ethical implications. Experts discussed how explainability intersects with transparency and accountability, and proposed socio-technical approaches to make AI systems comprehensible and usable under operational conditions.[65]

1.3.3.4 DILEMA Lecture Series

Next to activities aimed at academia and professionals, the project convened numerous public events aimed at the general public, which took place both online and in person in The Hague, and gathered a broad audience. In particular, the DILEMA Lecture Series regularly invited academics and experts to present their work and share insights on issues relevant to the project with a diverse audience of researchers, students, and professionals. The DILEMA Lecture Series featured a total of nine lectures by leading scholars. It covered a wide range of topics and disciplines, including international law, philosophy of technology, international relations, security studies, and political theory. To increase our reach, the video recordings of DILEMA Lectures have been made available online.[66] In September 2020, Prof. Rebecca Crootof (University of Richmond School of Law) delivered the inaugural DILEMA lecture titled 'Artificial Intelligence, Autonomous Weapon Systems, and Accidents in War', where she examined the legal accountability mechanisms for the harm caused by AWS, advocating for frameworks that balance innovation with responsibility.[67] In February 2021, Dr. William Boothby (Australian National University) presented 'Remote, Autonomous Weapons and Human Agency'. He explored whether existing IHL sufficiently addresses the complexities introduced by autonomous weapons, suggesting gaps and areas for further regulation.[68] Dr. Margarita Konaev (Georgetown's Center for Security and Emerging Technology) delivered a lecture in March 2021 titled 'Trusted Partners: Human–Machine Teaming and the Future of Military AI', analysing the transformative potential of AI in military strategy and operations, and emphasising the importance of understanding technological, strategic, and operational dynamics.[69] In April 2021, Prof. Peter-Paul Verbeek (University of Amsterdam) presented 'Artificial Intelligence and Ethical Disruption',

---

[64] See: https://www.asser.nl/dilema/news-and-updates/roundtable-international-governance-of-military-ai.

[65] See: https://www.asser.nl/dilema/news-and-updates/breakout-session-reaim-2024.

[66] See: https://www.asser.nl/dilema/events/dilema-lecture-series.

[67] See: https://www.asser.nl/dilema/news-and-updates/dilema-lecture-by-rebecca-crootof.

[68] See: https://www.asser.nl/dilema/news-and-updates/dilema-lecture-by-william-boothby.

[69] See: https://www.asser.nl/dilema/news-and-updates/dilema-lecture-by-margarita-konaev.

focusing on the ethical dimensions of technological design and how these considerations can shape the development of military AI in morally responsible ways.[70] Dr. Ingvild Bode (University of Southern Denmark) delivered a lecture in November 2021 titled 'Which Practices Shape Norms? Retaining Human Control over the Use of Force', highlighting the governance challenges surrounding military AI and stressing the importance of maintaining human agency and accountability in its deployment.[71] In November 2022, Prof. Sven Nyholm (Ludwig-Maximilians-Universität München) presented 'The Ethics of Human–Robot Interaction and Traditional Moral Theories'. He examined the moral complexities of human–robot interactions, particularly in military contexts, through the lens of traditional ethical theories.[72] Dr. Tim Sweijs (The Hague Centre for Strategic Studies) delivered a lecture in May 2024 titled 'Military AI and International Norms Development: Quo Vadis?', outlining emerging trends in military AI and discussing their potential implications for global security and strategic stability.[73] In July 2024, Dustin A. Lewis (Harvard Law School Program on International Law and Armed Conflict) presented 'Natural and Artificial Intelligence in Armed Conflict: Exploring Settled and Open Legal Questions', analysing the challenges of applying existing international legal frameworks to the regulation and governance of military AI technologies.[74] Finally, in November 2024, Dr. Rupert Barrett-Taylor (Alan Turing Institute) delivered a lecture titled 'Wither Clausewitz: How Artificial Intelligence and Automation is Making the State and War Incidental to Warfare', exploring how AI and automation are shifting warfare from a political act into an exercise of optimisation and efficiency.[75]

1.4 Overview of the Contributions to the Book

Organised into four parts, the book moves from foundational to applied questions. The first part explores the theoretical and conceptual premises that shape current debates (Chaps. 1–3). The second part delves into the legal and ethical dilemmas posed by the use of AI in armed conflict (Chaps. 4–7). The third part highlights technical considerations regarding systems design (Chaps. 8–10). Finally, the fourth part examines governance approaches and accountability frameworks to guide responsible development and use (Chaps. 11–13).

In **Chap. 2**, 'Normative Reasoning and Military AI: DILEMA's Dilemmas', Sadjad Soltanzadeh critically investigates the permissibility and feasibility of encoding legal and moral reasoning into military AI systems. Through an analysis of both fundamental normative obligations and the technical limitations of rule-based

[70] See: https://www.asser.nl/dilema/news-and-updates/dilema-lecture-by-peter-paul-verbeek.

[71] See: https://www.asser.nl/dilema/news-and-updates/dilema-lecture-by-dr-ingvild-bode.

[72] See: https://www.asser.nl/dilema/news-and-updates/dilema-lecture-by-sven-nyholm.

[73] See: https://www.asser.nl/dilema/news-and-updates/dilema-lecture-by-tim-sweijs.

[74] See: https://www.asser.nl/dilema/news-and-updates/dilema-hilac-lecture-by-dustin-a-lewis.

[75] See: https://www.asser.nl/dilema/news-and-updates/dilema-lecture-by-dr-rupert-barrett-taylor.

and data-driven approaches, the chapter argues that delegating normatively significant military decisions to AI systems remains ethically and legally impermissible and technically unfeasible.

In **Chap. 3**, 'Rhetoric and Regulation: The (Limits of) Human/AI Comparison in Legal Debates on Military AI', Klaudia Klonowska and Taylor Kate Woodcock analyse how analogies between human and AI performance shape legal and regulatory discussions. They argue that such comparisons, often focused on speed, accuracy, or compliance, obscure the complexity of AI systems and promote a reductive understanding of IHL. They instead propose an approach centred on the complexities of human–machine interactions to ensure legal compliance and accountability in AI-supported military decision making.

In **Chap. 4**, 'The Use of Autonomous Cyber Capabilities in Armed Conflict: Legal Appraisal from a Targeting Law Perspective', Marta Stroppa explores the compatibility of autonomous cyber capabilities with the core principles of IHL governing targeting. She argues that while such systems might be used lawfully in deliberate cyber operations under certain conditions, their use in dynamic targeting remains legally problematic without sustained human control.

In **Chap. 5**, 'ChatGPT for the Military? Large Language Models in the Military Domain and the Role of Article 36 Weapons Reviews', Elisabeth Hoffberger-Pippan investigates whether and how the legal obligation to conduct weapons reviews applies to large language models (LLMs) used in military contexts. She argues that while LLMs may not constitute weapons or weapon systems, they could qualify as means or methods of warfare depending on their design and deployment, thus necessitating broader interpretations of Article 36 to ensure compliance with IHL.

In **Chap. 6**, 'The AI-Augmented Super Soldier: An Interface-Based Approach to the Cognition of Enhanced Humans', Thomas Christian Bächle develops a theoretical framework to understand human–machine relations in military contexts through the lens of cognitive interfaces. Challenging dominant legal and ethical assumptions about agency, responsibility, and human intentionality, the chapter argues that the figure of the enhanced soldier reveals deep conceptual tensions and urges a shift towards relational, interface-centred models of cognition.

In **Chap. 7**, 'Artificial Decision-Making on Life-or-Death: Moral-Psychological Implications for Combatants with Increasing Autonomy in Weapon Systems', Tine Molendijk, Sofie van der Maarel, and Lonneke Peperkamp analyse the moral-psychological effects of AWS on military personnel. Drawing on empirical insights and theoretical debates, the chapter challenges assumptions that AWS reduce psychological harm, arguing instead that increased autonomy may amplify feelings of powerlessness, moral failure, and betrayal among operators.

In **Chap. 8**, 'Context-Driven Analysis for AI-Enhanced Solutions: Extracting Requirements for System Development and Operational Use', Iris Cohen, Gregor Pavlin and Rianne Gouman propose the Contextualised AI Onboarding Method (CAIOM) as a framework for systematically assessing the operational conditions and performance requirements for the use of AI systems deployed in military decision making. Departing from a one-size-fits-all approach to the use of military AI, CAICOM emphasises the need for contextual, multi-stakeholder assessment in order to maximise the benefits of AI whilst addressing operational, technical, legal and ethical challenges.

In **Chap. 9**, 'Iterative Assessment for Military Artificial Intelligence (AI) Systems', Jonathan Kwik proposes a new best practice for using AI in armed conflict: the iterative assessment of military AI across both legal review and operational deployment. Arguing that AI-induced uncertainty cannot be fully eliminated through *ex ante* controls, the chapter outlines how continuous monitoring, knowledge-sharing, and adaptive responses can reduce the risk of repeated failures and better protect civilians in compliance with IHL.

In **Chap. 10**, 'The Computational Representation of Rules of International Humanitarian Law in Military Autonomous Devices: Issues, Problems, and Controversies', Tomasz Zurek and Tom van Engers present a formal framework for integrating IHL compliance into military AI systems. Focusing on targeting decisions, they propose a hybrid model combining data- and knowledge-driven approaches to evaluate legal principles such as proportionality, distinction, and precautions. The chapter identifies core technical and normative challenges and outlines how structured reasoning modules can enable transparent, auditable, and legally compliant decision making in autonomous systems.

In **Chap. 11**, 'What's at the Core? The Quintessential Role of Responsibility in International Governance of Military Artificial Intelligence', Sofia Romansky and Tim Sweijs examine how the concept of responsibility underpins the current gridlock in international efforts to govern military AI. By analysing seven core focus areas within existing initiatives, the chapter argues that clarifying and operationalising responsibility in relation to relevant actors, specific contexts, and legal frameworks is essential for moving beyond high-level principles toward effective and actionable governance.

In **Chap. 12**, '"This is My Last Resort": Approaches to Overcome the Stalemate in Autonomous Weapons Regulation through National Legislation and Industry Self-Regulation', Marcel Schliebs and Vanessa Vohs assess alternatives to multilateral arms control in the face of geopolitical deadlock over AWS. They argue that while a global ban is unlikely in the short term, national legislation and industry self-regulation—especially when grounded in ethical design principles and supported by coalition-based cooperation—offer feasible pathways to mitigate the risks of unregulated AWS deployment.

In **Chap. 13**, 'Between Negligence and Malfunction: How to Address Responsibility for AI Failures', Bérénice Boutin examines how international legal obligations, particularly obligations of due diligence, apply to failures of AI systems used by States, with a focus on the blurred boundary between human errors and technical malfunctions. It proposes a comprehensive framework for rethinking due diligence in light of AI's unpredictability, offering guidance on how states can anticipate and mitigate risks throughout the AI lifecycle to fulfil their international responsibilities.

References

Articles, Books and Other Documents

Abraham Y (2023) A Mass Assassination Factory: Inside Israel's Calculated Bombing of Gaza. +972 Magazine in partnership with Local Call, 30 November 2023. https://www.972mag.com/mass-assassination-factory-israel-calculated-bombing-gaza. Accessed 1 September 2025

Abraham Y (2024) 'Lavender': The AI Machine Directing Israel's Bombing Spree in Gaza. +972 Magazine in partnership with Local Call, 3 April 2024. https://www.972mag.com/lavender-ai-israeli-army-gaza. Accessed 1 September 2025

Amoroso D (2017) Jus in Bello and Jus Ad Bellum Arguments Against Autonomy in Weapons Systems: A Re-Appraisal. Questions of International Law 43: 5–31

Amoroso D, Tamburrini G (2019) What Makes Human Control Over Weapons 'Meaningful'. ICRAC Report. https://www.icrac.net/wp-content/uploads/2019/08/Amoroso-Tamburrini_Human-Control_ICRAC-WP4.pdf. Accessed 1 September 2025

Anwar T, Klonowska K (2025) The Techno-Legal Co-Production of Terrorist Suspects. Law, Technology and Humans. https://doi.org/10.5204/lthj.3740

Asaro P (2013) On Banning Autonomous Weapon Systems: Human Rights, Automation, and the Dehumanization of Lethal Decision-Making. International Review of the Red Cross. https://doi.org/10.1017/S1816383112000768

Bhuta N, Beck S, Geiß R, Liu HY, Kreß C (eds) (2016) Autonomous Weapons Systems: Law, Ethics, Policy. Cambridge University Press, Cambridge.

Boutin B (2020a) Beyond AI Ethics: International Law and Human Rights for AI Accountability. I4ADA Accountability Paper Vision 2020: Taking Stock & Looking Forward, 47–48. https://i4ada.org/vision-2020. Accessed 1 September 2025

Boutin B (2020b) The Interplay of International Obligations Connected to the Conduct of Others: Toward a Framework of Mutual Compliance Among States Engaged in Partnered Warfare. International Law Studies (Naval War College) 96: 529–548

Boutin B (2021) Legal Questions Related to the Use of Autonomous Weapon Systems. Briefing Paper, Commissioned by the Advisory Committee on Public International Law (CAVV) in relation to the AIV/CAVV Advisory Report on Autonomous Weapon Systems: The Importance of Regulation and Investment, June 2021. https://www.asser.nl/media/795707/boutin-legal-questions-related-to-the-use-of-aws.pdf. Accessed 1 September 2025

Boutin B (2023a) State Responsibility in Relation to Military Applications of Artificial Intelligence. Leiden Journal of International Law. https://doi.org/10.1017/S0922156522000607

Boutin B (ed) (2023b) DILEMA 2023 Conference Materials. https://www.asser.nl/media/796748/dilema-2023-conference-materials.pdf. Accessed 1 September 2025

Boutin B, Klonowska K, Pacholska M, Soltanzadeh S, Woodcock TK, Zurek T (2023) DILEMA Statement on the Global Governance of Artificial Intelligence in the Military. https://www.asser.nl/dilema/research/dilema-statement. Accessed 1 September 2025

Boutin B, Woodcock TK (2024) Aspects of Realizing (Meaningful) Human Control: A Legal Perspective. In: Geiß R, Lahmann H (eds) Research Handbook on Warfare and Artificial Intelligence. Edward Elgar, Cheltenham, pp. 179–196

Crootof R (2016) A Meaningful Floor for 'Meaningful Human Control'. Temple International and Comparative Law Journal 30(1): 53–62

Ekelhof M (2018a) Autonomous Weapons: Operationalizing Meaningful Human Control. ICRC Humanitarian Law & Policy Blog. https://blogs.icrc.org/law-and-policy/2018/08/15/autonomous-weapons-operationalizing-meaningful-human-control. Accessed 1 September 2025

Ekelhof M (2018b) Lifting the Fog of Targeting: 'Autonomous Weapons' and Human Control Through the Lens of Military Targeting. Naval War College Review 71(3): 61–94

Grand-Clément S (2023) Artificial Intelligence Beyond Weapons: Application and Impact of AI in the Military Domain. UNIDIR. https://unidir.org/publication/artificial-intelligence-beyond-weapons-application-and-impact-of-ai-in-the-military-domain. Accessed 1 September 2025

Horowitz MC, Lin-Greenberg E (2022) Algorithms and Influence: Artificial Intelligence and Crisis Decision-Making. International Studies Quarterly. https://doi.org/10.1093/isq/sqac069

Horowitz MC, Scharre P (2015) Meaningful Human Control in Weapon Systems: A Primer. CNAS Working Paper. https://www.cnas.org/publications/reports/meaningful-human-control-in-weapon-systems-a-primer. Accessed 1 September 2025

Human Rights Watch, Harvard Law School (2015) Mind the Gap: The Lack of Accountability for Killer Robots. Report of Human Rights Watch and the Harvard Law School's International Human Rights Clinic. https://www.hrw.org/report/2015/04/09/mind-gap/lack-accountability-killer-robots. Accessed 1 September 2025

Human Rights Watch, Harvard Law School (2016) Killer Robots and the Concept of Meaningful Human Control: Memorandum to Convention on Conventional Weapons (CCW) Delegates. https://www.hrw.org/news/2016/04/11/killer-robots-and-concept-meaningful-human-control. Accessed 1 September 2025

ICRC (2016) Autonomous Weapon Systems: Implications of Increasing Autonomy in the Critical Functions of Weapons. https://www.icrc.org/en/publication/4283-autonomous-weapons-systems. Accessed 1 September 2025

ICRC, Geneva Academy (2024) Expert Consultation Report on AI and Related Technologies in Military Decision-Making on the Use of Force in Armed Conflicts. https://shop.icrc.org/expert-consultation-report-artificial-intelligence-and-related-technologies-in-military-decision-making-on-the-use-of-force-in-armed-conflicts-current-developments-and-potential-implications-pdf-en.html. Accessed 1 September 2025

Klaus M (2024) Transcending Weapon Systems: The Ethical Challenges of AI in Military Decision Support Systems. ICRC Humanitarian Law & Policy Blog. https://blogs.icrc.org/law-and-policy/2024/09/24/transcending-weapon-systems-the-ethical-challenges-of-ai-in-military-decision-support-systems. Accessed 1 September 2025

Klonowska K (2021) Article 36: Review of AI Decision-Support Systems and Other Emerging Technologies of Warfare. In: Gill TD, Geiß R, Krieger H, Mignot-Mahdavi R (eds) Yearbook of International Humanitarian Law, Volume 23 (2020). T.M.C. Asser Press, The Hague, pp. 123–153

Klonowska K (2022) Shifting the Narrative: Not Weapons, but Technologies of Warfare. ICRC Humanitarian Law & Policy Blog, 20 January 2022. https://blogs.icrc.org/law-and-policy/2022/01/20/weapons-technologies-warfare. Accessed 1 September 2025

Klonowska K (2024a) AI-Based Targeting in Gaza: Surveying Expert Responses and Refining the Debate. Articles of War, Lieber Institute West Point, Israel-Hamas 2024 Symposium, 7 June 2024. https://lieber.westpoint.edu/ai-based-targeting-gaza-surveying-expert-responses-refining-debate. Accessed 1 September 2025

Klonowska K (2024b) Designing for Reasonableness: The Algorithmic Mediation of Reasonableness in Targeting Decisions. Articles of War, Lieber Institute West Point, 23 February 2024. https://lieber.westpoint.edu/designing-reasonableness-algorithmic-mediation-reasonableness-targeting-decisions. Accessed 1 September 2025

Kwik J, Zurek T, van Engers T (2022) Designing International Humanitarian Law into Military Autonomous Devices. In: Ajmeri N, Morris Martin A, Savarimuthu BTR (eds) Coordination, Organizations, Institutions, Norms, and Ethics for Governance of Multi-Agent Systems XV. COINE 2022. Lecture Notes in Computer Science, vol 13549. Springer, Cham, pp. 1–18

Kwik J, Zwanenburg M, Took C, Aarts J (2025) Controlling Military Artificial Intelligence: Harnessing Rules of Engagement and Military Directives. Asser Policy Brief 2025–01. https://ssrn.com/abstract=5132731. Accessed 1 September 2025

Lewis DA, Blum G, Modirzadeh NK (2016) War-Algorithm Accountability. Research Briefing, Harvard Law School Program on International Law and Armed Conflict. https://pilac.law.harvard.edu/waa. Accessed 1 September 2025

Marauhn T (2018) Meaningful Human Control—And the Politics of International Law. In: Heintschel von Heinegg W, Frau R, Singer T (eds) Dehumanization of Warfare: Legal Implications of New Weapon Technologies. Springer, Cham, 207–218
McKernan B, Davies H (2024) 'The Machine Did It Coldly': Israel Used AI to Identify 37,000 Hamas Targets. *The Guardian*, 3 April 2024. https://www.theguardian.com/world/2024/apr/03/israel-gaza-ai-database-hamas-airstrikes. Accessed 1 September 2025
Nadibaidze A, Bode I, Zhang Q (2024) AI in Military Decision Support Systems: A Review of Developments and Debates. Report, AutoNorms Project. https://usercontent.one/wp/www.autonorms.eu/wp-content/uploads/2024/11/AI-DSS-report-WEB.pdf. Accessed 1 September 2025
Pacholska M (2022) Military Artificial Intelligence and the Principle of Distinction: A State Responsibility Perspective. Israel Law Review. https://doi.org/10.1017/S0021223722000188
Pacholska M (2023) Autonomous Weapons. In: Brozek B, Kanevskaia O, Pałka P (eds) Research Handbook on Law and Technology. Edward Elgar, Cheltenham, pp. 392–407
Pacholska M (2024) Many Hands in the Black Box: Artificial Intelligence and the Responsibility of International Organizations. In: Deplano R, Berkes A, Collins R (eds) Reassessing the Articles on the Responsibility of International Organizations: From Theory to Practice. Edward Elgar, Cheltenham, pp. 171–187
Rivera JP, Mukobi G, Reuel A, Lamparth M, Smith C, Schneider J (2024) Escalation Risks from Language Models in Military and Diplomatic Decision-Making. arXiv. https://arxiv.org/abs/2401.03408. Accessed 1 September 2025
Schwarz E (2021) Autonomous Weapons Systems, Artificial Intelligence, and the Problem of Meaningful Human Control. Philosophical Journal of Conflict and Violence. https://doi.org/10.22618/TP.PJCV.20215.1.139004
Soltanzadeh S (2022) Strictly Human: Limitations of Autonomous Systems. Minds and Machines. https://doi.org/10.1007/s11023-021-09582-7
Soltanzadeh S (2025) A Metaphysical Account of Agency for Technology Governance. AI & Society. https://doi.org/10.1007/s00146-024-01941-z
Soltanzadeh S, Mooney M (2021) Autonomy in the Context of Decision-Making Dilemmas. In: Pereira Martins C (ed) Do Desporto/On Sports: Theory vs. Praxis. Coimbra University Institute of Philosophical Studies and Fundação do Desporto, Coimbra, pp. 147–162
Stewart R, Hinds G (2023) Algorithms of War: The Use of Artificial Intelligence in Decision-Making in Armed Conflict. ICRC Humanitarian Law & Policy Blog. https://blogs.icrc.org/law-and-policy/2023/10/24/algorithms-of-war-use-of-artificial-intelligence-decision-making-armed-conflict. Accessed 1 September 2025
Williams AP, Scharre PD (eds) (2015) Autonomous Systems: Issues for Defence Policymakers. NATO Capability Engineering and Innovation Division, Norfolk, VA, USA
Woodcock TK (2021a) Artificial Intelligence: Is the Answer More Law? Asser Blog, 25 January 2021. https://www.asser.nl/about-the-institute/asser-today/blog-artificial-intelligence-is-the-answer-more-law. Accessed 1 September 2025
Woodcock TK (2021b) Eclipsing Human Rights: Why the International Regulation of Military AI Is Not Limited to International Humanitarian Law. Human Rights Here Blog, Doctoral Research Forum Blog Series, 13 July 2021. https://humanrightshere.com/post/doctoral. Accessed 1 September 2025
Woodcock TK (2023a) Decision-Support Systems and Human-Machine Interaction. Report of the Panel Discussion held at the REAIM Summit, 15 February 2023. https://www.asser.nl/dilema/news-and-updates/report-dss-and-hmi. Accessed 1 September 2025
Woodcock TK (2023b) Human/Machine(-Learning) Interactions, Human Agency and the International Humanitarian Law Proportionality Standard. Global Society. https://doi.org/10.1080/13600826.2023.2267592
Zurek T, Kwik J, van Engers T (2023) Model of a Military Autonomous Device Following International Humanitarian Law. Ethics and Information Technology. https://doi.org/10.1007/s10676-023-09682-1

Zurek T, Mohajeriparizi M, Kwik J, van Engers T (2022a) Can a Military Autonomous Device Follow International Humanitarian Law? JURIX 2022 Conference Paper, Legal Knowledge and Information Systems, pp. 273–278. https://ebooks.iospress.nl/volumearticle/62066. Accessed 1 September 2025

Zurek T, Woodcock TK, Pacholska M, van Engers T (2022b) Computational Modelling of the Proportionality Analysis under International Humanitarian Law for Military Decision-Support Systems. Working Paper. https://ssrn.com/abstract=4008946. Accessed 1 September 2025

Zurek T, Wyner A (2022) Towards a Formal Framework for Motivated Argumentation and the Roots of Conflict. Proceedings of the 22nd Workshop on Computational Models of Natural Argument (CMNA), CEUR-WS 3205: 39–50

Zwanenburg M (2021) Biometrics and International Humanitarian Law. Articles of War, Lieber Institute, 28 October 2021. https://lieber.westpoint.edu/biometrics-international-humanitarian-law. Accessed 1 September 2025

Bérénice Boutin is a Senior Researcher in International Law at the Asser Institute, University of Amsterdam (The Netherlands). She leads the DILEMA project on Designing International Law and Ethics into Military Artificial Intelligence, for which she secured a grant of over €600,000 from the Dutch Research Council (NWO). Her research explores the interplay between new technologies, such as artificial intelligence, and international law. This includes examining how international law shapes the governance and regulation of emerging technologies, as well as how these technologies challenge core notions and concepts of international law.

Taylor Kate Woodcock is a researcher in public international law at the Asser Institute, University of Amsterdam (The Netherlands). She researches international legal practices, human agency, and AI-enabled technologies. Her doctoral thesis, entitled *Human–Machine (Learning) Interactions: War and Law in the AI Era* and written as part of the DILEMA project, examines how the use of AI in military targeting operations can shape practices of legal reasoning and the exercise of human agency. Taylor has research experience in various fields of public international law, including international humanitarian law, international human rights law, international criminal law, and international arms control and disarmament law.

Sadjad Soltanzadeh is a Researcher in Philosophy of Technology at the University of Twente (The Netherlands). From 2020 to 2023, he was part of the DILEMA project, where his research explored the constituents of human autonomy, the limitations of autonomous systems, and the interaction between human and machine agency. In his book *Problem-Solving Technologies: A User-Friendly Philosophy* (2022), Soltanzadeh has introduced the *activity realist* approach, which argues that the study of technical systems must be accompanied by the study of the human activities they are intended to support.

Chapter 2
Normative Reasoning and Military AI: DILEMA's Dilemmas

Sadjad Soltanzadeh

Contents

Abstract As artificial intelligence (AI) systems are increasingly integrated into military operations, critical questions arise about the permissibility and feasibility of programming normative reasoning into AI systems. In this chapter, I address these issues in two main sections. First, I explore arguments that challenge the permissibility of delegating normative military reasoning to AI systems. I distinguish between concerns that stem from the characteristics of current AI technologies and the state of existing regulatory frameworks, and those that arise from fundamental moral and legal principles. The latter include inalienable obligations and activities that necessitate continuous human involvement. Second, I analyse the challenges of programming normative reasoning into AI, highlighting the constraints of rule-based and data-driven approaches. These constraints include the difficulties of modelling complex moral and legal reasoning, the risks associated with unreliable machine learning outputs, and the practical and ethical challenges of testing the reliability of high-stakes AI systems in real-world applications. In the face of these challenges, delegating normative military reasoning to AI systems remains impermissible and unfeasible.

S. Soltanzadeh (✉)
University of Twente, Enschede, The Netherlands
e-mail: s.soltanzadeh@utwente.nl

B. Boutin et al. (eds.), *Legal, Ethical, and Technical Dilemmas in Military Artificial Intelligence*, https://doi.org/10.1007/978-94-6265-759-5_2

Keywords Normative Reasoning · Inalienable Obligations · Responsibility Gap · Explainability · Artificial Intelligence (AI) · Knowledge-Based Systems · Data-Driven Systems · Empirical Evidence · International Humanitarian Law (IHL) · Simulation

2.1 Introduction

Not long after its official launch in September 2020, the DILEMA project developed an academic identity that is broader than, and perhaps even critical of, the narrow meaning of the phrase 'Designing International Law and Ethics into Military Artificial Intelligence'. The narrow meaning of DILEMA can give the impression that the project was about encoding international law and ethics into artificial intelligence (AI) systems, that the project members assumed such systems could perform military tasks in compliance with international law and moral principles, and devoted their research to deciphering how to make this happen. This narrow meaning of DILEMA is in line with a field of study that is known as machine ethics, where 'value alignment' has become one of its key principles. Machine ethics focuses on designing and programming AI and autonomous systems to behave in ways that align with human norms and values. But the fact that DILEMA's acronym resembles the English word 'dilemma' is significant and intentional, because the idea of designing international law and ethics into military AI inherently involves some dilemmas.[1] Designing AI systems whose behaviours are expected to align with those of legally compliant and morally virtuous humans may not be feasible, desirable, or even logically sound.

In this chapter, I highlight some of DILEMA's dilemmas by questioning the suitability of AI systems for performing normatively significant military decisions. Many military activities are normatively significant, and their permissible performance requires normative reasoning. Of course, not all interactions of military personnel with AI systems involve normative reasoning or are normatively significant. But those at the forefront of military operations, such as those that are used for committing acts of violence, are inherently normatively significant. I reserve the phrase 'military AI' to refer to such systems.

It is important to clarify that the distinction between decision-making systems and decision-support systems is irrelevant for my arguments.[2] A system capable

---

[1] This critical approach towards the narrow meaning of DILEMA is reflected in some of the project's publications, including the DILEMA Statement on the Global Governance of Artificial Intelligence in the Military, see Boutin et al. 2023.

[2] An AI system qualifies as a decision-making system when it makes decisions without any human interventions or inputs. In other words, the relationship between humans and AI decision-making systems is such that humans remain 'out of the loop' or 'on the loop'. Automated air-defence systems, which detect and intercept incoming aerial threats without any human intervention, are examples of decision-making systems. Decision-support systems, in contrast, require humans to remain 'in the loop'. These systems aid their users with cognitive tasks without fully replacing human decision making. A system that monitors the behavioural indicators of a person's level of

of making decisions can function as a decision-support system if it is always used under human supervision, with humans remaining on the loop. Conversely, a system initially employed as a decision-support system may effectively turn into a decision-making system if, for instance, due to automation bias, human users always follow the system's recommendations. More broadly, the distinction between decision-making and decision-support systems cannot be made outside the context in which the system is employed, without observing the specifics of human–machine interactions.[3] In any case, both types of systems may be used to perform normative reasoning in various ways and can therefore be relevant to the discussions of this chapter.

Here, I reason about military AI and question the normative reasoning of military AI. My analysis is structured around two distinct, yet related, perspectives: permissibility and programmability. I consider these 'DILEMA's dilemmas', as they reveal the extent to which designing international law and ethics into military AI is permissible or technically achievable. I first examine the permissibility of delegating normative military reasoning to AI systems (Sect. 2.2). To do so, I outline some moral and legal arguments that challenge the use of AI systems for military decision making by showing that such arguments have different scopes of validity: those that are applicable solely to current military technologies and regulatory frameworks, and those that are more fundamental and applicable to all AI systems, including future ones. The latter arguments are grounded in the nature of moral or legal obligations rather than the technical features of AI systems. I introduce the notion of 'inalienable obligations' to further clarify why delegating normative roles to AI systems can contradict the logical conditions that govern normatively significant activities. I will then discuss the challenges of encoding normative military reasoning by exploring both rule-based and data-driven techniques of programming AI systems (Sect. 2.3). I discuss the limitations of rule-based methods in modelling complex moral and legal reasoning, on the one hand, and expose the lack of relevant empirical evidence that could support the development and use of high-stakes data-driven systems, on the other.

2.2 Permissibility Dilemmas

In recent years, as many States have invested in using AI systems to conduct military activities, various arguments have emerged that question the moral and legal permissibility of using AI systems for military decision making. These arguments,

---

alertness to recommend when they should take a break, or one that analyses large amounts of data and presents patterns to its human users, would qualify as a decision-support system. Outside military AI literature, decision-support systems are also referred to as 'AI assistants'. For a taxonomy of AI-enabled decision-support systems, see Poszler and Lange 2024.

[3] I believe the way in which we particularly categorise technologies based on their functions (e.g., decision-making vs. decision-support systems) must be based on the actual consequences of their use. This approach, referred to as the 'belief-based consequentialist theory of function', results in a dynamic and non-binary categorisation. See Soltanzadeh 2022b, pp. 111–124.

referred to here as dilemmas of permissibility, are varied, but I believe that they can be categorised into two general groups based on their scopes of validity. Some arguments focus on current systems and existing regulatory frameworks to show that, given the present state of affairs, using AI systems to make life-and-death decisions is impermissible. The second group of arguments takes a more fundamental stance, suggesting that, regardless of technological advancements or the capabilities of AI systems, society should never permit the use of AI systems for making life-and-death decisions. I clarify these two lines of reasoning separately.

2.2.1 Dilemmas of Current Systems Within Current Social Structures

Some arguments that challenge the use of AI systems to perform military operations stem from the technical characteristics of current AI systems. For example, it can be argued that unexplainability is a feature of systems that are trained by feeding data into multi-layered neural networks.[4] The argument is that it is often extremely difficult to explain how an AI system developed using multi-layered neural networks generates a specific output, or why it produces that output rather than another. For example, it may be impossible to explain why an AI system classifies one person carrying a particular object as a civilian gathering wood to make fire, while classifying a similarly appearing individual who is carrying the same object as a combatant with a gun and hence a legitimate military target.[5] Unexplainability can in turn lead to lack of transparency and trust,[6] and create problems for attribution of moral or legal responsibility.[7] Each of these can, in itself, be used to argue against delegating normatively significant roles to AI systems.[8]

---

[4] Yampolskiy 2020.

[5] This example alludes to an event during the Israel-Gaza war. As reported by Al Jazeera, on 3 October 2024, an Israeli drone attack targeted a group of Palestinians when they were collecting wood to set up a fire and use it for cooking. See Mahmoud 2024.

[6] See, for example, von Eschenbach 2021, who explores how the opacity of AI systems, particularly those using deep learning, exacerbates trust issues. Lukyanenko et al. 2022 argue that when AI systems make decisions that are neither transparent nor understandable, users may find it difficult to trust the system's outputs. Yang et al. 2023 also review different approaches to explainable AI, their limitations and applications, and highlight the importance of transparency and explainability.

[7] For example, Coeckelbergh 2020 discusses the problem of responsibility attribution in AI and argues that explainability is crucial for addressing epistemic conditions related to transparency and accountability. Baum et al. 2022 too argue that explainable AI, particularly reason-giving AI, ensures that individuals can be held accountable for decisions made by AI systems by providing clear explanations for the system's recommendations. For further discussion of the relationship between explainability and accountability, see also discussions by Doshi-Velez et al. 2017.

[8] It is out of the scope of this chapter to spell out how the lack of explainability leads to the issues of transparency, trust, or responsibility attribution. But I believe that it is important to understand the connections between different concepts and issues, and how some problems arise from others.

In a similar vein, some argue that given the current state of regulatory frameworks, employing AI systems in military operations should be avoided. The arguments that point out the potential responsibility gaps arising from the use of AI systems follow this line of reasoning.[9] To clarify why I consider the scope of these arguments to be limited to the state of regulatory frameworks, I need to first clarify how I approach responsibility gaps.

The origin of the notion of the 'responsibility gap' has been attributed to Matthias, who discussed the problem of attributing responsibility for the operation of systems that are capable of learning from interactions with their environment.[10] One of the first authors to discuss this notion in relation to military applications of AI was Sparrow, who highlighted the difficulty of attributing responsibility for deaths caused by autonomous weapon systems, which are also known as 'killer robots'.[11] The argument is that the (semi-)autonomous operation of such systems means that humans lack sufficient control over the systems to be held responsible for their operation. At the same time, it does not make sense to hold the technical systems themselves responsible. Hence, responsibility gaps can occur because no one can be held responsible for the harms caused by autonomous weapon systems.

In the past twenty years, many intricacies have been added to this notion from moral, legal, and technical perspectives. And while highlighting responsibility gaps was initially intended to warn against using autonomous weapon systems, it has more recently been used to caution against a wider range of military AI systems, including those that may not be classified as autonomous weapon systems.

One of the intricacies of the notion of the responsibility gap is that such a gap should not be understood exclusively as a problem arising from certain technical systems alone. Rather, it is a *socio*-technical problem; i.e. it arises as a result of the interaction between technical systems and the social structures that shape how responsibility is attributed. Here I elaborate this point further, but specifically, I focus on accountability gaps, as a species of responsibility gaps. Accountability gaps arise when existing frameworks fail to hold any actor accountable for the harms caused by a given event. Understanding accountability gaps as a socio-technical problem entails, on the one hand, that a technical system may give rise to such a gap in one society but not in another, and on the other hand, that the gaps can stem from *any* technical system, be it an AI-powered one or any other technology.[12] To show that accountability gaps are not limited to AI systems, I use the example of a non-digital technology.

This understanding prevents a fragmented approach to the topic. It also enables us to recognise that addressing certain fundamental issues can automatically resolve others.

[9] In this volume, Chap. 11 by Romansky and Sweijs discusses the importance of addressing the issue of responsibility in the global governance of military AI.

[10] Matthias 2004.

[11] Sparrow 2007.

[12] In addition to the discussions that follow in this chapter, see also Santoni de Sio and Mecacci, who draw on examples from Simpson and Müller 2016, to argue that responsibility gaps can also arise in non-learning systems, such as buildings and bridges, see Santoni de Sio and Mecacci 2021, p. 1070.

Consider the case of lightning rods that are designed to protect buildings by attracting lightning strikes and safely directing electrical currents into the ground.[13] Prior to the invention of the lightning rod, lightning strikes could harm people in urban areas. Such accidents would not lead to any responsibility gap because they were uncontrollable natural events. With the advent of lightning rods, lightning strikes became more controllable. Currently, in many societies, accidents caused by lightning strikes in urban areas do not result in a responsibility gap because, on the one hand, such accidents have become controllable, and on the other hand, clear mechanisms for responsibility attribution are in place. That is to say, building companies and manufacturers of lightning rods must follow certain guidelines, and their failure to do so can make them accountable for accidents caused by lightning strikes. However, in some societies, there may not be clear mechanisms of responsibility attribution in place to account for the deaths or injuries caused by lightning strikes in urban areas. For example, building companies may not be required to install lightning rods, or there may not be reliable certification processes in place to ensure the effectiveness of the lightning rods that are produced and available on the market. In such societies, despite the availability of lightning rods, lightning strikes can lead to accountability gaps. They can lead to accountability gaps because although someone or a group of people are harmed, and despite the presence of means to prevent the harm, no one can be held accountable for the harm.

Similarly, whether AI systems used in the military lead to an accountability gap depends partly on how their production and use are regulated. One channel through which humans can impact the use of AI systems is regulation,[14] and one important dimension of regulation is establishing frameworks for responsibility attribution.[15] The absence of effective regulatory frameworks can lead to accountability gaps. Grey zones of underregulated technologies can be abused to avoid the responsible production or use of military AI systems.

Most people who argue that military AI systems do not lead to responsibility gaps also (implicitly) refer to the socio-technical nature of these gaps. They show that existing social institutions create mechanisms for holding wrongdoers accountable. Such institutions can ensure that technologies are not developed in a vacuum, and their development and use are subject to regulations. For instance, Boutin discusses State responsibility for violations of international law involving military AI technologies, and highlights how existing regulatory frameworks can provide mechanisms for accountability at the stages of development, acquisition, and use.[16] Bo also argues that the integration of AI in military targeting processes can create a responsibility gap because it complicates the determination of *mens rea* (i.e., the mental element of intentional wrongdoing under (international) criminal law).[17] She suggests that incorporating risk-taking mental elements, such as *dolus eventualis* (i.e., awareness

[13] This case builds on a similar discussion in Soltanzadeh et al. 2020.

[14] Soltanzadeh 2025, p. 1731.

[15] Ibid.

[16] Boutin 2023.

[17] Bo 2021.

of likely outcomes) and recklessness, into criminal procedures could help address this gap.[18] Oimann and Salatino also explore the doctrine of command responsibility and how it can be applied to hold human agents accountable for AI-induced outcomes in military contexts.[19]

In any case, the scope of the arguments that highlight potential responsibility gaps, similar to those linked to the unexplainability of current AI systems, is confined to the current generation of AI systems in current societies. These arguments are not necessarily valid for all AI systems in all societies. If systems were designed in ways that the problem of unexplainability did not arise, or if social mechanisms were in place to responsibly manufacture and use military AI systems, some of the arguments against the use of these systems for military operations may not be sound anymore as they would rest on false premises.

2.2.2 *Epistemic and Logical Dilemmas*

Moral and legal arguments against the use of AI for military operations (or other normatively significant purposes) can have a wider scope of validity. Some take a second approach and ground their arguments on the nature of moral or legal obligations rather than on the technical features of AI systems or the state of regulatory frameworks. These latter arguments can be applied to all systems, regardless of their design features or the social structures surrounding their production and use. The overarching point of these latter arguments is that outsourcing certain roles to AI systems may contradict the way in which humans should fulfil their moral or legal obligations, including obligations that militaries need to abide by in conducting their activities. I believe that although on the surface, these arguments seem to provide moral or legal arguments on the permissibility of delegating military decision making to AI systems, their underlying reasoning often rests on epistemic or logical considerations. So, I believe the general form of these arguments can be expressed as follows. (1) Fulfilling each moral or legal obligation requires specific logical and epistemic conditions to be met. (2) When these logical and epistemic conditions are not met, individuals are unable to fulfil some of their moral or legal obligations. (3) Some epistemic and logical conditions cannot be met by delegating the performance of certain tasks to AI systems. And therefore, (4) delegating the performance of certain tasks to AI systems can contradict the way in which humans should fulfil their moral or legal obligations or perform some military tasks.

---

[18] Ibid.

[19] Oimann and Salatino 2024.

For example, one of the concerns frequently raised in relation to the use of AI systems for military targeting is that these systems may not reliably distinguish between combatants and non-combatants, or more broadly, between legitimate and illegitimate military targets.[20] Distinguishing between combatants and non-combatants is a moral and legal obligation, and failure to do so would be morally and legally problematic. However, in essence, distinguishing between entities of different kinds is an epistemic task, pertaining to our knowledge about the world and the way we define our categories. So, in this context, the use of AI systems for military targeting may indeed be impermissible. Yet the core of this normative problem is epistemic: AI systems may not be able to reliably identify the different categories that their role requires them to. This epistemic problem is similar to the inability of an automatic door to distinguish between a human who intends to enter a building and a plastic bag that is being blown by the wind.

To further develop these arguments, I rely on the distinction between engaging in an activity and performing the actions required to achieve the goals of that activity.[21] When using machines, we delegate the performance of certain actions to them. However, the entities engaged in activities are not machines, but human users. Machines may be able to perform some tasks, but they cannot engage in activities, i.e., they cannot have goals or seek to fulfil obligations. From this distinction, we can derive two types of conditions: epistemic conditions of performance and logical conditions of engagement. The former conditions specify how a specific task should be performed to bring about the goal of the activity.[22] The latter specify the conditions that must be met for a person (or group of people) to be engaged in an activity. Each set of conditions can lead to a distinct argument against the delegation of certain normatively significant tasks, such as military decision making, to AI systems. Epistemic arguments show that AI systems cannot replace human decision making in the performance of certain tasks, and logical arguments show that humans cannot meaningfully fulfil their obligations if they outsource some of their tasks to AI systems.

2.2.3 Dilemmas of Epistemic Subjectivity

The epistemic conditions of performance and the logical conditions of engagement can be further clarified. Once again, I start with mundane examples before dealing with military uses of AI. For some activities, such as vacuuming a floor, it is possible to delegate most, or all, of the required tasks to machines and accomplish the goal

[20] Viveros 2024.

[21] This distinction is borrowed from Soltanzadeh 2022a, pp. 272–3.

[22] Note that the question of 'how should a task be performed?' can be answered through two distinct sets of conditions. Some conditions show how the task must be performed in order for the goal of the activity be achieved, while some others are general norms that are, or ought to be, considered in decisions made while performing the activity. The latter are normative frameworks that govern activities. See Soltanzadeh 2022b, p. 176.

of the activity. This is because the goal of such an activity is objectively clear, and the steps required to accomplish the goal of the activity can be objectively defined. It can be objectively determined whether a floor has been vacuumed, and the steps that can be taken to have the floor vacuumed can also be objectively described. But this is not the case with all activities. The point of some activities may not be about bringing about an objectively discernible state of affairs. Similarly, the steps required to achieve the goal of this latter type of activity may not be objectively definable. The point of some activities may be linked to *how* the activity is performed. Consider, for example, the activity of using one's car to go on a leisurely drive.[23] The goal of this activity is about the quality of the experience of driving itself. There is no objective way to tell whether the goal of leisurely driving has been fulfilled. Similarly, there is no objective recipe for performing the activity of leisurely driving. One is engaged in the activity of leisurely driving when one makes relaxed and often spontaneous decisions, which are triggered by spur-of-the-moment feelings and curiosities. These unpredictable momentary decisions constitute the activity of leisurely driving. So there is something epistemically different between the activity of leisurely driving, on the one hand, and vacuuming the floor, on the other. Unlike the latter, the former does not aim to bring about a particular physical change to the world, and no recipe can describe the steps that, once followed, will lead to the achievement of its goal. For these reasons, unlike vacuuming, the activity of leisurely driving cannot necessarily be delegated to others, including AI systems; it requires continuous subjective involvement.

Now, the above argument can be generalised to military AI and normative decision making in military activities. While achieving a military objective, viewed purely from a tactical or strategic perspective, may be objectively defined and hence, in principle, transferable to AI systems, the same cannot be said about all norms that govern military activities. The principle of precautions in International Humanitarian Law (IHL) is a good example here. This principle requires parties to a conflict to take all feasible precautions 'to avoid, and in any event to minimize, incidental loss of civilian life, injury to civilians, and damage to civilian objects'.[24] There are different ways to interpret the precautionary principle depending on how much discretion is given to commanders in deciding when and how to apply this principle. Under one interpretation, the precautionary principle is a subjective standard.[25] By subjective standard, I do not suggest that the content of this principle is subjectively determined. What I mean is that the application of the precautionary principle necessitates the commanders' continuous subjective involvement. Here, there is no obligation of

[23] This example, along with the related discussion of activities that cannot be delegated to machines for epistemic reasons, is further explored in Soltanzadeh 2022a, pp. 275–8.

[24] Henckaerts and Doswald-Beck 2009, p. 51. In addition to customary IHL, see also Article 57 of Additional Protocol I to the Geneva Conventions, which provides that '[i]n the conduct of military operations, constant care shall be taken to spare the civilian population, civilians and civilian objects'; Protocol Additional (I) to the Geneva Conventions of 12 August 1949, and Relating to the Protection of Victims of International Armed Conflicts, opened for signature 8 June 1977, 1125 UNTS 3, entered into force 7 December 1979 (API).

[25] Marchant 2020, p. 69.

result: instead, commanders are required to set up effective intelligence systems to gather and evaluate relevant information.[26] In other words, assessing whether the principle of precautions has been fulfilled cannot be achieved solely by examining the outcome of an operation and the objective states of affairs, such as the number of civilian deaths. Instead, this assessment depends on a range of factors, including the context of the conflict, the perspectives of those involved, and the commander's ongoing efforts to seek out reasonably available information. The nature of the precautionary principle renders it inherently reliant on continuous human judgement. Hence, complying with the precautionary principle cannot be achieved by relying on an AI system.[27]

2.2.4 Dilemmas of Inalienable Obligations

As I mentioned earlier, arguments against the use of AI systems for normative military decision making may be grounded in the nature of moral or legal obligations. In the previous Subsection, I discussed how the use of AI systems may contradict the epistemic conditions that stipulate active engagement of military commanders. Here, I discuss how the use of AI systems may contradict logical conditions that stipulate what is required for humans to be engaged in particular activities and fulfil their obligations. To illustrate this, I again begin with a non-military example.

Consider the activity of worshipping a deity.[28] According to some religions, engagement in the act of worship necessarily requires the worshipper to personally perform certain movements or recite specific words. Their active participation as a worshipper is a logical requirement for the goal of worshipping. One cannot send a robot to worship on one's behalf; if they do so, they are no longer engaged in the activity of worship themselves. This is not because robots cannot learn to 'recite' the words or perform the movements required for worshipping a deity. This is not an epistemic problem. This is a logical problem. Worshipping can be an *inalienable* activity: it must be carried out by the individual personally. Inalienable activities cannot be outsourced to others.

---

[26] Ibid., p. 70.

[27] Two points need to be added here. First, I do not consider the argument that I discussed here to be the only argument challenging the idea that the functioning of an AI system can suffice for the compliance with the precautionary principle. Another argument can be purely legal on the ground that ultimately abiding by the precautionary principle is the responsibility of States, which act through their organs and affiliated entities, including military commanders. This legal framework does not permit shifting responsibility and the burden of observing the precautionary principle onto AI systems. Second, I should acknowledge that different interpretations of the precautionary principle result in different assessments of whether AI systems can comply with its requirements. For example, Winter adopts an objective interpretation of the precautionary principle to argue that, if equipped with sufficiently advanced sensors and algorithmic intelligence, autonomous systems can outperform humans in discharging precautionary obligations concerning the 'choice of means' and 'choice of methods' of warfare. See Winter 2022, pp. 17–19.

[28] This example is borrowed from Soltanzadeh 2022a, pp. 278–283.

The above point can be extended to normatively significant activities that necessitate human involvement. In this vein, one might say that some of our obligations are *inalienable*; they cannot be delegated to others. For instance, it can be argued that respect is an inalienable obligation, meaning that showing respect to someone or something requires active behavioural and mental engagement in the respectful activity. The active engagement of a conscious and reflective subject is a logical condition for fulfilling the duty to respect. This can be the case for our duty to respect others or to respect our moral or legal obligations.

Respecting others means acknowledging their autonomy, considering their feelings, and recognising their intrinsic value in our interactions with them,[29] even if our interactions are hostile in nature, as in military operations. Respect is not merely about outward behaviour; it involves an internal commitment to valuing others and their rights.[30] Similarly, respecting social or legal norms requires awareness of those norms and recognition of their validity and significance in guiding behaviour. In this way, respecting social or legal norms requires more than seemingly compliant behaviour. It requires believing in the legitimacy of norms. It requires that individuals or institutions 'internalise' the norms and accept them as legitimate and worthy of adherence.[31]

Given the importance of the mental components of respectful behaviour, one can argue that respect is an inalienable obligation. AI systems lack the potential for respect. They cannot acknowledge others' worth, autonomy, or feelings, nor can they recognise the significance of norms and obligations. While AI systems may exhibit behavioural manifestations of respectful conduct or seemingly compliant behaviour, they are incapable of respecting humans or social and legal norms. Accordingly, tasks that must be performed with respect, such as military operations, cannot be delegated to AI systems. Once such tasks are delegated to technologies, the individuals or institutions expected to show respect are no longer doing so. They are neither showing respect toward the targeted humans nor showing respect to relevant international norms and regulatory institutions. More generally, inalienable obligations necessitate subjective engagement. When an inalienable obligation becomes an important dimension of normative reasoning, normative reasoning cannot be delegated to AI systems; otherwise, humans fail to fulfil their obligations.

---

[29] Here, I am referring to 'recognition respect', as distinct from 'appraisal respect', see Darwall 1977. Recognition respect is the respect owed to all persons simply by virtue of their status as persons.

[30] According to Dillon, respectful behaviour is merely an expression of respect; it is not respect itself. Hence, it is possible to 'behave in ways that are outwardly respectful without having respect for the object', see Dillon 2007, p. 204.

[31] Hart's notion of the 'internal point of view' can substantiate what I mean here by respecting the law. According to Hart, for individuals to truly respect and follow the law, they must not only comply with it out of habit or in response to external enforcement but also adopt a mental attitude that acknowledges and accepts the rules as legitimate and binding, see Hart 1961, pp. 55–57. Unlike mere compliance in a purely behavioural sense, respect for social or legal norms involves an internal commitment to the principles and values embodied by those norms.

2.3 Programming Dilemmas

For the rest of this chapter, I engage with the question of whether normative reasoning can be programmed into military AI systems. More specifically, I explore whether it is possible to program a form of algorithmic reasoning into AI systems that mimics the relevant moral and legal reasoning required for military decision making.

Reasoning refers to the process of drawing conclusions from a set of premises. For example, from the premise that 'Building X is a shelter zone and is full of displaced civilians', it can be concluded that 'Building X should not be targeted'. To design AI systems capable of exhibiting legally compliant and morally permissible behaviour, it is important to train them in a way that their outputs are functionally similar to human normative reasoning; e.g., the systems can differentiate between shelter zones and legitimate military targets and avoid targeting the former.

Normative reasoning rests on identification. Before determining whether a building can be legitimately targeted, it must first be identified. It needs to be determined whether it actually is a building; and it needs to be determined whether it is a shelter zone, a military compound, a hospital, or a different type of building. Identification is thus a crucial prerequisite for any decision making. While humans rely on their sensory organs and cognitive abilities to identify their surrounding objects, modern AI systems typically depend on neural networks to process what they detect through their sensors and group objects into distinct categories.

Neural networks belong to a general technique of creating AI that is known as 'data-driven'. Data-driven techniques primarily rely on large datasets, statistical methods, and machine learning techniques to make decisions or predictions. Data-driven techniques are contrasted with knowledge-based techniques, which rely on explicitly encoded knowledge, often symbolically represented by rules, facts, and relationships.

Unlike identification that is often exclusively tasked to data-driven systems, reasoning (i.e., the process of drawing conclusions and making military recommendations or decisions) can be encoded into machines by using either knowledge-based or data-driven, machine learning techniques. Here I do not discuss the dilemmas of identification; I will not discuss whether AI systems can perceive the world through the same normatively significant categories as humans do. Instead, I dedicate the remainder of this chapter to discussing the challenges of programming normative reasoning. I discuss challenges of using knowledge-based and data-driven techniques separately.

2.3.1 *Dilemmas of Knowledge-Based Reasoning*

Knowledge-based reasoning is structured around rules. These rules typically take the form of if–then statements designed to generate outputs based on specific conditions. Developing rule-based reasoning involves three main steps.

The first step is identification of the relevant legal and moral rules. Each activity is governed by different rules. Correctly identifying these rules ensures that AI systems are aligned with the relevant norms and principles. For example, in the case of military AI, applicable rules may include principles of IHL, international human rights law, or moral values relating to fighting a war for a just cause and fighting it justly. The second step involves formalising the identified rules by translating the relevant moral and legal rules into the language of formal logic. In this step, rules that are identified in the previous step are expressed in a language that can be codified into computers. In logic, this step requires defining inference rules. Inference rules specify what can be logically derived from a set of premises. For example, using natural language, one may reason from the premise 'Building X is a shelter zone and is full of displaced civilians' to the conclusion 'Building X should not be targeted'. This reasoning can be formalised using the inference rule '$A \rightarrow B$', where A stands for 'Building X is a shelter zone and is full of displaced civilians' and B for 'Building X should not be targeted'. The symbol '$\rightarrow$' indicates that B is inferred from A. Formalisation bridges the gap between human language and the language of machines. So, translating moral and legal rules into inference rules of logic serves as a stepping stone for the third step, which involves programming normative reasoning into computers. In this step, the inference rules are codified into computer programs so that AI systems can mimic the relevant legal and moral reasoning.

Each of these steps can face some challenges. The first step, i.e. the idea that law and ethics can be reduced to a set of rules, is itself an untenable assumption. More specifically, even if one assumes that all aspects of law and ethics can be linguistically expressed, rule-based approaches to normative decision making face at least three major criticisms. Firstly, rules may be ambiguous, and even those that use clearly defined terms inevitably stay at a level of generality, requiring further interpretation. This makes plain rules inherently insufficient. Secondly, rules often conflict with one another, creating confusion about which rule should take precedence. In military decision making, for example, many operations may be legally permissible according to the IHL principles of distinction, proportionality, and precaution.[32] But lawful military operations may still be morally wrong for resulting in the deaths of innocent humans or perpetuating cycles of violence. Here we have a conflict between different sets of rules, where one set permits an action, while the other forbids it. Determining which principle should be prioritised can itself be context dependent. Thirdly, rules can never be comprehensive. Even the most extensive rule sets may fail to account for unique situations that fall outside the predefined rules, leading to uncertainty and potential gaps in decision making. These critiques underline the insufficiency of rule-based approaches for capturing the complexity of normative reasoning.[33]

---

[32] Respectively, API, above n. 24, Articles 48, 51(5)(b) and 57.

[33] The limitations of rule-based approaches have been discussed by various authors across different fields. Schauer, for example, explores the limitations and challenges of relying solely on rules for decision making. He argues that while rules play a significant role, their application can be problematic due to ambiguities, conflicts, and the inability to cover every possible scenario. Schauer emphasises the need for flexibility and discretion in decision-making processes, especially in complex and dynamic contexts like law and ethics. See Schauer 1991. Horty explores the doctrine of precedent in

The second challenge concerns the limitations of formalism; i.e., the practice of translating sentences of ordinary languages into the language of formal logic. Formalism rests on the assumption that a logical structure lies beneath the sentences of ordinary language and the valid arguments that are used in different domains. Formalising any domain of human knowledge is the practice of uncovering the deep logical structure that underlies that domain and expressing it through symbols of formal logic. This practice may also involve inventing new symbols and inference rules specific to the domain in question.

Formalism was invented as a logical and philosophical method late in the nineteenth century and gained significant popularity during the early decades of the twentieth century. This method was particularly developed by philosophers and logicians, such as Russell, Frege, and the early Wittgenstein, and subsequently adopted and combined with empiricism by the logical positivists.[34] Some of these thinkers had grand ambitions of translating *all* forms of human knowledge into the language of formal logic, as they believed that logical analysis reveals the ultimate structure of reality.[35] Statements that could not be formalised and subsequently empirically verified were draconically labelled as 'pseudo-scientific' or 'meaningless'.[36] By the 1960s, however, formalism, at least in its ambitious form, faced substantial criticism. Critics argued that natural languages do not always work in formal logical ways and that, outside of certain limited domains, it is simply not possible to formalise many forms of human knowledge. Many aspects of human knowledge, including moral statements or legal judgments, are often context-dependent in ways that formal systems cannot adequately accommodate. Conflicting principles and cultural variations further complicate formalistic aspirations.[37] Nevertheless, formalism has survived not as the path to truth, but as a method of investigation and creating new possibilities for human knowledge. In recent decades, this method has regained popularity in research on algorithmic reasoning and in the development and training of AI systems. Within the context of training military AI, only limited studies have attempted to formalise the rules of IHL. These efforts, however, have

common law and the balance between rules and reasons in judicial decision making, highlighting the limitations of relying solely on rules. See Horty 2011. Similarly, Soltanzadeh and Mooney argue that from the practitioners' perspective, over-reliance on rules can create chaos and complicate decision making, as rules cannot account for the nuances and complexities of real-world situations. They note that rules may conflict with one another and require further interpretation. See Soltanzadeh and Mooney 2021.

[34] Empiricism is the idea that knowledge comes from sensory experiences. Logical positivists combined empiricism with logical analysis. Logical analysis was meant to clarify statements of ordinary language and break them down into elementary statements that can be independently empirically verified. See, for example, Schlick 1936.

[35] Magee 1971, p. 21.

[36] See, for example, Wittgenstein 1961 [1921]. See also Schlick 1936 who discusses the logical positivists' verification principle, according to which, a statement is only meaningful if it can be empirically tested or is analytically true.

[37] The strengths, features, and limitations of formal logic have been discussed by many philosophers of logic. For a general overview, see Hintikka 2019.

acknowledged that such formalisation is only possible after making several assumptions and simplifications, including the assumption that values (such as civilian lives or military advantage) can be represented by numbers,[38] or that human subjective uncertainties can be modelled through mathematical probabilities.[39]

Finally, the transition from the second to the third step, i.e. programming formalised logical inference rules into AI systems, involves additional challenges. Some of these are technical programming challenges relating to the complexity of logic and issues of scalability. Translating logical rules into a programming language in a way that ensures the system operates correctly under all conditions requires meticulous coding and extensive testing.[40] And as the system scales and the complexity of scenarios increases, the number of rules can exponentially grow. In cases where rules conflict, there needs to be additional higher-order rules to determine which rules take precedence. This expansion, in turn, adds further complexity and increases the likelihood of programming errors.[41]

Other challenges of rule-based systems go beyond programming challenges. Real-world environments can be dynamic and involve exceptions and unforeseen scenarios. A governmental building may turn into a shelter zone during an occupation, or a military base may turn into a vaccination centre during a pandemic. Such changes directly impact the rules that need to be taken into account during the conduct of military operations. Systems that operate according to fixed, predefined rules cannot cope with exceptions or respond appropriately in unforeseen situations and dynamic environments.

Handling exceptions and dynamic environments can potentially be achieved through data-driven techniques, as these techniques can allow machines to learn patterns from large datasets and generalise to new, unforeseen situations. But even these systems can pose great risks in handling exceptions and unforeseen situations. This is particularly the case in high-stakes contexts such as military operations. I discuss this point in the next and final section of the chapter.

2.3.2 *Dilemmas of Data-Driven Reasoning*

AI systems whose reasoning capabilities are developed through machine learning techniques do not require the formalisation of legal or moral norms. These systems

[38] See, for example, Zurek et al. 2023.

[39] See, for example, in this volume Chap. 10 by Zurek and van Engers.

[40] See, for instance, Ganesh et al. 2022, where the authors explore the intersection of machine learning and logical reasoning and highlight the complexities involved in integrating these two fields.

[41] In this volume, in Chap. 13, Boutin discusses several issues pertaining to programming errors. She argues that, in the case of AI systems, the distinction between what is a human error and what is a technical malfunction is often unclear. It is also questionable whether all errors should be attributed to the developers' negligence in the legal sense. The complexities of attributing responsibility to developers or operators can, in turn, result in other issues such as responsibility gaps.

are trained by large datasets. The underlying idea is that, through exposure to vast amounts of data during training, a neural network 'learns' the rules that determine input–output relationships and is able to reliably replicate them in real-world environments.[42]

While this approach may appear promising, relying on machine learning techniques is a risky way of making decisions in sensitive contexts, such as military operations. It is risky because algorithmic reasoning that is developed through machine learning techniques can be unpredictable. It can be unpredictable because strictly speaking, such systems never learn the governing rules of reasoning. They only learn the correct outputs in response to specific inputs and then generalise what they have learned in training to new inputs encountered in real-world environments. When inputs differ even slightly from those seen during training, the resulting outputs can become difficult to predict. The further real-world inputs diverge from the training data, the more unpredictable the system becomes.

The unpredictability of systems developed through machine learning techniques is further heightened when such systems are intended for use in high-stakes environments, such as military operations. This is because the training data for such systems should be limited to simulated environments that may or may not resemble real-world environments. The reason why such systems should not be trained in real-world environments is that their operation poses high risks of inflicting harm. It would be unethical to train military AI systems in real-world environments because that would amount to an extreme form of human experimentation in which the subjects may not consent to the experiment and are even likely to face serious injury or death as a result of the experiment. For these reasons, such systems should be developed in simulated environments.

While it is not morally permissible to train military AI systems during their deployment phase, data gathered during military operations can be retrospectively fed into AI systems. This approach (i.e., the use of historical operational data for training) would require extensive investment by militaries in equipping operations with various sensors to collect data, and in transferring and processing that data for AI training purposes. However, apart from the practical hurdles of collecting useful training data during turbulent armed conflicts, further ethical and regulatory issues, such as questions of data ownership and consent, need to be also considered.[43] Moreover, data gathered solely during military operations may also be insufficient to reliably train systems, as machine learning techniques typically require large-scale datasets.

Military operations, especially when performed in urban areas, can be significantly different from the simulations and training environments, including historical data gathered during previous operations. By significant, I mean significant for a system

[42] Different data-driven techniques may be used to train AI systems to follow normative rules. One candidate is reinforcement learning, which trains AI systems to make decisions through trial and error by receiving feedback (rewards or penalties) based on their actions. In this way, the system would 'learn' normative rules by interacting with a simulated environment and receiving feedback according to predefined normative outcomes, such as correct legal judgments or ethical behaviours.

[43] See, for example, Afina and Grand-Clément 2024, who argue that responsible AI governance should include responsible data governance.

where altering just a few pixels of an image can lead to considerably different identifications and behaviours by the system.[44] So it is very likely that the real-world environment in which the system is deployed will differ from its training environment. Many factors can contribute to such dissimilarities between the training environment and the real-world environments: the design of urban infrastructure, architectural styles, cultural dress codes, vehicle types, driving patterns, people's skin colours, or even air pollution, haze, sunlight, and atmospheric conditions. Each of these differences further heightens the likelihood and degree of unpredictability of systems developed through machine learning techniques. This heightened unpredictability would, in turn, increase the risk of violating legal and moral norms and obligations.[45]

The fact that some systems carry significant risks of violating legal and moral norms and obligations can imply that their use on the battlefield is morally impermissible. From a moral point of view, it can be argued that in high-stakes environments, such as military operations, if parties can reduce risk, then they ought to do so. Given that systems developed through machine learning techniques can be increasingly unpredictable, then there is a moral obligation not to use such systems in high-stakes environments. This moral argument also has a legal counterpart: it can be argued that militaries are legally obliged to use weapons and methods of warfare that allow higher degrees of compliance and pose less risk to civilians.[46] If it is possible to use less indiscriminate and more proportionate means and methods, then it might be argued that parties to a conflict have an obligation to do so. Hence, considering the learning limitations of machine learning systems, one can conclude that their use in high-stakes military environments is both morally and legally impermissible.

2.4 Conclusion

In this chapter, I have examined the dilemmas surrounding the permissibility and programmability of normative military reasoning into AI systems. I have highlighted that some concerns, such as responsibility gaps and issues of explainability, may be mitigated through regulation and technological advancements. However, more fundamental objections against the use of AI for normative military reasoning persist, particularly those arising from inalienable obligations and activities that necessitate continuous human involvement.

I also explored the programmability of normative military reasoning, demonstrating that both rule-based and data-driven approaches face challenges. Rule-based

---

[44] See, for example, Farkya et al. 2024, who discuss how pixel-level changes influence computer vision systems, particularly in dynamic sensing and neural networks.

[45] This is why some have suggested that the use of AI for target selection should be limited to naval or aerial operations, where the operational environment is less complex and more or less similar to the training environment.

[46] See, API, above n. 24, Article 57(2)(a)(ii).

systems struggle to capture the complexity and contextual nuances of moral and legal reasoning. Data-driven systems, on the other hand, introduce significant risks due to their unpredictability. This is especially the case in high-stakes military environments where real-world testing is impractical or ethically unacceptable.

While these challenges remain, AI systems cannot and should not perform normatively significant reasoning.

References

Articles, Books and Other Documents

Afina Y, Grand-Clément S (2024) Bytes and Battles: Inclusion of Data Governance in Responsible Military AI. https://www.cigionline.org/publications/bytes-and-battles-inclusion-of-data-governance-in-responsible-military-ai/. Accessed 10 January 2025

Baum K, Mantel S, Schmidt E (2022) From Responsibility to Reason-Giving Explainable Artificial Intelligence. Philosophy & Technology. https://doi.org/10.1007/s13347-022-00510-w

Bo M (2021) Autonomous Weapons and the Responsibility Gap in light of the *Mens Rea* of the War Crime of Attacking Civilians in the ICC Statute. Journal of International Criminal Justice. https://doi.org/10.1093/jicj/mqab005

Boutin B (2023) State responsibility in relation to military applications of artificial intelligence. Leiden Journal of International Law. https://doi.org/10.1017/S0922156522000607

Boutin B, Klonowska K, Pacholska M, Soltanzadeh S, Woodcock T, Zurek T (2023) DILEMA Statement on the Global Governance of Artificial Intelligence in the Military. www.asser.nl/dilema/research/dilema-statement. Accessed 20 May 2025

Coeckelbergh M (2020) Artificial Intelligence, Responsibility Attribution, and a Relational Justification of Explainability. Science and Engineering Ethics. https://doi.org/10.1007/s11948-019-00146-8

Darwall SL (1977) Two Kinds of Respect. Ethics. https://doi.org/10.1086/292054

Dillon RS (2007) Respect: A philosophical perspective. Gruppendynamik. https://doi.org/10.1007/s11612-007-0016-5

Doshi-Velez F, Kortz M, Budish R, Bavitz C, Gershman S J, O'Brien D, Scott K, Shieber S, Waldo J, Weinberger D, Weller A, Wood A (2017) Accountability of AI Under the Law: The Role of Explanation. arXiv. https://doi.org/10.48550/arXiv.1711.01134

Farkya S, Daniels ZA, Raghavan A, van der Wal G, Isnardi M, Piacentino M, Zhang D (2024) Data-Driven Pixel Control: Challenges and Prospects. arXiv. https://doi.org/10.48550/arXiv.2408.04767

Ganesh V, Seshia SA, Jha S (2022) Machine learning and logic: a new frontier in artificial intelligence. Formal Methods in System Design. https://doi.org/10.1007/s10703-023-00430-1

Hart HLA (1961) The Concept of Law. Oxford University Press, London

Henckaerts JM, Doswald-Beck L (2009) Customary International Humanitarian Law: Volume I: Rules. Cambridge University Press, Cambridge

Hintikka JJ (2019) Philosophy of logic. https://www.britannica.com/topic/philosophy-of-logic. Accessed 11 October 2024

Horty JF (2011) Rules and Reasons in the Theory of Precedent. Legal Theory. https://doi.org/10.1017/S1352325211000036

Lukyanenko R, Maass W, Storey VC (2022) Trust in artificial intelligence: From a Foundational Trust Framework to emerging research opportunities. Electronic Markets. https://doi.org/10.1007/s12525-022-00605-4

Magee B (1971) Modern British Philosophy. Secker & Warburg, London

Mahmoud H (2024) Israeli attacks continue across the Gaza Strip. https://www.aljazeera.com/news/liveblog/2024/10/3/live-beirut-bombed-as-hezbollah-battles-israeli-army-in-south-lebanon?update=3220638. Accessed 3 October 2024
Marchant EJ (2020) Insufficient Knowledge in Kunduz: The Precautionary Principle and International Humanitarian Law. Journal of Conflict and Security law. https://doi.org/10.1093/jcsl/krz033
Matthias A (2004) The responsibility gap: Ascribing responsibility for the actions of learning automata. Ethics and Information Technology. https://doi.org/10.1007/s10676-004-3422-1
Oimann AK, Salatino A (2024) Command responsibility in military AI contexts: balancing theory and practicality. AI and Ethics. https://doi.org/10.1007/s43681-024-00512-8
Poszler F, Lange B (2024) The impact of intelligent decision-support systems on humans' ethical decision-making: A systematic literature review and an integrated framework. Technological Forecasting and Social Change. https://doi.org/10.1016/j.techfore.2024.123403
Santoni de Sio F, Mecacci G (2021) Four Responsibility Gaps with Artificial Intelligence: Why they Matter and How to Address them. Philosophy & Technology. https://doi.org/10.1007/s13347-021-00450-x
Schauer F (1991) Playing by the Rules: A Philosophical Examination of Rule-Based Decision-Making in Law and in Life. Clarendon Press, London
Schlick M (1936) Meaning and Verification. The Philosophical Review. https://doi.org/10.2307/2180487
Simpson TW, Müller VC (2016) Just War and Robots' Killings. The Philosophical Quarterly. https://doi.org/10.1093/pq/pqv075
Soltanzadeh S (2022a) Strictly Human: Limitations of Autonomous Systems. Minds and Machines. https://doi.org/10.1007/s11023-021-09582-7
Soltanzadeh S (2022b) Problem-Solving Technologies: A User-Friendly Philosophy. Bloomsbury
Soltanzadeh S (2025) A metaphysical account of agency for technology governance. AI & Society. https://doi.org/10.1007/s00146-024-01941-z
Soltanzadeh S, Galliott J, Jevglevskaja N (2020) Customizable Ethics Settings for Building Resilience and Narrowing the Responsibility Gap: Case Studies in the Socio-Ethical Engineering of Autonomous Systems. Science and Engineering Ethics. https://doi.org/10.1007/s11948-020-00221-5
Soltanzadeh S, Mooney M (2021) Autonomy in the Context of Decision-Making Dilemmas. In: Pereira Martins C (ed) Do Desporto/On Sports: theoria vs praxis. IEF Coimbra and Fundação do Desporto, Coimbra, pp. 147–162
Sparrow R (2007) Killer Robots. Journal of Applied Philosophy. https://doi.org/10.1111/j.1468-5930.2007.00346
Viveros JSA (2024) The risks and inefficacies of AI systems in military targeting support. https://blogs.icrc.org/law-and-policy/2024/09/04/the-risks-and-inefficacies-of-ai-systems-in-military-targeting-support/. Accessed 20 May 2025
von Eschenbach WJ (2021) Transparency and the Black Box Problem: Why We Do Not Trust AI. Philosophy & Technology. https://doi.org/10.1007/s13347-021-00477-0
Winter E (2022) The Compatibility of Autonomous Weapons with the Principles of International Humanitarian Law. Journal of Conflict and Security Law. https://doi.org/10.1093/jcsl/krac001
Wittgenstein L (1961) *Tractatus Logico-Philosophicus* (Pears DF, McGuinness BF (transl)). Humanities Press, New York. (Original work published 1921)
Yampolskiy RV (2020) Unexplainability and Incomprehensibility of AI. Journal of Artificial Intelligence and Consciousness. https://doi.org/10.1142/S2705078520500150
Yang W, Wei Y, Wei H, Chen Y, Huang G, Li X, Li R, Yao N, Wang X, Gu X, Amin BA, Kang B (2023) Survey on Explainable AI: From Approaches, Limitations, and Applications Aspects. Human-Centric Intelligent Systems. https://doi.org/10.1007/s44230-023-00038-y
Zurek T, Kwik J, van Engers T (2023) Model of a military autonomous device following International Humanitarian Law. Ethics and Information Technology. https://doi.org/10.1007/s10676-023-09682-1

Sadjad Soltanzadeh is a Researcher in Philosophy of Technology at the University of Twente (The Netherlands). From 2020 to 2023, he was part of the DILEMA project, where his research explored the constituents of human autonomy, the limitations of autonomous systems, and the interaction between human and machine agency. In his book *Problem-Solving Technologies: A User-Friendly Philosophy* (2022), Soltanzadeh has introduced the *activity realist* approach, which argues that the study of technical systems must be accompanied by the study of the human activities they are intended to support.

Chapter 3
Rhetoric and Regulation: The (Limits of) Human/AI Comparison in Legal Debates on Military AI

Klaudia Klonowska and Taylor Kate Woodcock

Contents

Abstract The promise of artificial intelligence (AI) is ubiquitous and compelling, yet can it truly deliver 'better' speed, accuracy, and decision making in the conduct of war? As AI becomes increasingly embedded in targeting processes, legal and ethical debates often compare who performs better, humans or machines? In this chapter, we unpack and critique the prevalence of comparisons between humans and AI systems, including in analyses of the fulfilment of legal obligations under International Humanitarian Law (IHL). We challenge this binary framing by highlighting misleading assumptions that neglect how the use of AI results in complex human–machine interactions that transform targeting practices. We unpack what is meant by 'better performance', demonstrating how prevailing metrics for speed and accuracy can create misleading expectations around the use of AI given the realities of warfare. We conclude that holistic but granular attention must be paid to the

K. Klonowska (✉)
Sciences Po, Paris, France
e-mail: klaudia.klonowska@gmail.com

T. K. Woodcock
T.M.C. Asser Instituut, The Hague, The Netherlands

University of Amsterdam, Amsterdam, The Netherlands

T. K. Woodcock
e-mail: t.woodcock@asser.nl

B. Boutin et al. (eds.), *Legal, Ethical, and Technical Dilemmas in Military Artificial Intelligence*, https://doi.org/10.1007/978-94-6265-759-5_3

landscape of human–machine interactions to understand how the use of AI impacts compliance with IHL targeting obligations.

Keywords Artificial Intelligence · Military Targeting · Autonomous Weapons Systems · Decision-Support Systems · Legal Debates · Human–Machine Interaction

3.1 Introduction

Comparisons of artificial intelligence (AI) and human performance have become pervasive in debates on military AI.[1] When compared to humans, AI is often promised to offer superior speed, accuracy, and certainty, ostensibly enhancing compliance with International Humanitarian Law (IHL). The purported superiority of AI sustains broader hopes for 'overcoming one's own imperfections in the wielding of violence… a process of progress, improvement, rationalization, optimization, [and] ultimately the civilization of war-fighting'.[2] Unsurprisingly, the narrative that AI outperforms humans justifies and fuels large-scale investments in military AI technologies.[3] This chapter suggests that there is great urgency in critically interrogating the assumptions that underpin the human/AI comparison and its analytical value for legal analysis and argumentation regarding lawful targeting.

The human/AI comparison has roots in the inception of AI as a discipline. The terminology of 'intelligence' and 'neural networks' reflect the epistemic commitments of its forerunners, who sought to explore similarities with, and the replication of, human intelligence.[4] The Dartmouth Summer Research Project on Artificial Intelligence of 1956, widely considered to be the founding event of AI as a discipline, embraced the notion that every aspect of human intelligence can be registered, modelled, and simulated.[5] This mode of thinking facilitates analogical comparisons that drive desires to outperform human error and cognitive limitations.[6] As aptly put by Lepage-Richer, 'the history of AI is essentially that of mediating who or what is recognized as the bearer of intelligence'.[7]

[1] We acknowledge that 'AI' is a vague umbrella term encompassing a variety of algorithmic systems. The notion of an artificial kind of intelligence automatically invites a comparison between AI and human intelligence. Despite the conceptual assumptions and limitations of this term, we nevertheless use it in this chapter to engage with popular discourse and critically examine of its limitations.

[2] Kalpouzos 2020, p. 300; Jain 2022, p. 1111.

[3] United Kingdom Ministry of Defence 2023; United States Department of Defense 2023; Suchman 2023a, pp. 761–786; González 2024.

[4] For an in-depth historical account of the epistemic commitments underpinning the term 'neural networks', including its pre-computational origins and applications, as well as its evolving meaning in emergent AI projects, see Dhaliwal et al. 2024.

[5] Ibid.

[6] Ibid., pp. 87–107.

[7] Ibid., p. 47.

Nowadays, the discursive tendency to compare humans and AI technologies is a prominent feature of contemporary legal and regulatory debates. This is exemplified in the work of the Group of Governmental Experts on Lethal Autonomous Weapons Systems (GGE LAWS), an inter-governmental group addressing the regulation of AI-enabled weapons under the purview of the Convention on Certain Conventional Weapons.[8] At the GGE LAWS, actors deploy the human/AI comparison to both oppose and defend the need to regulate military applications of AI. States advocating for the development and use of such technologies frequently argue that AI offers military superiority, often 'emphasiz[ing] the promise and potential of autonomous military capabilities themselves: in performance and detachment, they *exceed* human soldiers, they insulate human soldiers from risk and they *enhance* IHL compliance and humanitarian protection'.[9] This narrative positions AI not only as a strategic asset, but as a tool for advancing legal and humanitarian aims. Conversely, the human/AI comparison also underpins some arguments for prohibiting these technologies, emphasising that humans are better suited to understand and address the complexities of warfare and to exercise the judgment required by IHL compared to autonomous weapons systems (AWS).[10]

Whilst the human/AI comparison continues to pervade discourse on military AI, it has been met with some criticism, reflected in a discernible shift towards interest in human–machine interaction in regulatory debates. Emphasising the interrelatedness of humans and technology, the concept of human–machine interaction has become increasingly prominent in debates on miliary AI.[11] For instance, despite much early discussion on 'meaningful human control', the 2019 Guiding Principles developed by the GGE LAWS replaced this concept with 'human–machine interaction'.[12] Some actors consider the notion of meaningful human control as unsuitable, arguing that it tends to isolate humans and machines, with 'control' being incongruous with the socio-technical relations that this concept seeks to explain and address.[13] Instead, the GGE LAWS report stresses that human–machine interaction in its various forms throughout the system lifecycle should ensure compliance with IHL.[14] References to human–machine interaction (teaming, integration, and collaboration) in national

[8] https://meetings.unoda.org/ccw-/convention-on-certain-conventional-weapons-group-of-governmental-experts-on-lethal-autonomous-weapons-systems-2024. Accessed 19 May 2025.

[9] Jain 2022, p. 1121 (emphasis added).

[10] See generally, Asaro 2012, p. 709; Heyns 2017, p. 60.

[11] The term human–machine interaction (sometimes referred to as 'human computer interaction') stems from early research on philosophy of science, human factors engineering, and computer science, amongst others. See generally, Dix 2017, p. 124. Whilst often used in those areas to examine human interaction with computing interfaces, the term is adopted more broadly in contemporary debates on military AI. Acknowledging these origins, it is in this broader sense—also informed by thinking on the socio-technical mentioned below—that we use it throughout this chapter.

[12] UN GGE LAWS 2019, para c.

[13] Jones 2018, p. 103; Jain 2022, p. 1105; Boutin and Woodcock 2024.

[14] Group of Governmental Experts on Emerging Technologies in the Area of Lethal Autonomous Weapons Systems 2019, para c.

policies and military doctrines are also increasingly used in relation to the regulation of AI beyond AWS, such as AI-enabled decision-support systems (DSS).

Beyond legal debates at the State level, it is also important to engage with the rich body of scholarship in cybernetics and science and technology studies (STS) that interrogates human/machine binaries as social constructs that sustain power structures.[15] Often predating debates around AI, abundant literature recognises the impossibility of separating technology from humans and vice versa, from post-phenomenology's acknowledgment of the extended nature of human senses and the mind,[16] to posthumanism's view that being human always implies entanglement with non-human others (including nature and technologies).[17] These theoretical approaches highlight the realities of socio-technical interdependence in which humans are never fully 'in control' or able to exercise agency independently from technological artifacts.[18] This socio-technical view has also been adopted, although sparsely, in legal scholarship where technological mediation is problematised in the emergence of new human-AI military practices.[19] We draw on this body of literature to develop an understanding of the limitations of human/AI comparisons in legal analysis.

This chapter demonstrates the fallacy surrounding direct comparisons of the 'human' and 'AI', which obscures the realities of warfare and neglects the trade-offs of framing legal debates predominately around 'enhanced performance'. While the human/AI comparison prioritises 'better' performance (e.g., in terms of speed or accuracy), IHL instead seeks the reasonable and context-specific balancing of military necessity and humanitarian protections. Human/AI comparisons often focus on narrow operational tasks, disregarding the varied range of obligations under IHL. We therefore argue that legal compliance does not necessarily result from 'better performance' by AI-enabled systems, as is often assumed. Legal analysis driven by the human/AI comparison is not only a simplification of targeting with the use of AI technologies but also risks obscuring the obligations and responsibilities of relevant actors and undermining the application of key IHL principles.

The objective of this chapter is to critically unpack the assumptions underlying the human/AI comparison, whilst also attending to what it ignores. As Lipp and Dickel fittingly remark, 'both approaches that essentialize the difference between human and machine as well as those that seek to overcome it by foregrounding hybridity, are in fact deficient'.[20] They continue by arguing that the biggest challenge is 'to grasp the simultaneity with which humans and machines are both separated and interconnected'.[21] As such, with this chapter we implore careful navigation of

[15] Haraway 1987.

[16] See, e.g., Introna 2014; Rosenberger and Verbeek 2015.

[17] See, e.g., Jones 2018; Arvidsson 2018.

[18] See, e.g., Suchman 2007; Jones 2018; Müller 2020.

[19] See, e.g., Arvidsson 2018; Sutton 2021; Mignot-Mahdavi 2023; Klonowska 2024; Woodcock 2024.

[20] Lipp and Dickel 2023, p. 2.

[21] Ibid.

the temptation to compare humans and AI systems in isolation, contributing to a more nuanced understanding of the limits and risks of the human/AI comparison specifically for legal and regulatory debates on military AI.

3.2 Misleading Assumptions in Human/AI Comparisons

In this section, we first argue that human/AI comparisons often presuppose that humans and AI-enabled systems are interchangeable, without acknowledgement of the broader picture of how socio-technical interactions transform practices. Second, we explore how human/AI comparisons often adopt homogeneous conceptions of both humans and AI technologies that neglect the diversities and dynamism of both entities, creating an unequal footing by comparing human past experiences with AI's future promises.

3.2.1 Replacement Fallacy

Within the military domain, some legal discourse hinges on the assumption that the legality of AI-enabled systems depends on whether they replicate or surpass human capabilities. This position adopts what we call the 'replacement fallacy', reflecting the idea that new technologies merely replace the role or specific tasks of actors without altering the overall practice in which they are situated. The replacement fallacy therefore obscures transformations in practices when AI-enabled systems are adopted.

Rhetoric embodying the replacement fallacy is reinforced by the tendency to anthropomorphise technical systems. One of the reasons for the perceived replaceability of humans with AI technologies, Johansen contends, is the term 'autonomy', which often generates misunderstandings by conflating the physical autonomy of machines with human-like qualities, such as self-awareness and perception of, and adaptation to, the environment.[22] She posits that machines do not 'become human-like entities with their own will', nor do they 'become a commander'.[23] Similarly, Russell argues that comparisons between humans and AI are fundamentally flawed, as technologies neither replicate nor replace human capabilities, but rather shift them.[24] Beyond discussions of autonomy in AI systems with robotic capabilities, we observe that there is a similar tendency to frame AI-enabled DSS as 'agents' or 'advisors' that could replace military analysts or even legal advisors.

The perspective that AI-enabled systems replace humans has led some to conceptualise a framework in which humans are 'out of the loop', suggesting that machines

[22] Johansen 2018, pp. 89–102.

[23] Ibid., p. 90.

[24] Russell 2023.

can perform critical functions without human intervention. However, as Jones argues, this framework is highly simplistic: 'the dichotomy between man and machine is a false one, but at a minimum, it is not reliable or stable enough to draft policy around'.[25] Instead, she suggests that humans perform a 'permanent role in the loop', not only because they design and develop technical systems, but also because of the various tasks required to maintain and enable the use of these systems.[26] As such, this humanness—'the subjectivity, the errors, the inexactness, and the carelessness'—can never be fully removed or replaced by the integration of AI.[27]

Another feature of the replacement fallacy is the selective allocation of tasks—deciding which 'tasks to automate versus what to allocate to humans'.[28] Developed in the 1950s, the MABA-MABA framework attempted to distinguish and categorise functions that 'Machine Are Better At' and 'Men Are Better At'.[29] The framework would, for example, distinguish between humans' 'ability to reason inductively', versus machines' 'ability to handle highly complex operations' and perform many tasks simultaneously.[30] This approach—which also reflects the gendered assumptions of its era—was accompanied by interest in ensuring that humans retain tasks that they are 'better' at performing. However, as Crootof et al. convincingly argue, MABA-MABA constitutes a trap emphasising the human/machine dichotomy, obscuring how human–machine interactions may 'hamper or amplify each other's weaknesses'.[31] Analytical approaches grounded in the idea of replacing humans with AI-enabled systems significantly misrepresent the complex realities of AI's implementation into military decision making.

The integration of AI technologies into military decision making does not simply replace humans in their tasks but rather transforms targeting practices in at least three core ways. First, the integration of AI technologies alters the role that humans perform in relation to emergent technological capabilities. The case of Predator drones serves as an example of these shifting practices, even though they do not have AI capabilities. As Gonzalez observes, the so-called '"unmanned" aerial Predator requires at least three human controllers: a pilot, a sensor operator, and a mission intelligence coordinator—plus an entire support team of data analysts and personnel who service the drone on the ground before and after flights'.[32] Unmanned systems did not just eliminate human pilots, but altered practices of surveillance and targeting, requiring a range of new roles for the humans involved in their operation.[33]

[25] Jones 2015, p. 102.

[26] Ibid., p. 104.

[27] Ibid., p. 92.

[28] Crootof et al. 2023, p. 472.

[29] Ibid., pp. 460–461; Jones 2015, pp. 104–105.

[30] Jones 2015, p. 105.

[31] Crootof et al. 2023, p. 467.

[32] González 2022, pp. 28–29.

[33] Highlighting the need to assess the lived experience of operators, in Chap. 7 of this volume Molendijk et al. argue that the use of both drones and autonomous systems 'require[s] technical knowledge and skills that differ from the previous roles and expectations of combatants': pp. 9–10.

Second, the integration of AI technologies alters the epistemic processes of how military actors sense, perceive, understand, and act upon collected information.[34] For example, predictive algorithms afford the possibility of connecting discrete behavioural traits to risk factors, resulting in the identification of individuals as 'suspected terrorists'.[35] Decision making by actors relying on AI-enabled systems is not simply enhanced but is transformed, being shaped according to the engineering approaches to problem-solving, in/visibilities afforded by sensors, algorithmic logics of the systems, and the human–machine interactions that emerge from their use.[36]

Third, the integration of AI technologies also affects adversary techniques and hence warfighting overall. For instance, reports of the use of small first-person view drones by Ukraine during the Russo-Ukrainian war suggest that this has led to changes in Russia's adversarial strategies. As a result, drone operator hubs were identified and engaged by Russian forces as 'high-value targets'.[37] This demonstrates that the implementation of new technologies not only alters how targeting is performed by those using these systems, but also shapes the warfighting practices of other actors.

The adoption of AI-enabled tasks thus requires critical 'reflection on how responsibilities shift as well, and whether values are protected through that shift'.[38] Human-AI interaction does not necessarily offer 'the best of both worlds', as some authors would suggest.[39] Rather, emergent socio-technical practices introduce issues and challenges of their own.[40] The focus on either one of these agents (human or AI) obscures the more complex challenges of human–machine interaction. Further empirical research into these changing practices is critical to better understand the transformations that occur and their potential long-term impacts on the conduct of hostilities.

3.2.2 *Homogeneity and Consistency*

Beyond the replacement fallacy, comparisons between humans and AI are fraught with generalisations, giving the impression that each are homogeneous and consistent entities. For example, it is argued that improvements in sensor technologies may enable autonomous systems to 'pierce the fog of war' and outperform humans in battlefield observation, leading to a reduction in civilian harm.[41] Sassòli suggests that humans commit more war atrocities and are worse than machines at following

---

[34] Klonowska 2026a.

[35] Anwar and Klonowska 2025.

[36] Klonowska 2026b; Woodcock 2026.

[37] Dickinson 2024.

[38] Jones 2015, p. 131.

[39] See for instance, Greipl 2024.

[40] Crootof et al. 2023, p. 438.

[41] Arkin 2013, p. 6.

rules.[42] Similarly, many others have flagged the 'human' characteristics of stress, fatigue, emotions, and the proclivity for mistakes as reasons to replace humans with machines.[43] Principally, such comparisons neglect the lack of homogeneity among human actors, not only in terms of their distinct cultural, ethical, and institutional backgrounds, but also their experiences, training, values, and personalities.

There is also a risk of portraying AI systems as homogeneous. 'AI' is a broad concept used to describe various approaches to computation and programming. This includes data-driven approaches (e.g., machine learning (ML)) that generate probabilistic predictions based on vast datasets. AI also encompasses knowledge-based systems using explicit rules, often referred to as 'Good Old-Fashioned AI'.[44] Both data- and knowledge-driven techniques raise nuanced—if sometimes related—issues regarding military applications of AI and autonomy in targeting. Much, though not all, of the current discourse around the opportunities and challenges of military AI relates to the use of probabilistic techniques of data-driven AI, such as ML. Nevertheless, in debates on AWS specifically, it is often acknowledged that automation through knowledge-driven techniques of AI is already used at present, such as in anti-missile defence systems or loitering munitions. Regarding the latter, some commentators argue that despite their general acceptance, these systems already raise issues concerning control over the use of force.[45]

Each technique entails programming models according to distinct algorithmic architectures, design choices, and goal parameters. Even within data-driven models, slight differences in training datasets can significantly impact algorithmic processing and generated outcomes. Other design choices may determine whether the system prioritises accuracy or explainability—two values that usually lead to output trade-offs, with related legal implications.[46] It is therefore important to recognise that 'AI' does not represent a homogenous group of technical systems from which insights can be generalised.

A corollary of this is that when comparing human versus AI decision-making processes in specific contexts or tasks, observations are not necessarily generalisable to human/AI comparisons more broadly. For example, in 2024, the National Security Institute Cyber and Tech Center Report reported that AI (in this case OpenAI's GPT-4) acted less aggressively than human participants in a simulated war game.[47] The report, however, fails to reflect on the influence of programming choices (e.g., training datasets, models, reinforcement learning with human feedback) on system outputs. For instance, it does not consider whether the system was designed to optimise for less 'aggressive' behaviours versus if it was trained to mimic more 'aggressive' tactics. The very use of the adjective 'aggressive' in the human/AI comparison here anthropomorphises the statistical calculations that are performed by these systems.

[42] Sassòli 2014.

[43] Arkin 2009; Müller and Simpson 2014, pp. 297–305; Heller 2023.

[44] Bench-Capon 2021.

[45] Watts and Bode 2023.

[46] Kwik and van Engers 2023, pp. 255–279.

[47] Jones and Jaffer 2024.

Sweeping statements about AI's superiority to human cognition obfuscates the underlying differences in how algorithms draw statistical inferences from available data and hinders meaningful discussion about the consequential differences between various AI systems.

Moreover, it is important to acknowledge and reflect on the implications of inconsistent behaviour and performance of humans and AI systems. Notwithstanding the neurological and physiological limitations of human minds and bodies, humans can and do improve performance, analysis, and judgement through experience, training, and education. For example, a study conducted by the International Committee of the Red Cross (ICRC) found that IHL training can result in greater combat restraint and emphasis on civilian protection.[48] Conversely, factors such as stress, fatigue, and traumatic experiences can undermine judgement. AI's performance is also not static, but can improve or deteriorate throughout deployment. This can be due to several factors, such as retraining models and software updates, human–machine interaction, changing environmental conditions, and countermeasures (explained in further detail below). The mutable nature of AI performance metrics may also render the results of system verification (e.g., accuracy rates) unreliable after iterative software updates or deployment in different environments.[49]

Ultimately, a comparison that lacks sufficient nuance places humans and AI systems on unequal footing. The 'human' featured in these comparisons is backward-looking and judged based on historically imperfect and error-prone performance. The potential for human development and progress is often neglected. In contrast, AI is portrayed as an imagined, future-oriented figure with open possibilities. After all, like any other technology, AI is a product of popular—and at times fictitious—vision, with the contours of what constitutes AI being limited only by our imagination. While such portrayals may be aspirational and advocate for technological advancement, they nevertheless obscure the reality of imperfect and fallible AI-enabled technologies.[50] Through the strategic vagueness of the term 'AI', companies producing and marketing these technologies blur the current state-of-the-art with fantasies of striking performance.[51] Much emphasis is placed on the 'superhuman' capabilities of AI,[52] with 'the proclaimed wonders of autonomous military capabilities obscur[ing] the old shortcomings that persist and the new shortcomings that they produce'.[53] For example, the GGE LAWS delegates persistently disagree on

48 Bell 2024.

49 Holland Michel 2024, p. 42. See the discussion in Sect. 3.2.2 below.

50 On how popular imaginings through film reproduce these ideas with respect to military data practices, see Krebs 2022.

51 Schwarz argues that as the ecosystem in which AI tech companies (e.g., Palantir, Anduril) emerge is in close connection to venture capital and startups, much of their work relies on speculation—startups sell 'fantasy' and it is through this marketing strategy that they are able to attract funding for projects before they are realised: Schwarz 2024. See also Elish and Boyd 2018, p. 7; Suchman 2023b, p. 2; Schwarz 2025.

52 Campolo and Crawford 2020.

53 Jain 2022, p. 1121.

whether the promise of future autonomous capabilities (e.g., artificial general intelligence)[54] undermine regulatory efforts. As the aspiration that AI will outperform human cognition is disseminated and reinforced in popular, commercial, and even governmental rhetorics, this comparison is sustained by the belief that this imagined future is attainable. At last, we hope that legal experts can put the human/AI comparison on an equal footing and ground analyses on the realities of human-AI interactions.

3.3 Unpacking 'Better Performance': Speed, Accuracy, and the Realities of Warfare

Contrasting human and AI performance often presupposes common metrics for comparison. Frequently, the speed and accuracy of military applications of AI is lauded as leading to 'better performance'. Claims about the superiority of military applications of AI rest on ideals and imaginaries about what AI is and how it functions. The vision of AI as 'superhuman' is actively promulgated both within popular culture and the industrial-military complex, driven by Big Tech as the gatekeepers of the latest developments in the field.[55] Yet, claims about AI superiority are often taken for granted, with very little empirical evidence indicating under what conditions these claims may materialise. As such, debates on military AI often overlook the conditions under which these systems perform 'better', what 'better' means, and who determines this, as well as whether and how this can be measured.

In this section, we unpack two metrics that are primarily used to compare humans and AI technologies, namely speed and accuracy. We argue that the reliability of these metrics is not only limited, but also that the realities of warfare reveal complex socio-technical interactions that often do not fulfil the promise of 'better performance'. We thus urge caution when relying on technical metrics in legal evaluation.

3.3.1 Cost of Speed

The increased speed of data processing is a frequently cited benefit of using military applications of AI. With the overarching strategic interest of outmanoeuvring enemies, militaries constantly seek ways to increase the pace of operations. As such, the speed of AI systems is not a side-effect, but is rather an objective driven by

[54] Artificial General Intelligence (AGI) is a hypothetical form of AI that matches or even outperforms human intelligence. Since AGI remains highly speculative and theoretical, it also lacks consistent definitions.

[55] Campolo and Crawford 2020.

the imaginary of faster military decision making and manoeuvre.[56] There are unintended costs associated with the increased tempo of military operations that are often neglected within these discourses. As we argue here, not only are verification and accountability mechanisms undermined when targeting is performed at high speed, but also faster target production may lead to a greater overall number of target engagements, inflating the risk of harm to civilians.

A primary cost of greater speed in targeting procedures is the curtailed time for deliberation over decisions and precautions. The accelerated tempo of operations shortens opportunities to understand and verify information and to apply appropriate precautionary measures.[57] The rapid nomination of targets may create a climate of risk, inducing action and response from military professionals.[58] At the same time, perceptions around the efficiency gained from the accelerated tempo of algorithmically-mediated targeting procedures may inhibit interventions, such as verification procedures, that could slow the process down.[59] Moreover, rapid decision making can also exacerbate human tendencies towards cognitive biases, such as automation bias, leading to greater trust in the perceived accuracy and objectivity of algorithmically-generated information.[60] This may lead to reduced attentiveness to alternative explanations and courses of action, and deskilling for tasks delegated to AI.

At face value, the accelerated pace of military operations may appear advantageous for giving militaries an edge over opponents not utilising AI technologies. However, speed should not be assessed in a vacuum. Rather, consideration of how speed impacts combat operations more broadly by examining the socio-technical interactions it produces provides a more operationally-grounded picture of speed as a metric for evaluation.

3.3.2 Conditional Accuracy

Accuracy is another frequently-cited feature in arguments anchored on the ostensibly superior performance of AI compared to humans. Particularly in legal debates, it is often repeated that humans are error prone and may underperform in stressful wartime conditions.[61] The use of AI-enabled systems not subject to psychological or physiological limitations, such as stress or fatigue, is expected to result in better targeting accuracy. This line of argumentation, however, rests on several assumptions about the reliability of accuracy rates, namely that accuracy in testing matches

[56] Suchman 2023a.

[57] Rosen 2023; Bo and Dorsey 2024; Klonowska 2024; Mimran and Dahan 2024; Woodcock 2026.

[58] Klonowska 2024.

[59] Woodcock 2026.

[60] Mosier and Skitka 2019, pp. 201–220; Cummings 2019, p. 20.

[61] See, for example, Arkin 2013, p. 6.

real-world performance and that external factors will not influence or diminish the reliability of accuracy rates.

Accuracy rates of AI models in training and testing only provide a limited indication of how the system performed in those specific conditions. A 90% accuracy rate does not guarantee that an AI-enabled system will always perform at that level in practice; rather, it reflects that the system achieved 90% accuracy under specific testing conditions, based on a particular training/testing dataset. Testing offers a controlled environment that cannot fully capture the complex nature of conditions 'in the wild', particularly when this relates to dynamic and unpredictable battlespace environments in armed conflict.[62] Due to these characteristics, the deployment of AI-enabled systems in conflict environments—where the conditions may differ substantially from those represented in training datasets—can lead to concept drift (a phenomenon of misalignment of algorithmic models and real-world data distribution) that significantly degrades algorithmic accuracy.[63]

This is compounded by limitations in creating training/testing datasets that can comprehensively represent the complexity and variability of these environments. Militaries often struggle to create sufficiently large and varied datasets to cover the diversity of possible scenarios, merge available data in different formats, or even to collect high quality data. Frequently, training and testing datasets are derived from two halves of the same set, raising questions about the generalisability of AI performance with new data.[64] While the development of synthetic data to train ML models is currently being explored as a potential solution to mitigate lack of data relating to complex environments, it can nevertheless inadvertently exacerbate biases from original datasets.[65]

Moreover, accuracy rates do not account for situations when models produce seemingly 'correct' outputs based on irrelevant factors as a result of 'spurious correlations' within training datasets.[66] AI models trained through supervised learning do not extrapolate beyond correlations from the training dataset.[67] Greater similarities between the conditions and input data with the training and testing process mean that accuracy rates will be more reliable for providing an indication of the

---

[62] Holland Michel 2021.

[63] Gama et al. 2014; Holland Michel 2024, p. 42.

[64] This is referred to as 'out-of-distribution data', referring to data that has not included in the training dataset and therefore deviates from the distribution. Out-of-distribution data can cause the system to underperform or to produce outputs that are incorrect but nevertheless have a high confidence score.

[65] Synthetic data refers to 'data points that have been generated by a machine-learning algorithm; data which in turn are used to train other machine-learning algorithms… The aim with generative models such as GANs is to produce synthetic outputs that are as proximate as possible to the training data without being an identical mapping of them': Jacobsen 2023, p. 2.

[66] Malik defines spurious correlations as '[n]on-causal correlations… i.e. a correlation that empirically exists and is robust not because of a direct causal link, but by some structure like a common cause': Malik 2020, p. 24. For example, in the case of a ML an image classifier for pneumonia, the system produced output on the basis of metal tokens used by hospitals for x-ray scans, rather than factors relevant to a diagnosis of pneumonia: Kirichenko et al. 2023.

[67] Malik 2020, p. 21.

performance of the system. The opacity of ML systems makes it difficult to assess whether (or to what extent) accuracy rates are reliable within a given context of use, increasing uncertainty around performance. Consequently, care should be taken in relying on accuracy rates to judge the expected performance of military applications of AI, requiring knowledge of the training/testing datasets and the compatibility of the design and development of these systems with their intended use.

Furthermore, the environment of use and adversaries can also disrupt the expected performance of AI-enabled systems, which is often not accounted for when accuracy rates are relied upon for human-AI comparisons. AI accuracy rates are always conditional upon intervening variables, such as the reliability of sensors, weather conditions, and adversarial tactics. For example, a drone camera malfunction and rain conditions can seriously deteriorate the performance of AI-enabled systems by creating dissimilarities between real-world conditions and those represented during training and testing. Likewise, adversaries can use countermeasures that interfere with the system's performance. The tendency of AI-enabled systems to base predictions on any statistical correlations, whether they are relevant or spurious, can be used to 'game' the model.[68] For instance, if an AI model is trained to identify enemy forces based on correlations that reflect a military uniform, the simple technique of wearing a baseball cap or other atypical accessory could lead to misidentification.[69]

Lastly, it bears mentioning that part of the appeal of AI-enabled systems is the prospect of continuously adapting models to changing conditions of use. To this end, developers may use continuous learning techniques to enable AI systems to learn from new data in the real world or alternatively they may be involved in manually retraining models on new datasets, reusing partially trained models, fine-tuning system parameters, and updating software.[70] The aim of these measures is to improve system performance, eliminate vulnerabilities, and enhance compatibility with the context of use. However, these measures can also introduce new uncertainties and risks. Changes in the interface or system behaviour can undermine human–machine interaction, coding mistakes can lead to classification errors, and updated training datasets can compromise the relevance of previously-observed accuracy rates.

Cumulatively, these factors demonstrate that accuracy rates are conditional and contextual rather than absolute. Understanding conditions in which accuracy rates

---

[68] An illustrative example is given by Athalye et al. 2017 testing adversarial attacks on deep learning neural networks, when a 3D printed turtle was misidentified as a rifle due to minor visual perturbations.

[69] On fashion that has been designed to specifically lead to misclassifications by AI models, see: Xu et al. 2019. See also Kwik 2024.

[70] This distinction refers to 'online' versus 'offline' learning systems. Online learning 'utilizes dynamic streams of data input to learn and update its predictions in real time'. If a system does not learn continuously from real-world deployment, it is sometimes referred to as a 'frozen' algorithm. This is a technique called 'offline learning', where the system does not learn continuously from patterns encountered in new data but is dependent upon manual changes and updates that are performed by system engineers and developers: Klonowska 2026a.

are reliable will lead to a better appreciation of AI-enabled systems' limitations and uncertainties in use, inform appropriate precautions, and mitigate unintended consequences.

3.3.3 Realities of Warfare

Historical accounts of warfare further illustrate that narratives of 'better' technological performance are often misplaced and that the metrics accompanying these statements are not a reliable basis for analysis. Again, examples of socio-technical interactions pre-dating contemporary AI demonstrate this point. Drone warfare is a well-studied example in which promises of greater precision did not materialise in practice. As Gonzalez observes:

> a major flaw in the latest iteration of automated war: the imprecision of the technologies, and the great margins of error that accompany even the most sophisticated new weapon systems... Although proponents argue that the weapons perform at levels comparable or even superior to humans, they rarely provide conclusive evidence to support their claims.[71]

The employment of drones has received much criticism precisely because it failed to deliver a 'cleaner war' and instead civilians continued to be frequent casualties in drone-enabled warfare.[72]

Another illustration is the integration of information technologies (IT) in the early 1990s, which promised greater connectivity and better certainty for decision making by military actors. As with drones, the aspirations surrounding IT technologies—and the results achieved in controlled testing environments—seem to have overpromised. Once implemented, these technologies produced similarly contrary effects in decreasing certainty due to connectivity failures, delaying data sharing in contested environments, equipment failures, and insufficient updates resulting in errors and a sense of insecurity amongst combatants.[73]

Once emerging technologies are taken out of controlled testing environments, the realities of warfare, combined with the challenges of common technological failures, show that promises of greater precision, speed, and accuracy are often less attainable than expected. At the very least, the integration of technical innovations requires careful planning, training, and adaptation with the context of conflict in mind.

The reality of warfare is also at odds with narratives of AI superiority that portray sanitised and enhanced targeting practices based on performance metrics. Given the lack of transparency around both militaries and technologies, little information is currently available regarding the actual use of AI-enabled DSS for targeting. Nonetheless, recent examples of the use of these systems by the Israel Defense Forces (IDF) foreshadow a reality in which the promise of enhanced targeting performance in terms of speed and accuracy stands in stark contrast to actual outcomes.

---

[71] González 2022, p. 7.

[72] McDonald 2021.

[73] Kim 2024.

A report published by +972 Magazine/Last Call discusses 'Lavender', an AI-enabled DSS used to identify individuals whose behavioural patterns match 'target profiles' of suspected Hamas operatives.[74] Operators of Lavender reportedly commented that they were informed that the system identified targets with 90% accuracy, in theory suggesting that 10% of the time the system misidentifies civilians as Hamas operatives. This accuracy rate is itself questionable; as discussed above, such metrics are often achieved in controlled environments and on select testing datasets, which may not capture the dynamic behaviour of individuals and general messiness of conflict. Situations that deviate from training/testing datasets—for example, data on the behaviour of children, journalists, or humanitarian workers—may significantly undermine the performance and reliability of the system. In other words, while accuracy rates refer to the overall performance of a system, they do not provide reliable assessment of each particular output without reference to the context of use.

When viewed in the context of the war in Gaza, Lavender's reported 90% accuracy rate is further questionable, given that a large majority of those killed have been civilians. Whilst a range of complex socio-political factors likely contribute to these high levels of civilian harm, the integration of AI into the targeting process appears to have facilitated—rather than improved— this situation. Despite a seemingly high accuracy rate, the increased speed of target nomination led to the production of more targets with less time for precautionary measures, which in turn contributed to a significant number of civilian casualties overall. If the use of AI-enabled systems by a technologically-advanced military such as Israel's is any indication, the use of AI in warfare has so far failed to deliver on its hypothetical promises of 'outperforming' human accuracy in conflict.

The reliability of simplistic metrics for the performance of new technologies is questionable at best. Instead of relying on metrics for speed and accuracy—especially in legal argumentation or regulatory debates—it is important to look at empirical evidence of the impact that such technologies have on warfighting. Cumulatively, technical malfunctions, data quality issues, changing warfare dynamics, and enemy countermeasures all contribute to an unstable and contested environment with heightened risk of mistakes. Human limitations such as technical aversion, a lack of technical understanding, or slow responses can also undermine the performance of technologies in practice. In such contexts, neither humans nor AI systems are acting in isolation, nor can 'better' performance be determined in controlled environments prior to conflict materialising. Instead, researchers need to carefully consider the realities of socio-technical interactions in warfare and critically question and empirically study whether the promises of enhanced accuracy at greater speeds match the results in practice in order to better support regulatory efforts for military AI.

[74] Abraham 2024.

3.4 Conflation of 'Better' with Lawfulness and the Dangers of Simplification

The question remains as to what implications inquiries into 'who makes better decisions, humans or machines?'[75] hold for legal debates on military AI. The danger of the human/AI comparison, we argue, is that it oversimplifies both the law as well as the implications of integrating AI into targeting. In this section, after a short explanation of IHL targeting principles, we first argue for a holistic understanding of IHL that does not reduce it to narrow or discrete tasks, and second, that legal compliance must centre on the complexities of human–machine interactions. We thus demonstrate that the comparison of AI versus humans alone cannot sustain a claim of 'better' IHL compliance.

IHL encompasses a carefully crafted set of targeting principles that seek to balance military necessity and humanitarian concerns. The principle of distinction primarily requires parties to a conflict to distinguish combatants and military objectives from civilians and civilian objects, with exceptional requirements regarding the targeting of civilians who are directly participating in hostilities and protections for combatants that are rendered *hors de combat*.[76] The principle of precautions requires parties to a conflict to take constant care to avoid harm to civilians and damage to civilian objects, including feasible precautions to ensure the lawfulness of targets and avoid or minimise civilian harm in attacks.[77] The principle of proportionality requires parties to a conflict to ensure that expected incidental harm to civilians and damage to civilian objects is not excessive in relation to the anticipated direct and concrete military advantage.[78] In general, these core IHL principles attempt to deal with the complexity of armed conflict by entailing a degree of indeterminacy that requires legal assessments adhering to the standard of the 'reasonable military commander', that is, what a commander would reasonably decide in the situation with the information available.[79]

Legal debates are saturated with human/AI comparisons, with scholars arguing that either humans or AI are better suited to fulfilling IHL obligations. The most problematic rhetoric, in our view, suggests that AI could be 'better' at reducing harm to civilians and as a result may ensure greater legal compliance.[80] For instance, Sassòli argues that AWS would commit less atrocities in warfare since, unlike humans, a

[75] For an example where this question is centred in legal analysis, see Harper 2024.

[76] Protocol Additional to the Geneva Conventions of 12 August 1949, and relating to the Protection of Victims of International Armed Conflicts (Protocol I), opened for signature 8 June 1977, 1125 UNTS 3, entered into force 7 December 1978 (API), Articles 41(1), 48.

[77] Ibid., Article 57.

[78] Ibid., Articles 51(5)(b), 57(2)(a)(iii), 57(2)(b).

[79] Woodcock 2026. The indeterminacy of these IHL principles is arguably also a product of the fraught debates and subsequent compromise that shaped the drafting and formulation of API: see, for example, Johansen 2019, p. 262.

[80] Sassòli 2014, p. 310; Arkin 2013, p. 8; Combe 2019, pp. 45–46; Jensen 2020; Howard 2022; Harper 2024.

machine 'cannot hate, cannot fear, cannot be hungry or tired and has no survival instinct,' and additionally 'can sense more information simultaneously and process it faster than a human being'.[81] Similarly, Heller critiques claims of human superiority for IHL compliance, suggesting that humans are not perfect as they do not perceive the world accurately or rationally, and may not be able to control negative emotions.[82] Instead, he argues that machines are better suited to performing distinctions in armed conflict. In another example, Müller argues that AWS are 'good news', as in comparison to humans they 'would probably reduce human suffering' and be less likely to lead to war crimes.[83] Arkin likewise contends that robots could potentially adhere to strict rules of engagement and IHL more rigorously than human combatants:

> If the baseline criteria becomes outperforming humans in the battlefield with respect to adherence to IHL (without mission performance erosion), I consider this to be ultimately attainable, especially under situational conditions where bounded morality (narrow, highly situation-specific conditions) applies, but not soon and not easily. The full moral faculties of humans need not be reproduced to attain to this standard.[84]

He goes as far as suggesting that if technical systems can 'exceed human performance with respect to IHL adherence' resulting in a reduction to harm to civilians, then a moral obligation to use them may arise.[85]

The human/AI comparison frames targeting obligations in terms of narrow tasks, resulting in a reductive understanding of IHL. It is often used to advance arguments in favour of the integration of AI into targeting processes through selective emphasis on particular aspects of IHL obligations. For instance, when the human/AI comparison is employed exclusively with respect to the principle of distinction, the legal obligation is then reduced to a task of recognition. By recognition, we mean the ability to identify something based on prior patterns in data. Developments in technologies, including sensors,[86] pattern recognition,[87] image classification,[88] and natural language processing,[89] contribute to enhancing military capabilities and situational awareness. These developments indicate an improvement in recognition capabilities, yet do not necessarily translate to compliance with obligations under IHL, as the narrow task of recognition of objects or individuals by AI-enabled systems cannot be automatically vested with legal meaning.

Legal categorisation of targetable individuals or military objectives entails contextualisation. For example, a tank-shaped structure that forms part of a children's

---

[81] Sassòli 2014, p. 310.

[82] Heller 2023, pp. 30–35.

[83] Müller and Simpson 2014, pp. 297–305.

[84] Arkin 2013, p. 7.

[85] Ibid.

[86] Arkin 2010, p. 333.

[87] Howard 2022, p. 234.

[88] Heller 2023, p. 21.

[89] Ibid., pp. 26–27.

playground can be recognised by an AI system as a tank, but this does not necessarily indicate its categorisation as a military objective. This example shows that AI-enabled systems may produce technically 'accurate' output for the narrow task they are performing and based on the specific dataset used to train the model. However, this narrow task does not equate to legal categorisation according to IHL due to the failure to consider relevant contextual factors. Note that instead of comparing whether AI is 'better' at distinction, we propose a more specific understanding of the task AI performs. This way we can avoid conflating the technical process of pattern recognition and its conditional accuracy with distinction assessments and the meaning ascribed to IHL categories.

Moreover, when AI-enabled systems are used to support specific tasks, they must not undermine the ability of decision makers to comply with targeting principles, all of which 'must be respected for an attack to be lawful'.[90] Therefore, when leveraging AI-enabled systems in targeting, besides a contextual assessment of legal categories, additional steps must be taken to minimise harm to civilians through feasible precautionary measures and to evaluate the proportionality of attacks. High accuracy of AI-enabled systems in recognition tasks does not relieve decision makers from the entire gamut of targeting law obligations. Recalling the replacement fallacy, it is therefore important to consider how the use of AI-enabled DSS transforms the conduct of hostilities. For example, one concern lies with the accelerated tempo of operations, where AI-enabled systems that support identification of targets rapidly and at scale may simultaneously undermine the ability of decision makers to engage in adequate precautionary measures.

Focusing on narrow tasks or specific aspects of legal assessments further neglects that targeting principles operate together rather than in isolation. Indeed, the 'three principles can fully perform their function only if respected cumulatively'.[91] IHL obligations are not a sequential, step-by-step procedure. While distinction may sometimes be mentioned as a starting point for targeting law assessments, it should not be taken to suggest that there is a linear order in which these obligations are fulfilled. IHL obligations operate as complementary components that together seek to ensure lawful, reasonable, and humane conduct during hostilities. For example, the obligation to take feasible precautions entails both duties to assess distinction and proportionality in attacks, as Article 57 API requires those launching an attack, *inter alia*, to verify the lawfulness of targets and to refrain from and cancel or suspend attacks that are disproportionate.[92] Therefore, decision makers must be vigilant to avoid a reductive understanding of IHL when using AI-enabled DSS and instead seek to make reasonable targeting assessments that appraise IHL holistically.[93]

Human–machine interaction, rather than a comparison of humans and AI, should be a central component of a comprehensive review of legal compliance with targeting

---

[90] ICRC 2019, p. 17.

[91] Daniele 2024, p. 28.

[92] API Article 57(2)(a)-(b).

[93] On reinforcing an 'irreducible' account of IHL that resists misrepresentation of the law as being reducible to code, see Kalpouzos 2020.

rules. Whether or not AI-enabled systems are purported to offer more accurate or 'better' performance, actual performance hinges on their effective implementation into operations. Poor interface design, distrust in system performance, information overload, or a lack of proper training with the system can cause human operators to disregard AI outputs, make mistakes, or even instil the system with feedback errors, undermining future reliability.[94] In other words, even a well-performing AI-enabled system can nevertheless lead to unintended consequences in targeting due to the complexities of human–machine interaction.

It is therefore important not to neglect several related uncertainties and errors stemming from human–machine interaction, such as technical malfunctions, data biases, and adversarial actions.[95] Errors may also result from external factors that undermine or temporarily impede the performance of an AI system. Technical malfunctions, such as sensor damage or connectivity issues, can cause AI systems to underperform and lead to mistakes in targeting. Changes in the context of use that expose the system to data that has not been introduced during training can undermine performance. AI systems can also lead to unintended consequences when their vulnerabilities are exploited by adversarial attacks. For example, as discussed above, an adversary can use simple methods to distort imagery and interfere with system recognition capabilities, which can lead to a series of identification mistakes.[96] As such, errors can emerge from the complex and dynamic nature of human–machine interaction and environments in which they interact.

In regulatory debates, the human/AI comparison, combined with the anthropomorphisation of AI, misdirects questions of accountability.[97] The binary choice between humans and AI systems leads lawyers to 'questions about hierarchy: Do humans ultimately rule over technology or the reverse?'.[98] Noll observes that 'it is premature, if not wrongheaded, to pose these questions'.[99] The assumed hierarchy underpinning this comparison simplifies complex socio-technical interactions. When decision makers conduct legal assessments with the support of AI-enabled DSS, accountability must account for the 'distributed agency' in military operations.[100] Some AI systems are also inherently unexplainable, which is a characteristic that can significantly hinder mechanisms of accountability.[101] This can have flow-on effects for human–machine interactions, requiring careful attention in order to develop mechanisms that enable the use of AI systems while ensuring compliance with, and rule of, law.

---

[94] Klonowska 2026a.

[95] For a more in-depth discussion of this issue, see Chap. 13 of this volume by Boutin.

[96] Kwik 2024.

[97] For an overview of key discussions on responsibility and accountability in the governance of military AI, see Chap. 11 in this volume by Romansky and Sweijs.

[98] Noll 2019, p. 77.

[99] Ibid.

[100] See, for example, Bode 2025, p. 7.

[101] Kwik and van Engers 2021.

3.5 Conclusion

In this chapter we unpacked and critiqued the rhetorics of human/AI comparisons, which today continue to be propagated with the development of generative AI and AI agents. We argued that the human/AI comparison reflects the assumption of static, hierarchical, and replaceable relations, as well as an oversimplification of the complex socio-technical interactions that characterise AI-enabled targeting practices. Whether AWS or DSS, AI technologies cannot be assessed *in abstracto*. Unless the whole AI-enabled targeting practice is evaluated iteratively and in a specific context of use,[102] the general human/AI comparison alone is an insufficient basis for claims about legal compliance. Only context-specific testing and evaluation can yield insights into potential errors stemming from human–machine interaction, adversarial action, technical malfunctions, and other uncertainties that need to be properly mitigated to prevent unintended or disproportionate civilian harm. Only time will tell whether general statements that AI-enabled targeting yields better legal compliance can be sustained. Unfortunately, the brief history of the use of AI systems in contemporary conflicts so far offers little reason for optimism.

Acknowledgements The drafting of this chapter, from ideation through to final writing, benefitted from an equal collaboration between both co-authors. Special thanks are given to Henning Lahmann and Shiri Krebs for their useful feedback and to Cheya Took for her astute editorial support.

Funding This chapter was partially developed in the context of the DILEMA Project on Designing International Lawand Ethics into Military Artificial Intelligence, funded by the Dutch Research Council Platform for Responsible Innovation (Nederlandse Organisatie voor Wetenschappelijk Onderzoek Maatschappelijk Verantwoord Innoveren (NWO-MVI)).

References

Articles, Books and Other Documents

Abraham Y (2024) 'Lavender': The AI Machine Directing Israel's Bombing Spree in Gaza. https://www.972mag.com/lavender-ai-israeli-army-gaza/

Anwar T, Klonowska K (2025) The Techno-Legal Co-Production of Terrorist Suspects. Law, Technology and Humans. https://doi.org/10.5204/lthj.3740

Arkin R (2013) Lethal Autonomous Systems and the Plight of the Non-combatant. AISB Quarterly 137:4–12

Arkin RC (2009) Governing Lethal Behavior in Autonomous Robots. CRC Press, New York

[102] On the need to iteratively assess AI systems, see Chap. 9 in this volume by Kwik.

Arkin RC (2010) The Case for Ethical Autonomy in Unmanned Systems. Journal of Military Ethics. https://doi.org/10.1080/15027570.2010.536402

Arvidsson M (2018) Targeting, Gender, and International *Posthuman*itarian Law and Practice: Framing The Question of the Human in International Humanitarian Law. Australian Feminist Law Journal. https://doi.org/10.1080/13200968.2018.1465331

Asaro P (2012) On banning autonomous weapon systems: human rights, automation, and the dehumanization of lethal decision-making. International Review of the Red Cross. https://doi.org/10.1017/S1816383112000768

Athalye A, Engstrom L, Ilyas A, Kwok K (2017) Synthesizing Robust Adversarial Examples. arXiv. https://doi.org/10.48550/arXiv.1707.07397

Bell A (2024) Can IHL training influence military conduct in war? https://blogs.icrc.org/law-and-policy/2024/05/07/can-ihl-training-influence-military-conduct-in-war/. Accessed 1 May 2025

Bench-Capon T (2021) The Need for Goold Old Fashioned AI and Law. Jusletter IT. https://doi.org/10.38023/cefe7081-e6dd-49de-9592-9adbb6063fd6

Bo M, Dorsey J (2024) Symposium on Military AI and the Law of Armed Conflict: The 'Need' for Speed—The Cost of Unregulated AI Decision-Support Systems to Civilians. https://opiniojuris.org/2024/04/04/symposium-on-military-ai-and-the-law-of-armed-conflict-the-need-for-speed-the-cost-of-unregulated-ai-decision-support-systems-to-civilians/. Accessed 1 May 2025

Bode I (2025) Human-Machine Interaction and Human Agency in the Military Domain. https://www.cigionline.org/publications/human-machine-interaction-and-human-agency-in-the-military-domain/. Accessed 1 May 2025

Boutin B, Woodcock T (2024) Aspects of Realising (Meaningful) Human Control: A Legal Perspective. In: Geiß R, Lahman H (eds) Research Handbook on Warfare and Artificial Intelligence. Edward Elgar Publishing, pp. 179–196

Campolo A, Crawford K (2020) Enchanted Determinism: Power without Responsibility in Artificial Intelligence. Engaging Science, Technology, and Society. https://doi.org/10.17351/ests2020.277

Combe PC (2019) Autonomous Doctrine: Operationalizing the Law of Armed Conflict in the Employment of Lethal Autonomous Weapons Systems. St Mary's Law Journal 51:35–68

Crootof R, Kaminski ME, Nicholson Price II W (2023) Humans in the Loop. Vanderbilt Law Review 76(2):429–510

Cummings ML (2019) Lethal Autonomous Weapons: Meaningful Human Control or Meaningful Human Certification? IEEE Technology and Society Magazine. https://doi.org/10.1109/MTS.2019.2948438

Daniele L (2024) Incidentality of the civilian harm in international humanitarian law and its *Contra Legem* antonyms in recent discourses on the laws of war. Journal of Conflict & Security Law. https://doi.org/10.1093/jcsl/krae004

Dhaliwal RS, Lepage-Richer T, Suchman L (2024) Neural Networks, In Search of Media. Meson Press and the University of Minnesota Press, Minneapolis

Dickinson P (2024) FPV Drones in Ukraine Are Changing Modern Warfare. https://www.atlanticcouncil.org/blogs/ukrainealert/fpv-drones-in-ukraine-are-changing-modern-warfare/. Accessed 1 May 2025

Dix A (2017) Human-computer interaction, foundations and new paradigms. Journal of Visual Languages & Computing. https://doi.org/10.1016/j.jvlc.2016.04.001

Elish MC, Boyd D (2018) Situating Methods in the Magic of Big Data and AI. Communication Monographs. https://doi.org/10.1080/03637751.2017.1375130

Gama J, Žliobaitė I, Bifet A, Pechenizkiy M, Bouchachia A (2014) A Survey on Concept Drift Adaptation. ACM Computing Surveys. https://doi.org/10.1145/2523813

González RJ (2022) War Virtually: The Quest to Automate Conflict, Militarize Data, and Predict the Future. University of California Press, California

González RJ (2024) How Big Tech and Silicon Valley Are Transforming the Military-Industrial Complex. https://watson.brown.edu/costsofwar/files/cow/imce/papers/2023/2024/Silicon%20Valley%20MIC.pdf. Accessed 1 May 2025

Greipl AR (2024) Artificial Intelligence Systems and Humans in Military Decision-Making: Not Better or Worse but Better Together. https://lieber.westpoint.edu/artificial-intelligence-systems-humans-military-decision-making-better-worse/. Accessed 1 May 2025

Group of Governmental Experts on Emerging Technologies in the Area of Lethal Autonomous Weapons Systems (2019) Report of the 2019 Session of the Group of Governmental Experts on Emerging Technologies in the Area of Lethal Autonomous Weapons Systems. https://documents.unoda.org/wp-content/uploads/2020/09/CCW_GGE.1_2019_3_E.pdf. Accessed 1 May 2025

Haraway D (1987) A Manifesto for Cyborgs: Science, Technology, and Socialist Feminism in the 1980s. Australian Feminist Studies. https://doi.org/10.1080/08164649.1987.9961538

Harper E (2024) Will AI fundamentally alter how wars are initiated, fought and concluded? https://blogs.icrc.org/law-and-policy/2024/09/26/will-ai-fundamentally-alter-how-wars-are-initiated-fought-and-concluded/. Accessed 1 May 2025

Heller KJ (2023) The Concept of 'The Human' in the Critique of Autonomous Weapons. Harvard National Security Journal 15(1):1–76

Heyns C (2017) Autonomous weapons in armed conflict and the right to a dignified life: an African perspective. South African Journal on Human Rights. https://doi.org/10.1080/02587203.2017.1303903

Holland Michel A (2021) Known Unknowns: Data Issues and Military Autonomous Systems. https://unidir.org/known-unknowns. Accessed 1 May 2025

Holland Michel A (2024) Decisions, Decisions, Decisions: Computation and Artificial Intelligence in Military Decision-Making. https://shop.icrc.org/decisions-decisions-decisions-computation-and-artificial-intelligence-in-military-decision-making-pdf-en.html. Accessed 1 May 2025

Howard D (2022) In Defense of (Virtuous) Autonomous Weapons. Notre Dame Journal on Emerging Technologies 3(2):230–260

ICRC (2019) International Humanitarian Law and the Challenges of Contemporary Conflicts. https://inee.org/sites/default/files/resources/ICRC%20Humanitarian%20Challenges%20Report%202019.pdf. Accessed 1 May 2025.

Introna LD (2014) Towards a Post-Human Intra-actional Account of Sociomaterial Agency (and Morality). In: Kroes P, Verbeek PP (eds) The Moral Status of Technical Artefacts. Springer Netherlands, Dordrecht, pp. 31–53

Jacobsen BJ (2023) Machine learning and the politics of synthetic data. Big Data & Society. https://doi.org/10.1177/20539517221145372

Jain AG (2022) International Law and the Regulation of Autonomous Military Capabilities. European Journal of International Law. https://doi.org/10.1093/ejil/chac064

Jensen ET (2020) The (Erroneous) Requirement for Human Judgment (and Error) in the Law of Armed Conflict. International Law Studies 96:26–57

Johansen SR (2018) So Man Created Robot in His Own Image: The Anthropomorphism of Autonomous Weapon Systems and the Law of Armed Conflict. Oslo Law Review. https://doi.org/10.18261/issn.2387-3299-2018-02-03

Johansen SR (2019) The Military Commander's Necessity: The Law of Armed Conflict and its Limits. Cambridge University Press, Cambridge

Jones E (2018) A Posthuman-Xenofeminist Analysis of the Discourse on Autonomous Weapons Systems and Other Killing Machines. Australian Feminist Law Journal. https://doi.org/10.1080/13200968.2018.1465333

Jones ML (2015) The Ironies of Automation Law: Tying Policy Knots with Fair Automation Practices Principles. Vanderbilt Journal of Entertainment and Technology Law 18(1):77–134

Jones J, Jaffer JN (2024) Artificial Instinct: AI vs. Human Decisionmaking in a Simulated Taiwan Strait Conflict. https://nationalsecurity.gmu.edu/wp-content/uploads/2024/06/Artificial-Instinct-AI-vs.-Human-Decisionmaking-in-a-Simulated-Taiwan-Strait-Conflict.pdf. Accessed 1 May 2025

Kalpouzos I (2020) Double Elevation: Autonomous Weapons and the Search for an Irreducible Law of War. Leiden Journal of International Law. https://doi.org/10.1017/S1566752907004612

Kim TH (2024) The ICT Revolution, 21st Century Warfare, and Honest Errors. In: Hayashi N, Lingaas C (eds) Honest Errors? Combat Decision-Making 75 Years After the Hostage Case. T.M.C. Asser Press, The Hague, pp. 217–31

Kirichenko P, Izmailov P, Wilson AG (2023) Last Layer Re-Training is Sufficient for Robustness to Spurious Correlations. arXiv. https://doi.org/10.48550/arXiv.2204.02937

Klonowska K (2022) Article 36: Review of AI Decision-Support Systems and Other Emerging Technologies of Warfare. In: Gill T D, Geiß R, Krieger H, Mignot-Mahdavi R (eds) Yearbook of International Humanitarian Law, Volume 23. T.M.C. Asser Press, The Hague, pp. 123–156

Klonowska K (2024) Designing for Reasonableness: The Algorithmic Mediation of Reasonableness in Targeting Decisions. https://lieber.westpoint.edu/designing-reasonableness-algorithmic-mediation-reasonableness-targeting-decisions/. Accessed 1 May 2025

Klonowska K (2026a) Elusive Reliability: Techno-Legal Considerations on the Challenges of Maintaining and Reviewing Performance of AI in Military Applications. Computer Law & Security Review (forthcoming)

Klonowska K (2026b) Techno-Legal Tinkering in War: AI Decision-Support Systems and International Humanitarian Law. DPhil Thesis, University of Amsterdam (forthcoming)

Klonowska K, van de Ven R, van der Kist J, van der Maarel S, Welfens N (2026) Collective Discussion: Sensing Security. International Political Sociology Journal (forthcoming)

Krebs S (2022) Drone-Cinema, Data Practices, and the Narrative of IHL. Zeitschrift fur Auslandisches Offentliches Recht und Volkerrecht. https://doi.org/10.17104/0044-2348-2022-2-309

Kwik J (2024) Is wearing these sunglasses an attack? Obligations under IHL related to anti-AI countermeasures. International Review of the Red Cross. https://doi.org/10.1017/S1816383124000067

Kwik J, van Engers T (2021) Algorithmic Fog of War: When Lack of Transparency Violates the Law of Armed Conflict. Journal of Future Robot Life. https://doi.org/10.3233/FRL-200019

Kwik J, van Engers T (2023) Performance or Explainability? A Law of Armed Conflict Perspective. In: Kornilakis A, Nouskalis G, Pergantis V, Tzimas T (eds) Artificial Intelligence and Normative Challenges: International and Comparative Legal Perspectives. Springer International Publishing, Cham, pp. 255–279

Lipp B, Dickel S (2023) Interfacing the Human/Machine. Distinktion: Journal of Social Theory https://doi.org/10.1080/1600910X.2021.2012709

Malik MM (2020) A Hierarchy of Limitations in Machine Learning. arXiv. https://doi.org/10.48550/arXiv.2002.05193

McDonald J (2021) Remote warfare and the legitimacy of military capabilities. Defence Studies. https://doi.org/10.1080/14702436.2021.1902315

Mignot-Mahdavi R (2023) Drones and International Law: A Techno-Legal Machinery. Cambridge University Press, Cambridge

Mimran T, Dahan G (2024) Artificial Intelligence in the Battlefield: A Perspective from Israel. https://opiniojuris.org/2024/04/20/artificial-intelligence-in-the-battlefield-a-perspective-from-israel/. Accessed 1 May 2025

Mosier KL, Skitka LJ (2019) Human Decision Makers and Automated Decisions Aids: Made for Each Other? In: Parasuraman R, Mouloua M (eds) Automation and Human Performance: Theory and Applications. CRC Press, Boca Raton, pp. 201–220

Müller O (2020) 'An Eye Turned into a Weapon': A Philosophical Investigation of Remote Controlled, Automated, and Autonomous Drone Warfare. Philosophy & Technology. https://doi.org/10.1007/s13347-020-00440-5

Müller V, Simpson TW (2014) Autonomous Killer Robots Are Probably Good News. Frontiers in Artificial Intelligence and Applications. https://doi.org/10.3233/978-1-61499-480-0-297

Noll G (2019) War by Algorithm: The End of Law? In: Liljefors M, Noll G, Steuer D (eds) War and Algorithm. Rowman & Littlefield International, London/New York

Ribeiro MT, Singh S, Guestrin C (2016) 'Why Should I Trust You? Explaining the Predications of Any Classifier. arXiv. https://doi.org/10.48550/arXiv.1602.04938

Rosen B (2023) Unhuman Killings: AI and Civilian Harm in Gaza. https://www.justsecurity.org/90676/unhuman-killings-ai-and-civilian-harm-in-gaza/. Accessed 1 May 2025

Rosenberger R, Verbeek P (2015) Postphenomenological Investigations: Essays on Human-Technology Relations, Postphenomenology and the Philosophy of Technology. Lexington Books, Lanham

Russell SJ (2023) Human Compatible: Artificial Intelligence and the Problem of Control. Penguin Books, London

Sassòli M (2014) Autonomous Weapons and International Humanitarian Law: Advantages, Open Technical Questions and Legal Issues to Be Clarified. International Law Studies 90(1):308–340

Schwarz E (2024) Unicorns for Uniforms: On the Problematic Allure of VC Investments in Defence. https://opiniojuris.org/2024/09/18/unicorns-for-uniforms-on-the-problematic-allure-of-vc-investments-in-defence/. Accessed 1 May 2025

Schwarz E (2025) From Blitzkrieg to Blitzscaling: Assessing the Impact of Venture Capital Dynamics on Military Norms. Finance and Society. https://doi.org/10.1017/fas.2024.18

Suchman L (2023a) Imaginaries of Omniscience: Automating Intelligence in the US Department of Defense. Social Studies of Science. https://doi.org/10.1177/03063127221104938

Suchman L (2023b) The Uncontroversial 'Thingness' of AI. Big Data & Society. https://doi.org/10.1177/20539517231206794

Suchman LA (2007) Human-Machine Reconfigurations: Plans and Situated Actions, 2nd edn. Cambridge University Press, Cambridge

Sutton R (2021) The Humanitarian Civilian: How the Idea of Distinction Circulates Within and Beyond International Humanitarian Law, 1st edn. Oxford University Press, Oxford

United Kingdom Ministry of Defence (2023) British Army's Approach to Artificial Intelligence: A Guide to Accelerate the Army's Adoption of AI and Get the Army AI Ready. https://www.army.mod.uk/media/24745/20231001-british_army_approach_to_artificial_intelligence.pdf. Accessed 1 May 2025

United States Department of Defense (2023) AUKUS Defense Ministers Meeting Joint Statement. https://www.defense.gov/News/Releases/Release/Article/3604511/aukus-defense-ministers-meeting-joint-statement/. Accessed 1 May 2025

UN GGE LAWS (2019) Final Report - Annex III 'Guiding Principles affirmed by the Group of Governmental Experts on Emerging Technologies in the Area of Lethal Autonomous Weapons System', CCW/MSP/2019/9

Watts TFA, Bode I (2023) Loitering Munitions and Unpredictability: Autonomy in Weapon Systems and Challenges to Human Control. Centre for War Studies. https://doi.org/10.5281/zenodo.7860761

Woodcock TK (2024) Human/Machine(-Learning) Interactions, Human Agency and the International Humanitarian Law Proportionality Standard. Global Society. https://doi.org/10.1080/13600826.2023.2267592

Woodcock TK (2026) Human-Machine (Learning) Interactions: War and Law in the AI Era. DPhil Thesis, University of Amsterdam (forthcoming)

Xu K, Zhang G, Liu A, Fan Q, Sun M, Chen H, Chen P, Wang Y, Lin X (2019) Adversarial T-Shirt! Evading Person Detectors in A Physical World. arXiv. https://doi.org/10.48550/arXiv.1910.11099

Klaudia Klonowska is a Postdoctoral Researcher at Sciences Po Paris and Managing Director of the West Point Manual on Artificial Intelligence. Her PhD thesis entitled *Techno-Legal Tinkering: AI Decision-Support Systems, Human–Machine Interaction, and International Humanitarian Law* was completed at the Asser Institute and the University of Amsterdam as part of the Designing International Law and Ethics into Military Artificial Intelligence (DILEMA) project funded by the Dutch Research Council.

Taylor Kate Woodcock is a researcher in public international law at the Asser Institute, University of Amsterdam (The Netherlands). She researches international legal practices, human agency, and AI-enabled technologies. Her doctoral thesis, entitled *Human–Machine (Learning) Interactions: War and Law in the AI Era,* written as part of the DILEMA project, funded by the Dutch Research Council, examines how the use of AI in military targeting operations can shape practices of legal reasoning and the exercise of human agency.

Part II
Legal and Ethical Challenges

Chapter 4
The Use of Autonomous Cyber Capabilities in Armed Conflict: Legal Appraisal from a Targeting Law Perspective

Marta Stroppa

Contents

Abstract Autonomous cyber capabilities (ACC)—software agents programmed to operate through cyberspace without real-time human oversight or intervention—are slowly becoming a tangible reality. States and regional organisations are increasing investment in the research and development of these technologies for both offensive and defensive applications. So far, discussions surrounding cyberspace and autonomous systems have neglected this emerging area. This chapter aims to fill this gap by exploring whether, and to what extent, ACC can be deployed to execute autonomous cyber attacks in compliance with targeting rules under International Humanitarian Law (IHL), focusing on the fundamental principles of distinction, proportionality, and precaution. Specifically, it considers ACC's application in *deliberate* and *dynamic* cyber attacks. It argues that, depending on the operational circumstances, a wide range of precautionary measures can be implemented to ensure that ACC accurately identify targets while avoiding or minimising incidental collateral damage. These measures range from embedding technical safeguards to retaining human control over ACC during deployment. As military reliance on autonomous

M. Stroppa (✉)
DIRPOLIS Institute, Sant'Anna School of Advanced Studies, Pisa, Italy
e-mail: marta.stroppa@santannapisa.it

B. Boutin et al. (eds.), *Legal, Ethical, and Technical Dilemmas in Military Artificial Intelligence*, https://doi.org/10.1007/978-94-6265-759-5_4

technologies increases, this chapter highlights the urgent need for further research to address the operational and legal challenges posed by ACC in future warfare.

Keywords Autonomous Cyber Capabilities (ACC) · Cyberspace · Artificial Intelligence (AI) · Autonomy · International Humanitarian Law (IHL) · Targeting · Human Control

4.1 Introduction

Over the last decade, artificial intelligence (AI) and autonomous technologies have played an increasingly significant role in the cyber military domain.[1] Autonomous cyber capabilities (ACC)—software agents programmed to operate through cyberspace without real-time human oversight or intervention—are slowly emerging from the realm of science fiction into tangible reality.[2] Applications of AI and autonomy within this domain are actively researched and developed by several states—including *inter alia* Australia,[3] France,[4] Germany,[5] Japan,[6] the Russian Federation,[7] the United Kingdom (UK),[8] and the United States (US).[9] Furthermore, the North Atlantic Treaty Organization (NATO) and the European Union (EU) have shown considerable interest in these technologies.[10] Indeed, there is little doubt that ACC will play a crucial role in the future of warfare.[11]

Discussions surrounding these technologies have so far eluded conversations on autonomous weapons systems (AWS)—weapons systems that, 'once activated, can select and engage targets without further intervention by a human operator'[12]—and cyberspace—'[t]he environment formed by physical and non-physical components to store, modify, and exchange data using computer networks'.[13] Debates on AWS primarily occurred within the framework of the Group of Governmental Experts on Lethal Autonomous Weapons Systems (GGE LAWS), established under the umbrella of the Convention on Prohibitions or Restrictions on the Use of Certain Conventional

[1] Bellasio and Silfversten 2020, pp. 90–91; Cristiano et al. 2023.

[2] Liivoja et al. 2019, p. 10.

[3] Australia 2023, p. 64; Haataja 2024a, p. 3.

[4] Delerue 2020, p. 159.

[5] Germany 2021, p. 47.

[6] Leyden 2012.

[7] Bendett et al. 2021, pp. 71–72.

[8] United Kingdom 2022.

[9] Scharre 2018, p. 95; US Cyberspace Solarium Commission 2020, p. 16; and US National Security Commission on Artificial Intelligence 2021, p. 79.

[10] Kott et al. 2019; EU Agency For Cybersecurity 2020; and EU 2022, p. 45.

[11] Perez 2023, p. 206.

[12] US Department of Defense 2012, pp. 13–14.

[13] Schmitt 2017, p. 564.

Weapons (CCW).[14] They largely focused on conventional robotic weapons and only referred to cyber in terms of AWS' cyber-security safeguards.[15] Meanwhile, discussions on cyberspace have occurred in different intergovernmental processes at the UN level: six Group of Governmental Experts (GGE) and two Open-Ended Working Groups have been established in the last two decades to discuss developments in the field of information and communication technologies and responsible State behaviour in cyberspace in the context of international security. Although few States acknowledged that ACC represent a 'new and potential severe threat to international peace and security',[16] discussions have predominantly focused on human-operated cyber capabilities. As a result, the significant interactions between autonomy and cyberspace have been mostly neglected.[17] Only recently, during a high-level meeting at the UN Security Council, did States acknowledge the potential detrimental impact of AI in cyberspace.[18] In this context, the NATO Cooperative Cyber Defence Centre of Excellence (CCDCOE) conducted a study raising awareness of the legal implications of ACC regarding international law.[19] However, further research is needed as the unpredictability, unreliability, and unexplainability of these technologies raise new legal hurdles *vis-à-vis* international law that must be urgently addressed.[20]

This chapter examines the key legal implications of deploying ACC in the conduct of hostilities by analysing autonomous cyber attacks from an International Humanitarian Law (IHL) perspective. IHL is the branch of international law that applies to armed conflicts (whether international (IAC) or non-international (NIAC)) and regulates the conduct of hostilities. It contains a set of provisions aimed at ruling when attacks—defined by Article 49 of Additional Protocol I (API) to the Geneva Conventions as 'acts of violence against the adversary, whether in offence or defence'[21] —are lawful, also known as targeting rules. When ACC are used by a party to an armed conflict to carry out an autonomous cyber attack, they need to comply with IHL rules on targeting.

---

[14] UN CCW 2013, para 32.

[15] UN CCW GGE LAWS 2018, p. 4, para 21 (2); UN CCW GGE LAWS 2019, p. 10, para (f).

[16] Netherlands 2020, p. 1. See also Brazil 2020, p. 1; and Ecuador 2020, p. 1.

[17] UNIDIR 2017, pp. 1–3; Liivoja et al. 2019, pp. 5–6.

[18] UN Security Council 2024.

[19] In 2019, the NATO CCDCOE published a 49-page working paper titled 'Autonomous Cyber Capabilities Under International Law', followed two years later by an edited volume with the same name, featuring 13 contributions on autonomy in cyberspace from experts in technical, legal, philosophical, and political fields. See, respectively, Liivoja et al. 2019; Liivoja and Väljataga 2021. In 2024, applications of machine learning and AI methods in cyberspace were discussed at CyCon, the annual conference organised by NATO CCDCOE: NATO CCDCOE 2024.

[20] Stroppa 2023a.

[21] Protocol Additional (I) to the Geneva Conventions of 12 August 1949, and Relating to the Protection of Victims of International Armed Conflicts, open for signature 8 June 1977, 1125 UNTS 3, entered into force 7 December 1979 (API), Article 49(1). It is important to note that the notion of attack under IHL is different from (and should not be confused with) the notion of 'armed attack' under Article 51 of the UN Charter, which belongs to the realm of the law on the use of force and is outside the scope of this chapter.

This chapter is structured as follows. Following a brief technical introduction to the notion of ACC in the military domain, it explores the legal implications autonomous cyber attacks pose in relation to the three key principles of IHL—*distinction*, *proportionality*, and *precaution*. In particular, it considers the deployment of ACC in deliberate and dynamic targeting. The chapter argues that, depending on the operational circumstances of an attack (deliberate *or* dynamic), militaries can implement a wide range of precautionary measures to ensure ACC operate in compliance with IHL. These measures range from embedding technical safeguards to exercising human control in cyberspace.

4.2 Autonomous Cyber Capabilities: A Technical Overview

ACC are software agents designed to perform specific tasks through cyberspace without requiring real-time interaction with a human operator.[22] They follow predefined instructions set during the programming stage, or in more advanced models, utilise sophisticated AI techniques, such as machine learning (ML), to adapt to dynamic environments.[23]

When deployed in the conduct of hostilities, ACC may be programmed to autonomously execute cyber operations and attacks, either in offence or defence.[24] The term 'cyber operation' is intended to refer to the 'employment of cyber capabilities to achieve objectives in or through cyberspace' in a broad sense.[25] With the term 'cyber attack', this chapter refers to the notion of attack under IHL, as defined by Article 49 of API, as previously mentioned. An ACC amounts to a cyber attack in the meaning of IHL when it causes (or is reasonably expected to cause) a certain degree of violence against the military forces of an opposing party to an armed conflict.[26] While to this day there is still no consensus on the level of harm that a cyber operation should reach in order to qualify as an attack under IHL, this chapter takes the view that ACC that cause, or are reasonably expected to cause, injury or death to persons or damage or destruction to objects clearly qualify.[27] It further acknowledges that,

---

[22] Stroppa 2023a, p. 1. See also Liivoja et al. 2019, p. 10.

[23] Tošić 2016; McFarland 2021, pp. 18–26.

[24] Ibid., pp. 7–13.

[25] Schmitt 2017, p. 564.

[26] API, above n. 21, Article 49(1).

[27] Schmitt 2017, Rule 92(10)–(12).

according to several States,[28] and the ICRC,[29] loss of functionality also reaches the necessary threshold of harm. By contrast, ACC merely causing inconvenience or irritation to the civilian population do not qualify and are therefore outside the scope of this chapter.[30] It remains unclear, however, whether cyber operations causing large-scale adverse consequences, but not physical damage or loss of functionality, would qualify as attacks under IHL.[31]

4.2.1 Offensive ACC

Offensive ACC are designed to *launch* cyber attacks against targets without real-time human oversight or intervention.[32] Autonomy can be integrated into every stage of the so-called 'cyber kill chain', from intelligence gathering to targeting.[33] For instance, an offensive ACC could be programmed to search for a specific target, and then autonomously launch a cyber attack without requiring real-time human intervention, either by strictly following pre-set instructions or employing AI techniques. One of the first known offensive ACC used was reportedly Stuxnet, a malware that targeted Iran's Natanz nuclear enrichment facility in 2009.[34] It was programmed to autonomously spread throughout Natanz's air-gapped network, identify software controlling the facility's centrifuges, and manipulate their operation by altering settings.[35] Stuxnet did not occur in the context of an ongoing armed conflict and experts are divided on whether it would have triggered the applicability of IHL.[36] Yet, it provides a good example of offensive ACC that may cause physical destruction.[37] Another recent example of offensive ACC is DeepLocker, a malware system developed by IBM that relies on ML to identify pre-selected targets based on predetermined trigger conditions (e.g., facial and voice recognition, geolocation) and autonomously launch a cyber operation without real-time human control.[38] Similar offensive ACC

---

[28] Albeit some States—notably, Denmark, Israel and Peru—have taken a more restrictive position, arguing that only cyber attacks resulting in physical damage qualify as attacks under IHL, several States—including Austria, Bolivia, Costa Rica, Ecuador, France, Germany, Guatemala, Ireland, Italy, Japan, and New Zealand—share the view that cyber operations may qualify as an attack under IHL without causing physical damage if they result in a loss of functionality. Relevant national positions and statements are available at: https://cyberlaw.ccdcoe.org/wiki/Attack_(international_humanitarian_law). Accessed 11 May 2025.

[29] ICRC 2020a, pp. 7–8.

[30] Schmitt 2017, Rule 92(14).

[31] Liivoja et al. 2019, p. 26.

[32] Stroppa 2023b, p. 7.

[33] Guarino 2013; Buchanan et al. 2020.

[34] Scharre 2018; Heinl 2018.

[35] Tyugu 2012, p. 337; Scharre 2018, pp. 213–215.

[36] ICRC 2018, p. 71.

[37] Liivoja et al. 2019, p. 27.

[38] Stoecklin et al. 2018.

may be deployed in the conduct of hostilities to execute cyber attacks against military objectives, such as command and control facilities or air-defence systems. Likewise, offensive ACC may be launched against an individual. Although cyber attacks against individuals might not be the most likely scenario, they are technically feasible. As underlined by Schmitt, indeed, 'it is, of course, possible to attack people by cyber means—for instance, by starting fires in facilities in which they are located, interfering with air-traffic control relied on by the aircraft transporting them, causing train collisions, and so forth'.[39] An offensive ACC may, for instance, be used to interrupt electricity in an hospital where a military commander is undergoing surgery, or even to disrupt a military commander's pacemaker, in order to target them.[40]

4.2.2 *Defensive ACC*

Defensive ACC are designed to *defend* a network or computer system from malicious cyber operations without real-time human control.[41] These systems can be programmed to detect malicious cyber threats and autonomously respond in real-time by executing passive, active, or combined defensive countermeasures.[42] While passive defensive measures do not raise particular concerns *vis-à-vis* international law, as they solely operate within the system they are defending,[43] active defensive measures involve proactive actions taken outside the defended system to prevent, block, or respond to malicious cyber operations.[44] One of the most well-known examples of active defensive ACC is Mayhem, a Cyber Reasoning System (CRS) that won the 2016 US Defence Advanced Research Projects Agency (DARPA) Cyber Grand Challenge.[45] Mayhem autonomously identified and patched vulnerabilities in flawed code that could be exploited by hackers, while also detecting and exploiting adversary vulnerabilities before they could respond.[46] While this capability did not reach the threshold of attack under IHL, similar defensive ACC could be designed to hack

[39] Schmitt 2015, p. 20.

[40] The example of the pacemaker was first formulated in the Tallinn Manual 2.0. According to the experts, it would be lawful to take the control of the Internet-addressable pacemaker devices of enemy combatants in order to kill them or render them *hors de combat*. However, it would be unlawful to conduct the operation in a manner that is intended to cause superfluous injuries and unnecessary suffering—such as stopping their hearts and then reviving them multiple times before finally killing them. Schmitt 2017, Rule 104(6).

[41] Stroppa 2023b, p. 7.

[42] Ibid.

[43] Passive cyber defence refers to measures designed to detect and mitigate intrusions, thereby enhancing the resilience of a network or system. Examples include firewalls and anti-virus software, which operate solely within the defended infrastructure. Schmitt 2017, p. 566.

[44] A notable example is the 'hack-back', where actions are taken against the source of a cyber threat to mitigate its impact or gather technical evidence for attribution of responsibility. Ibid., p. 565.

[45] https://www.darpa.mil/news/2016/cyber-grand-challenge-winners. Accessed 11 May 2025.

[46] Avgerinos et al. 2018.

back and incapacitate (or even destroy) the system from which the malicious cyber operation originates.[47] If similar active defensive measures are deployed, they would need to comply with the principles of distinction, proportionality, and precautions.

4.2.3 Prospects and Challenges of ACC in Warfare

The prospective uses of either offensive or defensive ACC in warfare hold particular appeal for States. The integration of AI applications into cyberspace has been suggested as a means to enhance the robustness and resilience of States' cyber networks while improving responses to malicious cyber operations. Additionally, it offers strong tactical and strategic advantages in the conduct of hostilities.[48] However, deploying ACC in warfare raises important challenges that warrant further examination.[49] ACC that rely solely on pre-programmed human instructions are unable to adapt to unforeseen circumstances not anticipated by humans in the programming phase.[50] ACC require extensive *a priori* knowledge of all potential circumstances they may encounter once deployed—a particularly challenging task in the complex environment of cyberspace.[51] For this reason, States are increasingly investing in AI-enabled ACC that can adapt to unforeseen changes in the operational environment.[52] Yet, such software agents introduce significant risks, including unpredictability, unreliability, and unexplainability.[53] Indeed, it is difficult to predict how AI-enabled ACC will respond to a particular input or ensuring consistent performance, especially when deployed in complex environments.[54]

4.2.4 ACC Versus *Other Automated/Autonomous Military Systems*

ACC share important features with other military systems that present a certain degree of autonomy, and in particular with AWS and automated decision-support systems

[47] Autonomous hack backs raise important challenges *vis-à-vis* a wide range of international law provisions, including those regulating the plea of necessity in self-defence. See, e.g., Tsagourias and Buchan 2017; Stroppa 2023b; Haataja 2024b.

[48] Taddeo et al. 2019, p. 557; McFarland 2021, p. 18; Burton and Soare 2019, pp. 9–10.

[49] ICRC 2020b, p. 467.

[50] Russell and Norvig 2022, pp. 67–69.

[51] Boulanin and Verbruggen 2017, p. 16.

[52] Shoaib 2020.

[53] Stroppa 2023a, p. 3.

[54] Boulanin and Verbruggen 2017; Holland Michel 2020; Taddeo 2021. On the inherent issues around AI unpredictability in complex operational environments, see also Kwik in this volume (Chap. 9).

(DSS). On the one hand, both ACC and AWS can engage targets without human control or intervention and have detrimental effects in the kinetic world.[55] On the other hand, both ACC and automated DSS rely on software and often sophisticated AI algorithms to recognise patterns and outline possible courses of action in the targeting process.[56] When these systems rely on advanced AI techniques, such as ML, they also share similar concerns in terms of unpredictability, unreliability, and unexplainability of the algorithms.[57] At the same time, however, ACC present some unique characteristics that deserve to be taken into consideration. Conversely to AWS, which are deployed in the physical world, ACC operates in a virtual domain where they can self-replicate and self-propagate at a very high speed, crossing the world and reaching their target within seconds.[58] This, combined with the fact that most cyber infrastructures are simultaneously used by both the military and civilians, increases the risk that the civilian population will be affected.[59] In addition, ACC may benefit from numerous obfuscation techniques to hide the original perpetrator of a cyber operation, rendering attribution particularly challenging.[60] Finally, while ACC may be programmed to engage targets through cyberspace without human oversight or intervention, automated DSS only support military personnel in decision making. They do not autonomously resort to the use of force.[61]

4.3 Autonomous Cyber Attacks and the Law of Targeting

In the conduct of hostilities, all attacks must respect the three cardinal rules of targeting law—the principles of *distinction*, *proportionality*, and *precaution*—including autonomous cyber attacks.[62] This section examines the legal challenges associated with ACC in targeting operations. First, it explores whether, and to what extent, ACC can be used to distinguish between lawful and unlawful targets (Sect. 4.3.1). Second, it assesses when an autonomous cyber attack on a lawful target risks collateral damage that would be excessive in relation to the anticipated military advantage (Sect. 4.3.2). Finally, it discusses the precautionary measures a commander should take during an autonomous cyber attack (Sect. 4.3.3).

---

[55] Perez 2023, pp. 192–197.

[56] In a report prepared for the ICRC, Arthur Holland Michel underlined how DSS are directly relevant to the ongoing debate on AWS, arguing that 'many of the tools that are currently used or will be used in the future to support human decisions in the use of force (such as automatic target recognition tools, planning and optimization tools) could play a critical function in autonomous weapon systems that execute those same "decisions" autonomously'. Michel 2024, p. 15. The same could be argued with respect to ACC.

[57] On the challenges arising from the use of AI and ML in AWS, ACC, and DSS, see ICRC 2020b.

[58] Anderson 2016, pp. 34–35; Delerue 2020, p. 160.

[59] Gisel et al. 2021, pp. 320–322.

[60] Anderson 2016, p. 29.

[61] Woodcock 2024, p. 101.

[62] Harrison Dinniss 2024, p. 271.

Before delving into the legal analysis, an important distinction must be made between two types of targeting processes. This chapter differentiates between deliberate and dynamic autonomous cyber attacks, each involving different levels of planning, oversight, and decision making. These targeting processes form the basis of the following analysis, where each will be examined in relation to the core principles of distinction, proportionality, and precaution. Under each principle, the analysis will first examine *deliberate* autonomous cyber attacks—pre-planned and authorised attacks against validated targets.[63] Second, it considers *dynamic* autonomous cyber attacks—unplanned attacks in which ACC autonomously detect and target emerging, unverified threats in line with broader operational objectives.[64]

In deliberate autonomous cyber attacks, legal assessments—in terms of target validation, collateral damage estimation, and capabilities analysis—are conducted before engagement by those who plan or decide upon the attack. ACC therefore execute the attack on the basis of the instructions imparted at the programming stage. In dynamic autonomous cyber attacks, however, part of these assessments cannot be performed in advance or must be adjusted to reflect the changes in the operational environment. Therefore, ACC may be expected to respond in real-time to evolving operational contexts, performing these assessments without human oversight or intervention.[65] This should not be regarded as anthropomorphising ACC but rather as acknowledging that cyberspace is a particularly complex environment that requires adaptability. Militaries will be tempted to rely on ACC in dynamic targeting, due to their speed of response and ability to analyse wide amounts of technical data.

It is therefore imperative to understand whether and to what extent ACC may be used in both deliberate and dynamic attacks. This does not mean that ACC bear legal responsibility for any IHL breaches resulting from their behaviour. As will be argued, legal responsibility remains with the military commander who has the due diligence obligation to take all feasible precautions to ensure compliance with IHL and prevent unintended violations, including embedding some safeguards and retaining human control, when necessary.[66]

4.3.1 Autonomous Cyber Attacks and the Principle of Distinction

The principle of distinction has been recognised by the International Court of Justice (ICJ) as a 'cardinal' principle of IHL and an 'intransgressible' tenet of customary

[63] NATO 2021, p. 12.

[64] Ibid.

[65] On the necessity to transfer decision-making to AI-enabled software agents, see Deeks et al. 2019, pp. 18–19.

[66] On responsibility and AI-enabled systems, see Romansky and Sweijs in this volume (Chap. 11).

international law (CIL).[67] It is codified under Article 48 of API,[68] which reflects CIL and applies to both IAC and NIAC.[69] This principle requires parties to an armed conflict to distinguish between civilians and combatants (or fighters in NIACs), as well as between civilian objects and military objectives, directing attacks only against the latter. The principle also applies, *ceteris paribus,* to cyber attacks (including those that are autonomous), which must only be directed against lawful targets.[70] In the conduct of hostilities, ACC may be deployed to target specific military objectives (*deliberate* targeting) or to identify and target unplanned emerging threats during operations (*dynamic* targeting).

4.3.1.1 Autonomous Cyber Attacks Against Military Objectives

To comply with the principle of distinction, ACC should be able to distinguish at *all* times between civilian objects and military objectives and to direct attacks only against the latter.[71] According to Article 52(2) API, military objectives are 'those objects which by their nature, location, purpose or use make an effective contribution to military action and whose total or partial destruction, capture or neutralisation, in the circumstances ruling at the time, offers a definite military advantage'.[72] However, applying this definition of military objectives in cyberspace may present unique challenges.[73] While ACC may be used to target a pre-determined military objective (e.g., a military network) using technical data, they raise several challenges in dynamic targeting. In a dynamic cyber attack, ACC may potentially identify the 'nature' of an object (e.g., a military IP address), but determining the 'location', 'purpose', or 'use' of an object is more difficult and inevitably requires a context-based analysis.[74] In addition, an ACC is not able *per se* to determine whether these objects 'make an effective contribution to military action' or whether their 'total or partial destruction, capture or neutralisation' offers a 'definite military advantage'. This determination requires the exercise of human judgement, as it relies on a qualitative and context-based assessment.[75] This is particularly evident in the following example.

---

[67] International Court of Justice, *Legality of the Threat or Use of Nuclear Weapons,* Advisory Opinion, 8 July 1996, ICJ Reports 226, para 78.

[68] API, above n. 21, Article 48.

[69] Henckaerts and Doswald-Beck 2009, Rule 1.

[70] Schmitt 2017, Rule 93.

[71] API, above n. 21, Article 48.

[72] Ibid., Article 52(2).

[73] Roscini 2014, p. 183.

[74] Tsagourias and Buchan 2017, pp. 230–231; Harrison Dinniss 2024, p. 272.

[75] As underlined by the Group of Experts Working on Schmitt, '[t]he term 'definite' does not imply any quantum of advantage. A cyber attack is lawful when the attacker reasonably concludes that the 'total or partial destruction, capture, or neutralisation' of the nominated target will yield an actual military advantage': Schmitt 2017, Rule 100(23).

One of the key challenges in applying the principle of distinction in cyberspace is the prevalence of dual-use infrastructures, which simultaneously serve both civilian and military purposes.[76] For example, servers, fibre-optic cables, satellites, and other software and physical hardware components of cyberspace are almost entirely dual-use.[77] The internet itself is inherently dual-use. This raises an important question: Would an ACC qualify dual-use objects as military objectives? For instance, according to some experts involved in the Tallinn Manual 2.0, a 'strict' application of the definition of military objectives could lead to the conclusion that the 'entire Internet' can become a military objective if used 'for military purposes'.[78] As such, in dynamic targeting, ACC could, in the extreme, conclude that the entire Internet is a legitimate target. Yet, to be a lawful target under the principle of distinction, ACC should also determine whether the 'destruction' or 'neutralisation' of the Internet would actually offer a definite military advantage. As previously mentioned, however, this assessment cannot be easily carried out without real-time human control as it relies on qualitative factors requiring the exercise of human judgment. Moreover, as underlined by Roscini, it is unlikely that the neutralisation of the entire Internet would offer a definite military advantage due to its high level of resilience.[79] As he notes, 'if certain channels become unusable as a consequence of a cyber or kinetic attack on servers, the data flow will simply find another path to reach its destination'.[80] Finally, it should be noted that even if the entire Internet would qualify as a military objective, an autonomous cyber attack against it would likely be in contrast with the principle of proportionality, as will be explored below.[81]

4.3.1.2 Autonomous Cyber Attacks Against Individuals

Although autonomous cyber attacks are more likely to be used to target military objectives, it is technically possible to use ACC to target individuals in cyberspace—although individuals attacked by cyber means could be affected only indirectly.[82] For instance, ACC may be used to cause a targeted computer explosion to kill its operator;[83] or to hack into a military commander's car in order to crash it and cause their death.[84] For this reason, it is crucial to explore whether and to what extent ACC

[76] Gisel et al. 2021, pp. 320–322.

[77] Roscini 2014, p. 185.

[78] Schmitt 2017, Rule 101(6).

[79] Roscini 2014, p. 190. On this point, see also Gisel et al. 2021, p. 321; Huang and Ying 2020, p. 359.

[80] Ibid.

[81] Roscini 2014, p. 190; Schmitt 2017, Rule 101(7).

[82] Schmitt 2015, p. 20; Roscini 2014, p. 193.

[83] Tsagourias and Buchan 2017, pp. 231–232.

[84] In 2015, Charlie Miller and Chris Valasek exposed the security vulnerabilities in automobiles by hacking into a car remotely, taking control of the car's transmission and brakes. Greenberg 2015.

can be used to target combatants (or fighters in NIACs) and civilians taking direct part into hostilities, in compliance with IHL.

In deliberate targeting, lawful targets are pre-identified by those responsible for the attack before engagement, with the ACC only tasked with carrying out the cyber attack based on such pre-determined instructions. If the target can be easily identified (e.g., through technical data) and the ACC is properly instructed and trained, no significant problems should arise *vis-à-vis* the principle of distinction. For instance, as mentioned above, ACC may be programmed to hack into a hospital network, identify a military commander through their medical record, and stop their pacemaker. However, given the complexity of operational environments and the widespread use of cyber obfuscation techniques (e.g., such as spoofing)[85] that might compromise the targeting process, human authorisation may be necessary if any doubt arises regarding target's identity.[86]

In dynamic targeting, real-time target identification and qualification may need to be performed by ACC. To comply with the principle of distinction, ACC must distinguish between lawful and unlawful targets. To determine the target's lawfulness, ACC must first identify different categories of persons by taking into account their status (e.g., whether they are members of the armed forces) and their conduct (e.g., whether they are directly participating in hostilities). Yet, the determination of the status of a person is not always easy in cyberspace given that individuals behind cyber operations are not always visible,[87] and most cyber operations are anonymous.[88] These complexities are further compounded when identifying members of militias or volunteer corps, as the criteria listed in Article 4(A)(2)(a)–(d) of the Third Geneva Convention[89] are not easily transposable to cyberspace.[90]

Likewise, assessing a person's conduct is particularly challenging in cyberspace, especially if assessments are carried out autonomously in real-time without human control. In order for ACC to determine whether a civilian is directly participating in hostilities, they would need to assess: (i) whether their actions cause or are intended to cause harm (threshold of harm); (ii) whether there is a causal link between the act and the harm (causation); and (iii) whether the act is directly related to the hostilities (belligerent nexus).[91] However, such assessments heavily rely on contextual elements that current AI-enabled technology cannot process effectively.[92] The output of AI (and especially ML) is indeed inherently 'decontextualised' and only

---

[85] In cybersecurity, *spoofing* is when a person or a program impersonalises 'a legitimate resource or user to gain unauthorised entry into an information system or to make it appear that some other organisation or individual has initiated or undertaken certain cyber activity'. Schmitt 2017, p. 567.

[86] Liivoja et al. 2019, pp. 28–29; Schmitt 2017, Rules 95 and 102, addressing doubt regarding the status of persons and objects, respectively.

[87] Schmitt 2017, Rule 95(4).

[88] Mavropoulou 2015, p. 68.

[89] Convention (III) relative to the Treatment of Prisoners of War, open for signature 12 August 1949, UNTS 972, entered into force 21 October 1959 (Third Geneva Convention), Article 4(A)(2)(a)–(d).

[90] Roscini 2014, pp. 196–199. See also D'Urso 2015.

[91] Melzer 2009. On ACC and direct participation into hostilities, see Singer 2017.

[92] Asaro 2012, pp. 696–698; Amoroso 2020, pp. 47–52.

reflects a 'technological rendering of the world as a statistical data relationship', not the current circumstances of the case.[93] Clearly, civilians who launch a cyber attack to contribute to the hostilities fulfil the criteria—but are ACC able to make this assessment? It should be noted that in cyberspace, civilians may unknowingly directly participate in cyber hostilities, such as in the case of botnets—networks of infected computers hijacked by external users without the owner's knowledge.[94] In such cases, the concerned civilians would not qualify as lawful targets since they are not intentionally participating in hostilities.[95] Yet, ACC are unlikely to detect such instances without human oversight or intervention. Finally, ACC must be able to determine the temporal aspect of the direct participation in hostilities. Notably, a civilian loses protection under IHL 'for such time as' they take direct part in hostilities.[96] However, this determination may require a qualitative assessment, especially when it comes to preparatory acts. Consider, for example, a civilian who penetrates the adversary's network in order to gather intelligence and identify a vulnerability that is subsequently exploited for an attack. An ACC would be required to identify the relevant preparatory acts and establish synergies with the related hostile act. This is not possible, however, without human intervention and a context-based analysis.[97] As underlined by Woodcock, indeed, as 'data-driven predictions are based on correlation and not causation', it is 'contextual grounding [that] allows human to determine what patterns and factors are casually relevant'.[98]

Thus, while ACC could potentially be used in compliance with the principle of distinction for deliberate targeting, provided the necessary precautions are in place, in dynamic targeting, it remains questionable whether they can be lawfully used. Indeed, the determination of lawful targets often requires a contextual assessment and the exercise of human judgement, especially if the autonomous cyber attack is carried out in complex environments.[99] For this reason, a certain degree of human control should always be retained over dynamic targeting.

4.3.2 *Autonomous Cyber Attacks and the Principle of Proportionality*

The principle of proportionality, the second pillar of IHL, is outlined in Article 51(5)(b) API. It prohibits attacks 'which may be expected to cause incidental loss of civilian life, injury to civilians, damage to civilian objects, or a combination thereof, which would be excessive in relation to the concrete and direct military advantage

[93] Schwarz 2021, p. 60. See also Woodcock 2024, pp. 108–109.

[94] Roscini 2014, pp. 210–211.

[95] Melzer 2009, p. 60.

[96] API, above n. 21, Article 51(3).

[97] Tsagourias and Buchan 2017, pp. 233–234.

[98] Woodcock 2024, p. 109.

[99] Tsagourias and Buchan 2017, p. 234.

anticipated'.[100] This principle applies, *ceteris paribus*, to cyberspace.[101] It should be noted, however, that assessing proportionality in cyberspace is not always easy. Determining whether an attack is expected to result in excessive collateral damage with respect to the military advantage is particularly difficult to predict, quantify, and assess in cyberspace due to the reverberating effects of cyber attacks in the long term—that is, collateral effects that are expected to materialise.[102] Moreover, the risk of collateral damage is higher in cyberspace, given that most cyber-infrastructures are interconnected and dual-use.[103] For these reasons, ensuring compliance with the principle of proportionality remains one of the major sources of concern when it comes to ACC.[104]

In deliberate targeting, the proportionality assessment is carried out by the military commander before engagement, based on the information available at the time, applying the standard of the 'reasonable commander'.[105] If the attack is carried out in a static and predictable environment, such as an air-gapped network,[106] ACC could, in theory, be deployed in compliance with the principle of proportionality, provided the necessary precautions have been taken.[107] For instance, Stuxnet was programmed to only target a piece of specific software (the Siemens Step 7) within a specific industrial control system.[108] Although it eventually infected thousands of civilian computers, it was instructed to deliver its destructive effects solely against the Natanz nuclear facility and to erase itself from any other computer after its expiration date.[109] However, if ACC are intended to be deployed over an extended period in more complex environments, such as the Internet, the proportionality assessment should be constantly updated by those responsible for the attack.[110]

In dynamic targeting, the proportionality assessment is delegated to ACC. To comply with the principle of proportionality, ACC would need to first determine the expected collateral damage of the cyber attack. From an operational perspective, it

---

[100] API, above n. 21, Article 51(5)(b). The principle of proportionality is also reaffirmed in Articles 57(2)(a)(iii) and 57(2)(b).

[101] Schmitt 2017, Rule 113.

[102] Ibid., Rule 113(13). On the principle of proportionality and reverberating effects, see also Henderson and Reece 2018.

[103] Schmitt 2017, Rule 113(3); Roscini 2014, p. 220.

[104] Liivoja et al. 2019, p. 29.

[105] International Criminal Tribunal for Former Yugoslavia (ICTY)'s Prosecutor Office, Final Report to the Prosecutor by the Committee Established to Review the NATO Bombing Campaign Against the Federal Republic of Yugoslavia, 13 June 2000, paras 48–50; ICTY, *Prosecutor v. Galić, Judgement* (Trial Chamber), 5 December 2003, Case No. IT-98-29-T, para 808.

[106] An air-gapped network is 'a network that has a physical separation from other networks that are not secure, such as the Internet. This allows the network to be more secure'. They are often used to prevent cyber operations from compromising classified or sensitive information: Mohamed et al. 2022, p. 2.

[107] Tsagourias and Buchan 2017, p. 235.

[108] For further technical information on Stuxnet, see Falliere et al. 2011.

[109] Scharre 2018, pp. 214–215.

[110] Tsagourias and Buchan 2017, p. 236.

might be feasible to determine the possibility of damage to civilians and civilian objects. States have already invested in computer systems capable of estimating these factors based on objective standards. For example, computer programmes that apply the US military's Collateral Damage Estimation Methodology (also known as CDEM) to identify any 'collateral concerns' within the 'collateral effects radius' of a weapon or means of warfare under consideration for use in the attack already exist.[111] However, these computer programmes differ from ACC in two main aspects. On the one hand, they are used to estimate collateral damage in the kinetic world, not in cyberspace. In the cyber domain, determining the estimated collateral damage may be more challenging due to its 'interconnectedness' and the reverberating effects of cyber attacks.[112] ACC would need to take into account both the direct and indirect consequences of the attack.[113] From a technical perspective, this might be possible if ACC are programmed with the necessary data at the design phase.[114] However, the more complex the environment in which the ACC operates, the more difficult it will be to programme the software agent accordingly. On the other hand, current computer programmes applying CDEM only support the decision-making process. They are used to decide at which level of command decision making should be escalated, but do not take the ultimate decision, which remains with the military commander.[115] The estimates these computer programmes generate derive from 'empirical data, probability, historical observations, and complex modeling',[116] but do not necessarily capture the contextual and qualitative nature of the proportionality assessments. For this reason, the ultimate decision is taken by the military commander on the basis of the available information at the time. The same arguments can be extended to ACC: even if they are programmed to carry out a quantitative assessment of the expected collateral damage, they still cannot perform any qualitative assessment without human intervention. Thus, human control should be exercised in order to determine the collateral damage.

Second, ACC would need to determine the 'anticipated military advantage'. Such assessment, however, intrinsically requires the exercise of human judgement. As underlined by Dinstein, indeed, 'the benefits accruing from an attack against a military objective depend on an interpretation of the operational picture at the time of action, and appraisal of the greater or lesser military advantage to be gained may be

[111] Cherry et al. 2021.

[112] On collateral damage estimation in cyberspace, see Romanosky and Goldman 2017.

[113] Notably, the effects of a cyber attack can be distinguished in (i) 'primary effects', those on the attacked computer or network (e.g., destruction, incapacitation of the computer); (ii) 'secondary effects', those on the infrastructure operated by the attacked computer or network (e.g., destruction or incapacitation of the infrastructure); and (iii) 'tertiary effects', those on the persons affected by the destruction or incapacitation of the attacked computer, network and/or infrastructure. In this respect, see Roscini 2014, pp. 220–221; and Schmitt 2017, Rule 113(6).

[114] Romanosky and Goldman 2017, pp. 248–253.

[115] Cannizzaro 2006, p. 786.

[116] Cherry et al. 2021.

debatable'.[117] It is a context-specific analysis that requires the exercise of reasonableness and good faith.[118] It cannot be performed by a computer on the basis of a mathematical formula. Thus, ACC are currently not able to determine the anticipated military advantage without human intervention.

Third, ACC would need to compare the expected collateral damage with the anticipated military advantage to understand whether the former is excessive in comparison to the latter. However, as also underlined by Kalshoven, 'weighing the expected collateral damage against the anticipated military advantage will never be a job for one's pocket calculator'.[119] This assessment is inherently 'subjective', influenced by 'social', 'historical', and situational 'factors', as well as the 'background' of those conducting the targeting process.[120] It must be carried out by a reasonable military commander who, based on the available information at the time, exercises human judgment.[121] As Dinstein famously stated, 'military advantage and civilian casualties have no common denominator. They are rather like the metaphorical apples and oranges. A comparison between them is therefore an art, not a science'.[122] They are different quantities and values that cannot be simply put into a mathematical formula.[123] While ACC can acquire, fuse, and process technical data, they are currently incapable of comprehending the broader operational context or predicting how it will evolve, especially in complex scenarios. For this reason, it is unlikely that ACC will be able to determine and balance the expected collateral damage with the anticipated military advantage without real-time human intervention.

In conclusion, ACC can be used in compliance with the principle of proportionality only in static and predictable environments to carry out deliberate attacks, provided all feasible precautions have been taken. However, in complex environments where civilian and military networks are highly interconnected, the proportionality assessment needs to be constantly updated by a human operator based on the available information. In contrast, in dynamic cyber attacks, ACC are currently unable to exercise proportionality assessments without human control, unless operating in a controlled, closed environment where no civilians or civilian objects are at stake.

[117] Dinstein 2022, p. 185.

[118] Ibid.

[119] Kalshoven 1992, p. 44.

[120] Roscini 2014, p. 228.

[121] On AWS and the principle of proportionality, see Amoroso 2020, pp. 88–96; Mauri 2022, pp. 149–153.

[122] Dinstein 2012, p. 271.

[123] As also highlighted in the Final Report by the Committee established to Review the NATO Bombing Campaign Against the Federal Republic of Yugoslavia, '[t]he intellectual process of balancing the various elements is so complicated, needs to take into account such a huge amount of data and so many factors, that any attempt to design formula which is both comprehensive and precise would be ridiculous'. See, in this respect, ICTY 's Prosecutor Office, Final Report to the Prosecutor by the Committee Established to Review the NATO Bombing Campaign Against the Federal Republic of Yugoslavia, 13 June 2000, para 48.

4.3.3 Autonomous Cyber Attacks and the Principle of Precaution

The principle of precaution, the third pillar of IHL, reflects CIL and fully applies in cyberspace.[124] Under this principle, parties to an armed conflict must adopt both precautions in an attack and measures to mitigate its harmful effects. While both are relevant to ACC, this section focuses on precautions in attack, as outlined under Article 57 API.

According to Article 57(1) API, '[i]n the conduct of military operations, constant care shall be taken to spare the civilian population, civilians and civilian objects'.[125] In other words, parties to an armed conflict must exercise 'constant care' throughout the entire military operation—including during 'any movements, manoeuvres and other activities whatsoever carried out by the armed forces with a view to combat'—to avoid harm to civilians.[126] This requirement is particularly relevant for ACC, as it would require States to not only exercise constant care during an autonomous cyber attack but also during software programming, as well as the preparation and planning of the attack.[127] Article 57(2) further provides a non-exhaustive list of precautions that military commanders may undertake in attack whenever feasible, in order to verify that targets are neither civilians nor civilian objects,[128] and to avoid (or at least minimise) collateral damage.[129] Whenever it becomes apparent that the target is not a legitimate military objective, or that the expected collateral damage exceeds the anticipated military advantage, commanders must cancel or suspend the attack.[130]

Accordingly, those planning and authorising an autonomous cyber attack must adopt all feasible precautions to ensure compliance with the principles of distinction and proportionality.[131] In addition, it would also require designing ACC in a way that enables military decision makers to cancel or suspend an attack whenever it is expected to be against an unlawful target or cause disproportionate harm.[132] Depending on the circumstances, different precautionary measures can be implemented to restrain ACC behaviour, ranging from embedding technical safeguards to exercising human control. According to Perez, technical safeguards include operational constraints (e.g., target profiles), parameters of use (e.g., deactivation or fail-safe mechanisms), and interaction controls (e.g., task termination or limits on self-learning capacities).[133] Coco and Dias further suggest that AI-enabled systems should

[124] Schmitt 2017, Rules 114–121.

[125] API, above n. 21, Article 57(1).

[126] Sandoz et al. 1987, para 2191.

[127] Harrison Dinniss 2024, p. 273.

[128] API, above n. 21, Article 57(2)(a)(i).

[129] Ibid., Article 57(2)(a)(ii).

[130] Ibid., Articles 57(2)(a)(iii) and 57(2)(b).

[131] Harrison Dinniss 2024, p. 273.

[132] Ibid., On this point, see also Jensen 2021, pp. 191–197.

[133] Perez 2023, pp. 204–205.

be trained to prioritise specific highly reliable data or set minimum accuracy thresholds before deployment to ensure decisions are appropriately informed.[134] Whenever technical safeguards are insufficient to ensure respect for IHL, States should retain a certain degree of human control over ACC, with the oversight threshold varying according to the circumstances of the attack. In this regard, Amoroso provides a particularly interesting perspective, suggesting that the duty to do 'everything feasible' would require States to develop 'human-weapons relationships that bring out the best in both machines and humans or—which is the same—that compensate their reciprocal weaknesses'.[135] If the exercise of human control is not technically feasible—for instance, when an ACC operates in an air gapped network where communication channels are unavailable—commanders must refrain from launching the cyber attack.[136]

In deliberate targeting within static and predictable environments, launching cyber attacks in compliance with the principle of distinction should not be difficult, provided the necessary technical safeguards are in place.[137] Likewise, ACC may also operate in compliance with the principle of proportionality if the military commander conducts the assessment based on their reasonable expectations immediately prior to the attack, and the operating environment remains predictable.[138] Consider, once again, the example of Stuxnet: it was embedded with sophisticated safeguards to restrict its behaviour and avoid harm to civilian systems while targeting a specific military objective.[139] However, when deliberate autonomous cyber attacks are carried out in complex and unpredictable environments, ensuring compliance with IHL solely through technical safeguards becomes more challenging.[140] While ACC may utilise AI to adapt to environmental changes, their behaviour risks becoming unpredictable, unreliable, and unexplainable, potentially resulting in unintended violations of IHL.[141] In these circumstances, retaining human control is crucial to ensure that the attack is carried out in compliance with the principles of distinction and proportionality.[142] By retaining human control, those who plan or decide upon the deliberate autonomous cyber attack may verify the target, avoid (or at least minimise) excessive collateral damage, and cancel or suspend the attack if it becomes apparent that it will be against an unlawful target or that it will cause collateral damage excessive to the anticipated military advantage.[143]

---

[134] Coco and Dias 2024, p. 254.

[135] Amoroso 2020, p. 109.

[136] In compliance with API, above n. 21, Article 57(2)(b).

[137] Guarino 2013, p. 11.

[138] Liivoja et al. 2019, p. 29.

[139] Scharre 2018, pp. 213–215.

[140] Liivoja et al. 2019, p. 29.

[141] Woodcock 2024; Viveros Álvarez 2024.

[142] Liivoja et al. 2019, p. 29.

[143] In compliance with API, above n. 21, Article 57(2)(a)(i)–(iii) and Article 57(2)(b).

With respect to dynamic targeting, ensuring that all feasible precautions are taken in compliance with IHL seems to require the exercise of human control over the entire targeting process. As previously mentioned, in dynamic targeting, part of the required legal assessments cannot be performed in advance or must be adjusted to reflect the changes in the operational environment. Therefore, ACC may be expected to respond in real-time to evolving circumstances, performing these assessments autonomously based on predefined, non-context-specific rules of engagement embedded in the software. As noted throughout this chapter, due to the current limitations of AI-enabled technology, ACC cannot reliably determine whether a target is lawful based on a contextual analysis (e.g., based on assessing the targets' conduct or an object's use or purpose).[144] Likewise, ACC cannot yet determine and balance the expected collateral damage with the anticipated military advantage without real-time human control.[145] Therefore, unless ACC are deployed in risk-free environments where there are no civilians or civilian objects at stake—which is unlikely in cyberspace given the interconnected and dual-use character of most infrastructures—those who plan or decide upon the attack must retain human control at *all* times to ensure the necessary precautions are in place both before and during engagement.[146]

4.4 Conclusion

The military domain is currently investing in the research and development of ACC for both offensive and defensive applications. Thus, as these technologies evolve, it is increasingly evident that ACC will play a crucial role in the future of warfare. For this reason, it is critical to understand whether, and to what extent, ACC can be deployed in compliance with IHL provisions, especially those regulating the targeting process.

This chapter has sought to outline the key legal implications that may arise from the deployment of ACC in both deliberate and dynamic attacks, with a particular focus on the principles of distinction, proportionality, and precaution. It has been contended that, at the current stage of technological development, ACC can be used in compliance with IHL only to carry out deliberate attacks, provided that: (i) all legal assessments are carried out immediately before engagement; (ii) the operating environment is static and predictable; and (iii) ACC have been embedded with technical safeguards as precautionary measures. When ACC are deployed to carry out deliberate targeting in complex and unpredictable environments, a certain degree of human control should be retained in order to validate targets and update proportionality assessments. By contrast, it has been contended that ACC can be deployed in dynamic targeting only in risk-free environments where there are no civilians or civilian objects at stake. In all other contexts, ACC cannot currently be deployed to carry out dynamic targeting unless human control is retained over legal assessments

---

[144] See Sect. 4.3.1.

[145] See Sect. 4.3.2.

[146] Liivoja et al. 2019, p. 29.

in order to ensure that the attack is directed against lawful targets and is not disproportionate. Whenever retaining human control is not feasible, commanders should refrain from launching the attack.

This chapter acknowledges that, from an operational perspective, exercising human control in cyberspace may be challenging, given the high speed at which operations occur and the large amount of data involved.[147] Yet, it is contended that 'human control' may still be the only available measure that military commanders have to ensure the use of ACC in compliance with IHL principles.[148] How human control may be exercised over ACC, however, remains an open question that future research on the topic should urgently address.

References

Articles, Books and Other Documents

Amoroso D (2020) Autonomous Weapons Systems and International Law: A Study on Human-Machine Interactions in Ethically and Legally Sensitive Domains. Edizioni Scientifiche Italiane/Nomos Verlag, Naples/Baden-Baden

Anderson K (2016) Why the Hurry to Regulate Autonomous Weapons Systems—But Not Cyber-Weapons. Temple International & Comparative Law Journal 30 (1):17–41

Asaro P (2012) On banning autonomous weapon systems: human rights, automation, and the dehumanization of lethal decision-making. International Review of the Red Cross 94(886):687–709

Australia (2023) National Defence: Defence Strategic Review. https://www.defence.gov.au/about/reviews-inquiries/defence-strategic-review. Accessed 11 May 2025

Avgerinos T, Brumley D, Davis J, Goulden R, Nighswander T, Rebert A, Williamson N (2018) The Mayhem Cyber Reasoning System. IEEE Security & Privacy: 52–60

Bellasio J, Silfversten E (2020) The Impact of New and Emerging Technologies on the Cyber Threat Landscape and Their Implications for NATO. In: Ertan A, Floyd K, Pernik P, Stevens T (eds) Cyber Threats and NATO 2030: Horizon Scanning and Analysis. NATO CCDCOE Publications, Tallinn, pp. 88–107

Bendett S, Boulègue M, Connolly R, Konaev M, Podvig P, Zysk K (2021) Advanced military technology in Russia: capabilities and implications. https://www.chathamhouse.org/2021/09/advanced-military-technology-russia. Accessed 11 May 2025

Boulanin V, Verbruggen M (2017) Mapping the Development of Autonomy in Weapon Systems. https://www.sipri.org/publications/2017/policy-reports/mapping-development-autonomy-weapon-systems . Accessed 11 May 2025

Brazil (2020) Comments Submitted by Brazil to the Initial "Pre-Draft" of the Report of the OEWG on Developments in the Field of Information and Telecommunications in the Context of International Security

Buchanan B, Bansemer J, Cary D, Lucas J, Musser M (2020) Automating Cyber Attacks: Hype and Reality. https://cset.georgetown.edu/publication/automating-cyber-attacks/. Accessed 11 May 2025

Burton J, Soare SR (2019) Understanding the Strategic Implications of the Weaponization of Artificial Intelligence. In: Minárik T, Alatalu S, Biondi S, Signoretti M, Tolga I, Visky G (eds)

[147] Crootof 2016, p. 56; Deeks et al. 2019, p. 9.

[148] Stroppa 2023a, p. 6.

11th International Conference on Cyber Conflict: Silent Battle. NATO CCD COE Publications, Tallinn, Estonia
Cannizzaro E (2006) Contextualizing proportionality: jus ad bellum and jus in bello in the Lebanese War. International Review of the Red Cross 88(864):779–792
Cherry J, Tinkler K, Schmitt M N (2021) Avoiding Collateral Damage on the Battlefield. https://www.justsecurity.org/74619/avoiding-collateral-damage-on-the-battlefield/. Accessed 11 May 2025
Coco A, Dias T (2024) 'Handle with care': due diligence obligations in the employment of AI technologies. In: Geiß R, Lahmann H (eds) Research Handbook on Warfare and Artificial Intelligence. Edward Elgar Publishing, Cheltenham/Northampton, pp. 234–260
Cristiano F, Broeders D, Delerue F, Douzet F, Géry A (2023) Artificial Intelligence and International Conflict in Cyberspace. Routledge, Oxon/New York
Crootof R (2016) A Meaningful Floor for 'Meaningful Human Control'. Temple International & Comparative Law Journal 30(1): 53–62
Deeks A, Lubell N, Murray D (2019) Machine Learning, Artificial Intelligence, and the Use of Force by States. National Security Law & Policy 10(1):1–29
Delerue F (2020) Cyber Operations and International Law. Cambridge University Press, Cambridge
Dinstein Y (2012) The Principle of Distinction and Cyber War in International Armed Conflicts. Journal of Conflict and Security Law 17(2):261–277
Dinstein Y (2022) The Conduct of Hostilities under the Law of International Armed Conflict, 4th edn. Cambridge University Press, Cambridge
D'Urso M (2015) The Cyber Combatant: a New Status for a New Warrior. Philosophy & Technology 28(3):475–478
Ecuador (2020) Ecuador Preliminary Comments to the Chair's "Initial Pre-Draft" of the Report of the United Nations Open Ended Working Group on Developments in the Field of Information and Telecommunications in the Context of International Security (OEWG)
European Union (EU) (2022) Strategic Compass for Security and Defence.https://www.eeas.europa.eu/sites/default/files/documents/strategic_compass_en3_web.pdf. Accessed 11 May 2025
European Union Agency for Cybersecurity (2020) AI cybersecurity challenges: threat landscape for artificial intelligence. https://www.enisa.europa.eu/publications/artificial-intelligence-cybersecurity-challenges. Accessed 11 May 2025
Falliere N, O Murchu L, Chien E (2011) W32.Stuxnet Dossier. https://docs.broadcom.com/doc/security-response-w32-stuxnet-dossier-11-en. Accessed 11 May 2025
Germany (2021) Cyber Security Strategy for Germany 2021. https://www.bmi.bund.de/EN/topics/it-internet-policy/cyber-security-strategy/cyber-security-strategy-node.html. Accessed 11 May 2025
Gisel L, Rodenhäuser T, Dörmann K (2021) Twenty years on: International humanitarian law and the protection of civilians against the effects of cyber operations during armed conflicts. International Review of the Red Cross 201(913):287–334
Greenberg A (2015) Hackers Remotely Kill a Jeep on the Highway—With Me in IT. https://www.wired.com/2015/07/hackers-remotely-kill-jeep-highway/. Accessed 11 May 2025
Guarino A (2013) Autonomous Intelligent Agents in Cyber Offence. In: Podins K, Stinissen J, Maybaum M (eds) 5th International Conference on Cyber Conflict. NATO CCD COE Publications, Tallinn, pp. 337–389
Haataja S (2024a) Autonomous Cyber Capabilities and International Law on the Use of Force, Self-Defence, Intervention, and Sovereignty. Australian Army Occasional Paper No. 25. https://researchcentre.army.gov.au/sites/default/files/Occasional-Paper-25-Haataja-Autonomous-Cyber-Capabilities.pdf. Accessed 11 May 2025
Haataja S (2024b) Cyber Operations and automatic hack backs under international law on necessity. Computer Law & Security Review 55:1–9
Harrison Dinniss HA (2024) AI and military cyber operations. In: Geiß R, Lahmann H (eds) Research Handbook on Warfare and Artificial Intelligence. Edward Elgar Publishing, Cheltenham/Northampton, pp. 262–280

Heinl C (2018) Maturing autonomous cyber weapons systems: implications for international security and autonomous weapons systems regimes. In: Cornish P (ed) Oxford Handbook of Cyber Security. Oxford University Press, Oxford, pp. 702–722

Henckaerts J-M, Doswald-Beck L (2009) Customary international humanitarian law. Volume 1: Rules, 3rd edn. Cambridge University Press, Cambridge

Henderson I, Reece K (2018) Proportionality under International Humanitarian Law: The "Reasonable Military Commander" Standard and Reverberating Effects. Vanderbilt Journal of Transnational Law 51(3):835–855

Holland M A (2020) The Black Box, Unlocked: Predictability and Understandability in Military AI. https://unidir.org/publication/the-black-box-unlocked/. Accessed 11 May 2025

Huang Z, Ying Y (2020) The application of the principle of distinction in the cyber context: A Chinese perspective. International Review of the Red Cross 102(913):335–365

ICRC (2018) The Potential Human Cost of Cyber Operations. ICRC Expert Meeting 14–16 November 2018—Geneva. https://www.icrc.org/en/publication/potential-human-cost-cyber-operations. Accessed 11 May 2025

ICRC (2020a) International Humanitarian Law and Cyber Operations during Armed Conflicts: ICRC Position Paper Submitted to the "Open-Ended Working Group on Developments in the Field of Information and Telecommunications in the Context of International Security" and the "Group of Governmental Experts on Advancing Responsible State Behaviour in Cyberspace in the Context of International Security". International Review of the Red Cross 102:481–492

ICRC (2020b) Artificial intelligence and machine learning in armed conflict: A human-centred approach. International Review of the Red Cross 102:463–479

Jensen ET (2021) Autonomy and Precautions in the Law of Armed Conflict. In: Liivoja R, Väljataga A (eds) Autonomous Cyber Capabilities under International Law. NATO CCD COE Publications, Tallinn, pp. 181–204

Kalshoven F (1992) Implementing Limitations on the Use of Force: The Doctrine of Proportionality and Necessity. American Society of International Law Proceedings 86: 39–45

Kott A, Théron P, Drašar M, Dushku E, LeBlanc B, Losiewicz P, Guarino A, Mancini LV, Panico A, Pihelgas M, Rzadca K (2019) Autonomous Intelligent Cyber-defense Agent (AICA) Reference Architecture, Release 2.0. Devcom Army Research Laboratory. https://apps.dtic.mil/sti/pdfs/AD1080471.pdf. Accessed 11 May 2025

Leyden J (2012) Japan tasks Fujitsu with creating search-and-destroy cyber-weapon. The Register. https://www.theregister.com/2012/01/03/japan_cyber_weapon_research/. Accessed 11 May 2025

Liivoja R, Naagel M, Väljataga A (2019) Autonomous Cyber Capabilities under International Law. NATO CCDCOE Publications, Tallinn

Liivoja R, Väljataga A (2021) Autonomous Cyber Capabilities under International Law. NATO CCDCOE Publications, Tallinn

Mauri D (2022) Autonomous Weapons Systems and the Protection of the Human Person. Edward Elgar Publications, Cheltenham/Northampton

Mavropoulou E (2015) Targeting in the Cyber Domain Legal Challenges Arising from the Application of the Principle of Distinction to Cyber Attacks. Journal of Law & Cyber Warfare 4(3):23–93

McFarland T (2021) The Concept of Autonomy. In: Liivoja R, Väljataga A (eds) Autonomous Cyber Capabilities under International Law. NATO CCD COE Publications, Tallinn, pp. 12–35

Melzer N (2009) Interpretative Guidance on the Notion of Direct Participation in Hostilities under International Humanitarian Law. https://www.icrc.org/en/publication/0990-interpretive-guidance-notion-direct-participation-hostilities-under-international. Accessed 11 May 2025

Michel AH (2024) Decisions, Decisions, Decisions: Computation and Artificial Intelligence in Military Decision Making. Report prepared for the International Committee of the Red Cross. https://www.icrc.org/en/publication/decisions-decisions-decisions-computation-and-artificial-intelligence-military-decision. Accessed 11 May 2025

Mohamed N, Almazerouei S K, Oubelaid A, Elsisi M, Basem M E, Ghoneim S S M (2022) Air-Gapped Networks: Exfiltration without Privilege Escalation for Military and Police Unites. Wireless Communications and Mobile Computing: 1–11
NATO (2021) Allied Joint Doctrine for Joint Targeting (AJP–3.9). https://assets.publishing.service.gov.uk/media/618e7da28fa8f5037ffaa03f/AJP-3.9_EDB_V1_E.pdf. Accessed 11 May 2025
Netherlands (2020) Position Paper on the UN Open-Ended Working Group "on Developments in the Field of Information and Telecommunications in the Context of International Security" and the UN Group of Governmental Experts "on Advancing Responsible State Behavior in Cyberspace in the Context of International Security".
Perez L (2023) Is Stuxnet the next Skynet? Autonomous cyber capabilities as lethal autonomous weapons systems. In: Cristiano F, Broeders D, Delerue F, Douzet F, Géry A (eds) Artificial Intelligence and International Conflict in Cyberspace. Routledge, Oxon/New York, pp. 186–222
Romanosky S, Goldman Z (2017) Understanding Cyber Collateral Damage. Journal of National Security Law & Policy 9: 233–257
Roscini M (2014) Cyber Operations and the Use of Force in International Law. Oxford University Press, Oxford
Russell S, Norvig P (2022) Artificial Intelligence: A Modern Approach, 4th edn. (Global Edition). Pearson Education, Inc., New Jersey
Sandoz Y, Swinarski C, Zimmermann B (1987) Commentary to Protocol Additional to the Geneva Conventions of 12 August 1949, and relating to the Protection of Victims of International Armed Conflicts (Protocol I). Martinus Nijhoff, Geneva
Scharre P (2018) Army of None: Autonomous Weapons and the Future of War. W. W. Norton & Company, New York
Schmitt MN (2015) The Law of Cyber Targeting. Naval War College 48(2):10–29
Schmitt MN (ed) (2017) Tallinn Manual 2.0 on the International Law Applicable to Cyber Operations, 2nd edn. Cambridge University Press, Cambridge
Schwarz E (2021) Autonomous Weapons Systems, Artificial Intelligence, and the Problem of Meaningful Human Control. The Philosophical Journal of Conflict and Violence 1: 53–72
Shoaib M (2020) AI-Enabled Cyber Weapons and Implications. Journal of Strategic Affairs
Singer T (2017) Update to Revolving Door 2.0: The Extension of the Period for Direct Participation in Hostilities Due to Autonomous Cyber Weapons. In: Rõigas H, Jakschis R, Lindström L, Minárik T (eds) 9th International Conference on Cyber Conflict: Defending the Core. NATO CCD COE Publications, Tallinn
Stoecklin MPh, Jang J, Kirat D (2018) DeepLocker: How AI Can Power a Stealthy New Breed of Malware. https://securityintelligence.com/deeplocker-how-ai-can-power-a-stealthy-new-breed-of-malware/. Accessed 11 May 2025
Stroppa M (2023a) Legal and ethical implications of autonomous cyber capabilities: a call for retaining human control in cyberspace. Ethics and Information Technology 25(1):1–7
Stroppa M (2023b) Autonomous cyber capabilities and unilateral measures of self-help against malicious cyber operations. NATO CCD COE Publications, Tallinn
Taddeo M (2021) On the risks of trusting artificial intelligence: the case of cybersecurity. In: Cowls J, Morley J (eds) The 2020 Yearbook of the Digital Ethics Lab. Springer, Cham, pp. 97–108
Taddeo M, McCutcheon T, Floridi L (2019) Trusting artificial intelligence in cybersecurity is a double-edged sword. Nature Machine Intelligence 1(12):557–560
Tošić PT (2016) Understanding Autonomous Agents: A Cybernetics and Systems Science Perspective. FTC 2016—Future Technologies Conference, pp. 121–129
Tsagourias N, Buchan R (2017) Automatic Cyber Defence and the Laws of War. German Yearbook of International Law 60:203–237
Tyugu E (2012) Command and Control of Cyber Weapons. In: Czosseck C, Ottis R, Ziolkowski K (eds) 2012 4th International Conference on Cyber Conflict. NATO CCD COE Publications, Tallinn

UN CCW (2013) Final Report of the 2013 Meeting of the High Contracting Parties to the Convention on Prohibitions or Restrictions on the Use of Certain Conventional Weapons Which May Be Deemed to Be Excessively Injurious or to Have Indiscriminate Effects, CCW/MSP/2013/10

UN CCW GGE LAWS (2018) Report of the 2018 Session of the Group of Governmental Experts on Emerging Technologies in the Area of Lethal Autonomous Weapons Systems, CCW/GGE.1/2018/3

UN CCW GGE LAWS (2019) Final Report—Annex III 'Guiding Principles affirmed by the Group of Governmental Experts on Emerging Technologies in the Area of Lethal Autonomous Weapons System', CCW/MSP/2019/9

UNIDIR (2017) The Weaponization of Increasingly Autonomous Technologies: Autonomous Weapon Systems and Cyber Operations. https://unidir.org/files/publication/pdfs/autonomous-weapon-systems-and-cyber-operations-en-690.pdf. Accessed 11 May 2025

United Kingdom (2022) National Cyber Strategy. https://www.gov.uk/government/publications/national-cyber-strategy-2022/national-cyber-security-strategy-2022. Accessed 11 May 2025

United Nations Security Council (2024) High-Level Debate on "Maintenance of International Peace and Security: Addressing Evolving Threats in Cyberspace". https://webtv.un.org/en/asset/k1c/k1cifeuu9g. Accessed 11 May 2024

United States Cyberspace Solarium Commission (2020) Final Report. https://cybersolarium.org/wp-content/uploads/2022/05/CSC-Final-Report.pdf. Accessed 11 May 2025

United States Department of Defense (2012) Autonomy in Weapons Systems (Directive 3000.09). https://ogc.osd.mil/Portals/99/autonomy_in_weapon_systems_dodd_3000_09.pdf. Accessed 11 May 2025

United States National Security Commission on Artificial Intelligence (2021) Final Report. https://reports.nscai.gov/final-report/. Accessed 11 May 2025

Viveros Álvarez JS (2024) The risks and inefficacies of AI systems in military targeting support. https://blogs.icrc.org/law-and-policy/contributor/jimena-sofia-viveros-alvarez/. Accessed 11 May 2025

Woodcock TK (2024) Human/Machine(-Learning) Interactions, Human Agency and the International Humanitarian Law Proportionality Standard. Global Society 38(1):100–121

Marta Stroppa is a post-doctoral researcher in international law at the Sant'Anna School of Advanced Studies (Pisa, Italy), where she also obtained her Ph.D. She has been a Visiting Scholar at the NATO Cooperative Cyber Defence Centre of Excellence and at the University of Westminster, where she carried out extensive research activities on the legal implications of autonomous cyber capabilities in the use of force and conduct of hostilities.

Chapter 5
ChatGPT for the Military? Large Language Models in the Military Domain and the Role of Article 36 Weapons Reviews

Elisabeth Hoffberger-Pippan

Contents

Abstract The advent of ChatGPT and large language models (LLMs) has heralded a new era in generative artificial intelligence (AI). While commercial applications of LLMs abound, the military is now exploring their potential across various areas, including battlefield operations. This chapter investigates whether, and under what parameters, LLMs used in the military domain fall under the purview of Article 36 of Additional Protocol I to the Geneva Conventions, enshrining the obligation for all States Parties to conduct a weapons review. It examines whether LLMs qualify as weapons, means, or methods of warfare by analysing relevant state practice in the interpretation and implementation of Article 36. Although LLMs do not directly inflict harm on combatants or military objects, their potential role in supporting targeting decisions may subject them to the obligation of a weapons review, as demonstrated by parallels in the cyber domain. The chapter concludes with the observation that, although in their infancy, LLMs herald a general trend toward increased military reliance on non-weaponised AI, in turn, raising critical questions regarding compliance with International Humanitarian Law.

E. Hoffberger-Pippan (✉)
Peace Research Institute Frankfurt (PRIF), Frankfurt, Germany
e-mail: hoffberger.pippan@prif.org

B. Boutin et al. (eds.), *Legal, Ethical, and Technical Dilemmas in Military Artificial Intelligence*, https://doi.org/10.1007/978-94-6265-759-5_5

Keywords Large Language Models (LLMs) · Generative Artificial Intelligence (AI) · Decision-Support Systems (DSS) · International Humanitarian Law (IHL) · Weapons Review · Means or Methods of Warfare

5.1 Introduction

When OpenAI's ChatGPT—a large language model (LLM), a type of artificial intelligence (AI)—was released to the public in 2022, the world was mesmerised by this novel, if not revolutionary, technology.[1] While initial problems with GPT-3, the first neural network behind ChatGPT, occupied OpenAI for some time, the updated and significantly larger GPT-4 now operates far more effectively, having passed, *inter alia*, the bar exam.[2] In 2024, the latest version 'GPT-4o mini' was launched, supporting text and image functions, with future versions expected to expand these capabilities to include audio and video input and output.[3] There is, understandably, significant excitement surrounding this technology. Students, for instance, frequently utilise LLMs to draft or pre-formulate assignments and theses. They leverage these systems for convenient access to extensive information, which can serve as a resource during examinations. Beyond academic settings, many people turn to ChatGPT for everyday tasks, such as drafting emails or letters, organising events, or even seeking personal life advice.[4] However, at the same time, this rapid advancement has also prompted concern among AI researchers, with some calling for a pause in the training of AI models.[5]

It did not take long for militaries and industry to invest time and resources into exploring the potential application of LLMs in the defence sector. One of the first projects (or rather experiments) was Scale AI's Hermes, an experimental AI-enabled LLM decision-support system (DSS) used for military planning.[6] Hermes was developed in cooperation with the United States (US) Marine Corps School of Advanced Warfighting, allowing students to use the model for a simulated military operation exercise.[7] Other prominent real-world projects include Scale AI's Donovan,[8] as well as Palantir's Artificial Intelligence Platform and Gotham system.[9] Furthermore, the

---

[1] Marr 2023.

[2] https://openai.com/index/gpt-4-research/. Accessed 30 July 2024. For critical reflections, see Sloan 2023.

[3] https://openai.com/index/gpt-4o-mini-advancing-cost-efficient-intelligence/. Accessed 30 July 2024.

[4] New Digital Age 2024.

[5] The Future of Life Institute 2023.

[6] Jensen and Tadross 2023.

[7] Ibid.

[8] https://scale.com/donovan. Accessed 30 July 2024.

[9] https://www.palantir.com/offerings/defense/. Accessed 30 July 2024.

US has established Project Lima to study the potential benefits and risks of generative AI in the military domain.[10]

This chapter examines the potential role of weapons reviews, as set out in Article 36 of Additional Protocol I (API) to the Geneva Conventions,[11] in relation to LLMs. This provision obliges States Parties to review the legality of new weapons, means, or methods of warfare, to ensure compliance with International Humanitarian Law (IHL). For a weapon to comply with IHL, it must adhere to the core principles of distinction, proportionality, precaution, and the prohibition to cause superfluous injury or unnecessary suffering. Weapons that inherently violate these principles, such as chemical or biological weapons, are prohibited. Given the potential role of LLMs in military decision making, particularly targeting, it is crucial to assess whether their use could unintentionally breach these standards. It is important to bear in mind, however, that LLMs can be employed across a range of domains for varying purposes, depending on their design and intended use. For example, some LLMs may directly influence targeting processes by generating recommendations or providing relevant operational information,[12] while others may only have an *indirect* effect—or no implications for targeting at all. Thus, depending on the design of an LLM, different legal questions arise, especially regarding the applicability of Article 36.

Cognisant of these facts, Sect. 5.3 discusses the definition of LLMs and explores their potential role within the military. While most projects investigating LLMs remain under development, relevant public information on their potential applications and concomitant risks remains scarce. Two projects—Donovan and Gotham—will be examined to gain initial insights into how LLMs might be integrated into future military operations. In doing so, it also considers the potential role of weapons reviews should such systems be deployed in armed conflict. It is important to note that Donovan and Gotham are intended for use within the US military. Although the US is not a State Party to API, it has enacted one of the most rigorous weapons review processes.[13] Developments in the US may serve as a catalyst for States Parties to API to similarly explore the potential military utility of LLMs. Thus, a brief overview of Donovan and Gotham is imperative to identify the various legal obligations that may arise for States Parties to API considering the deployment of LLMs. Section 5.4 then discusses whether, and under what parameters, LLMs may fall within the scope of Article 36.

The central legal question examined in this chapter is whether LLMs could qualify as weapons, means, or methods of warfare. The fact that most States Parties to API

[10] Demarest 2023.

[11] Protocol Additional to the Geneva Conventions of 12 August 1949, and relating to the Protection of Victims of International Armed Conflicts (Protocol I), opened for signature 8 June 1977, 1125 UNTS 3, entered into force 7 December 1978. The question of whether Article 36 reflects customary law remains contested and will not be further elaborated upon in this chapter. For further reading, see Jevglevskaja 2018.

[12] For a definition of the targeting process (or targeting cycle) see US Joint Chiefs of Staff Joint Targeting 2018, pp. 3–60.

[13] US Department of the Army 2019.

interpret and implement Article 36 differently has led to significant inconsistencies in practice, thereby adding further complexity to the ensuing legal assessment. This chapter demonstrates that not all LLMs will trigger the obligation to conduct a weapons review. It concludes, however, by asserting that Article 36 reviews may be crucial where LLMs are integrated into military operations, depending on their design and intended use. While most LLMs will not directly exert force, they may still qualify as a means of warfare. Their increasing use within the military domain highlights the increasing role—and potential operational value—of non-weaponised AI-enabled technologies on the battlefield. A comprehensive reading of IHL, and of Article 36 in particular, is necessary to ensure that States Parties remain legally compliant while adapting to the evolving technological landscape.

Before proceeding, it is important to note that most LLMs and other generative AI models are still in the early stages of development. Hence, their design and prospective use in future conflicts remain uncertain. Nonetheless, their eventual deployment in some capacity appears almost certain, necessitating a thorough, albeit *preliminary*, legal analysis.

5.2 LLMs in Context: Technological Foundations and Military Applications

To effectively analyse the legal challenges associated with using LLMs in the military, it is essential to first understand the underlying technology, including the broader field of AI. Additionally, exploring emerging projects, such as Donovan and Gotham, is crucial for addressing the various legal and practical implications of LLMs in the military domain.

5.2.1 Defining LLMs

Before assessing what constitutes a LLM, it is essential to first briefly explain and contextualise other key terms, such as AI, machine learning (ML), deep learning, foundation models, transformer architecture (which also stands for the "T" in ChatGPT), and generative AI. In the broadest sense, 'AI encompasses the set of all (computer-based) processes that mimic human capacities'.[14] According to IBM, one of the largest technology companies in the US, ML is a subset of AI 'focused on enabling computers and machines to imitate the way that humans learn, to perform

[14] Reinhold et al. 2024, p. 2.

tasks autonomously, and to improve their performance and accuracy through experience and exposure to more data.'[15] Deep learning, a further subset of ML, refers to 'algorithms that build on machine-learning concepts to simulate human brain cells (neurons) and their interconnections in artificial neural networks'.[16] Deep learning is based on artificial 'neural networks', which can be described as a specific type of model architecture used for deep learning. They typically consist of three or more layers and do not require any form of human intervention during the learning process. According to Marcus,

> Deep learning, as it is primarily used, is essentially a statistical technique for classifying patterns, based on sample data, using neural networks with multiple layers. Neural networks in the deep learning literature typically consist of a set of input units that stand for things like pixels or words, multiple hidden layers (the more such layers, the deeper a network is said to be) containing hidden units (also known as nodes or neurons), and a set [of] output units, with connections running between those nodes.[17]

Foundation models, in turn, denote deep neural networks trained on vast datasets. They represent a significant shift in the development of ML systems, enabling data scientists to build AI applications more efficiently by adapting pre-trained models rather than constructing systems from scratch.[18] The term 'foundation model' was introduced to describe ML models pre-trained on diverse, generalised, and unlabelled data, capable of performing a broad spectrum of common tasks, such as language comprehension, text and image generation, and natural language dialogue.[19]

LLMs are part of the broader category of so-called generative AI—an umbrella term referring to technology capable of creating various forms of content, such as text, images, audio, and even video.[20] LLMs, however, are not necessarily a completely new phenomenon. Their conceptual foundations were laid decades ago, particularly during the 1980s, when computer scientists began applying statistical models to natural language processing. One of the most important models developed at that time was the recurrent neural network (RNN),[21] which processes sequential data step-by-step. Although RNNs are not modern LLMs *per se*, they played a foundational role in the evolution of deep learning-based language models. Transformer models, in turn, are the model architecture that comprise LLMs. These models use attention mechanisms for simultaneous data processing improving efficiency and scalability.[22] The first LLM in the contemporary sense was Open AI's Generative Pre-trained Transformer (GPT) introduced in 2018. Over the years, LLMs have become increasingly

---

[15] IBM, https://www.ibm.com/topics/machine-learning. Accessed 30 July 2024.

[16] Reinhold et al. 2024.

[17] Marcus 2018, p. 4.

[18] https://aws.amazon.com/what-is/foundation-models/?nc1=h_ls. Accessed 30 July 2024.

[19] Ibid.

[20] https://research.ibm.com/blog/what-is-generative-AI. Accessed 30 July 2024.

[21] https://www.ibm.com/topics/recurrent-neural-networks. Accessed 30 July 2024; Vaswani et al. 2017.

[22] Khan Raiaan et al. 2024, p. 2684; Vaswani et al. 2017.

sophisticated, capable, and efficient. This progress is largely due to the greater availability of data and significant improvement in computing power.[23] Today, models such as GPT-2, GPT-3, GPT-4, ChatGPT, and GPT-4o-mini can perform complex tasks quickly and efficiently, prompting militaries to take a keen interest in this technology. For instance, the US Military is currently testing several LLMs that offer a range of potential advantages. Their ability to process vast amounts of information rapidly and communicate results to decision makers in an accessible and comprehensible manner renders them particularly valuable. In the military realm, LLMs could basically serve as AI-driven tools that provide decision support to commanders.[24]

In civilian applications, LLMs typically use data gathered from a wide range of publicly available sources across the internet. However, military applications differ in that decision makers must rely on internal data when using LLMs or resort to closed environments to protect privacy, safeguard national security, and counter adversarial attacks.[25] While commercial applications of LLMs leverage virtually all publicly available data, the military must use 'a trusted, verified military dataset inside a secure, firewalled environment'.[26]Although not unique to LLMs, this reliance could lead to several negative consequences, such as the unavailability of sufficient (real-world) training data, resulting in increased reliance on synthesised data.[27]

5.2.2 Donovan

Donovan is not an LLM in and of itself, but rather a platform leveraging LLMs as part of a broader DSS.[28] It is primarily designed for use in the early stages of military decision making within the 'OODA' loop.[29] Developed in the late twentieth century by US Air Force Colonel John R. Boyd,[30] the OODA loop stands for 'observe—orient—decide—act'.[31] According to Scale AI, Donovan is intended to play a role in the first two stages (observe and orient) of this loop. However, decision making—especially involving the selection of potential targets—remains a human prerogative. Thus, Donovan is designed to enhance human intelligence and support,

---

[23] Manson 2023. This aspect also holds true for data-driven AI more generally. For example, see Marcus 2018.

[24] Luckenbaugh 2023.

[25] An adversarial attack refers to the process of disrupting a ML model by training it with inaccurate or intentionally falsified data, or by externally manipulating the model with such data. See Data Scientist 2023.

[26] Ibid.

[27] Luckenbaugh 2023. It is important to note, however, that this issue is not distinct to LLMs, but applies to all forms of data-driven AI, including in the military domain.

[28] For more information, see Hoijtink and Planqué-van Hardeveld 2022, pp. 1–19.

[29] Richards 2020, p. 143.

[30] Boyd 1976.

[31] Richards 2020, p. 144.

particularly in the US military context, by assisting with the Joint Operation Planning Process and the Military Decision Making Process.[32] For example, Donovan could be used to provide information on previous strikes by State A against the territory of State B, then analyse the data to calculate the most probable location for future strikes by State A. Donovan could also provide recommendations on which tactics should be employed to subdue enemy combatants or identify the most effective weapons systems that would offer the best defence against incoming attacks.[33] Scale AI has already partnered with the US XVIII Airborne Corps to, *inter alia*, provide '[l]ive context of friendly and enemy force operations by ingesting live data, such as orders, situation reports, and intelligence reports'.[34] Additionally, Scale AI is tasked to provide '[c]ontext for intelligence-operations fusion by ingesting reporting, unit observations, and reducing the operational planning cycle time.'[35] Given these functionalities, Donovan appears primarily intended to serve as a DSS.

5.2.3 Gotham

Palantir describes Gotham as an AI-enabled system primarily to provide decision support. On its website,[36] Palantir presents a video demonstrating how Gotham could be used in a military context. In this fictional scenario, Gotham monitors a Chinese military exercise in the South China Sea. Over time, Gotham detects the build-up of several vessels near the island of Taiwan, indicating a potential naval blockade. An alert from Japanese intelligence reports the sudden disappearance of a Chinese destroyer. By relying on a sophisticated array of sensors and data, Gotham locates the vessel and predicts its most likely route—the port of Taiwan. Gotham then recommends that the US deploys its closest military vessel, stationed in the port of Okinawa. As the US vessel approaches the port of Taiwan, the Chinese destroyer alters its course, heading North and deviating from its initial route to Taiwan. In the scenario, Palantir presents Gotham as an early warning system designed to help prevent escalation and support deterrence.[37]

In 2024, Palantir was chosen by the US Army 'to provide one of two prototype contracts for the Common Data Fabric and Data Security solution to support the network design experimentation for the next network modernization set of technology'.[38] Gotham will not only detect and fuse data but also analyse it, providing

[32] For more details, see US Department of the Army, Department of the Navy, Marine Corps, United States Department of the Air Force, United States Coast Guard, and United States Space Force 2020 Joint Planning. For more information, see Shortland et al. 2019, pp. 15–33.

[33] https://scale.com/donovan. Accessed 30 July 2024.

[34] Business Wire 2023.

[35] Ibid.

[36] https://www.palantir.com/offerings/defense/. Accessed 30 July 2024.

[37] Ibid.

[38] Boguslavsky 2020.

decision makers with concrete recommendations, who, in turn, should be able to gain better situational awareness and adjust their military operations accordingly.[39]

5.2.4 Prospects and Limitations of LLMs in the Military Domain

Undoubtedly, LLMs have the potential to play a substantial role in military decision-making. Given the vast amount of available battlefield data, humans are often simply overtasked with analysing swathes of information and it takes a comparatively long time to reach final and most importantly *actionable* intelligence.[40] LLMs could play a substantial role as they would be able to gather, fuse, and analyse data in seconds and at the same time be able to make recommendations to human operators. The ability of LLMs to communicate with human decision makers make LLMs a useful tool for wargaming as well.

Despite the promising benefits of LLMs, significant challenges remain. LLMs pose substantial risks, such as hallucinations and stochastic parroting, which can undermine their reliability. Hallucinations are 'a 'phenomenon' in which an LLM 'perceives patterns or objects that are non-existent or imperceptible' to humans, resulting in outputs that are 'nonsensical' or 'inaccurate'.[41] Another limitation is stochastic parroting, which refers to the idea that LLMs, 'despite their remarkable capabilities, don't truly comprehend language'. They are like mere parrots, replicating human speech patterns without truly grasping the essence of the words they utter'.[42] These shortcomings can undermine the reliability of LLM-generated outputs in high-stake military environments.

Another challenge, not confined to LLMs but also relevant for AI-enabled technologies in general, is the amplification of biases (either by biased training data or by biases inherent to the programmers of AI-enabled technologies).[43] Furthermore, there are challenges surrounding the effective training of LLMs for military contexts and the broader issue of AI brittleness. When testing LLMs for military use, challenges include ensuring the models are trained on secure and relevant data while maintaining resilience against adversarial manipulation and misinformation. Additionally, the issue of AI brittleness—where systems may fail or behave unpredictably under novel or stressful conditions—is especially concerning in operational settings where failure can have potentially serious consequences. It is not the aim of this

39 Ibid.

40 This has been referred to in the literature as 'information overload': see Horlings et al. 2023, pp. 221–236.

41 https://www.ibm.com/topics/ai-hallucinations. Accessed 30 July 2024.

42 Feuillade-Montixi and Peigné 2023.

43 Bender et al. 2021.

chapter to provide solutions for the abovementioned problems. Rather, it seeks to clarify whether and according to what parameters LLMs could fall under the purview of Article 36.

5.3 The Potential Role of Article 36

This section examines the potential role of Article 36 in relation to the military applications of LLMs. The central guiding question of this inquiry is whether and how LLMs could fall within the scope of Article 36, which mandates a review of new weapons, means, and methods of warfare. First, Sect. 5.3.1 will explore whether LLMs could be considered a 'weapon' or even a 'weapon system' within the meaning of Article 36, thereby triggering the obligation to conduct a corresponding legal review. Second, Sect. 5.3.2 will address whether, and according to which parameters, LLMs might be classified as a 'means of warfare', thus also invoking the obligation of review. Finally, Sect. 5.3.3 will consider whether LLMs could be considered a 'method of warfare' and outline the criteria necessary for such a classification.

The interpretative methodology adopted follows the framework established by the Vienna Convention on the Law of Treaties, with the terms 'weapon,' 'means,' and 'methods' in Article 36 interpreted in accordance with Articles 31 and 32, which reflect customary international law.[44] A distinction is made between general and supplementary treaty interpretation. General interpretation includes the ordinary meaning of the wording of the text, the systematic, and the teleological interpretation (the purpose objective of the provision). Supplementary means of interpretation include the historical context at the time of the treaty's conclusion, for example. Additionally, literature can and should be used as an auxiliary tool for treaty interpretation, as explicitly mentioned by the International Court of Justice under Article 38(c) of its Statute.[45]

Discussions on the utility of weapons reviews are already prominent in the debate on the potential regulation of autonomous weapon systems (AWS) within the United Nations Group of Governmental Experts (GGE) on Lethal Autonomous Weapons Systems,[46] Principle (e) of the 2019 Guiding Principles affirms that:

> [i]n accordance with States' obligations under international law, in the study, development, acquisition, or adoption of a new weapon, means or method of warfare, determination must be made whether its employment would, in some or all circumstances, be prohibited by international law.[47]

The terminology of Guiding Principle (e) is similar to Article 36, according to which:

---

[44] Vienna Convention on the Law of Treaties (VCLT), 23 May 1969, UNTS Vol. No. 1155 18232, entry into force 27 January 1980. See also Dörr and Schmalenbach 2018, pp. 559–634.

[45] Statute of the International Court of Justice, opened for signature 26 June 1945, 33 UNTS 993, entered into force 24 October 1945.

[46] GGE on LAWS 2023

[47] GGE on LAWS 2019.

> [i]n the study, development, acquisition or adoption of a new weapon, means or method of warfare, a High Contracting Party is under an obligation to determine whether its employment would, in some or all circumstances, be prohibited by this Protocol or by any other rule of international law applicable to the High Contracting Party.

The relevance of weapons reviews extends beyond the AWS debate and has also been central to broader discussions on the responsible use of AI.[48] For example, when the US adopted its 2022 Responsible AI Strategy and Implementation Pathway it raised the question of 'whether or how review processes can support implementation of the DoD AI Ethical Principles, including the review of the legality of weapons per DoD [Directives] 2311.01. 5.000, 3000.03E and 3000.09'.[49] Additionally, legal scholarship has also explored the potential role of Article 36 reviews in the context of (non-weaponised) AI-enabled technologies. Scholars such as Klonowska,[50] Copeland, Liivoja, and Sanders,[51] Boulanin and Verbruggen,[52] and Meier,[53] have argued that the obligation to conduct a review under Article 36 extends to AI-enabled technologies, provided certain conditions are met. Although their contributions do not specifically address LLMs, they all advocate an expansive interpretation of Article 36.

5.3.1 LLMs: Neither Weapons nor Weapon Systems

This chapter builds on these arguments to consider whether, and under what parameters, LLMs may also trigger such review obligations. The first question under consideration is whether LLMs qualify as a 'weapon' under Article 36. Article 36 does not define the term 'weapon'. API itself does not provide for a definition of the term weapon but Art 36 only refers to various *types* of weapons, such as 'surface-to-air weapons systems',[54] 'light individual weapons',[55] and 'weapons capable only of repelling hostile action against the protected works or installations'.[56] According to the Cambridge Dictionary, a weapon is 'any object used in fighting or war, such as a gun, bomb, knife, etc.'.[57] This definition offers little guidance on how to interpret the term and leaves several questions unanswered: Do chemical or biological agents also qualify as weapons? Do weapons have to be *tangible* objects, or can they be digital, or only analogue? Does the term 'weapon' cover new technologies as well? The

[48] Meier 2022.

[49] US Department of Defense 2022, p. 21.

[50] Klonowska 2020, pp. 123–153.

[51] Copeland et al. 2023, pp. 285–316.

[52] Boulanin and Verbruggen 2017a.

[53] Meier 2022.

[54] API, above n. 12, Article 25.

[55] Ibid., Article 65(3).

[56] Ibid., Article 56(5).

[57] Cambridge Dictionary 2024.

ordinary meaning of the term 'weapon', along with the preamble and the object and purpose of API, suggest that the term within the meaning of Article 36 should be interpreted expansively to ensure maximum protection for victims of armed conflict.[58] Thus, arguably, the term 'weapon' in Article 36 covers a wide range of objects and substances that can cause harm to humans or damage to objects. Furthermore, a broad interpretation of Article 36 suggests that weapons can be either analogue or digital, traditional, or novel.[59] This interpretation is further supported by existing state practice. Only a limited number of States Parties to API have adopted national legislation that *defines* the term 'weapon' in the context of legal reviews, including Australia, Germany, and Denmark.[60] For example, Australia defines a weapon as '[a]ny device, whether tangible or intangible, designed or intended to be used in warfare to cause: a. injury to, or death of, persons; or b. damage to, or destruction of, objects'.[61] Germany's Joint Service Regulation A-2146/1 defines weapons as 'objects that are designed or suitable to kill or injure persons or objects'.[62] Similarly, Denmark's Service Regulation CIR1H defines weapons as encompassing 'conventional weapons... cyber weapons... delivery systems and instruments designed to kill, destroy, wound, or otherwise incapacitate personnel and equipment'.[63] In the context of the debate on the potential regulation of AWS, the Netherlands and Sweden have clarified that weapons 'are intended to cause harm to persons (including injury or death) or damage to objects (including destruction, capture, and neutralization) as well as incapacitation of persons or objects'.[64]

In light of these observations, it can be concluded that to qualify as a weapon under Article 36, there must be a clear correlation between the object (or substance) in question and the specific harm caused to people or objects.[65] This reasoning is supported by scholarly literature. According to McClelland, the term weapon 'connotes an offensive capability that can be applied to a military object or enemy combatant'.[66] According to publicly available information and as discussed in Sect. 5.2 above, LLMs are primarily designed to *support* military decision makers by providing relevant information, including on potential targets, but are not intended to exert force. These observations lead to the preliminary conclusion that LLMs do not qualify as

[58] See VCLT, above n. 45, Article 31(1). See also Dörr and Schmalenbach 2018, pp. 559–616.

[59] Cf. ICJ, *Legality of the Threat or Use of Nuclear Weapons*, Advisory Opinion, 8 July 1996, ICJ Reports 1996, p. 226, para 86.

[60] Jevglevskaja 2021, p. 96.

[61] Seen in Jevglevskaja 2021, p. 98.

[62] German Federal Ministry of Defence 2016. Seen in Jevglevskaja 2021, p. 97.

[63] Danish Ministry of Defence 2018, pp. 97–98.

[64] Weapons Review Mechanisms 2017, para 27.

[65] See also Klonowska 2020, p. 123.

[66] McLelland 2003, p. 404; see also Boulanin and Verbruggen 2017a. It is important to note, however, that some scholars argue that only weapons causing *direct* damage or destruction should be considered weapons under Article 36, while those causing *indirect* damage are excluded from this definition. For instance, legal scholars argue that the term 'weapon' under Article 36 only applies to those that directly inflict harm. For example, see Biller and Schmitt 2019, p. 204.

weapons under Article 36. However, it is important to note that predicting technological developments in the field of LLMs is challenging, and this assessment should be seen as a preliminary guide or starting point.

The discussion within the GGE has mainly focused on weapon *systems*.[67] The term 'weapon system' reflects the fact that, from a military perspective, it is the combination and interaction of various components—ranging from hardware to software, such as sensors and algorithms—that lead to the intended result. However, only those components *critical* for the use of force and an *integral* part of a weapon system are considered to qualify as a weapon system.[68] A LLM would mainly function as an *auxiliary* tool to support decision makers by performing tasks such as 'automatic summarization, sentiment analysis, and topic modelling'.[69] If LLMs are used solely to support decision makers without involvement in the process of target identification, they would likely not qualify as a weapon or weapon system. However, the situation would differ if LLMs were to play a role in target identification. In such cases, it could be argued that LLMs would form *part* of a weapon system within the meaning of Article 36.

5.3.2 LLMs as a Means of Warfare

While LLMs may not qualify as weapons or weapon systems, they could be considered a means of warfare. Article 36 does not define this term, and although 'means' is referenced in several provisions of API, these references do not provide sufficient clarity to draw any generalisable conclusions.[70] Moreover, state practice regarding the interpretation of 'means of warfare' is limited. Only a few states, such as Denmark and Germany, explicitly define 'means' of warfare as objects that, while not classified as weapons, directly influence a state's offensive or defensive capabilities.[71] New technologies, however, often inflict harm *indirectly*. In the cyber context, this is typically referred to as second-order effects.[72]

---

[67] GGE on LAWS 2023.

[68] Klonowska 2020, pp. 123–124.

[69] Caballero and Jenkins 2024.

[70] For example, according to API, above n. 12, Article 35(1): '[i]n any armed conflict, the right of the Parties to the conflict to choose methods or means of warfare is not unlimited'. According to API Article 55(1), '[c]are shall be taken in warfare to protect the natural environment against widespread, long-term and severe damage. This protection includes a prohibition of the use of methods or means of warfare which are intended or may be expected to cause such damage to the natural environment and thereby to prejudice the health or survival of the population'.

[71] Danish Ministry of Defence 2018 in Jevglevskaja 2021, p. 97; German Federal Ministry of Defence 2016 in Jevglevskaja 2021, p. 97.

[72] Colatin and Väljataga 2020.

When discussing computer code and whether the obligation to undertake weapons reviews applies to such technology, Biller and Schmitt argue that a technology qualifies as either a weapon or a means of warfare if it causes *direct* harm.[73] In their view, means of warfare must, for example, 'deliver a terminal effect directly on a target'.[74] However, the Tallinn Manual does not share this view.[75] According to Rule 103, a cyber means of warfare, for example, 'encompasses both cyber weapons and cyber weapon systems Cyber means of warfare, therefore, include any cyber device, materiel, instrument, mechanism, equipment, or software used, designed, or intended to be used to conduct a cyber attack'.[76] The Tallinn Manual, therefore, does not stipulate that *direct* damage to enemy combatants or military objects must be inflicted. Rather, it is the combination of *different* technologies and capabilities that, taken together, *contribute* to inflicting injury or death on enemy combatants or damage to military objects.[77] The United Kingdom (UK) has listed examples of technologies that qualify as means of warfare, such as 'sighting equipment, laser designators, target acquisition equipment, data links and software used for processing data'.[78] This suggests once again that means of warfare are not limited to those that inflict *direct* damage but involve the combination or interaction of several technologies.[79]

Similar discussions have taken place in relation to DSS. DSS have been defined as a 'model-based set of procedures for processing data and judgments to assist decision-makers' in military operations.[80] DSS may operate at various 'levels in the chain of command' addressing 'semi-structured and unstructured decision tasks'.[81] The applicability of Article 36 to DSS has been explored in the literature, most notably by Klonowska, who developed a four-stage test to determine whether Article 36 applies to DSS. First, the use of the DSS must raise questions in terms of IHL compliance. Second, for the system to fall under the purview of Article 36, it must be an *integral* part of military decision making. Third, the technology must provide *actionable* intelligence to human decision makers. Finally, the technology must be intended to achieve *direct* or, at a minimum, *indirect* effects on the battlefield.[82]

Klonowska's four-stage test provides a useful framework for investigating whether certain LLMs qualify as DSS that meet the criteria of a means of warfare under Article 36. It seems undisputed that the use of systems like Gotham or Donovan, as described above, raises fundamental questions about compliance with IHL, particularly when used in the context of target production. This is because classic targeting rules, such as the principles of distinction and proportionality, would apply. LLMs for target

[73] Biller and Schmitt 2019, p. 210.

[74] Ibid.

[75] Schmitt 2017.

[76] Ibid., Rule 103(2).

[77] Klonowska 2020, pp. 124–126.

[78] United Kingdom 2016.

[79] Klonowska 2020, pp. 124–126.

[80] Little 1970, pp. 466–485.

[81] Şuşnea 2012, pp. 132–133.

[82] Ibid.

production could be used to make concrete recommendations regarding the question of whether a specific object qualifies as a military target and thus, potentially, challenge the principle of distinction, especially if the system malfunctions. Or the system may be used to provide recommendations or background information on potential collateral damage. Any system failure could, potentially, challenge the principle of proportionality, among others. However, determining whether these systems constitute an 'integral' component of military decision making is more complex. Notably, there is no universally accepted definition of what constitutes an 'integral' part of military decision-making *per se*. As Klonowska rightly warns, DSS can influence human decision makers in various ways, which may, in turn, affect decisions related to target identification.[83] Therefore, she emphasises the need for an urgent critical examination of human–machine interaction in this context. While an 'integral' part of military decision making remains open to interpretation, this chapter argues that a system can be considered 'integral' if it plays at least a certain role in the identification or selection of military targets. In principle, LLMs should be regarded as integral components of military decision-making processes if they contribute—even indirectly—to target identification, the decision to initiate an attack, or proportionality assessments. Such a comprehensive interpretation is essential to ensure that obligations under IHL are not circumvented by delegating specific functions to LLMs. Admittedly, the application of this principle will often necessitate a case-by-case analysis.

In the cases of both Donovan and Gotham, it seems safe to conclude that these systems could be regarded as an integral part of military decision making, particularly when used to gather information on potential targets or to determine the most effective military tactics for achieving specific objectives. Whether the information provided by Donovan and Gotham constitutes actionable intelligence is more straightforward. Current evidence suggests that both systems are designed to enable centralised data collection, processing, and dissemination in a format understandable to human decision makers. If these systems even partially contribute to the generation of targets, as noted earlier, they would influence—at least indirectly—battlefield outcomes. Consequently, both Gotham and Donovan appear to satisfy the criteria for a DSS as they may challenge various norms of IHL, play an integral part of military decision making, have significant impacts on military operations and contribute to critical offensive capabilities. In light of this, they in principle qualify as means of warfare under Article 36.

5.3.3 LLMs as a Method of Warfare

LLMs that do not qualify as means of warfare could still be considered methods of warfare. Again, Article 36 does not define this term. An analysis of the provisions of API that reference 'method of warfare' yields limited guidance. For example, Article

[83] Klonowska 2020, pp. 124.

54(1) API prohibits the '[s]tarvation of civilians as a method of warfare'. In this case, the term 'method of warfare' has no connection with a weapon or weapon system, yet it remains difficult to draw generalisable conclusions from this provision. Similarly, Article 35(2) API prohibits the employment of 'weapons, projectiles and material and methods of warfare of a nature to cause superfluous injury or unnecessary suffering'. According to the ICRC, the term 'methods of warfare' refers to 'tactics and strategies used in hostilities to defeat the enemy'.[84] However, the obligation to undertake reviews is limited to the question of 'how certain weapons and means are intended to be deployed in the operational circumstances', excluding 'rules of engagement, military concepts and doctrines more generally' from these reviews.[85]

State practice regarding Article 36 and the term 'methods of warfare' presents an incoherent picture.[86] The majority of States Parties to API interpret this term as referring to *how* a weapon or weapon system is used.[87] However, some states have adopted a broader understanding, viewing methods of warfare as encompassing 'a plan, concept or doctrine for a military *modus operandi* that is intended to support certain military operations and capabilities to impair those of an adversary'.[88] For example, the UK views methods of warfare as referring to how 'warfare is conducted', rather than how a weapon or weapon system is used.[89] Denmark includes military doctrine under the term 'method of warfare',[90] while Germany extends the term to include 'planning, concepts or doctrines for the military operations designed to counter, interfere, or support enemy military operations and capabilities to interfere or support their own military operations and capabilities'.[91]

Given their capability to analyse vast amounts of data and relatively complex content, LLMs could be employed to compare various military-relevant documents, ensuring coherence across them. If LLM-driven decisions influence tactical-level operations, this may, in turn, necessitate a formal review of these systems. However, as always, the impact of such systems depends on how the respective system is used and the capabilities it possesses. It is still too early to draw general conclusions, and it remains to be seen which technological developments will ultimately prevail. Most importantly, whether LLMs qualify as methods of warfare largely depends on how States Parties to API interpret and implement Article 36. It would, however, be in the best interests of potential victims of armed conflict to interpret Article 36 broadly, including LLMs that impact military doctrine more generally.

[84] Verri 1992, in Jevglevskaja 2021, p. 102.

[85] Jevglevskaja 2021, p. 102.

[86] See also Klonowska 2020, p. 126.

[87] Ibid.; Daoust et al. 2002, p. 352.

[88] Boulanin and Verbruggen 2017b; Klonowska 2020, p. 126.

[89] United Kingdom 2016.

[90] Danish Ministry of Defence 2018.

[91] German Federal Ministry of Defence 2016.

5.4 Conclusion

Rapidly changing technological developments will severely alter the dynamics of armed conflict. Both the military and the private sector, such as Scale AI and Palantir, have already started to explore potential military applications of LLMs and generative AI more broadly. A brief analysis of projects like Donovan and Gotham reveals that LLMs yield numerous military benefits, such as the ability to rapidly gather, fuse, and analyse vast amounts of data. This, in turn, provides decision makers with the most relevant information and concrete recommendations, such as identifying potential targets. However, LLMs also present inherent challenges, including hallucinations and a lack of deeper understanding of the information they process, highlighting the need for rigorous testing and evaluation before deployment in military operations.

From a legal perspective, the use of LLMs in the military domain raises significant challenges regarding the applicability and interpretation of the obligation to undertake legal reviews under Article 36 API. The emergence of new military technologies certainly supports an extensive reading of this provision. However, the current stage of development of most LLMs, combined with the limited publicly available information on their use, only allows for a preliminary legal assessment.

The tentative legal analysis carried out in this chapter led to the conclusion that LLMs do not qualify as weapons or weapon systems. Based on the available information, there will be no direct causal link between the system and the infliction of harm to individuals (rather than to enemy combatants) and objects (rather than military objects). However, LLMs could potentially qualify as a means of warfare. Evidence from other technological domains, such as cyber, suggests that to qualify as a means of warfare, the causation of *indirect* harm may be sufficient to invoke Article 36.

The question of whether Article 36 would also apply to non-weaponised AI has already been addressed in the context of DSS, described as a 'model-based set of procedures for processing data and judgments to assist decision-makers'.[92] Some LLMs appear to meet the characteristics of a DSS, particularly if the system *inter alia* forms an integral part of military decision making and provides actionable intelligence to human decision makers.[93] However, not all LLMs meet these criteria. LLMs that do not provide actionable intelligence but influence military doctrine could, arguably, be classified as a method of warfare. However, a more detailed understanding of these systems and their actual use is necessary for a complete legal analysis.

While the exact role of LLMs in the military domain remains uncertain, a clear trend is emerging: AI-enabled technologies are increasingly being integrated into military operations, and not all of them will be weaponised. Although the theoretical development of a military-specific 'ChatGPT' may not be immediately plausible or foreseeable, its potential impact raises critical questions in terms of whether such an LLM would fall under Article 36 and comply with IHL. As AI technologies become

[92] Little 1970, p. 466.

[93] Klonowska 2020, p. 126.

more embedded in decision-making processes, it is essential to adopt a forward-thinking and expansive interpretations of IHL, particularly Article 36 API, to ensure that human decision makers keep pace with these developments and fulfil their legal obligations in an increasingly complex technological landscape.

References

Bender EM, Gebru T, McMillan-Major A, Shmitchell S (2021) On the Dangers of Stochastic Parrots: Can Language Models Be Too Big? https://dl.acm.org/doi/10.1145/3442188.3445922

Biller JT, Schmitt MN (2019) Classification of Cyber Capabilities and Operations as Weapons, Means, or Methods of Warfare. International Law Studies 95:179–225

Boguslavsky E (2020) Palantir to support US Army's modernization of mission command capabilities. https://www.israeldefense.co.il/index.php/en/node/46671. Accessed 30 July 2024

Boulanin V, Verbruggen M (2017a) Article 36 Reviews: Dealing with the challenges posed by emerging technologies. https://www.sipri.org/sites/default/files/2017-12/article_36_report_1712.pdf. Accessed 30 July 2024

Boulanin V, Verbruggen M (2017b) SIPRI Compendium on Article 36 Weapons Reviews. https://www.sipri.org/sites/default/files/2017-12/sipri_bp_1712_article_36_compendium_2017.pdf. Accessed 30 July 2024

Boyd RB (1976) Destruction and Creation. https://www.coljohnboyd.com/static/documents/1976-09-03__Boyd_John_R__Destruction_and_Creation.pdf. Accessed 30 July 2024

Business Wire (2023) Scale AI Partners with XVIII Airborne Corps for First LLM Deployment to a U.S. Government Classified Network. https://www.businesswire.com/news/home/20230510005630/en/Scale-AI-Partners-with-XVIII-Airborne-Corps-for-First-LLM-Deployment-to-a-U.S.-Government-Classified-Network. Accessed 30 July 2024

Caballero WN, Jenkins PR (2024) On Large Language Models in National Security Applications, arXiv:2407.03453

Cambridge Dictionary (2024) https://dictionary.cambridge.org/dictionary/english/weapon

Colatin SDT, Väljataga A (2020) Data as a Weapon: Refined Cyber Capabilities Under Weapon Reviews and International Human Rights Law. https://ccdcoe.org/uploads/2020/05/Data_as_a_weapon_-_reviews_and_oversight_FINAL_PDF.pdf. Accessed 30 July 2024

Copeland D, Liivoja R, Sanders L (2023) The Utility of Weapons Reviews in Addressing Concerns Raised by Autonomous Weapon Systems. Journal of Conflict and Security Law 28: 285-316

Danish Ministry of Defence (2018) Cirkulære om folkeretlig vurdering i forbindelse med udforskning, udvikling, erhvervelse eller valget af et nyt våben og af metoder eller midler i krigsførelse [Service Regulation on the International Legal Evaluation in Connection to the Study, Development, Acquisition, or Adoption of a New Weapon, Means, or Method of Warfare], CIR1H nr 9494 (29 May 2018)

Daoust I, Coupland R, Ishoey R (2002) New wars, new weapons? The obligation of States to assess the legality of means and methods of warfare. International Review of the Red Cross 84:345–363

Data Scientist (2023) Adversarial Attack: Definition and protection against this threat. https://datascientest.com/en/adversarial-attack-definition-and-protection-against-this-threat. Accessed 30 July 2024

Demarest C (2023) Pentagon establishes Task Force Lima to study generative AI issues. https://www.c4isrnet.com/artificial-intelligence/2023/08/10/pentagon-establishes-task-force-lima-to-study-generative-ai-issues/. Accessed 30 July 2024

Dörr O, Schmalenbach K (2018) Vienna Convention on the Law of Treaties: A Commentary, 2nd edn. Springer, Berlin

Feuillade-Montixi Q, Peigné P (2023) The Stochastic Parrot Hypothesis is debatable for the last generation of LLMs. https://www.lesswrong.com/posts/HxRjHq3QG8vcYy4yy/the-stochastic-parrot-hypothesis-is-debatable-for-the-last. Accessed 30 July 2024

Future of Life Institute (2023) Pause Giant AI Experiments: An Open Letter. https://futureoflife.org/open-letter/pause-giant-ai-experiments/. Accessed 30 July 2024

German Federal Ministry of Defence [Bundesministerium der Verteidigung] (2016) Zentrale Dienstvorschrift, Prüfung neuer Waffen, Mittel und Methoden der Kriegführung [Joint Service Regulation A-2146/1] (13 June 2016)

Group of Governmental Experts of the High Contracting Parties to the Convention on Prohibitions or Restrictions on the Use of Certain Conventional Weapons Which May Be Deemed to Be Excessively Injurious or to Have Indiscriminate Effects (2017) Weapons Review Mechanisms, submitted by the Netherlands and Switzerland, Group of Governmental Experts of the High Contracting Parties to the Convention on Prohibitions or Restrictions on the Use of Certain Conventional Weapons Which May Be Deemed to Be Excessively Injurious or to Have Indiscriminate Effects, 7 November 2017, CW/GGE.1/2017/WP.5

Hoijtink M, Planqué-van Hardeveld A (2022) Machine Learning and the Platformization of the Military: A Study of Google's Machine Learning Platform TensorFlow. International Political Sociology 16/2:1–19

Horlings T, Lindelauf R, Rietjens S (2023) Battling information overload in military intelligence & security organisations. In: Pijpers PBMJ, Voskuijl M, Beeres RJM (eds) Towards a Data-Driven Military: A Multidisciplinary Perspective. Leiden University Press, Leiden, pp. 221–236,

Jensen B, Tadross D (2023) How Large Language Models Can Revolutionize Military Planning. https://warontherocks.com/2023/04/how-large-language-models-can-revolutionize-military-planning/. Accessed 30 July 2024

Jevglevskaja N (2018) Weapons Review Obligation under Customary International Law. International Law Studies 94:187–221

Jevglevskaja N (2021) International Law and Weapons Review: Emerging Military Technology under the Law of Armed Conflict. Cambridge University Press, Cambridge

Khan Raiaan MA (2024) A Review on Large Language Models: Architectures, Applications, Taxonomies, Open Issues and Challenges. https://ieeexplore.ieee.org/stamp/stamp.jsp?tp=&arnumber=10433480. Accessed 30 July 2024

Klonowska K (2020) Article 36: Review of AI Decision-Support Systems and Other Emerging Technologies of Warfare. In: Gill TD, Geiß R, Krieger H, Mignot-Mahdavi R (eds) Yearbook of International Humanitarian Law Vol. 23. T.M.C. Asser Press, The Hague, pp. 123–153

Little JDC (1970) Models and Managers: The Concept of a Decision Calculus. Management Science 16:466–485

Luckenbaugh J (2023) Army Hopes AI Will Give Soldiers an Information Advantage. https://www.nationaldefensemagazine.org/articles/2023/7/21/army-hopes-ai-will-give-soldiers-an-information-advantage. Accessed 30 July 2024

Manson K (2023) The US Military Is Taking Generative AI Out for a Spin. https://www.bloomberg.com/news/newsletters/2023-07-05/the-us-military-is-taking-generative-ai-out-for-a-spin. Accessed 30 July 2024

Marcus G (2018) Deep Learning: A Critical Appraisal. arXiv. https://arxiv.org/pdf/1801.00631. Accessed 30 July 2024

Marr B (2023) A Short History of ChatGPT: How We Got To Where We Are Today. https://www.forbes.com/sites/bernardmarr/2023/05/19/a-short-history-of-chatgpt-how-we-got-to-where-we-are-today/?sh=46141dc9674f. Accessed 30 July 2024

McLelland J (2003) The review of weapons in accordance with Article 36 of Additional Protocol I. International Review of the Red Cross 85:397–420

Meier MW (2022) Responsible AI Symposium—Responsible AI and Legal Review of Weapons. https://lieber.westpoint.edu/responsible-ai-legal-review-weapons/. Accessed 30 July 2024

New Digital Age (2024) Incredibly helpful or incredibly hyped? Chat GPT one year on. https://newdigitalage.co/technology/incredibly-helpful-or-incredibly-hyped-chat-gpt-one-year-on/. Accessed 30 July 2024
Reinhold T, Hoffberger-Pippan E, Blanchard A (2024), Artificial Intelligence in the Military Domain: Technical, Legal and Ethical Perspectives. EU Non-Proliferation and Disarmament Brief No. 35 https://www.sipri.org/sites/default/files/2025-01/eunpdc_no_92_0.pdf. Accessed 20 July 2024
Richards C (2020) Boyd's OODA Loop. Necesse 5:142–165
Schmitt MN (ed) (2017) Tallinn Manual 2.0 on the International Law Applicable to Cyber Operations. Cambridge University Press, Cambridge
Shortland ND, Alison LJ, Moran JM (2019) Military Decision-Making: Doctrine, Rationality, and Field-Based Approaches. In: Shortland N D, Alison L J, Moran J M (eds) Conflict: How Soldiers Make Impossible Decisions. Oxford University Press, Oxford, pp 15–33
Sloan K (2023) Stellar or so-so? ChatGPT bar exam performance sparks differing opinions. https://www.reuters.com/legal/transactional/stellar-or-so-so-chatgpt-bar-exam-performance-sparks-differing-opinions-2023-05-31/. Accessed 30 July 2024
Şuşnea E (2012) Decision-Support Systems in Military Actions: Necessity, Possibilities and Constraints. Journal of Management Resources 2:131–140
United Nations Group of Governmental Experts on Emerging Technologies in the Area or Lethal Autonomous Weapons Systems (GGE on LAWS) (2019) Report of the 2019 session of the Group of Governmental Experts on Emerging Technologies in the Area of Lethal Autonomous Weapons Systems, 25 September 2019, UN Doc. CCW/GGE.1/2019/3, Annex IV
United Nations Group of Governmental Experts on Emerging Technologies in the Area or Lethal Autonomous Weapons Systems (GGE on LAWS) (2023) Report of the 2023 session of the Group of Governmental Experts on Emerging Technologies in the Area of Lethal Autonomous Weapons Systems, 6 May 2023, UN Doc. CCW/GGE.1/2023/CRP.2
United Kingdom (2016) Ministry of Defence (2016) UK Weapon Reviews. https://assets.publishing.service.gov.uk/media/5a80bf5f40f0b62305b8cec5/20160308-UK_weapon_reviews.pdf. Accessed 30 July 2024
US Department of the Army (2019) Legal Review of Weapons and Weapon Systems. Army Regulation 27–53. https://armypubs.army.mil/epubs/DR_pubs/DR_a/pdf/web/ARN8435_AR27-53_Final_Web.pdf. Accessed 30 July 2024
US Department of the Army, Department of the Navy, Marine Corps, United States Department of the Air Force, United States Coast Guard, United States Space Force (2013) Joint Targeting. https://jfsc.ndu.edu/Portals/72/Documents/JC2IOS/Additional_Reading/1F4_jp3-60.pdf. Accessed 30 July 2024
US Department of the Army, Department of the Navy, Marine Corps, United States Department of the Air Force, United States Coast Guard, United States Space Force (2020) Joint Planning. https://irp.fas.org/doddir/dod/jp5_0.pdf. Accessed 30 July 2024
US Department of Defense (2022) Responsible Artificial Intelligence Strategy and Implementation Pathway. https://media.defense.gov/2022/Jun/22/2003022604/-1/-1/0/Department-of-Defense-Responsible-Artificial-Intelligence-Strategy-and-Implementation-Pathway.PDF. Accessed 30 July 2024
US Joint Chiefs of Staff Joint Targeting (2018) Joint Publication 3-60, II-3. Available at https://www.esd.whs.mil/Portals/54/Documents/FOID/Reading%20Room/Joint_Staff/21-F-0520_JP_3-60_9-28-2018.pdf?utm_source=chatgpt.com
Vaswani A et al. (2017) Attention is all you need. arXiv. https://doi.org/10.48550/arXiv.1706.03762
Verri P (1992) The Dictionary of the International Law of Armed Conflict (Markee E, Mutti S (transl))

Other Documents

Report of the 2019 session of the Group of Governmental Experts on Emerging Technologies in the Area of Lethal Autonomous Weapons Systems, Convention on Prohibitions or Restrictions on the Use of Certain Conventional Weapons Which May Be Deemed to Be Excessively Injurious or to Have Indiscriminate Effects, 25 September 2019, CCW/GGE.1/2019/3, Annex IV

Report of the 2023 session of the Group of Governmental Experts on Emerging Technologies in the Area of Lethal Autonomous Weapons Systems, Group of Governmental Experts on Emerging Technologies in the Area of Lethal Autonomous Weapons System, 06 May 2023, CCW/GGE.1/2023/CRP.2

Elisabeth Hoffberger-Pippan is Policy Advisor for Security Policy and International Order at the Konrad Adenauer Foundation in Vienna. Her main areas of research include questions related to new technologies in the military domain, including AI-enabled weapon systems and military robotics. Prior to joining the Konrad Adenauer Foundation, she was Senior Researcher at the Peace Research Institute in Frankfurt (PRIF) focussing on arms controlling and emerging technologies. Before that she was the head of iPRAW, the International Panel on the Regulation of Autonomous Weapons Systems, a project funded by the German Foreign Office.

Chapter 6
The AI-Augmented Super Soldier: An Interface-Based Approach to the Cognition of Enhanced Humans

Thomas Christian Bächle

Contents

Abstract The concepts of responsibility, control, and accountability serve as a reassuring foundation for operational, ethical, and legal questions regarding the employment of military AI and autonomous weapon systems. This normative terminological scaffolding, however, is often at odds with the complex dynamics of agency and human–machine interactions. Focussing on the figuration of the enhanced or augmented soldier, this contribution develops a theoretical framework that takes into account the role of interfaces and cognitive processes, shedding new light on these normative assumptions. First, this chapter looks at human/machine configurations within modern warfare paradigms. It discusses the idea of human augmentation, which reflects a deliberate vision of an ever-stronger hybridisation of humans and machines: human soldier or weapon? Second, the chapter proposes an interface-centred approach to cognitive processes, modelling cognition as a continuous re-establishment of relations between the body and its environment. Cognitive processes and interface effects often remain underexplored when theorising military AI. They are, however, central to the dynamics of the human–machine relationship, which makes them so meaningful for questions of intention, control, or responsibility. Third, this framework will be applied to the cognition of the enhanced or augmented human

T. C. Bächle (✉)
University of Bonn, Bonn, Germany
e-mail: thomas.baechle@hiig.de

Humboldt Institute for Internet and Society (HIIG), Berlin, Germany

B. Boutin et al. (eds.), *Legal, Ethical, and Technical Dilemmas in Military Artificial Intelligence*, https://doi.org/10.1007/978-94-6265-759-5_6

soldier, highlighting three areas: (a) human agency, nonconscious decision-making and (de)skilling, (b) situational awareness, and (c) prediction. Overall, the interface-centred approach to human augmentation and cognition developed in this chapter calls into question normative presuppositions and reframes theoretical certitudes around the reference objects of responsibility, control, accountability, or rationality, which also has implications for ethical and legal debates.

Keywords Human Agency · Human–Machine Interaction · Cognitive Science · Interface Theory · Military AI · Human Augmentation · Human Enhancement · Extended Cognition

6.1 Introduction

The terms 'military artificial intelligence' (military AI) and 'autonomous weapon systems' (AWS) typically evoke ideas of technologies that operate largely without human supervision or intervention. The autonomy of these systems, however, is much more complex than the common 'in, on or out of the loop' or 'meaningful human control' (MHC) vocabularies imply. Nonetheless, these terms are common reference points for establishing a normative scaffolding of responsibility, control, and accountability. They serve as a reassuring foundation for operational, ethical, and legal questions regarding the employment of military AI and AWS. In this context, it is important to look at the essential and complex dynamics of agency and human–machine interactions, which often elude normative—or positivist—categorisations. They are to be understood as normative, as they generally ask for an unambiguous agent, namely, the 'who' in 'who is responsible or accountable?' and 'who is in control?'. What is often implicitly voiced in these larger categories of accountability, responsibility and control are normative extensions, including human intentionality, the operator/user as a rational subject or a clear-cut human/machine divide. This chapter aims to challenge the normative assumptions made in human/machine relationships, by developing an interface-based approach to cognition in the context of human augmentation within military settings.

First, this chapter will look at human/machine configurations within modern warfare paradigms—particularly Network-Centric Warfare (NCW)—and concepts such as human–machine teaming, which promote a particular understanding of the human and human agency. The idea of the 'enhanced' or 'augmented soldier' has emerged as a necessary consequence of these conceptualisations, emblematic of a particular shift: rather than focusing primarily on how to adapt increasingly autonomous technologies to ensure their compliance with legal and ethical standards—thereby enabling effective human oversight—the human soldier becomes the central point of attention. The 'enhanced' or 'augmented' soldier describes the enhancement of performance and capabilities through, among other methods, neurological, biological, or technological interventions, which also include media technologies.[1] These technologies of augmentation and enhancement create new possibilities for (inter-)actions and perceptual spaces. As will be demonstrated, the figuration of the enhanced or augmented soldier serves a dual function in military discourse. It is both an expression—and deliberate vision—of an ever-stronger hybridisation of humans and machines, a trend that long predates current technological possibilities. It also highlights how legal and ethical discourses necessitate a normative approach and—through a counter-movement—reintroduce an unambiguous (rhetorically maintained) distinction between the technological and the human. Is it a human soldier, or a weapon? (Sect. 6.2).

Second, to tackle the contradictory movements of hybridisation and essentialism, this chapter proposes an interface-centred approach to cognitive processes, that accounts for a relational model. While acknowledging that the categories of human and technology are distinct, it argues that this distinction becomes functionally less relevant when enhancement or augmentation is fundamentally regarded as a rearrangement of cognitive processes. Simply put, human cognition must be understood as an incessant re-establishment of relations between the body and its environment. These relations are constitutive of cognition and rely on mediating forms that establish and maintain them. As will be argued, the interface—as an entity that both connects and separates—therefore fulfils a central role in cognitive processes. This approach also emphasises the idea of continuity, as human cognition has always relied on social interactions and symbolic systems. At the same time, it accounts for new possibilities for interactions and perceptual spaces. Both cognitive processes and interface effects often remain underexplored when theorising human/machine relations in military contexts. These dynamics not only play a major role when discussing the autonomy of a system, as the relations between the system, its environment, and a human operator are co-determined by specific interfaces. In the dynamic, performative settings of human–machine interactions, interfaces are an integral element, extending far beyond mere control units or screens. They rather co-produce the dynamics of the human–machine relationship, a circumstance that makes them so meaningful for questions of intention, control, or responsibility (Sect. 6.3).

Third, this interface-centred theoretical framework will be applied to the cognition of the enhanced or augmented human soldier, highlighting three areas in particular that all point to illusions that need to be questioned in connection with the augmented soldier: (a) in the area of human agency, (un)conscious decision-making and (de)skilling, the discussions point to the illusion of the soldier as a rational subject whose decisions are always conscious; (b) in the area of situational awareness, the human/machine figuration of the augmented soldier evokes the illusion of an objective reality that is made available to the human operator, optimising situational awareness and the ability to make predictions with greater accuracy; and (c) in the area of prediction, the ideal of the augmented human creates the self-assuring

[1] de Boisboissel and Le Masson 2021.

illusion of a knowable future, providing a delusive sense of control in the face of the abhorrence of war (Sect. 6.4).

The interface-centred approach to human augmentation developed in this chapter also contributes to reframing theoretical certitudes, such as the seemingly self-evident reference objects of responsibility, control, accountability, or rationality. It may, therefore, also have implications for ethical and legal discussions surrounding human augmentation in military contexts.

6.2 Augmentation, Enhancement, and the Upgraded Soldier: Human/Machine Configurations in Late Modern Warfare

Military paradigms of recent years—such as NCW, human–machine teaming, platform-centric warfare, enhancement, or augmentation—have not only been reflective of the dominant technological discourses of their respective time. They have, more or less explicitly, always constructed and perpetuated a particular understanding of human/machine relations, and hence, the human itself. As will be argued in this section, the discussion cannot be reduced to mere machines (i.e., 'robots', AI, and AWS) and variations of the question of how to equip them with ethical functions or ensure their compliance with legal frameworks. The line that is historically drawn from an anthropocentric to a robocentric or mechanistic view of warfare lies more in the discursive re-balancing of the hybrid nature of the human/machine relationship. Simply put, for centuries, the focus was on how technological equipment could be utilised to improve the performance of human soldiers. Now, the emphasis shifts to the technology itself and, as a consequence, the discursive mechanisation of the human who—when measured against the technological benchmark—necessarily becomes deficient. This shift becomes particularly palpable in the figuration of the enhanced or augmented soldier: human insufficiency is compensated with technology.

The shifting conceptualisation of the human/machine hybrid is particularly evident with the increasing degrees of automation and autonomy of weapons systems. Common questions of MHC over these weapons inevitably reflect the human/machine relationship.[2] The idea of machine autonomy construes a likeness between machines and humans, reinforcing a particular understanding of the human.[3] It reiterates the cybernetic paradigm and its understanding of humans and machines, which views living and non-living systems as (at least functionally) equivalent.[4]

[2] See, for example, Scharre 2018. Autonomous systems, in more general terms, can be conceptualised by their various degrees of self-directedness and self-sufficiency, see Bradshaw et al. 2013. Such systems remain necessarily dependent on external factors, such as their energy supply or infrastructural factors that ensure their functioning.

[3] See also the contribution by Klonowska and Woodcock in this volume (Chap. 3, Sect. 3.2.2).

[4] Cf. Suchman 2007; Suchman and Weber 2016. Current discourses on AI and the human originate in these larger conceptual histories, such as cybernetics, and model both machines and humans as

Besides the concept of autonomy, the military paradigm of NCW has also been instrumental in shaping human/machine relations. NCW's key goal is to seek permanent information dominance by connecting the whole range of military systems, consisting of both human and technical agents. More specifically, it is envisioned

> as an information superiority-enabled concept of operations that generates increased combat power by networking sensors, decision makers, and shooters to achieve shared awareness, increased speed of command, higher tempo of operations, greater lethality, increased survivability, and a degree of self-synchronization. In essence, NCW translates information superiority into combat power by effectively linking knowledgeable entities in the battlespace.[5]

Later military interpretations describe NCW similarly as 'the combination of strategies, emerging tactics, techniques, and procedures, and organizations that a fully or even a partially networked force can employ to create a decisive warfighting advantage'.[6]

The United States (US) military report quoted here quickly turns to emphasise that the 'implementation of NCW is first of all about human behaviour as opposed to information technology',[7] and that 'Soldiers, Sailors, Airmen, and Marines conducting military operations at the tactical and operational levels of war gain a significant advantage over adversaries because of shared situational awareness'.[8] While there is an explicit acknowledgement of the importance of information-centred technologies, the role of the human (soldier) is clearly shaped within this network model of warfare, by pointing to factors such as shared situational awareness (e.g., perception and cognition in a technological environment) or self-synchronisation. Self-synchronisation refers to a 'mode of interaction between two or more entities',[9] where the 'combination of a rule set and shared awareness enables the entities to operate in the absence of traditional hierarchical mechanisms for command and control'.[10] In this context, the human (soldier) is not only attributed with the functionality of internalised rule sets that can be automatically processed based on a shared awareness and information pool. The soldier is also constructed as a highly mechanistic human, on par with other non-human elements of the network.

These links are deepened in the idea of *human/machine teaming*, a metaphor that constructs the human and the machine as effectively seeing eye to eye. Military strategy documents—such as the 2013 Strategy Brief developed by the US Army

---

operating on the same principle of information processing. The idea of brain/computer interfaces (see Sect. 6.4) is one of the most recent examples of this premise, reinforced by political imaginaries that promote a kinship between the human mind and machine intelligence, see Edwards 1997.

[5] Alberts et al. 1999, p. 2.

[6] Cebrowski 2005, p. 3.

[7] Ibid.

[8] Ibid., pp. 3–4.

[9] Alberts et al. 1999, p. 175.

[10] Ibid., pp. 175–176. In practical terms, this mode increases the 'opportunity for low-level forces to operate nearly autonomously and to re-task themselves through exploitation of shared awareness and the commander's intent'; see Cebrowski 2005, p. 9.

Aviation Center of Excellence (USAACE)—define manned-unmanned teaming (MUM-T) as 'the synchronized employment of Soldiers, manned and unmanned air and ground vehicles, robotics, and sensors to achieve enhanced situational understanding, greater lethality, and improved survivability'.[11] This conceptual integration of machines and humans is further advanced by notions of the 'soldier as a system', exemplified by the United Kingdom (UK) military's 2012 Generic Soldier System (GSA) and expressed in many of today's research and development goals within military industries (see also Sect. 6.4).[12] These paradigms are extensions of the idea of scientific and technological rationality—manifesting in the particular tools, weapons, and machinery of any given time—in an attempt to steer the dialectic of order and chaos on the battlefield.[13] The discourse of clean, rational, and effective warfare, along with the computable human element, is also echoed in studies of war that attempt to hold an empirical grip on entropy.[14]

The discursive construction of a fluid human/machine (soldier/weapon) continuum is maintained not only by the notion of the technically enhanced human but also through the terminological equation of machines as humans in legal or ethical discourses. The claim 'of a radical transition from the usual anthropocentric warfare to a *robocentric* warfare with the belief that the transition has moral advantages', introduces the contestable idea of programming 'ethics into smart soldiers'.[15] What makes these arguments noteworthy is the explicit terminological fusion of humans and machines,[16] while conceptualising human and machine agency as emphatically distinct.[17] The enhancement in question is a vague, functional element of the machine, understood as 'ethically enhanced smart soldiers (EeSS) for an ethical warfare'.[18] In the wake of this shift, responsibility or intention seemingly become problems that are (at least in part) issues of the technological domain.

---

[11] Quoted in Taylor 2014, p. 5; see also Eshel 2019.

[12] The more recent concept of *human-autonomy teaming* (HAT) acknowledges the concept of autonomy even more by describing HAT as 'at least one human working cooperatively with at least one autonomous agent, where an autonomous agent is a computer entity with a partial or high degree of self-governance with respect to decision-making, adaptation, and communication'; see O'Neill et al. 2022, p. 904. Especially with the advent of AI, 'autonomous agents can perform a greater number of dynamical functions in both teamwork and taskwork than ever before, and they are beginning to be viewed as teammates rather than tools', ibid.

[13] Bousquet 2022. From 2005 onward, for example, the 'U.S. Army has developed and implemented the Human Terrain System (HTS) Project as part of the U.S. counterinsurgency strategy in the Middle East' by deploying 'social scientists to areas of conflict to develop social and cultural understanding of local populations as an aid to military decision-making', employing 'ethnographic methods to collect data on local customs, kinship structures, economics, and politics', see Ellison and Wellner 2013. It was widely regarded as a failure, not least because it was based on the premise of the predictability of social and cultural factors, see Connable 2018.

[14] Bousquet et al. 2020.

[15] Omotoyinbo 2023, p. 1485.

[16] 'I will refer to autonomous weapons, and autonomous weapon system (AWS) broadly, as smart soldiers'; see Omotoyinbo 2023, p. 1488.

[17] Ibid., p. 1485, n. 1.

[18] Ibid., p. 1488.

While the focus shifts away from human actors to technology, the concepts of *augmentation* and *enhancement* reflect an interesting counterpoint: the emphasis on the human soldier, though emphatically made, is framed through the lens of technology. In a somewhat paradoxical pattern, AWS are discussed in terms of their human-like qualities; while the human, on the other hand, is conceptualised in a mechanised form. The 'enhanced soldier' is described as one 'whose capacities are improved, either stimulated or created, to strengthen his or her operational efficiency. Such enhancements can range from a physiological modification or a change of the soldier's psychological condition to other means, embedded in the soldier, that provide a consistent improvement of his or her sensorial, physical, or cognitive capacities'.[19] In short, the term 'enhanced soldier' describes the enhancement of a soldier's performance and capabilities through, among others, neurological, biological, or technological interventions, targeting sensorial, physical, or cognitive capacities. All three domains point to cognitive processes that can be interpreted within an interface-centred framing (see Sects. 6.3 and 6.4).

Augmentation, a more general and overarching concept, is defined as 'the application of science and technologies to temporarily or permanently improve human performance'.[20] This idea can be further divided into human performance optimisation and enhancement. Optimisation improves 'human performance up to the limit of biological potential without adding new capabilities'; enhancement, by contrast, pushes human performance to go '**beyond** the limit of biological potential and can include additional capabilities beyond those innate to humans (for example, night vision)'.[21] Enhancement is developed here as distinct from optimisation techniques, such as physical or cognitive training, nutrition, or education. It should be noted, however, that these understandings are not universally shared in research and development (R&D) literature, where the idea of the enhanced soldier still often implies transcending biological limitations through technological means.

The strategic joint paper by the Bundeswehr German Armed Forces and the UK Ministry of Defence applies another metaphor of contemporary technological structures: 'Conceptualising the human as a platform is fundamental to thinking about human augmentation'.[22] This metaphor juxtaposes humans and machines along the following premises:

> The performance of traditional military platforms—vehicles, aircraft and ships—is routinely monitored and analysed but it is remarkable that our ability to understand our most critical

[19] de Boisboissel and Le Masson 2021, pp. 2–3: The goal is to render 'him or her more efficient during military operations by strengthening intellectual skills (mental, psychological, cognitive) and/or physical abilities, or by letting the soldier acquire new skills; using technologically advanced equipment worn by the soldier to enhance performance; using nontherapeutic substances or using static dynamic implants (nanomaterials, prostheses) or applying suitable gene therapeutic treatment; and applying enhancement for short- or long-term usage that can even be irreversible provided its effects are controlled'.

[20] Bundeswehr German Armed Forces and UK MoD 2021, p. 18.

[21] Ibid., emphasis in original.

[22] Ibid., p. 19.

> capability—people—is so under-researched... Successful application of human augmentation demands a more sophisticated approach to understanding our people and a way of achieving this is to define the key elements that collectively represent the human platform; these are physical, psychological and social in nature. It is recognised that it is impossible to neatly separate the human into three distinct areas and that this model is a conscious oversimplification.[23]

For the authors of the strategic paper, the triad of physical ('affect the physical environment and move within it'), psychological ('cognition, emotion and motivation'), and social ('ability to perceive oneself as part of a group and the readiness to act as part of the team') performance serves to pinpoint the spheres of influence of different augmentation technologies.[24] These include exoskeletons, sensory augmentation, tele-existence (such as the remote operation of robots), genetic engineering, bioinformatics, brain interfaces, pharmaceuticals, neurostimulation, and augmented reality.[25] The human augmentation paradigm refocuses on the human—or rather a particular version of the human—despite the ubiquitous vision of future warfare: '[w]ar is, by its nature, a human endeavour. So far, technology has not changed the nature of war, but it has changed its character. People will still be central to war but the way in which they play this role will change'.[26] Despite this emphasis, the enhanced or augmented soldier is emblematic of the much wider idea of the technological completion of the human as a deficient entity. This concept aligns with long-standing traditions of countering human deficiencies through technological means. More recently, it bears a strong resemblance to posthumanism and the cybernetic paradigm, which prioritises information over matter.[27]

The general ideas of enhancement and augmentation are historical constants, iteratively adapted to contemporary technological paradigms or trends, with AI representing the latest instantiation. This is especially true for technologies labelled as emerging and disruptive—those 'capable of overturning previous power structures and [that] might allow weaker challengers to overtake the militaries of previously stronger players through innovations'.[28] Examples of such technologies include

---

[23] Ibid.

[24] Ibid., p. 20.

[25] Ibid., p. 28.

[26] Ibid., p. 21: The focus on humans also acknowledges that they 'remain unrivalled (for now) for general intelligence' and when 'the unforeseen happens, people will be required to step in to fulfil the mission, avert crises or seize unforeseen opportunities'.

[27] Hayles 1999. The line can be drawn further back to tools such as shields, spears, or swords in Antiquity or armour plates, bows, and arrows in the Middle Ages used to enhance human capabilities in the military context, see Shunk 2015, p. 92. In many 20th century wars, stimulants such as amphetamines or khat were used to counter fatigue, enhance performance, fight depression or anxiety, ibid., p. 93.

[28] According to the Cluster for Natural and Technical and Science Arms Control Research quoted here, these emerging disruptive technologies include 'hypersonic missiles, military robotics, remotely piloted as well as autonomous and semi-autonomous weapon systems, nanotechnology, various forms of human enhancement, cyber operations, militarily used Artificial Intelligence (AI) and Machine Learning, and even the military use of quantum computers'. https://www.cntrarmscontrol.org/research. Accessed 24 September 2024.

'bio and cognition-inspired designs for robots', 'social/cognitive network science to improve cognitive performance for enhanced distributed collaboration and decision-making in complex network-enabled operations', and 'neuroscience to optimize soldier performance through system design that is consistent with brain function'.[29] These technologies are intended to alleviate the limitations of human cognitive abilities. With the idea of the 'super soldier', these imaginaries borrow inspiration from the realm of fiction.

These imaginaries are also constructed and upheld in ethical and legal discourses, often framed in hypotheticals:

> ...[if] an enhanced soldier's behavior goes out of control and violates the laws of war, who is at fault? Who is responsible? Is it the soldier, the combat leader, or the medical team that created him? Do the laws of war need to be modified to account for enhanced soldiers? Will enemy forces be reluctant to take our enhanced soldiers as prisoners?[30]

As the enhanced soldier seems to transcend human limitations, becoming more machine than soldier, these questions challenge categorisations that are usually non-negotiable: '[w]hat are the ethics of fighting an enemy enhanced soldier who does not feel pain? Will the only way to stop that soldier in battle be to cause severe trauma or death?'[31] Some commentators offer a succinct answer to the question of whether human enhancement could transform soldiers into weapons in violation of international law—namely, a distinct 'Yes'.[32] Other legal scholarship, however, insists that '[d]espite the enhanced status of members of the military or any other person who is the subject of an enhancement (whether pharmacological, cybernetic, genetic or otherwise), they remain, at their core, fundamentally human'.[33]

This is a reminder that in legal and ethical discourses, a normative stance is necessary. Accountability, agency, and intentionality generally require a clear reference object. The purpose of ethical and legal discussions is to restore clarity to the technological and human components, engaging in an epistemological process that disentangles these categories.

In no other technology does this become more of an issue than in the idea of brain-computer interfaces (BCI), which also highlights that human augmentation and enhancement point to an interface problem. The core issue of enhancement is

---

[29] Savage-Knepshield et al. 2016, p. xxv. Nanotechnology is predicted to modify the human body by allowing biochemical control or sensing, influencing cognitive performance, or mechanical enhancement, see Altman 2006, p. 89. Pharmacological interventions through drug stimulants or hormones have undergone many trials and are discussed quite critically: 'the perceived need to improve human biology with drugs may be solving the wrong problem, trying to fit the human to the demands of poorly conceived tactics, tasks, and equipments', see Friedl 2015, p. 71; 'CBRN hardened super soldiers' see Heslop 2019, are envisioned to counter chemical, biological, radiological, and nuclear threats. The imaginary of the 'soldier of the future' is envisioned as 'enhanced through neuroscience, biotechnology, nanotechnology, genetics and drugs' by way of (neural) implants, bionic parts or exoskeletons, see Shunk 2015.

[30] Shunk 2015, p. 96.

[31] Ibid., p. 97.

[32] Lin 2013.

[33] Harrison Dinniss and Kleffner 2016, p. 452.

not the improvement of 'sensorial, physical, or cognitive capacities', but rather the extension or readjustment of relations between the human and their environment—specifically in terms of perception, materiality, and cognition, with interfaces playing a central role. BCIs easily count as the most invasive practice in this regard, elevating the questions of human or machine, and weapon or soldier, to a new level:

> While military human enhancements generally raise questions about the dividing line between the weapon and the human operator, it is hard to conceive of a greater blurring of the lines than that created by the human-machine symbiosis of brain-computer interfaces. Moreover, the use of brain-computer interfaces raises many of the challenging legal questions posed by AI and the growing use of data as well as complex new issues specific to the unique brain-computer connection.[34]

The envisioned potential applications of BCIs 'range from one-way transfer of sensory data from the brain to a computer, to two-way data exchanges between the brain and artificial intelligence systems, providing the human with almost instantaneous access to the power of AI'.[35] This conceptual blurring has significant legal implications for the application of International Humanitarian Law (IHL) (also known as the Law of Armed Conflict). If, for example, an enhanced soldier is captured, it is unclear whether the 'BCI is still active and if the soldier should be considered *hors de combat* and entitled to protection, or whether the soldier's brain is still transmitting data back to headquarters; indeed, it is possible that the soldier may still be able to launch a strike through the BCI'.[36]

A fundamental prerequisite of legal and ethical discourses is the necessary quest for categorical clarity, which often conflicts with the hybrid ambiguity inherent in emerging technologies. Distinctions, such as human/machine, soldier/weapon, and cognition/computation are more heuristic models than accurate reflections of reality.[37] This heuristic approach is performative rather than analytical, ultimately singling out individual humans as the sole sources of agency, intention, or responsibility.

---

[34] Lubell and Al-Khateeb 2022, p. 3.

[35] Ibid., p. 2.

[36] Ibid. According to Protocol Additional to the Geneva Conventions of 12 August 1949, and relating to the Protection of Victims of International Armed Conflicts (Protocol I), opened for signature 8 June 1977, 1125 UNTS 3, entered into force 7 December 1978, Article 31: '1. A person who is recognized or who, in the circumstances, should be recognized to be 'hors de combat' shall not be made the object of attack. 2. A person is 'hors de combat' if: (a) he is in the power of an adverse Party; (b) he clearly expresses an intention to surrender; or (c) he has been rendered unconscious or is otherwise incapacitated by wounds or sickness, and therefore is incapable of defending himself; provided that in any of these cases, he abstains from any hostile act and does not attempt to escape'. Lubell and Al-Khateeb 2022, p. 10, elaborate on the challenges for regulation: 'Perhaps the most obvious one surrounds their categorisation as a means or method of warfare and how they are to be regulated under the weapon review process. But the issues to be addressed are far wider. The aforementioned blurring of the human-machine divide also creates challenges in relation to the rules on targeting and complex new problems in the protection of individuals hors de combat, as well as concerns over accountability for violations'.

[37] See Liivoja and Chirop 2018 for a legal discussion of enhanced warfighters as 'weapons, means, or methods of warfare'.

In this field of conflicting requirements, the interface-centred approach to cognitive processes presented below is not tied to the degree of invasiveness associated with any one technology. Instead, it considers the differing and dynamic ways in which interfaces and technologies are co-constitutive of cognition. This approach does not disregard legal or ethical consequences but suggests rethinking some of their foundational premises. By modelling the role of interfaces in cognitive processes, it provides an analytical framework for human/machine relations.

6.3 An Interface-Centred Approach to Cognition

Technologies of augmentation and enhancement create new modes of (inter)actions and perceptual spaces. This section will discuss the interrelatedness of interface effects—serving as defining components of human/machine relations—and cognition, both of which should be understood as dynamic processes.[38] As a quite general premise: cognitive processes should be modelled as not limited to the human brain—or, functionally speaking, the mind. Instead, they are constituted through dynamic situatedness (the body), relatedness (to the environment external to the body), and performativity (e.g. interactions and movements etc.). Cognitive processes, therefore, depend on mediating forms which enable these relations to be established. The interface—as a functional entity to facilitate a connection between two or more entities—can therefore be utilised to theorise these aspects of mediation in cognitive processes. This prompts several questions, such as: what are the parameters for how the environment is represented via the computer system when addressing human senses? How is the relationship between humans—their senses—and the technical system initiated and maintained? Or, what are the means the system is equipped with to interact with the environment? The last question points to another defining factor, when the system is a proxy for human senses and cognition.[39] The idea of 'distributed cognition' accounts for the increased complexity found in human–computer interactions.[40] Modelled in terms of situatedness and relations (e.g., as mediation and cultural form), cognition and interfaces are close—somewhat complementary—acquaintances.

First, cognition is *not* an isolated processing of sensory stimuli predominantly located in the brain and separate from the external environment. Cognitive processes

[38] It is necessary to note—in a manner that explicates the limitations of the theoretical scope that can be covered here—that this interrelatedness particularly presents itself with a specific set of models reflective of one field of cognitive science combined with an understanding of interfaces that is not merely technical, but entails a much broader range of relations that are established in the mediating effects of interfaces, an approach developed (yet again) in a particular field of media studies.

[39] Cognition is situated in complex sociocultural contexts. It is not limited to declarative knowledge (that is language) and boundaries between the inside (the brain) and the outside have mainly been 'erected for analytical convenience', see Hutchins 1995, p. xiii. It is 'intrinsically a cultural phenomenon', as a co-effect of the organising resources offered by this environment of which media representations are an important part, ibid., pp. xiv–xvi.

[40] Hollan et al. 2000.

are rather instantiated in a complex web of relations, captured in the term 4E cognition, differentiating its embodied, embedded, extended, and enacted aspects.[41] These attributes underline that cognitive processes cannot be split from the human body, as they are inseparably instantiated in its materiality,[42] including sensory capabilities and motor skills (embodied). They are situated within social, cultural, or material settings, constantly redefining the relations to these environments (embedded). As such, they are not reducible or limited to symbolic processing but are instead shaped by external conditions.[43] Cognition is also a dynamic process, never static, and continuously maintained through interactions with the environment (enacted). It also relies on these external factors to be effective (extended). The well-known extended mind hypothesis,[44] emphasises that the environment is not external to cognition but rather an active element within it. The mind of a person is extended in the form of 'a new problem-solving architecture built from an array of resources spanning brain, body, and world'.[45]

Second, cognition does not presuppose consciousness. Most cognitive tasks are solved non-consciously—for example, when grabbing a coffee mug, you normally do not consciously plan the individual steps; it is rather a script that is unconsciously processed. This combination of 4E modelling and the absence of consciousness forms a theoretical premise that functionally dissolves the human/machine divide in the modelling of cognition. The concept of 'cognitive assemblages' captures this functional understanding in lieu of a materialist interpretation of cognition.[46] It allows for an analytical approach to the deep entanglement with a mediated environment that shapes human interactions and perceptions (offering both a social and aesthetic argument) and also points to the repercussions for cognitive processes, expanded by technological agents that are becoming increasingly autonomous.[47]

These assemblages become particularly powerful 'when they function as *systems*, with well-defined interfaces and communication circuits between sensors, actuators, processors, storage media, and distribution networks, and which include human, biological, technical, and material components', pointing to 'the cognitive nonconscious, a term that crucially includes technical as well as human cognizers'.[48] To clarify human/machine relations in this approach, it is helpful to turn to Hayles' illustration, which explains why an assemblage is more than a network, as:

---

[41] It should be noted that the conceptual set, which is summarised under the label of 4E cognition, is far from being a widely shared understanding within cognitive science, see Carney 2020.

[42] The debate between functionalists and materialists in modelling consciousness and cognition is ongoing (e.g., see Chalmers 2022 and Seth 2021). The argument made here takes a materialist approach.

[43] See Shapiro 2014.

[44] Clark and Chalmers 1998.

[45] Clark 2023, p. 169.

[46] Hayles 2016.

[47] See Bächle 2026.

[48] Hayles 2017, pp. 2–3: this presents 'a definition for cognition that applies to technical systems as well as biological life-forms'.

> the configurations in which systems operate are always in transition, constantly adding and dropping components and rearranging connections. For example, when a person turns on her cell phone, she becomes part of a nonconscious cognitive assemblage that includes relay towers and network infrastructures, including switches, fiber optic cables, and/or wireless routers, as well as other components. With the cell phone off, the infrastructure is still in place, but the human subject is no longer a part of that particular cognitive assemblage.[49]

This also clarifies why a model of cognitive processes that acknowledges a techno-media environment is a relevant approach for the study of human enhancement.

In an extension of the 'extended mind' model, Clark also describes the mind as 'coupled systems combining brain, body, and technology', including 'apps, tools, and other 'beyond the brain' resources'.[50] These may 'replicate or bolster skills and abilities' of 'our biological brains' or might be 'enhancing and transforming them'.[51] It is important to note, for the purpose of this argument, that invasive implants are not explicitly needed to create 'cyborg or hybrid minds', because 'the brain learns to simply expect the presence of those resources, factoring their effects into all our planning and actions'.[52] This has significant repercussions for two of the brain's main functions—experiencing and predicting—and their epistemic relevance in the production of knowledge.[53]

These approaches offer a dynamic, decentralised, and hybrid understanding of cognition that is established in relations between humans, (media) technologies, and their epistemic consequences. The next step, then, is to ask the question of how these relations are initiated, maintained, and characterised. The interface—and its major, somewhat contradictory functions of simultaneously separating and connecting different entities—gains a particular relevance as the locus of mediation. It must be emphasised, to prevent a common misunderstanding, that interfaces are not to be simply taken for controllers, keyboards, or computer screens. The interface is better theorised as 'a form of relation that obtains between two or more distinct entities, conditions, or states such that it only comes into being as these distinct entities enter into an active relation with one another'.[54] Contrary to common assumptions, the interface is not simply a device (or its surface) but comes into being within an active relation.[55] Another important conceptualisation is the performative quality of this relation, as interfaces 'perform a distinction or boundary between at least two entities while at the same time establishing relations between those entities'.[56]

[49] Ibid., pp. 2–3.

[50] Clark 2023, p. 148.

[51] Ibid.

[52] Ibid.

[53] See also Sect. 6.4.

[54] Hookway 2014, p. 4.

[55] While this common understanding of interfaces can also be useful, it is important to note that design theories of interfaces usually stress the underlying relations rather than an understanding of the interface as a mere object, see Bonsiepe 1999. For the theorisation of cognition or perception, an (albeit metaphorical) play with the understanding of the interface as an object, turns out to be an unnecessarily limiting approach, cf. Hoffman et al. 2015.

[56] Lipp and Dickel 2022; Galloway 2012.

Thus, the interface becomes part of this relation, shapes it, but can still be distilled as an analytical entity: 'the interface is that form of relation which is defined by the simultaneity and inseparability of its processes of separation and augmentation, of maintaining distinction while at the same time eliding it in the production of a mutualism that may be viewed as an entity in its own right'.[57]

The theorisation of cognitive processes and interfaces (or interfacing) not only presents a degree of mutualism but also complementarity. Interfaces are constitutive factors in the relations established by the embodied and extended mind. Their impermanence is mirrored in the adaptability and constant performative re-establishing, characterised by the enacted aspect of cognition. Analytically, the relational model of cognitive processes allows for the integration of interfaces, which can be treated as entities in their own right, having their share in shaping and augmenting these relations, and, in turn, cognition itself. Functionally, the interface establishes a human/machine relation even before a role, such as 'user' or 'operator', is performatively engaged.

As an 'entity in its own right' that can be analytically foregrounded, the relevant parameters involve the material structure, aesthetic qualities, and functionality of the interface. The relations are manifold, encompassing not only general human/machine figurations (e.g., the possibilities of control or intervention) but also the ways in which the processes of symbolic conversion translate back and forth across the computer system's boundary between internal and external elements (i.e., human/machine/environment). The study of interfaces reflects on the many modes in which human perception, agency, or decision-making is partly shaped by the design of interfaces, thereby structuring human cognition.

The psychological 'theory of affordances' introduced an interactionist model, prioritising the situatedness of perception and agency in a given environment that 'offers', 'provides', or 'furnishes' something to the perceiving agent.[58] As a consequence, any particular situation prioritises particular relations, thus shaping certain actions and perceptions. The idea of affordances has also been embraced in design theory, where it captures the quality of an object to communicate how the object can be used.[59] While the relation between user and object is acknowledged, the concept—as it is applied in the design of digital environments, robotic or software systems—often locates specific properties within the object itself:[60] some perceptions are 'ready-made' to be seen. This can tempt the observer to ascribe an essentialist quality to certain perceptions, mistakenly interpreting them as natural, which leads to an 'error in *post hoc propter hoc* reasoning by assuming that properties located

---

[57] Hookway 2014, p. 4.

[58] Gibson 1979.

[59] Norman 2002.

[60] This can be exemplified by the design affordances discussed in robotics, where a 'robot's appearance' is seen as 'an important affordance because people tend to assume that the robot's capabilities will be commensurate with its appearance. If a robot looks like a human, it is expected to act like a human; if it has eyes, it should see; if it has arms, it should be able to pick up things and might be able to shake hands', see Bartneck et al. 2020, p. 45.

by actors in contexts of use must somehow have been there prior to their use case, thereby making them perspicuous for action in the first place'.[61]

The ensuing insight is highly relevant for the study of human augmentation as a military technology practice, as it also highlights the need to address 'the user's situated accomplishment in producing or making perspicuous qualities of use relevant to their problem at hand. There is, of course, a parallel, no less situated accomplishment on behalf of the designer(s) that make such qualities appear to be natural, psychological, or decontextualized, and otherwise devoid of politics'.[62] This lays bare a tension that is difficult to grasp analytically, namely between the 'taxonomies and assumptions about the material or political conditions of software usage' on the one hand, and 'the creative, flexible, and sometimes unexpected things that actors do with such technologies' on the other.[63]

This is also applicable to the discourse on augmentation and the repercussions for agency and autonomy. The act of employing support systems functionally equals corresponds to a 'scaffolding' of human abilities that also includes devices such as wheelchairs, prostheses, or exoskeletons. A reflection of human autonomy and disability also provides an important reminder that referring to 'human abilities' *per se* that are being 'augmented' bears a normative stance: the context sensitivity and functionality of human (dis)abilities 'opens up space for thinking of "scaffolded" capacities as not thereby necessarily less genuine'.[64] The second continuity—rather than a categorical shift—in human/machine abilities is the historicity of 'mediality' (i.e., the particular aesthetics of media forms) in cognitive processes. The flashy character of digital media environments, augmented reality, or smartphone displays should not distract us from the fact that the agential or perceptual modes of human/machine relations predate digital technologies by far.[65] Calculators, media-specific aesthetics (e.g., photography), or the extension of human senses (e.g., field glasses) have long shaped cognitive relations with the world, with the interface as part of this relation.[66]

An interface-centred framework for conceptualising the augmentation of cognitive processes therefore accounts for the different dimensions of relations that are relevant

---

[61] Vertesi 2019, p. 371.

[62] Ibid.

[63] Ibid.

[64] Anderson 2022, p. 160.

[65] Krämer 2015.

[66] Post-phenomenological approaches, in an effort to extend the hybrid modelling of Science and Technology Studies and the material turn in phenomenology, emphasise the importance of 'studying how human beings make technologies epistemologically, ethically, and metaphysically relevant in conversations and interactions', putting the emphasis back on human beings and the ways in which they 'give meaning to their mediating roles', see Verbeek 2016, p. 5. Its goal is to better understand the 'dynamics of human-technology relations, and the interplay between technological mediations and human appropriations', ibid., p. 6. The interface theory-based approach to cognitive processes proposed here neither prioritises materiality nor 'human beings' but rather the mediated relations that co-create these elements.

for cognitive processes (extended, embodied, enacted, and embedded), while particularly reflecting on the role of interfaces in mediating these relations. It sheds a unique light on reference terms often evoked in the legal and ethical debates surrounding military AI, as it conceptually—and out of epistemic necessity—renounces the 'de-hybridisation' of categories. Consequently, it is at odds with the idea of fixed reference objects for responsibility or intentionality in agency or decision-making. Historically, law and ethics have always been able to performatively establish responsibility, accountability, intention, or guilt, for example via case-based applied ethics or as the result of court proceedings. There is an obvious incongruity with current technological discourses that seek to integrate ethical or legal compliance directly into the technology, a technological *a priori* fuelled by AI-solutionist expectations. The conceptual hybridity, however, is diametrically opposed to this quest.

The interface-based framework prioritises a perspective that emphasises the default state of cognitive relationality, rather than promoting clear shifts driven by technological advances, such as through digitalisation or the invasiveness of brain-computer interfaces. In essence, it also argues against a normative stance of human augmentation that implies a set of human capabilities as a benchmark—a homogenous idea of human capabilities—extended with the help of technologies.

In light of these premises, the concluding section explores three key fields of cognition that are frequently evoked as major areas of human augmentation in the military context: agency, decision-making, and (de)skilling; situational awareness; and predictions.

6.4 The Cognition of Human/Machine Soldiers

The interface-centred framework developed in the previous section provides an approach to enhancement and augmentation that foregrounds technologies associated with cognitive processes. The NCW paradigm discussed above places particular emphasis on the cognitive domain, which:

> . . .is in the mind of the warfighter. This is the realm of EBO [effects-based operations].[67] Many, though not all, battles, campaigns, and wars are won in this domain. The intangibles of leadership, morale, unit cohesion, level of training and experience, and situational awareness are elements of this domain. This is the domain where commander's intent, doctrine, tactics, techniques, and procedures reside. This is also where decisive battlespace concepts and tactics emerge.[68]

[67] Explanation added by T.C.B.

[68] Cebrowski 2005, p. 20. Other fields include the physical ('the traditional domain of warfare where a force is moved through time and space') and information ('where information is created, manipulated, and shared') domains. It also extends to the social, 'where humans interact, exchange information, form shared awareness and understandings, and make collaborative decisions' and cultural ('the set of values, attitudes, and beliefs held and conveyed by leaders to the society, whether military or civil'), ibid.

The network is seen as a means to synchronise individual cognitive processes and render them to form an effective collective: 'shared sensemaking—the process of going from shared awareness to shared understanding to collaborative decision making—is a socio-cognitive activity'.[69]

The augmentation of cognitive processes particularly concerns how the environment is represented via the computer system or how it enables intervention by offering human senses the modalities in which the relationship between humans and the system is initiated or maintained. Brunyé et al. identify a long list of organisations, accounting for 'over 15,000 scientists and engineers' that are involved in 'research and development targeting human cognitive performance enhancement' in the US military context.[70] Cognitive enhancement is not limited to technological interventions but is pursued 'across the pharmaceutical, dietary, neuroscientific, instructional, technological, and sleep-related domains'.[71] Companies like Neuralink showcase high-profile advancements in the field of BCI, such as chips or threads containing electrodes that are implanted into the human brain.[72] What occurs much more frequently—and even subtly—is a wide range of non-invasive BCIs, including augmented reality (AR) glasses or even smartphones, by the help of which perceptions and sensations are enhanced with information and mediated social interactions, which in turn, extend cognitive relations.[73]

The following aspects of augmented cognition focus on the use of digital augmentation and enhancement technologies envisioned for the enhanced/augmented human soldier. The act of looking at augmentation through the prism of cognition reveals often implicit premises beneath the surface of these seemingly 'new' technologies.

---

[69] Ibid.

[70] Brunyé et al. 2020, pp. 453–454. The shared goal 'is to increase the ability to achieve and sustain military dominance through accelerated training and skill acquisition, targeted assessment and feedback, and increased vigilance, threat detection, situation awareness, decision-making, teamwork, and emotional control', ibid., p. 454. The scope of the projects that Brunyé et al. 2020, p. 454, identify as having a 'a primary emphasis on cognitive enhancement' ranges widely and includes topics such as 'Soldier Tactical Readiness and Effectiveness', 'Restorative Sleep for Performance and Health' or 'Sleep-on-Demand', 'Noninvasive Neuromodulation for Warfighter Performance Enhancement' and 'Biomedical Performance Enhancement'.

[71] Brunyé et al. 2020, p. 463. Regarding mainly technological means of optimisation, European projects such as the German Bundeswehr 'Infantryman of the Future' or the UK's Generic Soldier Architecture focus on 'soldier systems'. These initiatives strive for the integration of human soldiers with military equipment, framed as a problem of interfaces and software standards, see Thadani 2022. See also GOSSRA 2018, which seeks to develop standards that cover 'electronics, voice and data communication, software, human interface devices, sensors, and effectors'.

[72] The Neuralink mission statement reads as follows: 'Our Mission. Create a generalized brain interface to restore autonomy to those with unmet medical needs today and unlock human potential tomorrow'. https://neuralink.com/. Accessed 03 May 2025.

[73] The DARPA project 'Next-Generation Nonsurgical Neurotechnology' seeks to develop 'high-performance, bi-directional brain-machine interfaces for able-bodied service members. Such interfaces would be enabling technology for diverse national security applications such as control of unmanned aerial vehicles and active cyber defense systems or teaming with computer systems to successfully multitask during complex military missions'. https://www.darpa.mil/program/next-generation-nonsurgical-neurotechnology. Accessed 26 September 2024.

This is the case for (at least) the following three key areas: (i) agency, non- and (un)conscious decision-making (pointing to the illusion of the soldier as a rational and conscious subject); (ii) situational awareness (pointing to the illusion of an objective reality made available to a rational operator); and (iii) predictions (pointing to the illusion of a predictable future).

6.4.1 Agency, Non- and (Un)conscious Decision-Making[74]

The German Bundeswehr and UK MoD Strategy Paper on Human Augmentation explains that 'the role of people is being challenged in three key areas: data, complexity and speed'.[75] The vast amounts of data generated in today's computer and media environments can no longer be processed by humans alone, which is why they increasingly rely on machines to alleviate cognitive burdens and filter relevant information.[76] The networked character of technology and the interconnectedness of devices, media, and users result in a potentially infinite complexity. Additionally, the heightened role of machine learning (ML) and AI-based automated decision-making increases the necessary speed required to act.

The Defense Advanced Research Projects Agency's (DARPA) Biological Technologies Office offers insight into how human augmentation is envisioned to solve these challenges, particularly via 'new capabilities for intuitively interfacing with complex systems. For example, emerging technologies such as noninvasive neural interfaces are imagined to, in the future, allow pilots to control groups of unmanned aircraft by delivering high-level commands and maintaining oversight while the systems adjust to rapidly changing conditions to complete the mission' (see Fig. 6.1 below).[77]

Interfacing constitutes these relations and instantiates cognitive processes, making it the core of human augmentation:

> Human beings are embedded much more intricately into the military technological systems logic, as operator and functional element, in the pursuit of speed and optimization... there is considerable interest in developing technologies that facilitate smoother and more functional teaming between the human and computational systems through so-called neural interface technologies.[78]

---

[74] This terminology distinguishes the states of conscious and unconscious for human acts of cognition. Technology, however, is neither conscious nor unconscious, which is why neither term applies. As discussed above, Hayles introduces the 'cognitive nonconscious' as a model of cognition that 'includes technical as well as human cognizers' (see Sect. 6.3). Based on this idea, the term *nonconscious decision-making* is proposed here to more accurately reflect the nonconscious processes of decision-making that are negotiated within the complex relations between human and technological elements.

[75] Bundeswehr German Armed Forces and UK MoD 2021, p. 20.

[76] Horlings et al. 2023.

[77] DARPA 2018, p. 78.

[78] Favaro and Schwarz 2022.

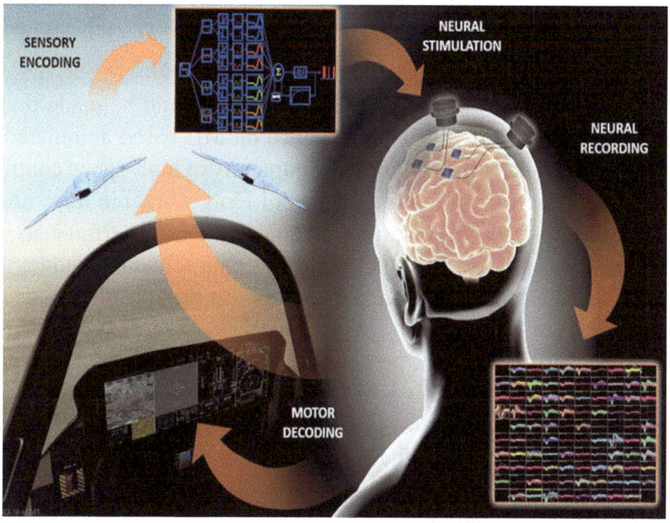

Fig. 6.1 DARPA's vision of 'intuitively interfacing with complex systems' through 'non-invasive neural interface', as 'the pace and complexity of modern combat increases' and 'warfighters require new tools to help them stay meaningfully engaged'.[79] *Source* DARPA 2018, p. 78

The efficiency of interfacing, with the design gold standard of being intuitive, is both the problem and the solution in these complex, high-speed, and automation-heavy technological environments.

The synchronisation of 'manned and unmanned platforms', as promoted by NCW and MUM-T (see Sect. 6.2), makes commentators wonder: '[h]ow do units, teams, and crews get to the point where they can synchronize, combine, and produce synergy? I know this is coming from an "old guy" but TRAINING is the key'.[80] Training—as the internalisation of rules that make the system work effectively and in sync—not only conceptually overlaps with NCW. It is functionally equivalent to extending the algorithmic logic of linear, step-by-step problem-solving to the human agent as one element within a larger whole. The processing of recipe-style knowledge, a skill, is the result of internalised scripts. This even extends to situations that are, by definition, uncertain.

One of the major downsides of cognitive augmentation is the danger of losing non-supported human capabilities in the wake of increased reliance on automated knowledge production or decision-making. Contrary to the desired effect, additional sources of information may even render human decision-making more difficult or produce unique biases:

> When human decision-makers get used to trusting the technology to detect threats, instead of exercising their own judgement and skill, it leads to de-skilling or diminished risk assessment capabilities. This means, for example, that when a sensor is damaged, the aircrew (who have

[79] Ibid.

[80] Taylor 2014, p. 5.

been trained to rely on that sensor) may be less capable of exercising human judgement based on other sources of information.[81]

A plausible but also somewhat foreseeable argument could be made that this type of de-skilling only intensifies with overreliance on ML-based automated decision-making. The frenzy of data, the networked complexity of high-speed communication and knowledge production all require the use of tools which, in turn, often leave a mark that goes unnoticed.[82] AI is used to analyse data, determine its relevance, and prompt specific options. Still, the totality of data remains opaque, the bias of relevance criteria is usually unknown, and the options provided may curtail creative problem-solving.[83]

While this concern should not be discounted, what is sometimes overlooked in this line of argument is that AI is still (only) a tool. The human decision-making process depends on the level of trust placed in the AI system.[84] This also models the human operator as a conscious subject, or in other words: a figuration of a rational subject making conscious decisions—an idealisation against a vision that is seen as marred by AI-enabled technology.

Turning to the idea of the technical nonconscious, introduced above, the human operator's cognitive processes may become part of a complex assemblage that is continuously in flux. Human nonconscious cognitive processes (not the conscious ones, as the quest for responsibility and intent implies) are analogous to the technical nonconscious: 'Like human nonconscious cognition, technical cognition processes information faster than consciousness, discerns patterns and draws inferences... Moreover, technical cognitions are designed specifically to keep human consciousness from being overwhelmed by massive informational streams so large, complex, and multifaceted that they could never be processed by human brains'.[85] Modelled as analogues, the human and the technical nonconscious cannot be distinguished by a before-and-after technical development, the degree of intervention, or invasiveness (e.g., along the lines of external interfaces and implants), but rather form a continuum. As Hayles states, 'biological and technical cognitions are now so deeply entwined that it is more accurate to say they interpenetrate one another'.[86]

---

[81] Krebs 2023, p. 1702.

[82] Recent events and reports at the time of writing are stark reminders of the risks this entails. A report by '+972 magazine' (Abraham 2024), on the use of automated systems by the Israel Defense Forces (IDF) to select human targets in Gaza details a particular (unconfirmed) practice. One of the operators of the Lavender system is quoted as saying: 'At first, we did checks to ensure that the machine didn't get confused. But at some point we relied on the automatic system, and we only checked that [the target] was a man—that was enough. It doesn't take a long time to tell if someone has a male or a female voice'.

[83] See Marcus 2018 for a discussion of some of these issues.

[84] Roesler et al. 2024. For a discussion of the 'moral-psychological implications for combatants with increasing autonomy in weapon systems', including the 'illusion of control' and 'sentiments of distrust in technology', see also the contribution by Molendijk et al. in this volume (Chap. 7).

[85] Hayles 2017, p. 11.

[86] Ibid.

The concept of bounded rationality—well-recognised in military contexts—aptly points to the fact that decision-making processes are always limited in their rationality by factors such as time, information, or cognitive ability, among others. Still, the discourse on de-skilling or the crippling of human agency often reverts to an ideal that never existed: the illusion of the soldier, not just as a *rational* subject but also one whose decisions are always *conscious*. Regarding the latter, it is especially noteworthy to address the question of how computer- and AI-enabled 'rapid processing is traded-off against consciousness'.[87] This becomes particularly consequential when a BCI enables the circumvention of human consciousness. Simply put, perceptions and sensations occur subconsciously, with only a fraction becoming conscious. For instance, human cognition may subconsciously detect an incoming enemy missile long before a conscious decision can be made on whether or how to engage it. Based on this latency, Noll presents the following scenario:

> A military mastering the integration of that subconscious signal into a weapon system would be able to save time by bypassing human consciousness. Such a military would possess an across-the-board superiority over enemy forces still relying on the traditional pathway from human perception over human consciousness to a human command to the weapons system. I will call 'neuroweapons' those weapons systems that (i) integrate neuronal and synaptic activities of the human brain into a weapons system, and (ii) in doing so, significantly reduce the role of human consciousness before engaging a target.[88]

The performative de-hybridisation of concepts such as responsibility or intent is a largely language-based endeavour, always requiring a complex transfer from unconscious and nonconscious processes into consciousness. Noll concludes that 'IHL cannot be applied by operators of BMI weapons systems of this kind, unless the deploying military takes the time for a human review of all targeting decisions through a superior before the target is engaged'.[89] But even the modelling of these processes is fragile, as it implies a seemingly clear-cut and traceable distinction between the conscious, unconscious, and nonconscious realms.

Astonishingly, this type of cognitive enhancement reduces the human mind to a mere function, namely that of a sensor within a larger computational network where the actual machine-based decision-making takes place. Paradoxically, it is not the human who is being enhanced—it is the computational system that is augmented by the human brain.

6.4.2 *Situational Awareness*

Another imaginary drawn from the idea of augmentation is the enhancement of human situational awareness, expanding it into a technologically objectified version

---

[87] Noll 2014, p. 203.

[88] Ibid., p. 207. Consequently, 'IHL cannot be applied where neuroweapons disintegrate the cognitive unity of man and downgrade the role of language in cognition', as language is necessary to retrospectively reconstruct a decision, ibid., p. 204.

[89] Ibid., p. 215.

for rational and conscious human operators. In military contexts, 'cross reality' serves as an umbrella term for 'virtual reality, mixed reality, and augmented reality', envisioned as a broad set of applications that can be used for training or for 'improving situational awareness on operations'.[90] Military strategy papers voice the expectation that augmented reality systems (such as AR glasses) 'could include overlaid information on friendly, enemy and civilian locations, geography and weapon engagement zones. This enhanced understanding could improve the speed and quality of decision-making, as well as the application of military capability'.[91] As developed above, the augmentation of human capabilities is to be understood as part of the idea of NCW, which is characterised 'the ability of geographically dispersed forces to attain a high level of shared battlespace awareness that is exploited to achieve strategic, operational, and tactical objectives in accordance with the commander's intent. This linking of people, platforms, weapons, sensors, and decision aids into a single network creates a whole that is clearly greater than the sum of its parts'.[92]

Within this larger NCW framework, human cognitive abilities have been identified as weak spots, with augmentation being the solution. Aspirations of the military industry therefore share the tendency to mirror this human-centric approach in the development of military technologies, framing the soldier as part of the 'system'. This human-centred rhetoric is utilised as a marketing strategy to promote AWS while highlighting the interfacing problem between humans and machines.[93]

Even though insinuated otherwise by current technological and military strategy discourses, the discussion of situational awareness as a critical factor in system operation has a long conceptual history.[94] Circling back to the interface-centric approach to cognitive processes developed above: Clark theorises the brain as an 'experience machine', underlining the idea of the 'natural-born cyborg',[95] reminding us that it is a 'mistake to think that human–machine hybridization must always depend on wires and implants. Instead, what matters is the reliance of the biological parts on capacities made available by the nonbiological parts'—analytically always catering towards 'a larger hybrid whole'.[96] The biological brain is entangled with symbolic and material structures, 'nonbiological' media environments that nonetheless constitute cognition.

---

[90] Bundeswehr German Armed Forces and UK MoD 2021, p. 36.

[91] Ibid., p. 37.

[92] Cebrowski 2005, p. 1.

[93] As of 2024, the German arms manufacturer Rheinmetall praises the 'open, modular and scalable architecture' of its GLADIUS 2.0 product, which it claims 'remains unrivalled worldwide for its user-centric soldier system solution. An up-to-date situational awareness with a consistent, stable communication infrastructure enables operational sensor-to-shooter networks. GLADIUS 2.0 guarantees a decisive advantage on the digital battlefield under even the most challenging of conditions!'. https://www.rheinmetall.com/en/products/c4i/soldier-system-gladius. Accessed 25 September 2024. In 2024 XTEND Defense frames its products as providing 'Human-centric interface for complex decision-making', in a paradoxical marketing move, even labelling autonomous systems as 'human-guided'. https://defense.xtend.me/. Accessed 25 September 2024.

[94] Cf. Endsley 1995.

[95] Clark 2023. See also Clark 2004.

[96] Clark 2023, p. 153.

Following the premise of the hybrid mind, Clark identifies two perspectives—essentially two key functions—that are characteristic of what, in his model of human cognition, he calls 'the predictive brain'.[97] First, there is the function of 'epistemic actions', described as 'actions selected to improve our state of knowledge rather than to directly achieve some practical goals' (e.g., checking the bus schedule first when your overarching goal is to reach the airport in time for a flight). The second function is 'thinking about action—including epistemic actions—as controlled by prediction'.[98]

The idea of augmentation—extending beyond military contexts through the imaginary of mixed reality environments—strongly points to the need for conceptual continuity rather than a drastic redesign of human cognitive abilities. While the technological promises of heightened situational awareness may be accurate, they do not change the brain's fundamental constant functions: processing information from internal and external resources to reach goals and predict outcomes. Still, a distinct interface modality shapes the relations of cognitive processes. When media change, the modality of cognitive mediation changes.

For the cognition of the augmented soldier, this human/machine figuration evokes the illusion of an objective—or at least more valid—reality that is made available to the human operator, optimising situational awareness and the ability to predict outcomes more accurately. What it does not account for, however, is that present awareness is not reducible to a technological problem or one of interface optimisation; it is rather shaped within relational cognitive processes. In other words, situational awareness should not be equated with knowledge provided through symbolic representations via user interfaces that strive for an ever-increasing degree of information-rich perfection. While the modality of the cognitive relations may change, the basic functions of epistemic action and prediction persist. Therefore, let us turn now to the latter.

6.4.3 Predictions

One of the starkest visions of AI in combat is the idea that

> the primordial elements of violence and passion, which intensely influence human judgments in war, will be mitigated by a greater reliance on objective criteria programmed into machine learning (ML) algorithms to aid human judgement and decision making. The element of chance will always remain in war, but artificially intelligent machines are becoming increasingly adept at forecasting probabilities and could reduce some of war's inherent fog and friction.[99]

Leveraging AI directly to enhance analytic strategies, awareness, and prediction capabilities lies at the core of the promise of the augmented soldier. The current discourse

---

[97] Ibid., p. 151.

[98] Ibid., p. 148.

[99] Gorman 2019, p. 45.

on AI-assisted systems often presupposes the superiority of certain knowledge. In other words, it is reflective of a promise of more precise predictions, seemingly providing a firmer grasp of control over the future.

This gesture of projecting control onto simulation techniques is also not without a long tradition. Wargaming, a practice that began in early 19th century Prussia, sought to anticipate the complex decision-making necessary in battleground scenarios as part of military training. Clausewitz's 'fog of war' element was later added to the simulation through chance scenarios determined by the roll of a dice. Contemporary AI discourses echo this tradition, as evidenced by emphatic postulations such as 'It Is Time to Democratize Wargaming Using Generative AI', fitting witness to the gist of contemporary AI-tech discourses, where the authors explain that

> rather than directly relying on human players sitting around a table to play a game, the twenty-first-century analyst can use generative AI and LLMs to create game agents... Imagine a new type of wargame where a collection of decision-makers—human players—interacts with AI-generated role players, similar to most modern video games.[100]

Even though the interface—the virtual video game environment—may make this seem like a giant leap from the original wargame, this shift is not too significant of a step when conceptualised in terms of the epistemic actions and predictions involved in human cognition. This is especially true when considering that the whole of human experience is based on informed predictions, which mediate between mind and reality.

The machine is not capable of eliminating ambiguity or uncertainty. Nonetheless, it seems to be quite effective in performatively reducing the feeling of uncertainty and compensating for a lack of control. This cognitive relation between human and machine is the actual site of augmentation—irrespective of whether there is a digital or AI element. It is based on a particular way of forming cognitive processes through adaptation that takes shape in human/machine interactions. This general process of adaptation is subjected to particular trajectories in military contexts, namely through the use of formalised training.[101] Simulations, media environments, and interfaces are widely employed for 'targeted training', which is 'designed to directly influence the rate or extent of knowledge or skill acquisition in a specialized domain'.[102] These include 'multimedia learning experiences that increase the realism and vividness of learning materials, integrate multiple sensory modalities', or 'simulation-based training that emulates real-world training tasks and environments to increase the realism, fidelity, and user engagement'.[103]

---

[100] Jensen et al. 2024

[101] These techniques include 'inhibitory control training' to 'improve shooting performance', 'visual search training', which 'might improve security screening', and 'raw intelligence processing' or 'working memory training'. Such methods may be applied to 'high cognitive workload tasks such as flying modern military aircraft, and attention training', which 'might have applications for watchstanding duties', see Blacker et al. 2019, p. 30.

[102] Brunyé et al. 2020, pp. 455–456. Feedback methods 'encourage critical self-reflection and growth, error recognition and correction, and deeper understanding'.

[103] Ibid.

Again, it is a new type of interfacing, which introduces multimodal (i.e., visual, auditory and haptic) environments to increase the 'realism and vividness' that makes the difference for cognitive augmentation. This training is similar to the linear—algorithmic—processing of well-defined steps to fulfil a task. From the perspective of the brain as a 'prediction machine', this training is a drill of epistemic actions that functionally leads to the retrieval and execution of predefined expectations. The simulated process knowledge is internalised and determines future predictions. On the one hand, this speaks to a continuous development, namely the necessary 'artificiality of the human mind',[104] which is formed through social interactions, technological support systems, and acts of mediation. On the other hand, a change in the modality of what enables these relations has an effect on the mind and cognitive processes. The hypermedia, interactive environment is designed to closely engage the human senses, offering a high degree of immersion for human perception. Hence, cognitive training that implements particular epistemic actions and abilities to predict a specific version of reality in the human soldier's mind could already be seen as challenging the precarious line between human and machine—soldier and weapon—which so far had only been a purely hypothetical scenario in the context of BCI.

The AI-assisted creation of knowledge about future scenarios, combined with self-proclaimed realism in experiencing the simulation, creates yet another chimaera—the reassuring illusion of a predictable future, or rather, the illusion of control in the face of what is, by definition, void of rules, norms, and security: the chaos that is met in the dismal fog of war.

6.5 Conclusion

The approach presented in this chapter outlines an interface-based conceptualisation of cognitive processes to theorise the idea of human augmentation in military contexts. The relational character of human cognition is to be regarded as a historical constant, continuously reestablished under any contemporary socio-technical circumstances. The augmentation of human cognition not only challenges the desired meanings of responsibility or agency. The act of identifying the substrate of 'the human' in the augmented figuration even calls into question the very foundational notion that there has *ever* been a normative idea of human intentionality, the abstraction of human agency as a clear and rational form or a clear-cut divide between machine and human.

When examining the ethical and legal implications, one often encounters a strikingly counter-intuitive contradiction. On the one hand, in the wake of AI, there seems to be a growing tendency to treat questions of ethical decision-making and legal accountability as matters of *technological* design that are to be solved *before* employment. This marks a departure from previous technologies—such as AI-free guns, missiles, and mines—which were never expected to be ethically or legally

[104] Krämer 2022.

conforming agents. The reason for this shift lies in the major expectations placed on AI, effectively treating it as an intelligent entity, which suffices to make a special case for this technology. On the other hand, the established performative techniques in ethical and legal meaning-making remain intact, despite the seemingly novel possibilities introduced by AI, by tracing responsibility or intentionality in case-based ethical analyses or court proceedings.

The performative de-hybridisation of concepts, characteristic of these endeavours to stabilise categories, has become an even greater challenge in light of the increased invasiveness and ubiquity of technology, particularly relevant in human augmentation. These challenges range from normative ideas such as human intentionality (often implicitly designed as a product of a conscious state) and the abstraction of human agency as a clear and rational form, to the fundamental divide between machine and human. The act of focusing on the relational characteristics of human cognition lays bare a range of illusions, including the concepts of the conscious subject, objective reality, or the rationally proceeding operator.[105]

The model of the human mind as forming a nonconscious assemblage, with its dynamic dependencies on external relations, emphasises that the sought-after conceptual stability—such as machine vs. human, combatant vs. non-combatant, weapon vs. soldier, responsibility, and intention—is more of a gesture than a realistically achievable goal. Many of the legal and ethical discourses are based on this quest for conceptual clarity. This overlooks, however, that the human/machine relationship has always been messy, raising the question of why AI debates demand a clarity that has, for the large part, been unattainable with preceding types of technology. AI-enabled weapons and augmented soldiers are markedly different from the bow-and-arrow fighters of previous eras. The question, however, on the 'essence of combatants'—and the equation of soldier and weapon—is not new to our AI-laden times, neither in the epistemological nor in the ethical or legal sense.[106]

Acknowledgements This text was written within the framework of the research network *Meaningful Human Control —Autonomous Weapon Systems between Regulation and Reflection*, funded by the German Federal Ministry of Research, Technology and Space (BMFTR) (grant number 01UG2206C).

---

[105] This is not to say that there is no technological change or a shifting balance in the human/machine assemblage which—as argued—is largely a consequence of new modes of interfacing cognitive processes.

[106] See Chamayou 2015 for a contemporary discussion of 19th-century philosopher Georg Wilhelm Friedrich Hegel's position on war.

References

Books, Articles, and Other Documents

Abraham Y (2024) Lavender: The AI machine directing Israel's bombing spree in Gaza. https://www.972mag.com/lavender-ai-israeli-army-gaza/. Accessed 24 September 2024

Alberts DS, Garstka JJ, Stein FP (1999) Network centric warfare: Developing and Leveraging Information Superiority. https://apps.dtic.mil/sti/citations/ADA406255. Accessed 23 September 2024

Altman J (2006) Military Nanotechnology. Potential applications and preventive arms control. Routledge, London/New York

Anderson J (2022) Scaffolding and Autonomy. In: Colburn B (ed) The Routledge Handbook of Autonomy. Routledge, London, pp. 158–166

Bächle TC (2026) Autonomous systems, Concepts of the digital society. Internet Policy Review (forthcoming)

Bartneck C, Belpaeme T, Eyssel F, Kanda T, Keijsers M, Sabanovic S (2020) Human-robot interaction: An introduction. Cambridge University Press, Cambridge

Blacker KJ, Hamilton J, Roush G, Pettijohn KA, Biggs AT (2019) Cognitive Training for Military Application: A Review of the Literature and Practical Guide. Journal of Cognitive Enhancement. https://doi.org/10.1007/s41465-018-0076-1

Bonsiepe G (1999) Interface: An Approach to Design. Uitgeverij De Balie, Amsterdam

Bousquet AJ (2022) The Scientific Way of Warfare: Order and Chaos on the Battlefields of Modernity, 2nd edn. Hurst, London

Bousquet A, Grove J, Shah N (2020) Becoming war: Towards a martial empiricism. Security Dialogue. https://doi.org/10.1177/0967010619895660

Bradshaw JM, Hoffman RR, Woods DD, Johnson M (2013) The Seven Deadly Myths of 'Autonomous Systems'. IEEE Intelligent Systems 28:54–61

Brunyé TT, Brou R, Doty TJ, Gregory FD, Hussey EK, Lieberman HR, Loverro KL, Mezzacappa ES, Neumeier WH, Patton DJ, Soares JW, Thomas TP, Yu AB (2020) A Review of US Army Research Contributing to Cognitive Enhancement in Military Contexts. Journal of Cognitive Enhancement. https://doi.org/10.1007/s41465-020-00167-3

Bundeswehr German Armed Forces, UK Ministry of Defence (MoD) (2021) Human Augmentation. The Dawn of a New Paradigm. A strategic implications project. https://assets.publishing.service.gov.uk/media/609d23c6e90e07357baa8388/Human_Augmentation_SIP_access2.pdf. Accessed 25 September 2024

Carney J (2020) Thinking avant la lettre: A Review of 4E Cognition. Evolutionary studies in imaginative culture. https://doi.org/10.26613/esic/4.1.172

Cebrowski AK (2005) The Implementation of Network-Centric Warfare. https://apps.dtic.mil/sti/citations/ADA446831. Accessed 7 March 2024

Chalmers D J (2022) Reality+: Virtual Worlds and the Problems of Philosophy. W. W. Norton & Company, New York City

Chamayou G (2015) Drone Theory. Penguin, London

Clark A (2004) Natural-Born Cyborgs: Minds, Technologies, and the Future of Human Intelligence. Oxford University Press, Oxford

Clark A (2023) The Experience Machine. How Our Minds Predict and Shape Reality. Penguin, London

Clark A, Chalmers D (1998) The Extended Mind. Analysis 58:7–19

Connable B (2018) Human Terrain System is Dead, Long Live … What? Building and Sustaining Military Cultural Competence in the Aftermath of the Human Terrain System. Military Review January-February:24–33 https://www.armyupress.army.mil/Journals/Military-Review/English-Edition-Archives/January-February-2018/Human-Terrain-System-is-Dead-Long-Live-What/. Accessed 26 September 2024

DARPA (2018) Defense Advanced Research Projects Agency: 60 years, 1958–2018. https://www.darpa.mil/attachments/darapa60_publication-no-ads.pdf. Accessed 23 September 2024

de Boisboissel G, Le Masson, J-M (2021) The Enhanced Soldier. Definitions. Military Review. https://www.armyupress.army.mil/Journals/Military-Review/Online-Exclusive/2021-French-OLE/Part-2-Definitions/. Accessed 23 September 2024

Edwards PN (1997) The Closed World. Computers and the Politics of Discourse in Cold War America. MIT Press, Cambridge MA

Ellison K, Wellner K (2013) Social Scientists and the Human Terrain System (HTS) Project. Online Ethics Center. https://doi.org/10.18130/f90z-zp13

Endsley MR (1995) Toward a Theory of Situation Awareness in Dynamic Systems. Human Factors. https://doi.org/10.1518/001872095779049543

Eshel T (2019) Manned-Unmanned Teaming. European Security & Defence 10:53–57

Favaro M, Schwarz E (2022) Human Augmentation and Nuclear Risk: The Value of a Few Seconds. Arms Control Today 52:20–25

Friedl KE (2015) U.S. Army Research on Pharmacological Enhancement of Soldier Performance: Stimulants, Anabolic Hormones, and Blood Doping. Journal of Strength and Conditioning Research. https://doi.org/10.1519/JSC.0000000000001027

Galloway A R (2012) The Interface Effect. Polity, Cambridge

Gibson JJ (1979) The Ecological Approach to Visual Perception. Houghton Mifflin, Boston

Gorman RR (2019) Next Generation Intelligence Integration: Leveraging Artificial Intelligence to Enhance Human-Machine Analytic Collaboration. Marine Corps Gazette 103:45–49

GOSSRA (2018) Generic Open Soldier System Reference Architecture (GOSSRA), EDA Project Sheet. https://eda.europa.eu/docs/default-source/projects/padr-gossra-projectweb_v2.pdf. Accessed 24 September 2024

Harrison Dinniss HA, Kleffner J K (2016) Soldier 2.0: Military Human Enhancement and International Law. International Law Studies 92:432–482

Hayles NK (1999) How we Became Posthuman: Virtual Bodies in Cybernetics, Literature, and Informatics. The University of Chicago Press, Chicago

Hayles NK (2016) Cognitive Assemblages: Technical Agency and Human Interactions. Critical Inquiry 43:32–55

Hayles NK (2017) Unthought: The Power of the Cognitive Nonconscious. The University of Chicago Press, Chicago

Heslop DJ (2019) Beyond traditional CBRN force protection - a future of CBRN hardened super-soldiers? Global Biosecurity. https://doi.org/10.31646/gbio.3

Hoffman DD, Singh M, Prakash C (2015) The Interface Theory of Perception. Psychonomic bulletin & review 22:1480–1506. https://doi.org/10.3758/s13423-015-0890-8.pdf. Accessed 23 September 2024

Hollan J, Hutchins E, Kirsh D (2000) Distributed cognition: toward a new foundation for human-computer interaction research. ACM Trans. Comput.-Hum. Interact https://doi.org/10.1145/353485.353487

Hookway B (2014) The Interface Effect. The MIT Press, Cambridge MA

Horlings T, Lindelauf R, Rietjenset S (2023) Battling information overload in military intelligence & security organisations. In: Pijpers PBMJ, Voskuijl M, Beeres RJM (eds) Towards a Data-Driven Military: A Multidisciplinary Perspective. Leiden University Press, Leiden, pp. 221–236

Hutchins E (1995) Cognition in the Wild. The MIT Press, Cambridge MA

Jensen B, Atalan Y, Tadross D (2024) It Is Time to Democratize Wargaming Using Generative AI. https://www.csis.org/analysis/it-time-democratize-wargaming-using-generative-ai. Accessed 26 September 2024

Krämer S (2015) Media, Messenger, Transmission. An Approach to Media Philosophy. Amsterdam University Press, Amsterdam

Krämer S (2022) The Artificiality of the Human Mind: A Reflection on Natural and Artificial Intelligence. In: Nagl-Docekal H, Zacharasiewicz W (eds) Artificial Intelligence and Human Enhancement. De Gruyter, Berlin/Boston, pp. 17–32

Krebs S (2023) Above the law: Drones, aerial vision and the law of armed conflict - a socio-technical approach. International Review of the Red Cross 105:1690–1728. https://doi.org/10.1017/S1816383123000413

Liivoja R, Chirop L (2018) Are Enhanced Warfighters Weapons, Means, or Methods of Warfare? 94 International Legal Studies 161

Lin P (2013) Could Human Enhancement Turn Soldiers Into Weapons That Violate International Law? Yes. The Atlantic. https://www.theatlantic.com/technology/archive/2013/01/could-human-enhancement-turn-soldiers-into-weapons-that-violate-international-law-yes/266732/. Accessed 23 September 2024

Lipp B, Dickel S (2022) Interfacing the human/machine. Distinktion: Journal of Social Theory. https://doi.org/10.1080/1600910X.2021.2012709

Lubell N, Al-Khateeb K (2022) Cyborg Soldiers: Military Use of Brain-Computer Interfaces and the Law of Armed Conflict. In: Dickinson L A, Berg E (eds) Big Data and Armed Conflict: Legal Issues Above and Below the Armed Conflict Threshold. Oxford University Press, Oxford, pp. 1–20

Marcus G (2018) Deep Learning: A Critical Appraisal. arXiv. https://doi.org/10.48550/arXiv.1801.00631

Noll G (2014) Weaponising neurotechnology: international humanitarian law and the loss of language. London Review of International Law. https://doi.org/10.1093/lril/lru009

Norman DA (2002) The Design of Everyday Things. Basic Books, New York

Omotoyinbo FR (2023) Smart soldiers: towards a more ethical warfare. AI & Soc. https://doi.org/10.1007/s00146-022-01385-3

O'Neill T, McNeese N, Barron A, Schelble B (2022) Human-Autonomy Teaming: A Review and Analysis of the Empirical Literature. Human Factors. https://doi.org/10.1177/0018720820960865

Roesler E, Vollmann M, Manzey D, Onnasch L (2024) The dynamics of human-robot trust attitude and behavior. Exploring the effects of anthropomorphism and type of failure. Computers in Human Behavior. https://doi.org/10.1016/j.chb.2023.10800

Savage-Knepshield P, Martin J, Lockett J, Allender L (2016) Designing Soldier Systems. Current Issues in Human Factors. Routledge, London/New York

Scharre P (2018) Army of None: Autonomous Weapons and the Future of War. W. W. Norton & Company, New York City

Seth A (2021) Being You: A New Science of Consciousness. Faber, London

Shapiro L (2014) The Routledge Handbook of Embodied Cognition. Routledge, London

Shunk D (2015) Ethics and the Enhanced Soldier of the Near Future. Military Review January-February:91–98. https://www.armyupress.army.mil/Portals/7/military-review/Archives/English/MilitaryReview_20150228_art017.pdf. Accessed 23 September 2024

Suchman LA (2007) Human-Machine Reconfigurations. Plans and Situated Actions, 2nd edn. Cambridge University Press, Cambridge

Suchman LA, Weber J (2016) Human-Machine-Autonomies. In: Bhuta N C, Beck S, Geiß R, Liu H-Y, Kreß C (eds) Autonomous Weapons Systems. Law, Ethics, Policy, Cambridge, 2nd edn. Cambridge University Press, Cambridge, pp. 75–102

Taylor M (2014) Manned-Unmanned Teaming Training is the Key Ingredient. Aviation Digest - United States Army Aviation 2:5–6. https://home.army.mil/novosel/application/files/2415/6026/6933/AVN_DIG_2014_07-09.pdf. Accessed 23 September 2024

Thadani A (2022) Equipped to win. Defence & Security Systems International. https://www.defence-and-security.com/analysis/equipped-to-win-9743423/?cf-view. Accessed 24 September 2024

Verbeek PP (2016) Toward a Theory of Technological Mediation: A Program for Postphenomenological Research. In: Berg J K, Friis O, Crease R C (eds) Technoscience and Postphenomenology: The Manhattan Papers. Lexington Books, London, pp. 89–204

Vertesi J (2019) From Affordances to Accomplishments: PowerPoint and Excel at NASA. In: Vertesi J, Ribes D (eds) digitalSTS: A Field Guide for Science & Technology Studies. Princeton University Press, Princeton, pp. 369–392

Thomas Christian Bächle is Head of the Digital Society Research Programme at the Alexander von Humboldt Institute for Internet and Society (HIIG) in Berlin. He is also senior researcher at the University of Bonn as part of the research network 'Meaningful Human Control', which studies autonomous weapon systems.

Chapter 7
Artificial Decision-Making on Life-or-Death: Moral-Psychological Implications for Combatants with Increasing Autonomy in Weapon Systems

Tine Molendijk, Sofie van der Maarel and Lonneke Peperkamp

Contents

Abstract The increasing autonomy of military technologies has sparked intense ethical debates, particularly regarding the morality of lethal autonomous weapons systems (AWS). Central questions include whether the shift from human to autonomous targeting reduces or increases moral-psychological harm, and more generally, how we should examine the moral-psychological dimensions of AWS. Currently, legal and ethical discussions predominantly rely on Just War Theory,

T. Molendijk · S. van der Maarel · L. Peperkamp
Faculty of Military Sciences, Netherlands Defence Academy, Breda, The Netherlands
e-mail: tine.molendijk@ru.nl

S. van der Maarel
e-mail: sofie.vandermaarel@ru.nl

T. Molendijk · S. van der Maarel
Centre for International Conflict Analysis and Management (CICAM), Radboud University Nijmegen, Nijmegen, The Netherlands

L. Peperkamp (✉)
Radboud University Nijmegen, Nijmegen, The Netherlands
e-mail: lonneke.peperkamp@ru.nl

B. Boutin et al. (eds.), *Legal, Ethical, and Technical Dilemmas in Military Artificial Intelligence*, https://doi.org/10.1007/978-94-6265-759-5_7

related abstract principles, and hypothetical scenarios. While these offer important normative arguments regarding AWS, they provide limited insights into the daily realities of combatants operating such systems. Our approach focuses on the lived experiences of AWS operators to explore moral judgment as a lived process of meaning-making by these practitioners. While some advocates suggest AWS could shield combatants from moral-psychological harm, our analysis challenges this assumption. By integrating abstract ethical arguments with insights from combatants' lived experiences, including a secondary analysis of an empirical case study, we identify both persistent and additional moral-psychological risks associated with AWS. Furthermore, our analysis yields a preliminary framework for future research and practice. Control, responsibility, and trust emerge as key concepts bridging abstract and empirical research, essential for comprehensively examining and mitigating moral-psychological harm in the context of AWS.

Keywords AWS · Military · Meaning-Making · Lived Experience · Moral Injury · Responsibility · Trust · Control · Drones

7.1 Introduction

The increasing autonomy of military technologies has sparked intense debates about its ethical aspects, particularly regarding the morality of lethal autonomous weapons systems (AWS). AWS can independently identify, select, and engage targets with minimal or no human intervention, for instance, operating based on pre-programmed descriptions and constraints. Three common classifications of human control are: human-in-the-loop (where a human initiates action, thus not fully autonomous), human-on-the-loop (where a human can intervene or halt the action), and human-out-of-the-loop (where no human involvement occurs).[1] On the one hand, there are those who argue that AWS are simply an extension of the evolution of warfare, not fundamentally differing from other weapon systems, nor inherently immoral. Their deployment and use, they contend, remains subject to existing rules and principles. On the other hand, critics argue that AWS are instrumentally different and inherently immoral.

One line of argument in defence of AWS focuses on the moral obligations of States *vis-a-vis* their armed forces, generally building on frameworks such as Just War Theory and focusing on hypothetical thought experiments. Just War Theory is a foundational ethical framework that assesses the morality of engaging in war (*jus ad bellum*) and conduct during war (*jus in bello*). As such, it underpins debates on AWS by engaging with principles such as distinction, proportionality, necessity, and legitimate authority, while also establishing new specific principles tailored to the unique challenges posed by artificial intelligence (AI) technologies. For instance, Strawser's principle of unnecessary risk (PUR) asserts that States have a moral obligation to

[1] Horowitz 2016; Noone and Noone 2015.

prevent unnecessary physical harm to their own troops.[2] The PUR argues that a military engaged in a 'just war' has a moral obligation to protect its soldiers. A 'just war' is one that meets specific moral and legal criteria under Just War Theory. This theory is divided into two main components. *Jus ad bellum* governs the justification for going to war and includes principles such as just cause, legitimate authority, right intention, and last resort. *Jus in bello* governs conduct within war and includes principles like proportionality and distinction, which ensure that military actions are measured and that civilians are not deliberately targeted. According to the PUR, as long as a military operates within these ethical constraints—i.e., if protection does not compromise adherence to *jus ad bellum* and *in bello* principles—it is justified in taking measures to protect its soldiers.[3] That is, according to the PUR, since remote warfare eliminates physical risks—such as injury or death—States have a *prima facie* duty to deploy remotely piloted armed drones when feasible. Further, advocates extend the application of the PUR, arguing that AWS not only avoid unnecessary physical risk but also prevent moral-psychological harm in operators.[4] It is assumed that the deployment of AWS will reduce feelings of guilt and shame—also called moral injury—by relieving combatants of the responsibility for life-or-death decisions. But how likely is it that the shift from human to increasingly autonomous targeting truly reduces moral-psychological harm? Relatedly, how should we examine the moral-psychological dimensions of AWS?

These are the central questions we address in this chapter. There is increasing debate on the harmful moral-psychological effects of this type of remote warfare.[5] Operators, for instance, can develop feelings of shame and guilt in response to automated violence, coupled with a feeling of powerlessness.[6] Thus, physical removal from the battlefield does not guarantee that combatants will actually feel more emotionally or psychologically detached. Similarly, reduced responsibility for life-or-death decisions according to formal moral and legal criteria does not necessarily mean that combatants will *feel* less responsible or guilty. However, as suggested, the ethics of AWS have mostly been debated within frameworks such as Just War Theory. While certainly relevant, in such normative debates based on abstract thought experiments, the specific moral-psychological impact on combatants has either not been a significant concern or has been too readily inferred from researchers' own judgments about the morality of combatants' actions. To answer the questions above, it is crucial to increase understanding of the lived experience of those who operate AWS. This approach moves beyond merely relying on abstract ethical arguments and hypothetical scenarios, encompassing the real-life experiences of operators. While the former provides important normative insights into AWS by assessing where and when responsibility should lie, as well as the objective meaning of concepts like 'control', it does not account for individual perspectives. Examining operators'

[2] Strawser 2010.

[3] Ibid., pp. 458–459.

[4] Riesen 2022.

[5] Enemark 2019; Enemark 2023.

[6] McKernan and Davies 2024.

subjective experiences sheds light on how they perceive and ascribe meaning to issues such as control, trust, and responsibility in practice.

Hence, in this chapter we focus on moral judgment not just as the result of *reasoned deliberation* done by *scholars*, but also as a lived experience of *meaning-making* by *practitioners*, operators in particular.[7] Lived experience involves 'personal knowledge about the world gained through direct, first-hand involvement in everyday events rather than through representations constructed by other people'.[8] Moral judgment as a lived experience is thus a process of *meaning-making*, involving basic assumptions about living in a meaningful and coherent world, where actions and outcomes are connected.[9] It is well-documented that all humans possess basic assumptions with which they navigate the world. Among these assumptions is the belief that they live in a world where good intentions lead to good outcomes, and vice versa. This understanding renders the world intelligible and predictable, not random.[10] Rather than treating abstract arguments and real-life experiences as two opposing perspectives, we aim to bridge these domains. This approach allows us to integrate practical insights into the moral-psychological experience of operators within existing theoretical debates on AWS. To achieve this, we focus on three concepts central in both theoretical debates on AWS and practical research on moral-psychological experience: control, responsibility, and trust. By linking these concepts to concrete practices and the lived experiences of operators, we aim to shed new light on the moral-psychological impact of increased autonomy in weapon systems.

In debates surrounding AWS, the phenomena of control, responsibility, and trust are generally approached from a rational, objectified standpoint. These discussions focus on notions of power balance, zero-sum assessments, and risk calculation.[11] However, linking these perspectives to research on personal meaning-making brings into focus themes such as the tension between a sense of control and powerlessness or fatalism, adherence to values versus moral failure or disengagement, and trust versus distrust and betrayal. Empirical research on the actual experiences of operators—as even so-called fully autonomous systems still require human oversight—offers further insight into how changes in autonomy and responsibilities can affect moral and psychological well-being. Due to the scarcity of empirical material on AWS operator experiences, we draw on the limited empirical insights from remotely piloted drones, particularly Rauch and Ansari's study on United States (US) drone operations, to inform our discussion.[12] The connection between remotely piloted drones

[7] Molendijk 2024; Van der Maarel et al. 2023; Van der Maarel 2025.

[8] Chandler and Munday 2011.

[9] Janoff-Bulman 1992.

[10] Ibid.

[11] Amoroso and Tamburrini 2020; Horowitz 2016; Ma 2020.

[12] See Rauch and Ansari 2022. These researchers gathered 43 personal diaries kept by military professionals and complemented their findings with 43 interviews with the diarists, ethnographic observations conducted at a military base, and archival documents. For our intended purposes, we undertook a secondary, explorative coding process, organising the quoted material according to our theoretical framework.

and AWS can be understood as a matter of degree of autonomy, with drones representing a precursor to the challenges posed by AWS. Both systems raise similar issues of control, responsibility, and trust, yet AWS arguably magnify these concerns due to their higher levels of autonomy. Analysing the impact of increased autonomy for drone operators thereby helps us understand potentially similar dynamics for those working with AWS. At the same time, as autonomy can be understood as a gradual process,[13] we can learn from systems with limited autonomy—such as remotely piloted drones—to better understand the potential dynamics and impacts of fully AWS. While our understanding of operators' lived experiences remains preliminary due to limited empirical data, our initial findings challenge the assumption that deploying AWS mitigates moral and psychological harm. Moreover, they represent an important step towards a more comprehensive understanding of the real-world ethical issues related to increasing autonomy in weapon systems. By integrating abstract ethical theory on moral-psychological experience, our analysis serves as a framework for future empirical research.

First, we discuss in more detail the PUR arguments for a moral obligation on States to deploy AWS. We then explore the intersection of abstract ethical principles with the tangible experiences of combatants, focusing on themes of control, responsibility, and trust. We then employ an empirical case study to further flesh out these concepts, providing concrete insights into how these concepts manifest in the lived realities of combatants. This leads us to challenge arguments that support AWS solely based on reducing moral-psychological harm through the transition from human to autonomous targeting. To conclude, we argue for the importance of bridging abstract ethical principles with real-life practices and experiences, proposing a preliminary framework for future research.

7.2 AWS, Just War Theory, and the Principle of Unnecessary Risk

As discussed in the introduction, AWS are generally described as systems with a high level of autonomy.[14] Debates within Just War Theory often focus on remotely piloted drones as systems primarily controlled by human operators, but which could become more automated with the integration of AI. The key distinction between AWS and remotely controlled drones lies in their level of autonomy and the extent to which operators directly control their functionalities in real-time. The use of remotely piloted drones has been described as a form of 'riskless' warfare. As Walzer notes, drone operators are not 'vulnerable', making targeted killing 'politically easier'. This creates the perception of a war with 'no casualties (on our side), no veterans

[13] Strawser 2010.

[14] https://disarmament.unoda.org/the-convention-on-certain-conventional-weapons/background-on-laws-in-the-ccw/. Accessed 14 June 2024.

who spend years in VA hospitals, no funerals'.[15] While such 'riskless' warfare has been criticised for undermining the 'equality of combatants'[16]—or at the very least for making killing so effortless that it evokes discomfort,[17]—the reduction of risk to one's own troops remains a compelling moral reason to deploy drones. Instead, States must equip their armed forces with weapons and materials that best allow them to perform the task they are trusted with: to protect national and international safety and security through the use of force. Thus, when certain weapon systems eliminate or reduce combatant risk while demonstrating comparable effectiveness and precision in armed conflict to alternative options, States should provide these to their armed forces.

Building on Strawser's PUR, it follows that if States deploy their armed forces to achieve a just cause, they must select means that align with the demands of justice, do not worsen the world, and do not expose their combatants to unnecessary lethal risk.[18] Using remotely piloted drones removes combatants from harm's way, effectively eliminating the risk of death or injury in battle. Consequently, when States are engaged in a just war, the deployment of drones instead of traditional manned vehicles is not only justified but may even be required, provided there is no significant loss of operational capability.

The question of whether drones (or remote warfare more generally) truly eliminate combatant risk remains a subject of debate.[19] Several studies argue that whilst remote targeting clearly protects combatants against physical harm, it does not necessarily shield them from moral-psychological harm. Drone warfare, despite the absence of any physical threat, can induce stress and trauma-related problems.[20] Moreover, it has been argued that the combination of physical distance and virtual proximity to targets might even increase moral-psychological risks.[21] While combat-related trauma may be less prevalent among drone operators compared to physically deployed troops, the limited empirical research on this phenomenon indicates that burnout and psychiatric symptoms are higher among drone crews than pilots operating manned aircrafts, such as F-16s.[22] Additionally, there are indications that drone operators are especially vulnerable to experiencing moral injury.[23] Moral injury refers to the psychosocial impact of facing situations that violate one's moral beliefs and expectations.[24]

---

[15] Walzer 2016, p. 15.

[16] Kahn 2002.

[17] Walzer 2016.

[18] Strawser 2010, p. 344: 'If X gives Y an order to accomplish good goal G, then X has an obligation, other things being equal, to choose a means to accomplish G that does not violate the demands of justice, make the world worse, or expose Y to potentially lethal risk unless incurring such risk aids in the accomplishment of G in some way that cannot be gained via less risky means'.

[19] Enemark 2019; Clark 2019; Huntington and Eckert 2022; Enemark 2023.

[20] Phelps 2021.

[21] Enemark 2023, p. 158.

[22] Saini et al. 2021; Chappelle et al. 2014.

[23] Enemark 2023, pp. 172–173.

[24] Molendijk 2021.

Notably, research indicates that the 'most problematic sources of distress' for drone operators are 'operational in nature' rather than 'combat-related'.[25] While these findings partly nuance the exclusive focus on combat as the primary source of trauma, they also affirm new insights into military stress and trauma: that shocking, distressing situations can never be fully understood without considering the context in which they emerge.[26] For example, distress always arises in the context of unit and leadership dynamics and organisational stressors, which may contribute to exhaustion and can significantly affect moral decision making and behaviour during combat operations.

Moral injury from remote warfare is linked to the heightened sense of 'intimacy' that operators experience—rather than a 'videogame-like' detachment—due to the use of high-quality sensors.[27] Sophisticated imagery allows operators to observe intimate details, and seeing the enemy as (too) human can make the use of force more morally challenging.[28] At the same time, this virtual proximity strips operators of the experience of 'moral permission' to use force, an authorisation combatants typically experience when directly confronted with lethal danger on the battlefield.[29] As such, technological innovations—such as drones, sensors, and advanced interfaces—lead to 'distant-intimate killing' or 'tele-intimate violence',[30] which lacks personal justification, as it does not arise from a direct threat posed by the enemy combatant or a legitimate need for self-defence. The drone operator is simultaneously present and not present,[31] being physically safe while the enemy remains defenceless. This leads some to advise States to acknowledge these risks, prioritise the well-being of combatants, and grant them the discretionary power to refuse to engage in lethal actions involving AWS.[32]

Others, however, argue that the moral-psychological risks of remote warfare further justify removing combatants from direct participation in hostilities. They propose transferring control from human combatants to AWS, thus sparing combatants from the burden of killing and minimising the remaining non-lethal risks. For example, MacIntosh argues that the use of AWS can be justified as they protect the combatant's 'moral self'.[33] He argues that engaging unjust enemy combatants morally harms the just combatant conducting the attack, as making these hard life-or-death decisions can result in guilt and other trauma-related symptoms. Thus, the conscience of combatants fighting a just war would be protected by removing them from the loop.

---

[25] Norrholm et al. 2023, p. 47.

[26] Molendijk 2018; Molendijk 2021.

[27] Demmers and Gould 2018; Holmqvist 2013.

[28] Enemark 2019; Enemark 2023.

[29] Enemark 2019; Molendijk 2024.

[30] Enemark 2019; Enemark 2023.

[31] Clark 2019, p. 173; Phelps 2021, pp. 133–134.

[32] Enemark 2023.

[33] MacIntosh 2021, p. 14.

Riesen explicitly builds on Strawser's PUR by proposing an 'extended' framework, E-PUR.[34] This extension argues that States ought to avoid not only unnecessary lethal risks to combatants but also moral and psychological risks that can negatively affect the well-being of combatants.[35] This results in a 'strong *prima facie* moral reason' for deploying AWS in a just war, as they 'decrease psychological and moral risk both by decreasing the number of soldiers making life-or-death decisions and by spreading responsibility for mistakes more widely'.[36] Whilst Riesen acknowledges that this remains an assumption, he argues that the use of AWS is likely to 'save' combatants 'from the guilt, culpability, and psychological distress' they would otherwise experience when piloting armed drones.[37]

Whilst both accounts rely on the rights and duties central to Just War Theory, the *prima facie* duty of States to protect the well-being of combatants by using AWS has also been grounded in virtue ethics. Cappuccio et al. view moral injury as an inherently undesirable form of moral character deterioration that must be prevented by just institutions if possible.[38] They too expect that deploying AWS will be effective in preventing moral injury. Although combatants supervising AWS would remain aware of the use of force:

> The impacts of guilt, shame, and remorse generated by simply knowing about the killing that machines have done in a given military context is likely less severe than that coming from performing such killings firsthand, which would incorporate a vivid experience and memories, direct agency, and immediate decision-making.[39]

Thus, Cappuccio et al. argue that autonomous systems alleviate combatants from what they perceive as two major contributing factors: the act of killing *and* the moral decision to do so.

All the arguments above assume that combatants will be better off if a weapon autonomously selects and engages a target. Indeed, it may be that, as stated above, it is 'easier' to have a machine perform killings. With the option of using AWS, combatants could transfer control over life-or-death decisions—and the subsequent act of killing—to a system that autonomously decides and acts based on predefined criteria. In this scenario, combatants would only have to trust the system to make the right decisions on their behalf, which is automatically assumed to occur when the system is designed to operate reliably and provide operators with the necessary information to make reasonable decisions. AWS would then alleviate operators' responsibility in two ways: first, the operator controls the deployment of the system, but does not directly engage individual targets (i.e., making the causal chain less

[34] Riesen 2022, p. 136.

[35] Ibid.: 'If X gives Y an order to accomplish good goal G, then X has an obligation, other things being equal, to choose a means to accomplish G that does not violate the demands of justice, make the world worse, or expose Y to potential lethal, moral, or psychological risk unless incurring such risk aids in the accomplishment of G in some way that cannot be gained via less risky means'.

[36] Ibid., p. 135.

[37] Ibid., p. 139.

[38] Cappuccio et al. 2022, pp. 8, 13.

[39] Ibid., p. 10.

direct); second, the operator shares control over what happens with other agents who all contribute to the 'kill chain' in some way. Compared to remote warfare with armed drones, this relatively indirect and diffused operator responsibility is thought to shield combatants from the risk of moral-psychological harm and moral injury. But is this truly the case? What do concepts such as control, responsibility, and trust mean in the experience of the operator?

7.3 Abstract Ethics Versus Lived Experience

This section turns to the lived experience of combatants, drawing on research on meaning-making and moral injury, which often encompasses feelings of powerlessness, guilt, and mistrust. As has already become clear, these feelings are closely related to important concepts in ethical debates on AWS: control, responsibility, and trust.

7.3.1 Control

Legal and ethical debates concerning the role of control in AWS typically focus on the extent of human involvement, distinguishing, as discussed in the introduction, between human-in-the-loop, human-on-the-loop, and human-out-of-the-loop.[40] Relatedly, a key term in these debates is 'meaningful human control' (MHC).[41] MHC is often presented as a solution to the 'problem' of control, ensuring that humans retain essential oversight and authority over automated systems, thereby addressing concerns related to accountability, safety, and ethical decision making. However, critics argue that the concept of MHC is often approached intuitively as if its meaning is self-evident.[42] As a result, despite its significance, the definition of 'meaningful', 'human', and 'control' risk remaining rather vague.[43] Control is generally framed in terms of decision making based on rational calculations, often focusing on whether a human is supervising or merely 'pushing the button'. At the same time, marginal attention is given to what the 'human' element actually entails, what is considered 'meaningful', and to whom.[44] Below, we explicitly focus on how human operators experience control, or lack thereof, over their actions.

First, as discussed, we build on existing studies on remotely controlled drones and autonomy to better understand the potential dynamics of AWS. Both systems require technical knowledge and skills that differ from the previous roles and expectations

[40] Horowitz 2016; Noone and Noone 2015.

[41] Amoroso and Tamburrini 2020; Ferl 2024; Williams 2021.

[42] Ekelhof 2019; Robbins 2023; Schwarz 2021.

[43] Robbins 2023.

[44] Ekelhof 2019; Schwarz 2021.

of combatants. Remotely controlled drones, such as the MQ-9 Reaper, are equipped with numerous sensors, requiring operators to not only analyse visual imagery but also control sensors, targeting decision processes, and weapons guidance—a task far more demanding than before.[45] Operators' work in this context is shaped by heightened responsibilities and the need to oversee complex processes. Increased autonomy in AWS may reduce the overall number of tasks. However, responsibility may increase due to the expanded operational area of these systems and the need to monitor autonomously executed tasks. This shift inherently impacts operators' experience of control, as they face increased expectations of control alongside less actual control. Moreover, this dynamic increases risks such as automation bias, where operators overly rely on automated systems despite errors or misleading information. It also contributes to alert fatigue, as operators become desensitised to frequent alarms or alerts, reducing their ability to respond effectively.[46]

The question of how operators may experience control brings us to our second point. As discussed, moral judgment as lived experience involves basic assumptions about living in a meaningful and coherent world, where actions and outcomes are connected. Related to these basic assumptions are the concepts of 'locus of control' and 'self-efficacy', which refer to the degree to which individuals perceive themselves as having control over events that impact their lives.[47] Locus of control specifically concerns the extent to which individuals believe that events are within their control through their own actions (internal locus of control), or are predominantly influenced by external factors beyond their control (external locus of control). Importantly, while the prevailing argument in the aforementioned debates suggests that less human involvement leads to less trauma, research indicates that a greater external locus of control has been associated with greater vulnerability to physical illness, including symptoms associated with Post-Traumatic Stress Disorder and moral injury.[48] Hence, internal locus of control acts as a protective factor against mental health problems, while an external locus of control is a risk factor. Indeed, the prevailing sentiment frequently reported by soldiers who have experienced trauma during deployment is a pervasive sense of powerlessness.[49]

At the same time, to complicate matters, humans are never passive agents. Research suggests that in complex situations, individuals with an external locus of control may paradoxically create situations that actually heighten their perception of control over their ability to cope with challenges. When they perceive their problems as complex and unpredictable, they deliberately seek external support to manage them effectively.[50] This pattern is particularly discernible among soldiers who experience shock and trauma during deployment, where feelings of powerlessness can

[45] Asaro 2013.

[46] Soltanzadeh 2025.

[47] Bandura et al. 1999; Karstoft et al. 2015.

[48] Karstoft et al. 2015; Wheeler 2020.

[49] Molendijk 2021.

[50] Ryan and Carr 2010.

coexist with proactive efforts to seek external assistance in managing challenging circumstances.

7.3.2 *Responsibility*

As with discussions on control, in ethical and legal debates concerning AWS, the issue of responsibility is often framed in rational, outsider-view terms. Accordingly, responsibility is typically approached in zero-sum terms, centred around what is commonly referred to as 'responsibility ascription issues'.[51] This applies to matters of ethical and judicial accountability, raising questions about whether 'the programmer', 'the state', or 'the soldier' can be held responsible.[52] However, the actual experiences and subjective feelings of responsibility among operators are rarely explored, and when they are, the analysis is often based on assumptions or speculations. For instance, common arguments regarding responsibility highlight that weapons and robots lack 'situational understanding',[53] are incompatible with 'human dignity',[54] remove the opportunity for 'human compassion',[55] and cannot be 'punished like humans' for violations.[56] These normative ethical arguments focus on who should be held responsible in a legal or ethical sense.

However, from a lived experience and meaning-making perspective, the question of responsibility shifts to how operators themselves experience responsibility and the ethical weight of their decisions. From this perspective, responsibility is not just about fulfilling one's duty and upholding values; it involves living up to moral commitments. Drawing from moral injury research, failing in this regard is not merely an outcome of a zero-sum calculation, but hinges on whether values and commitments are violated.[57] A person may also experience 'moral failure' in situations where it is objectively indicated they did nothing wrong, yet still struggle with the psychological effects of a moral dilemma.[58] While terms like 'error' or 'violation' imply quantifiable transgressions, 'moral failure' simply refers to the feeling of having morally failed, no matter how unavoidable the situation was. Accordingly, while straightforward transgressions may lead to unequivocal feelings of guilt, shame, and anger, the psychological outcome of moral failure is often closer to 'tragic remorse'.[59] Tragic remorse differs from other forms of remorse in that it pertains to actions—or the failure to act—that the individual does not perceive as blameworthy. It is the regret

[51] Amoroso and Tamburrini 2020; Horowitz 2016; Ma 2020.

[52] Ibid.

[53] Etzioni 2018.

[54] Sharkey 2019.

[55] Heller 2023.

[56] Schröder 2021, p. 195.

[57] Molendijk 2018; Molendijk 2021.

[58] Ibid.

[59] de Wijze 2005; Molendijk 2018.

that, morally, the best available option was still the least terrible one. Only moral disengagement or indifference can protect against the pain of moral failure.[60]

This feeling of moral failure can be reinforced by technological innovations such as AWS, particularly as their increased autonomy exposes operators to a wider array of concrete responsibilities and tasks. As Asaro describes:

> The traditional compartmentalization and separation of intelligence analysis and interpretation and target designation and killing has been broken down and reconfigured [which] places greater psychological demands on [operators] because it becomes more difficult to shift responsibility to others or to ignore the consequences of one's own decisions and actions.[61]

Concrete changes in operators' tasks can thus cause moral-psychological stress. These transformations are shaped by emerging technologies and may concern something as basic as the 'poor design of interfaces', which complicates information coordination and dissemination, thereby influencing operators' feelings of responsibility.[62]

Accordingly, as AWS complicate issues of responsibility, they may also heighten the likelihood of complex moral-psychological experiences in operators, such as 'moral failure' and 'tragic remorse'. Operators face the constant challenge of managing a system that may act in ways beyond their control. This combination of intimacy and detachment can result in a form of moral failure that is both deeply pronounced and profoundly alienating—where operators feel they have morally failed, even when they have followed procedures or have not technically committed any violations. The tragic remorse they will then experience arises not from blame for a specific error but from the sense of responsibility for actions that, while procedurally correct, remain morally ambiguous, heightened by the difficulty of being unable to pinpoint where ethical accountability ultimately lies.

7.3.3 Trust

Finally, in legal and ethical debates on AWS, the concept of 'trust' is primarily framed within the context of risk assessment. Discussions typically revolve around questions such as 'can we trust robots?' and whether humans or machines are more reliable and forgivable when errors occur.[63] Such questioning stimulates normative discussions about the degree to which autonomous systems should be trusted and the appropriateness of delegating certain tasks to them. However, from the perspective of lived experience and human meaning-making, trust is not about certainty in outcomes but

[60] Bandura et al. 1999.

[61] Asaro 2013, pp. 207–208.

[62] Ibid., p. 213.

[63] Hauer 2021; Coeckelbergh 2012; Sullins 2020. See Chap. 3 in this volume by Klonowska and Woodcock, which discusses the limitations of framing debates around whether humans or AI systems are 'better'.

arises precisely because of the absence of such certainty.[64] Trust as human experience is not an educated guess, but rather an emotionally and morally charged social expectation. It embodies an individual's willingness to embrace vulnerability in relation to another person or entity.[65] Trust, by its very nature, is a leap of faith, inherently involving a relationship of dependence, wherein one relies on another person or entity for their well-being and safety.[66] This is particularly relevant in contexts where combatants need to trust others to survive high-stakes, life-or-death situations. It is due to these emotional and moral aspects of trust that a betrayal of trust can inflict immense pain, even resulting in trauma. Betrayal constitutes a violation of fundamental moral principles and what is morally right.[67] Interestingly, research indicates that people's aversion to betrayal is so strong that they would rather accept greater safety risks than face the potential breach of a promise of protection.[68] Therefore, on this basis individuals are willing to face heightened risks of the very harm they seek protection from, merely to evade the possibility of betrayal.

Here again, these experiences are mediated by the implementation of technologies such as drones or AWS. The transformation or accumulation of tasks, combined with 'poorly designed interfaces',[69] not only alters the experiences of control and responsibility among operators but also introduces new complexities. Removing drone operators from the traditional battlefield to a geographically distant location forces them to solely rely on the information provided by or through these technologies.[70] Being dependent on and having to place trust in distant sensors or AI-generated predictions, presents a completely different experience of warfare compared to experiencing it firsthand through one's own 'senses' of smelling, hearing, and seeing.[71] To reiterate, these issues are not entirely new, as the use of sensors in military technologies predates both drones and AI, and warfare has long been mediated by technology. However, the scale, speed, and sophistication of contemporary technologies—combined with the physical distance of operators from the battlefield and their limited understanding of the AWS they oversee but do not directly control—arguably intensify and complicate the moral issues involved.

To recap, in current discussions on the ethics of AWS, the concepts of control, responsibility, and trust are generally approached from a rational standpoint, seen as principles on which actors or institutions must base their actions. In contrast, research on moral judgment and injury shows that these concepts also relate to a sense of control versus powerlessness or fatalism, the conflict between upholding values versus moral failure or disengagement, and the tension between trust versus distrust and betrayal. By exploring both strands of research, we have taken steps

[64] Hosmer 1995; Lewis and Weigert 1985.

[65] Weckert and Soltanzadeh 2020.

[66] Molendijk 2021.

[67] Shay 1994.

[68] Koehler and Gershoff 2003.

[69] Asaro 2013, p. 208.

[70] Ibid.

[71] Gusterson 2016.

Integrated framework for moral-psychological risk and AWS			
	Control	**Responsibility**	**Trust**
Abstract military ethics: ***Just war theory, PUR***	Meaningful human control, human in/on/out of the loop	Accountability, zero-sum matter	Risk assessment, system reliability
Military ethics in practice: ***Lived experience, meaning-making***	Perception of control over events, shaped by beliefs about underlying causes	Sense of fulfilling duty, upholding values and moral commitments	Leap of faith in uncertainty and relations of dependence
Moral-psychological risks: ***Moral injury***	Feelings of guilt, shame, anger, moral disorientation		
	Powerlessness or fatalism	Moral failure or disengagement	Distrust and feelings of betrayal

Fig. 7.1 Integrated framework for moral-psychological risk and AWS. *Source* The authors

towards developing a framework that integrates both abstract and empirical perspectives on control, responsibility, and trust, as relevant factors for the risk of moral-psychological harm among operators. Our synthesising discussion of these issues, including the below analysis of an empirical case, resulted in the framework shown in Fig. 7.1 above. This framework integrates abstract military ethics, primarily framed by Just War Theory and related principles, with military ethics in practice, which focuses on lived experiences and meaning-making processes. Bringing these domains together reveals the specific moral-psychological risks of AWS, collectively known as moral injury, which involve feelings of guilt, shame, anger, and moral disorientation. To further flesh out these dynamics, the following section provides an empirical case of their meaning in the actual experience of combatants.

7.4 Empirical Case: Drone Operators

There is a notable lack of empirical data on the actual experiences of combatants working with AWS, which underscores the emphasis on abstract discussions rather than the lived experience of operators. To examine this gap, below we draw on a study by Rauch and Ansari, which focuses on military personnel engaged in drone operations for the US Air Force.[72] This study provides valuable data and clear insights into operators' perceptions of control, responsibility, and trust. While their study focuses on remotely controlled weapon systems (drones) rather than fully AWS, the insights gained are highly pertinent for understanding the moral-psychological mechanisms of operating weapon systems with increased autonomy.

The operators in this study are part of the Unmanned Combat Aerial Vehicles (UCAV) programme of the US Air Force. Their everyday practices encompass the collection and dissemination of updated information between the control crew and

[72] Rauch and Ansari 2022.

the troops deployed on the field, as well as a reciprocal exchange of intelligence. Depending on the situation, surveillance operations may quickly transform into lethal missions. The following example presents a record of an internet relay chat among the individuals involved in the operations, including the sensor screener, pilot, mission coordinator, and others.

> **00:24 (JAG25):** Roger those two vehicles they appear to be moving south to the left are they staying close to the green zone or are they moving out into the open?
>
> **00:24 (Slasher03):** We are now tracking three vehicles and standby we will give you an update.
>
> **00:25 (JAG25):** Copy.
>
> **00:25 (Slasher03):** They're on the move and we will try to get you the distance between them. ...
>
> **03:48 (JAG25):** Kirk97, Good copy. If they close distance with our location at [redacted] base, and at Ground force commander's orders we may have them come up, action those targets, and let you use your hellfire for clean-up shot.
>
> **03:49 (Pilot):** Kirk97, Good copy on that, sounds good.[73]

One drone operator commented on such human–machine interactions:

> You see your buddies down there moving, or other friendlies and the insurgents, all through monitors displayed across the room. You cannot talk to them directly, there is no sound or smell, you don't feel the heat and weather on the ground, but you are still in the middle of all and interact with them.[74]

This underscores how technology mediates the experiences of drone operators. In the following sections, we specifically examine how this mediation shapes their experiences and perceptions of control, responsibility, and trust.

7.4.1 Illusion of Control

A first theme that emerged in the accounts of drone operators concerns perceptions and experiences of control. Some operators strongly conveyed a sense of being in control when using drone technologies:

> I have a live feed of all the movement 24/7, 365. Technology plays a much more central role now because it allows interactions with insurgents directly.[75]

> We have now new relationships with the objects we target and surveil. It's like Big Brother, just in the military sense.[76]

[73] Ibid., p. 87.

[74] Ibid., Interview 12.

[75] Ibid., Informal Conversation 22.

[76] Ibid., Interview 11.

These accounts demonstrate how operators are immersed in a constant flow of information via live feeds, revealing the potential risks that, as increased information enhances perceptions of control, moments of inadequate situational awareness may leave combatants feeling particularly powerless. Conversely, an overload of excessive information can also lead to cognitive overload. In both cases, the operators' locus of control is affected. These risks are evident in the following accounts from other operators who were more ambivalent about how drones influenced their sense of control, or who unequivocally expressed a lack of control:

> We sent it [the missile] down and we are live right with the action… For half a minute the monitors are filled with smoke, and nothing is to be seen because of the thick clouds. Only then I see the outcome of the action and things getting moving. Did we get it right? Target alive or dead? Another package [missile] to be sent down? Any other incidents to report? Civilians or children? Chaos?[77]

> We have our fixed criteria and tick the boxes with the help of video screeners and lots of people involved calling PID [positive identification] and MAMs [military-aged men]. But with the live and constantly developing situation, intel, video feed, radio chatter, IRC [Internet Relay Chat], finding accurate answers to this question is complex… [I]t doesn't always feel like it is the most just version of the truth we are doing here.[78]

Thus, displays and monitors may foster an increased sense of control by providing aerial oversight, even as tasks on the battlefield become increasingly distributed. However, when crucial ground-level information is lacking, or when operators are overwhelmed by the sheer volume of information, this illusion of control can quickly dissolve. As a result, operators may come to realise that their perceived control was partly illusory, leading to a stark sense of diminished *actual* control over the situation.

7.4.2 Responsibility and Moral Failure

This leads us to an important question: what about perceptions and experiences of responsibility among drone operators? Again, the data shows a diverse range of perspectives. On the one hand, some operators felt their work was completely aligned with their personal sense of duty, upholding values, and meeting moral obligations. Or at least, these operators did not view the potentially problematic aspects of their job as their responsibility.

> It is the responsibility of others to make decisions who we target. I am just the one who exercises what has been decided after lengthy processes and mountains of information.[79]

On the other hand, some operators expressed more uncertainty, conveying feelings of shame and guilt:

---

[77] Ibid., Diary 10.

[78] Ibid., Interview 30.

[79] Ibid., Interview 18.

> Wasn't it supposed to be that a war has a mission or purpose? If I worked through the pile of targets, there will be a new one. If not in country X, then country Y, without a clear pattern or rationale for me to understand.[80]

> Often, I take anger or a sense of guilt and embarrassment to my house... This feeling is there when things get messed up but also because of the absence of 'an eye for an eye.' We sneak up on them and, boom, party is over.[81]

These examples illustrate how technologically-mediated experiences can heighten the likelihood of detachment, both positively and negatively. On the negative side, there is a risk of estrangement where operators might be assigned specific tasks without fully understanding or defining their scope, thereby lacking true accountability. However, as the testimonies above reveal, this does not prevent operators from developing sentiments of guilt and shame. As research on moral injury has shown, such feelings can lead to either moral disengagement or profound experiences of moral failure.[82]

7.4.3 (Dis)trust and Betrayal

Finally, the following quotes exemplify various perceptions and experiences of trust among drone operators. Some operators felt that using drones did not fundamentally alter their military role, while others found that advanced technologies increased their confidence in successfully performing their tasks. Many operators expressed strong trust in the technologies they worked with and the information provided by these systems:

> We have used missiles and bombs as part of our strategy for many decades. It's just a different technology that does it now.[83]

> We can be more efficient now. We have moved to being a surveillance company and have amazing situational awareness now... And we can precisely target [those] that need to be removed from the world, because we can really see now their movements 24/7.[84]

> This new technology allows us to bomb... from a safe distance without putting any of our boys in harm's way. This is the way to go forward.[85]

In contrast, other operators expressed doubts or explicit distrust:

---

[80] Ibid., Field Note 65.

[81] Ibid., Field Note 32.

[82] Molendijk 2021.

[83] Rauch and Ansari 2022, Interview 7.

[84] Ibid., Interview 29.

[85] Ibid., Diary 31.

> Where will we land if we question each and every step of the chain? This is how it ran over hundreds of years. We have to trust the system, although this sometimes is of course not so easy when you are paid to watch children die.[86]

> How do I know that this is actually an insurgent and the stuff in his truck under the sheet isn't stuff for the harvest in his backyard and not to blow someone up? Just cause [he] wears a greyish kameez shalwar [traditional male clothing in parts of Afghanistan and Pakistan] like everybody else? ...This blind trust that I had before for the AF I don't have any more since UAV is in town.[87]

> Very ashamed we define any male above 12 as a combatant. This cannot be legal. If so, half of the US is a military aged male.[88]

This operator distrust extended not only to the technology itself but also to the predefined criteria upon which it operates. For them, witnessing the outcomes of their actions through a screen can provoke uncertainty about the moral principles of their profession. They are expected to place 'blind trust' in these systems, yet their experiences with drone footage may raise doubts about the objectives of their organisation. This sense of disillusionment can, in turn, foster distrust and even feelings of betrayal towards military superiors or political decision makers who, for example, define what constitutes a target or who is considered a terrorist.

Indeed, research on moral injury shows that in the case of civilian casualties or wrongful targeting, the ensuing distrust could lead to feelings of betrayal by one's own military organisation and superiors, and more broadly of 'what's right'.[89] This is particularly problematic in the context of both the growing autonomy of weapons systems, where tasks and responsibilities becoming increasingly distributed, and in the case of weapon systems becoming more and more autonomous.

7.5 Conclusion and Discussion

Ethical debates surrounding AWS typically revolve around rights and obligations rooted in Just War Theory and related abstract moral principles. While important, they provide limited insight into the day-to-day realities faced by individual combatants who must navigate increasingly autonomous weapon systems in both current and future modes of warfare. Several arguments in defence of AWS build on the assumption that AI-enabled decision making on life-or-death situations will protect combatants from moral-psychological harm. However, grasping this harm requires an understanding of how combatants themselves experience their work. To evaluate these arguments in light of combatants' lived experience and contribute to a comprehensive view of the ethics of AWS, we juxtaposed abstract discussions about control,

[86] Ibid., Interview 13.
[87] Ibid., Diary 4.
[88] Ibid., Diary 21.
[89] Shay 1994; Enemark 2019; Molendijk 2021.

responsibility, and trust with ideas about the lived moral-psychological experiences faced by combatants.

Returning to our primary question—how likely is it that the shift from human targeting to increased autonomous targeting truly reduces moral-psychological harm?—our analysis identifies mechanisms of moral-psychological harm that are particularly relevant in the context of AWS. We identified several risk factors, such as the illusion of control, feelings of responsibility without accountability, sentiments of distrust in technology, and betrayal by superiors. While it may initially seem plausible that the deployment of AWS minimises the risk of moral-psychological harm for combatants—and in some cases, it may indeed do so—our analysis shows that this assumption does not hold universally. In fact, for many combatants, the risk of moral-psychological harm may even increase. Our analysis of the lived experience of combatants demonstrates how these actors navigate morally complex experiences.

Of course, technology in its many forms is as old as humankind. Indeed, in many ways AWS reflect ongoing technological trends, with the ethical issues they raise stemming largely from increases in speed and scale, thereby compounding existing challenges. These technologies increasingly alter human control over their actions, complicate responsibility for outcomes, and reshape trust in the very machines that mediate their work. However, AWS also introduce a significant, perhaps exponential, escalation in complexity. By progressively removing humans from the decision-making loop, AWS create a dual dynamic that simultaneously enhances and diminishes the operator's sense of control, responsibility, and trust, profoundly complicating the ethical terrain of autonomous warfare.

Our second main question was: how should we examine the moral-psychological dimensions of AWS? To comprehensively discuss the ethics of AWS, it seems vital to integrate both objective, normative theory-based insights and empirical findings from psychology and sociology. We identified the concepts of control, responsibility, and trust as essential concepts for bridging abstract and empirical-based research, as these concepts are relevant in both domains. As our analysis has shown, while prevailing debates on AWS often frame control, responsibility, and trust in rational and abstract ways, human experience reveals that these concepts also relate to more nuanced and complex emotions, such as powerlessness, moral failure, and betrayal. These dynamics are also visualised in the framework presented in Fig. 7.1 above.

Control, as discussed in abstract ethics, centres on concepts like MHC and human 'in the loop'. In contrast, in military ethics in practice, perceptions of control emerge when actors attribute events to internal or external factors, shaped by individual beliefs about underlying causes. Specific moral-psychological risks regarding control include powerlessness or fatalism. Responsibility, when examined through abstract ethics, typically revolves around themes of accountability and the zero-sum nature of decision making. Yet, in military ethics in practice, responsibility is about whether one can fulfil their duty, uphold values, and adhere to moral commitments. When operators of AWS are unable to do so, they may face moral-psychological risks such as a sense of moral failure, or alternatively, resorting to moral disengagement as a form of self-protection. Finally, trust within abstract ethics is usually evaluated in terms of risk assessment and system reliability. However, when considered as lived experience, trust is a leap of faith amidst uncertainty and relationships of dependence. Accordingly, specific moral-psychological risks in this regard are the development of mistrust and feelings of betrayal. Understanding such real-life dynamics is not only crucial for comprehending the moral-psychological implications of AWS but also for more effectively mitigating these harmful implications in practice.

References

Articles, Books and Other Documents

Amoroso D, Tamburrini G (2020) Autonomous Weapons Systems and Meaningful Human Control. Ethical and Legal Issues. Current Robotics Reports 1:187–194

Asaro PM (2013) The Labor of Surveillance and Bureaucratized Killing. New Subjectivities of Military Drone Operators. Social Semiotics 23:196–224

Bandura A, Freeman WH, Lightsey R (1999) Self-Efficacy: The Exercise of Control. Journal of Cognitive Psychotherapy 13: 158–166

Cappuccio ML, Galliott JC, Alnajjar FS (2022) A Taste of Armageddon: A Virtue Ethics Perspective on Autonomous Weapons and Moral Injury. Journal of Military Ethics 21:19–38

Chandler D, Munday R (2011) A Dictionary of Media and Communication. Oxford University Press, New York

Chappelle W, McDonald K, Prince L, Goodman T, Ray-Sannerud BN, Thompson W (2014) Assessment of Occupational Burnout in United States Air Force Predator/Reaper 'Drone' Operators. Military Psychology 26:376–385

Clark L (2019) Gender and Drone Warfare. A Hauntological Perspective. Routledge, London

Coeckelbergh M (2012) Can We Trust Robots? Ethics and Information Technology 14:53-60

Demmers J, Gould L (2018) An Assemblage Approach to Liquid Warfare: AFRICOM and the 'Hunt' for Joseph Kony. Security Dialogue 49:364–381

de Wijze S (2005) Tragic-Remorse – The Anguish of Dirty Hands. Ethical Theory and Moral Practice 7:453–471

Ekelhof M (2019) Moving Beyond Semantics on Autonomous Weapons: Meaningful Human Control in Operation. Global Policy 10:343–348

Enemark C (2019) Drones, Risk, and Moral Injury. Critical Military Studies 5:150–167

Enemark C (2023) Moralities of Drone Violence. Edinburgh University Press, Edinburgh

Etzioni A (2018) Pros and Cons of Autonomous Weapons Systems (with Oren Etzioni). In: Etzioni A (ed) Happiness is the Wrong Metric. Library of Public Policy and Public Administration, vol 11. Springer, Cham, pp. 253–263

Ferl A (2024) Imagining Meaningful Human Control: Autonomous Weapons and the (De-) Legitimisation of Future Warfare. Global Society 38: 139–155

Gusterson H (2016) Drone: Remote Control Warfare. MIT Press, Cambridge, MA

Hauer C (2021) Should We Trust Robots? The Ethical Perspective. In: Nam CS, Lyons JB (eds) Trust in Human-Robot Interaction. Academic Press, pp. 531–551

Heller KJ (2023) The Concept of 'The Human' in the Critique of Autonomous Weapons. Harvard National Security Journal. https://doi.org/10.2139/ssrn.4342529

Holmqvist C (2013) Undoing War: War Ontologies and the Materiality of Drone Warfare. Millennium 41:535–552

Horowitz MC (2016) The Ethics & Morality of Robotic Warfare: Assessing the Debate over Autonomous Weapons. Daedalus 145:25–36

Hosmer LT (1995) Trust: The Connecting Link Between Organizational Theory and Philosophical Ethics. Academy of Management Review 20:379–403

Huntington TJ, Eckert AE (2022) 'We Watched His Whole Life Unfold... Then You Watch the Death': Drone Tactics, Operator Trauma, and Hidden Human Costs of Contemporary Wartime. International Relations 36:638–657
Janoff-Bulman R (1992) Shattered Assumptions. Free Press, New York
Kahn PW (2002) The Paradox of Riskless Warfare. Faculty Scholarship Series 22:2–8
Karstoft KI, Armour C, Elklit A, Solomon Z (2015) The Role of Locus of Control and Coping Style in Predicting Longitudinal PTSD-Trajectories after Combat Exposure. Journal of Anxiety Disorders 32:89–94
Koehler JJ, Gershoff AD (2003) Betrayal Aversion: When Agents of Protection Become Agents of Harm. Organizational Behaviour and Human Decision Processes 90:244–261
Lewis JD, Weigert A (1985) Trust as a Social Reality. Social Forces 63:967–985
Ma EH (2020) Autonomous Weapons Systems under International Law Notes. NYU L Rev 95:1435–1474
MacIntosh D (2021) Fire and Forget: A Moral Defence of the Use of Autonomous Weapons Systems in War and Peace. In: Galliott J, Ohlin JD, MacIntosh D (eds) Lethal Autonomous Weapons. Re-Examining the Law and Ethics of Robotic Warfare. Oxford University Press, pp. 9–23
McKernan B, Davies H (2024) 'The machine did it coldly': Israel used AI to identify 37,000 Hamas targets. https://www.theguardian.com/world/2024/apr/03/israel-gaza-ai-database-hamas-airstrikes. Accessed 21 September 2024
Molendijk T (2018) Moral Injury in Relation to Public Debates: The Role of Societal Misrecognition in Moral Conflict-Colored Trauma Among Soldiers. Social Science & Medicine 211:314–320
Molendijk T (2021) Moral Injury and Soldiers in Conflict: Political Practices and Public Perceptions. Routledge, London
Molendijk T (2024) Moral Coping or Simply Uncomplicated Soldiering? How Soldiers Avoid Moral Injury Through Simplification, Justification, Rationalization, and Compartmentalization. Armed Forces & Society 50:977–999
Noone GP, Noone DC (2015) The Debate over Autonomous Weapons Systems. Case Western Reserve Journal of International Law 47: 25–35
Norrholm SD, Maples-Keller JL, Rothbaum BO, Tossell CC (2023) Remote Warfare with Intimate Consequences: Psychological Stress in Service Member and Veteran Remotely-Piloted Aircraft (RPA) Personnel. Journal of Mental Health & Clinical Psychology 7:37–49
Phelps LCW (2021) On Killing Remotely. The Psychology of Killing with Drones. Little, Brown and Company, New York
Rauch M, Ansari S (2022) Waging War from Remote Cubicles: How Workers Cope with Technologies That Disrupt the Meaning and Morality of Their Work. Organization Science 33:83–104
Riesen E (2022) The Moral Case for the Development and Use of Autonomous Weapon Systems. Journal of Military Ethics 21:132–150
Robbins S (2023) The Many Meanings of Meaningful Human Control. AI Ethics. https://doi.org/10.1007/s43681-023-00320-6
Ryan S, Carr A (2010) Applying the Biopsychosocial Model to the Management of Rheumatic Disease. In: Dziedzic K, Hammond A (eds) Rheumatology. Churchill Livingstone, pp. 63–75
Saini RK, Raju MSVK, Chail A (2021) Cry in the Sky: Psychological Impact on Drone Operators. Industrial Psychiatry Journal 30:S15–S19
Schröder WM (2021) Robots and Rights: Reviewing Recent Positions in Legal Philosophy and Ethics. In: von Braun J, Archer S, Reichberg M, Sánchez Sorondo M (eds) Robotics, AI, and Humanity. Springer, pp. 191–203
Schwarz E (2021) Autonomous Weapons Systems, Artificial Intelligence, and the Problem of Meaningful Human Control. Philosophical Journal of Conflict and Violence 5:53–72
Sharkey A (2019) Autonomous Weapons Systems, Killer Robots and Human Dignity. Ethics and Information Technology 21:75–87
Shay J (1994) Achilles in Vietnam: Combat Trauma and the Undoing of Character. Simon and Schuster, New York

Soltanzadeh S (2025) A Metaphysical Account of Agency for Technology Governance. AI & Society 40. https://doi.org/10.1007/s00146-024-01941-z
Strawser BJ (2010) Moral Predators: The Duty to Employ Uninhabited Aerial Vehicles. Journal of Military Ethics 9:342–368
Sullins JP (2020) Trust in Robots. In: Simon J (ed) The Routledge Handbook of Trust and Philosophy. Routledge, Abingdon, pp. 313–325
Van der Maarel S (2025) 'Drones for Good': Innovation, Meaning and Remoteness in the Dutch Police Drone Team. Critical Studies on Security 1–18
Van der Maarel S, Verweij D, Kramer EH, Molendijk T (2023) 'This Is Not What I Signed up for': Sociotechnical Imaginaries, Expectations, and Disillusionment in a Dutch Military Innovation Hub. Science, Technology, & Human Values. https://doi.org/10.1177/01622439231211032
Walzer M (2016) Just & Unjust Targeted Killing & Drone Warfare. Daedalus 145:12–24
Weckert J, Soltanzadeh S (2020) Trust in Nanotechnology. In: Simon J (ed) The Routledge Handbook of Trust and Philosophy. Routledge, Abingdon, pp. 391–404
Wheeler J (2020) Locus of Injury: The Relationship Between Moral Injury and Locus of Control. Mercer University, Doctoral dissertation. Macon, Georgia
Williams J (2021) Locating LAWS: Lethal Autonomous Weapons, Epistemic Space, and 'Meaningful Human' Control. Journal of Global Security Studies 6:1–18

Tine Molendijk anthropologist, is professor by special appointment of Moral Dilemmas of Military Operations at Radboud University and associate professor at the Faculty of Military Sciences of the Netherlands Defence Academy. Her interdisciplinary research focuses on violence, political practices, and societal perceptions of the armed forces, military culture, ethics, post-traumatic stress disorder, and moral injury.

Sofie van der Maarel is assistant professor at the Faculty of Military Sciences of the Netherlands Defence Academy. Her research focuses on the socio-technical dimensions of moral injury and how expectations of innovative technologies shape military and police practice. She draws from cultural anthropology, Science and Technology Studies (STS), and critical security studies. Her themes include military technology, drones, (semi-)autonomous systems, data science, moral injury, and the future of warfare.

Lonneke Peperkamp is professor of Military Ethics and Leadership at the Faculty of Military Sciences of the Netherlands Defence Academy. She is affiliated with iHub at Radboud University Nijmegen and the Centre for Military Ethics at King's College London. Her research focuses on just war theory, peace building, global justice, human rights, new technologies in warfare, and space security.

Part III
Technical Approaches

Chapter 8
Context-Driven Analysis for AI-Enhanced Solutions: Extracting Requirements for System Development and Operational Use

Iris Cohen, Gregor Pavlin and Rianne Gouman

Contents

Abstract Artificial Intelligence (AI)-enhanced decision-support systems (DSS) in the military domain can improve the speed, quality, and geographical coverage of critical decisions, resulting in operational advantages. Development and deployment of such DSS bring interdisciplinary challenges that must be systematically addressed. Technical challenges focus on determining and achieving the required performance levels of a DSS (e.g., accuracy, resolution, and speed), how to allocate functions between automation and humans, and how to avoid the cognitive costs of automation. Legal and ethical challenges regarding the use of AI-enhanced DSS focus on compliance with targeting law, control, agency and responsibility. The key to successfully tackling these challenges is understanding the decision making within the context in which a DSS would be used. Our solution to tackling these challenges is a contextual

I. Cohen · G. Pavlin · R. Gouman (✉)
Thales Netherlands B.V., Delft, The Netherlands
e-mail: rianne.gouman@nl.thalesgroup.com

I. Cohen
e-mail: iris.cohen@nl.thalesgroup.com

G. Pavlin
e-mail: gregor.pavlin@nl.thalesgroup.com

B. Boutin et al. (eds.), *Legal, Ethical, and Technical Dilemmas in Military Artificial Intelligence*, https://doi.org/10.1007/978-94-6265-759-5_8

analysis of decision-making processes and the operational environment in which they take place. Operational, technical, legal, and ethical experts should understand the end-users' Decision-Making Process (DMP) in various contexts and at different abstraction levels, the contextual factors influencing the decisions, their impact in the real world, and potential risks involved. Knowledge about the operational and contextual settings can be used to: (i) extract technical requirements; (ii) systematically study the potential impact of a DSS in the DMP and safe onboarding into the larger operational system; and (iii) analyse the potential benefits and negative side effects of the DSS under relevant conditions from the operational, legal, and ethical perspectives. The Contextualised AI Onboarding Method (COAIM) provides various tools to extract the context-based knowledge needed to tackle challenges related to AI-enhanced DSS development and onboarding.

Keywords Decision-Support Systems (DSS) · Military Artificial Intelligence (AI) · Naturalistic Decision-Making (NDM) · System Requirements · Rules of Deployment · Responsible Use of AI (RAI) · AI Life Cycle

8.1 Introduction

Within the military domain, defence systems and applications increasingly rely on artificial intelligence (AI) to improve the effectiveness and efficiency of complex operations, while reducing adverse impacts on civilians and the environment. Technical solutions enhanced with AI operate across different operational levels and can leverage a wide range of techniques for automated inference, problem-solving, and machine learning (ML).[1] These solutions rely on AI methods that can be broadly categorised into: (i) symbolic AI (sometimes called rule-based or classical AI) and (ii) methods that rely on various statistical models, typically obtained through ML. From a high-level operational perspective, AI methods can be categorised into: (i) those that support situation awareness (maintaining a constantly updated understanding of the environment and its present and future consequences), which is needed to formulate optimal decisions,[2] and (ii) those that automate the determination of the best course of action in a given situation and the preceding execution. Examples of AI methods supporting situation awareness include various detectors, classifiers, and prediction functions based on (Deep) Neural Networks (DNNs),[3] Probabilistic Graphical

[1] Russell and Norvig 2010.

[2] Endsley 1995; Endsley et al. 2003.

[3] Goodfellow et al. 2016; Mitchell 1997; Bishop 2006.

Models,[4] Decision Trees,[5] and Support Vector Machines. Moreover, the decision-making steps can be automated with the help of problem solvers and optimisers, such as various search algorithms and variants of Reinforcement Learning.[6]

In general, as AI techniques mature they are increasingly integrated at different operational levels, boosting the speed, geographical coverage, and quality of decision-making processes. The level of automation in AI applications varies greatly. For example, autonomous weapon systems (AWS) that can identify and engage targets without a human in the loop—a much-debated topic in the military domain—typically require a high level of automation based on integrating different types of AI techniques to enable automated situation awareness, as well as decision-making. Some militaries have already rejected the deployment of AWS due to ethical, legal, and operational concerns.[7] In contrast, this chapter focuses on a different application of AI in the military: AI-enhanced decision-support systems (DSS). DSS support the establishment of situation awareness and can automate related tasks.[8] However, unlike AWS, they do not automatically choose and execute a course of action based on situation awareness. AI-enhanced DSS support the establishment of situation awareness both for individual operators as well as distributed situation awareness across individual human and artificial agents.[9] Despite the lack of a clear definition of DSS, scholarship identifies several key characteristics of these systems. DSS are systems that support human decision making rather than replacing it.[10] DSS use models and analytical techniques designed to handle ill-structured, complex situations.[11] Most importantly, DSS still require human operators to perform an action within an operational setting. In military operations, sense- and decision-making within the Command and Control process is often described as the Observe, Orient, Decide, and Act loop (OODA loop).[12] This framework outlines the process in which data and information are *observed* and *analysed* (including the assessment of uncertainty), followed by an appropriate *decision*, and selecting a course of *action*.[13] The OODA loop describes human sense- and decision-making behaviour at the individual and higher organisational levels: individual operators engage in the OODA loop, and the outcome of their decisions serves as input for decision makers at higher organisational levels.[14] To gain an advantage over adversaries, military decision makers aim to reduce the time required to complete an OODA loop while also improving the quality of decision outcomes. Many technologies already support steps of the OODA

---

[4] Pearl 1988; Jensen and Nielsen 2007.

[5] Russell and Norvig 2010.

[6] Sutton and Barto 2018.

[7] Koch and Keisinger 2024.

[8] Endsley 2015.

[9] Jiang et al. 2023.

[10] Er 1988.

[11] Ibid.

[12] Richards 2020.

[13] Hammond 2018.

[14] Omarova et al. 2012.

loop, such as observation (e.g., radar or infrared cameras) and taking action within an environment. AI can further support human operators by, for example, performing reasoning tasks that improve situation awareness—rapidly processing vast amounts of data to identify patterns and anomalies at speeds beyond human capability. Integrating such AI techniques within a DSS can produce relevant information, enabling human operators to establish situation awareness individually and within teams.

The development of AI-enhanced DSS introduces a range of challenges to various stakeholders, such as AI experts, Human Factors specialists, system developers, and end-users or their representatives. To tackle these challenges, stakeholders need a common understanding of the operational environment and the expert's decision-making process within it. More precisely, stakeholders need to understand the effects, risks, and environmental constraints of the operational context and integrate these factors throughout the AI-enhanced DSS life cycle. The Contextualised AI-Onboarding Method (CAIOM) provides various methods that help extract this critical knowledge. This novel approach aims to ensure that common Human Factors (Sect. 8.2.1), AI considerations (Sect. 8.2.2), and ethical and legal challenges (Sect. 8.2.3), are systematically and comprehensively addressed.

The central premise of CAIOM is that a contextual analysis of the DSS and the operational context in which it will operate is needed throughout the system's life cycle. At the start of a life cycle, contextual analysis can help the development team determine the optimal allocation of functions between machine and human operators, as well as the appropriate level of automation. Additionally, insights into the impact of the decisions on the operational context (such as implications and risks) help determine minimum performance and accuracy levels for the automation. The analysis also helps create awareness among stakeholders about legal and ethical issues. Depending on what tasks are automated within the overall operation, human responsibility or accountability might be diminished or lost. Therefore, the complexity and criticality of the situation determine whether more or less human agency is needed, and how human control can be exercised. An analysis should go as far as to investigate the entire socio-technical context in which humans interact with the system, to fully understand how the OODA loop takes effect at individual and higher organisational levels.[15] A similar analysis can be performed after development using knowledge of the system's performance levels and the factors influencing them. At this stage, an analysis helps determine robust rules of deployment, specifying the circumstances under which the AI-enhanced DSS can, or cannot, be used during the mission.

To illustrate the use of CAIOM, we provide simplified example scenarios that are introduced and elaborated upon in Sect. 8.3. For example, let us assume a (fictitious) AI-enhanced DSS that can automate the task of identifying perceived subjects and objects (e.g., humans, vehicles, and aircraft) moving within the operational environment. From an operational perspective, identifying subjects and objects creates team situation awareness which is needed to decide on follow-up actions within a mission. Such an automated identification function can support human operators in performing (parts of) the identification task.

[15] Assaad and Boshuijzen-van Burken 2023.

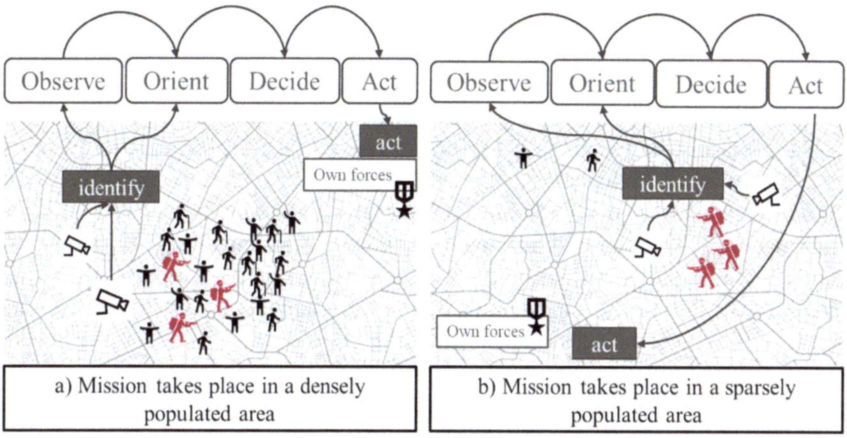

Fig. 8.1 Two example scenarios in which a mission can take place. Both scenarios can be enhanced with the same AI-enhanced DSS. Situation (**a**) is a densely populated area, and Situation (**b**) is a sparsely populated area. *Source* The authors

Figure 8.1 (see above) visualises two urban areas (a and b) where similar missions are taking place and adversary forces are suspected. These forces need to be identified, and if posing a threat, own forces need to defend the area and engage the adversaries. After initial detection, suspicious subjects and objects within relevant areas are tracked (i.e., their positions are continuously monitored). Moreover, each subject must be associated with an identity, classified as 'friendly', 'neutral', or 'hostile'. Different sources (e.g., sensors in the field and intelligence) are used to collect, analyse, and combine information about subjects that helps determine their identity. In Fig. 8.1, the red icons represent actual adversary tracks (although not necessarily identified as such), while the black icons denote civilians.

The task of identifying tracks can result in two types of classification errors: false alarms (where a neutral or friendly track is mistakenly identified as hostile) and misses (where a hostile track is mistakenly identified as neutral or friendly). Additionally, there are two types of correct classifications: hits (where hostile identities are correctly identified) and correct rejections (where friendly or neutral identities are accurately classified).[16] Due to the inherent limitations of AI models, the automated approach may occasionally yield erroneous results (e.g., false alarms or misses). Although such cases are rare, they are not impossible (see Sect. 8.2.2). Let us apply this approach to two distinct operational environments and explore how context influences deployment rules and system requirements.

Figure 8.1 depicts a scenario during a mission in a densely populated area (in the left panel), where many tracks observed by the sensors feeding the DSS (represented by surveillance camera icons) correspond to civilians moving within the operational area. This means there is a higher *a priori* chance that observed tracks correspond

[16] Macmillan 2002.

to civilians. This results in a non-negligible risk of false alarms (i.e., mistakenly identifying civilians as adversary forces). Consequently, the deployment rules for this DSS supporting automated identification must be conservative (e.g., requiring manual verification) to prevent inadvertent harm to civilians.

The scenario depicted in the right panel of Fig. 8.1 takes place in a sparsely populated area, with no civilians located within the operational environment. The risk of mistaking civilians for hostile forces—and thereby causing civilian casualties during an engagement—is extremely low. In this context, an AI-enhanced DSS can significantly increase the likelihood of a successful engagement by rapidly identifying hostile tracks, thus improving situation awareness without endangering civilians and own forces. As a result, deployment rules can be less stringent, fewer verification steps are required, and automation outcomes can be trusted more readily.

8.2 Challenges

Throughout the life cycle of an AI-enhanced DSS, stakeholders from different disciplines experience common and recurring challenges. Technical challenges are addressed from both Human Factors and AI perspectives. These challenges include, but are not limited to, determining the appropriate allocation of functions between the human operator and the systems (or automation), taking into account the cognitive costs of automation, and operators' trust in the system. AI experts face the challenge of achieving an appropriate level of performance for the DSS they are developing, which depends on the risks and consequences associated with the DSS's output. We propose that these challenges can only be solved by considering the range of relevant contexts in which each specific DSS will be deployed. From a legal and ethical perspective, adherence to International Humanitarian Law (IHL) and ethical principles during deployment, as well as ensuring human agency in system design, are among the key challenges. Although many more challenges arise throughout AI life cycles, the following sections focus on those mentioned above. In Sect. 8.3, the use of CAIOM is revisited in relation to these challenges, using the example scenarios provided.

8.2.1 Human Factors Challenges

The Human Factors discipline is an applied research field focused on ensuring users' safety, health, well-being, comfort, and efficiency in the design of tools, systems, jobs, and processes. This aim can be approached from physical, organisational, sensory, behavioural, and cognitive perspectives.[17] When introducing AI-enhanced DSS into

[17] https://www.hfes.org/About/What-Is-Human-Factors-and-Ergonomics. Accessed 2 December 2024.

well-established operational and cognitive work processes, various challenges arise for organisational and cognitive Human Factors experts. The operational workflow might require a redesign, especially considering the redistribution of tasks between the human operator and the system. As Roth highlights, determining function allocation requires work domain analysts to explore and accommodate not only straightforward situations but also more complex ones, such as when system boundaries are exceeded or sensors fail.[18] In the military domain, system failures are not the only risks to consider; the voluntary shutdown of systems is also a possibility (e.g., systems emitting signals that expose one's location). Since risk analyses are common practice for major organisational decisions, deciding on functional allocation between human operators and automation should also be based on a risk analysis.[19]

The allocation of functions between humans and automation, based solely on their relative capabilities, ignores the variability in cognitive and affective factors that influence operators' capabilities throughout different mission phases.[20] A better approach is to perform a context-based risk analysis that includes cognitive issues introduced by automation. These issues arise when manual jobs shift from actively performing tasks to passively observing a machine's performance. During prolonged automation usage, human operators tend to lose the manual skills required to perform tasks, which becomes crucial when automation fails.[21] Next, when humans are out-of-the-loop, they tend to lose oversight of the task and process, leading to a significant reduction of situation awareness. In the event of system failure, it becomes increasingly difficult to manually take over the task (the 'out-of-the-loop performance problem').[22] Furthermore, observing a machine's performance is known as a vigilance task, requiring sustained operator attention, which is characterised by the performer's readiness to detect rare and unpredictable events.[23] This ability to detect rare events decreases over time, a phenomenon known as the vigilance decrement.[24] Introducing automation can lead to vigilance decrements, reducing the human operator's ability to perform (system) failure detection. Therefore, proper function allocation between humans and machines should be based on a thorough understanding of the operational context, along with the risks and consequences of manual and automation failures or shutdowns.

Another challenge in the Human Factors domain is the concept of trust in automation. Cho et al. 2015 have consolidated trust definitions from various domains into a common definition:

> Trust is the willingness of the trustor (evaluator) to take risk based on a subjective belief that a trustee (evaluatee) will exhibit reliable behavior to maximize the trustor's interest under uncertainty (e.g., ambiguity due to conflicting evidence and/or ignorance caused by

[18] Roth et al. 2019.

[19] Challenger et al. 2013.

[20] Wickens et al. 2004; Cohen et al. 2016.

[21] Breton and Bossé 2002.

[22] Endsley and Kiris 1995.

[23] Endsley and Kiris 1995, p. 383; Hancock et al. 2016.

[24] Hancock et al. 2016, p. 152.

complete lack of evidence) of a given situation based on the cognitive assessment of past experience with the trustee.[25]

Trust is an attitude, not a behaviour, that affects and guides how much reliance is placed on automation.[26] Some disciplines question whether trust can be placed in digital systems, arguing that trust is actually placed in the developers of the automation.[27] Whether aimed at the developers or the system, trust depends on the dynamic interaction between the user, the automation, its developers, and its behaviour. Consequently, trust influences the interaction between individuals and automation.[28] Continuous interaction provides insights into an automation system's reliability at a given moment. The alignment between a system's reliability and the trust placed in it is referred to as calibrated trust.[29] Misalignment between trust and system reliability could lead to *misuse* (overreliance in automation, using automation when it should not be used), *disuse* (underutilising available automation), or even *abuse* (intentional inappropriate application of automation).[30] Furthermore, the domain and context in which automation is used determine the level of system reliability and trust required for a human operator to accept advice from a system.[31] In high-risk domains, human operators require a higher baseline of trust before fully relying on the automation.

Overall, determining which tasks to automate and how to allocate functions between systems and human operators should be based on a thorough understanding of various operational scenarios and their associated risks. Collaboration between stakeholders and end-users in conducting this contextual analysis can help establish a baseline of trust with end-users and provide a foundation for appropriate function allocation.

8.2.2 Artificial Intelligence Challenges

AI-enhanced DSS that improve situation awareness rely on inference algorithms and world models that describe the relations between relevant phenomena in the world. These algorithms use world models to infer states or events in the world that (i) have materialised but cannot be observed directly, or (ii) could take place in the future. The former type of inference is used for detection, classification, and identification, while the latter is used for predicting the evolution of relevant phenomena. For example, the identification process shown in Fig. 8.1 could use a model that encodes data on how hostile forces typically wear specific types of uniforms and move in predictable

25 Cho et al. 2015, p. 5.

26 Lee and See 2004.

27 Taddeo 2009.

28 Lee and See 2004.

29 McDermott and Brink 2019; McDermott et al. 2018.

30 Parasuraman and Riley 1997, p. 233.

31 Appelganc et al. 2022.

patterns (e.g., speed, group formation, etc.). Moreover, the classification of these uniforms, an important element in the overall identification process, could be based on a DNN model, which encodes relations between different types of uniforms and patterns observed in surveillance imagery.

World models critically influence the accuracy and speed of automated inference processes. Thus, constructing adequate world models that support performant AI-enhanced solutions is a critical step in the life cycle of an AI-enhanced DSS. In this chapter, performance is defined in terms of accuracy, resolution, and the speed of inference.

Accuracy refers to the 'truthfulness' of the inference results. For example, if the image fed to the AI-enhanced DSS (e.g., an AI solution embedded within the DSS using an image classifier) includes a hostile soldier, and the classifier correctly identifies the soldier as wearing the uniform of hostile forces, the result is accurate. However, if the classifier mistakenly identifies the uniform as belonging to friendly forces or civilians, the result is inaccurate (i.e., the answer is not 'truthful'). In general, models are not perfect as they cannot account for all possible conditions in the operational domain, meaning that inference errors may occur. For AI-enhanced detectors and classifiers, accuracy and error rates are captured by a confusion matrix,[32] which is obtained through systematic and rigorous testing with real-world data. Optimal performance for a given set of data sources is highly dependent on the domain, operational context, and conditions. For example, under certain lighting conditions (e.g., at twilight), distinguishing between the uniforms of hostile and friendly troops in imagery may be challenging. In such cases, even the best model cannot support accurate classification based solely on images. Therefore, prior to deploying any AI-enhanced DSS solution, the system must be evaluated using real-world data collected under the specific conditions expected during operations. While overall inference accuracy can often be improved by introducing more sophisticated models capable of handling a greater variety of input types, this typically demands considerable development effort, as it involves larger quantities of more complex training data. Moreover, the evaluation effort for such solutions often increases exponentially with the number of inputs.

Resolution refers to the granularity of the results. For example, classifiers that differentiate between multiple types of uniforms offer higher resolution than models that can only distinguish between civilian outfits and military uniforms. The higher the resolution, the more complex the model becomes, requiring greater development effort.

Speed refers to the time it takes for an AI solution to process inputs. Typically, the more complex the model, the longer the processing time required.

The development of effective AI-enhanced DSS solutions and their responsible use critically depends on reconciling the performance elements mentioned above with the performance requirements. These requirements are key to determining the

[32] Alpaydin 2020.

required model sophistication and, consequently, the development effort involved. In addition, they are indispensable for establishing clear deployment rules, which can be achieved by systematically investigating the conditions under which the actual performance elements satisfy the performance requirements. However, determining useful performance requirements is often challenging. These requirements must be based on an understanding of decision-making processes within the operational context. Such performance requirements must also consider the fact that decisions are based on one's situation awareness, with the intention to influence the physical world to one's advantage. Several factors at the mission level must be considered, particularly the criticality of the mission, as well as the benefits and potential adverse impacts of an AI-enhanced DSS. The greater the potential adverse effects of erroneous or delayed DSS outputs—such as civilian harm—the more stringent the performance requirements. Hence, the performance requirements should be derived from a contextual analysis of the decision-making process.

Another challenge related to performance requirements is the evaluation of AI-enhanced DSS. The evaluation requires clear metrics and processes that encompass all major factors influencing performance. It can take different forms, such as exhaustive black box testing to derive statistical inferences about performance levels, knowledge-based analysis with qualitative evaluations, or most likely, a combination of both. Generally, if the evaluation is not conducted appropriately, it is likely to be both time-consuming and costly. The evaluation depends on three factors: (i) the technologies employed; (ii) the performance requirements specific to the application; and (iii) the complexity of the domain in which the AI-enhanced DSS operates. The complexity of the domain corresponds to the variety of operational contexts, such as the number of distinct physical situations in which the required performance must be ensured. The more relevant operational contexts there are, the greater the evaluation effort required. In complex settings, pure black-box testing may not be tractable, as obtaining sufficient data for all relevant situations can be challenging. In such cases, qualitative and knowledge-based analyses, which consider the theoretical properties of the models and algorithms used, become indispensable.

8.2.3 Legal and Ethical Challenges

Finally, AI-enhanced automation in military applications is often associated with substantial legal and ethical challenges. In scholarly research, a range of challenges is being debated. Though an extensive review is beyond the scope of this chapter, we briefly focus on the legal principles of distinction, proportionality, and precautions in relation to human oversight, agency, and responsibility, as well as on ethical considerations regarding the subjective experience of operators with respect to control and responsibility.

Sense- and decision-making activities within the military OODA loop must comply with IHL, regardless of whether they are conducted by human (e.g., a commander or operator) or artificial actors. As illustrated by the example in Fig. 8.1, situation assessment involves the identification of sensor tracks as friendly, hostile, or neutral. The action of identification is a first step in the targeting process: the selection and prioritisation of objects and installations (targets) to define an appropriate response (capture, attack or destroy). The central principles of targeting law under IHL are: (i) distinction, (ii) proportionality, and (iii) precautions. In general, the principle of *distinction* requires that parties to an armed conflict always distinguish between combatants and non-combatants (e.g., civilians) and military objectives and civilian objects.[33] In case of doubt regarding the identification of an individual or an object, they shall be presumed to be civilian in nature and, as such, are protected from attack.[34] The principle of *proportionality* dictates that even when the target is a military objective, attacks are prohibited when they are expected to cause harm to civilians and/or damage to civilian objects, that is considered excessive in relation to the direct military advantage anticipated.[35] The principle of *precautions* requires that all feasible precautions are taken by the attacking party to avoid or minimise harm to civilians and damage to civilian objects.[36] This means the commander and his/her command team should carefully assess target verification, means of engagement, and possible effects of the attack.[37]

There is ongoing debate about whether the use of AI undermines the ability of military actors to comply with IHL obligations. Other contributions in this volume address this issue. Boutin, for example, questions how States can fulfil obligations under international law in military contexts where AI systems are susceptible to failures.[38] Technical malfunctions and unpredictability of AI systems, and also the risk of human errors by operators related to the speed and complexity of AI outcomes, could result in harmful consequences or even inability to comply with the law.[39]

Human agency is a key concept in this respect,[40] as it involves the capacity of an individual to act based on intentional choices, as well as the ability to control oneself and influence the environment.[41] The issue of human agency in relation to AI-enhanced DSS is contentious. As Canca highlights, human value judgements and decision making are complex and highly context-dependent processes, which are

33 Protocol Additional to the Geneva Conventions of 12 August 1949, and relating to the Protection of Victims of International Armed Conflicts (Protocol I), 1125 U.N.T.S. 3, 8 June 1977 (API) Article 51(1); Henckaerts and Doswald-Beck 2005, Rule 6 of the ICRC's Customary IHL Study.

34 API, n. 30, Article 52(3); Henckaerts and Doswald-Beck 2005, Rules 5 and 10 of the ICRC's Customary IHL Study.

35 API, n. 30, Article 51(5)(b); Henckaerts and Doswald-Beck 2005, Rule 14 of the ICRC's Customary IHL Study.

36 API, n. 30, Article 57; Henckaerts and Doswald-Beck 2005, Rule 15 of the ICRC's Customary IHL Study.

37 https://casebook.icrc.org/highlight/targeting-under-international-humanitarian-law. Accessed 2 April 2025.

38 See Boutin, Chap. 13 in this volume.

39 Ibid.

40 Boutin and Woodcock 2024.

41 Goller and Harteis 2017.

difficult for AI to grasp.[42] Moreover, characteristics of AI models (e.g., the amount of data processed, model complexity, etc.) could make it impossible for humans to comprehend them, as they surpass human cognitive abilities. In addition, the speed of AI-enhanced decision-making processes may also exceed human abilities. For operators and commanders, it may be more challenging to judge a situation, exercise human agency and control, and consider ethical and legal aspects, especially under time-critical and stressful circumstances. Users of AI-enhanced DSS should be able to participate in and retain control over decision-making processes while exercising autonomy free from undue influence or manipulation by the system.[43]

The debate on human control tended towards the concept of Meaningful Human Control (MHC), basically defined as a sufficient degree of cognitive awareness of the operator using the autonomous system, that makes the exercise of human judgement possible in the process of informed decision-making.[44] Boutin and Woodcock point out that the nature and purpose of MHC in relation to international law remains under debate: while MHC is not a formal principle in international legal frameworks, it serves as a useful lens through which to consider human agency and responsibility. These authors argue that insights from Human–Machine Interaction and related disciplines should be used to investigate human agency throughout the life cycle of AI systems, accounting for the distributed nature of decision making in military operations within broader sociotechnical contexts involving human and artificial actors.[45]

The ability of humans to make intentional choices and understand the outcomes of AI-enhanced DSS relates to challenges in holding individuals, or States, responsible for the potentially harmful consequences of military actions. Scholarly discussions on individual responsibility consider the challenge of holding individuals responsible for risks taken during the employment of AI in an attack in which civilians are harmed. The deployment of military AI could result in erroneous target identification and the risk of harm to civilians during an attack as a consequence. For an individual to be held responsible his/her criminal intention or knowledge of a wrongful act (*mens rea*) needs to be established. When for example, during targeting, errors in the identification of objects, and risks of harming civilians are knowingly accepted, an individual operator or commander would be responsible for these decisions and their consequences. However, under international law, it is currently challenging to prosecute a human employing AI in the targeting process and prove criminal intent.[46] Boutin points out that State responsibility in relation to military AI is important because States form the broader institutional structure in which AI systems are developed, evaluated, implemented and deployed. Benefits of this regime are that under it States have the obligation to offer remedies such as compensation, or restitution, it can impact the governance of AI throughout its entire life cycle (e.g., also

[42] Canca 2023.

[43] Nadibaidze et al. 2024.

[44] Boutin and Woodcock 2024.

[45] Ibid.

[46] See Bo 2021 for an analysis on individual criminal responsibility.

design, development, procurement, etc.), and it complements other responsibility frameworks.[47]

Ethical considerations enrich these notions of control, agency and responsibility from a legal perspective. As an example, Molendijk et al. notice that the concepts of control, responsibility and trust are central in debates on autonomous technologies (such as AWS) and moral-psychological harm to combatants.[48] These concepts are mostly considered from a rational perspective based on abstract principles and hypothetical thought experiments (e.g., the Just War Theory framework). That is, operators are expected to be in control of a system, to be responsible for autonomous targeting, and to trust the system to a certain degree. As these authors demonstrate, such abstract and rational interpretations of these concepts overlook the way in which operators *feel* in control of ongoing events.[49] The rational approach also overlooks how operators *experience* moral failures in relation to consequences of autonomous targeting, even when they are not responsible according to procedures. Moreover, it ignores how trust and risk assessment are shaped over time in relation to others, involving social expectations, vulnerability and interdependence. Empirical research into the lived experiences of operators can deepen understanding of the complexity and dynamics of autonomous technologies in military practice.[50] This also benefits developers' understanding of what human control, responsibility, trust, etc. mean to the users of AI-enhanced DSS.

To summarise, in ongoing debates, scholars question whether human control and agency are required when deploying AI-enhanced DSS for IHL compliance, whether AI use undermines control and agency, and how technical standards can benefit the development and adoption of AI systems.[51] Scholars also question whether new international regulations are needed to address these concerns and reflect on the ethical consequences of military AI. In light of these debates, AI-enhanced DSS developers should take responsibility for considering legal and ethical challenges by recognising and understanding them early on in the AI life cycle and addressing them throughout the AI development and deployment stages.[52] This requires robust mechanisms to ensure safety, mitigate risks, and avoid unintended consequences of AI applications. From a legal and ethical perspective, users such as the operator or commander should maintain sufficient cognitive awareness while using an AI-enhanced DSS to assess its outcomes within a specific situation to make informed decisions. In line with the DSS description in Fig. 8.1, the human operator should be making the final decision, with the AI-enhanced system serving as a support tool.

---

[47] Boutin 2023.

[48] See Molendijk et al., Chap. 7 in this volume.

[49] Ibid.

[50] Ibid.

[51] See Boutin, Chap. 13 in this volume.

[52] Boutin and Woodcock 2024.

8.3 Contextualised AI Onboarding Method (CAIOM)

The challenges described above are affected by contextual factors present in the environment in which the AI-enhanced DSS and human operator will interact. Therefore, it is not feasible to develop a one-size-fits-all set of standards as guidance for developers and users of AI-enhanced DSS (e.g., standardised levels of model performance). Instead, we propose the Contextualised AI Onboarding Method (CAIOM), a standardised approach to the analysis and evaluation of an AI-enhanced DSS within its envisioned context. With the help of CAIOM, multidisciplinary teams can gain a deeper understanding of the operational benefits and risks associated with using AI-enhanced DSS in various contexts. This process helps determine system requirements for the development of AI-enhanced DSS, as well as establish robust deployment rules that maximise the benefits of these systems while minimising associated risks.

CAIOM consists of four steps, each relying on different types of analysis methods (see Fig. 8.2 below). The first two steps, the Application Domain (App) Scan and the Decision-Making Process (DMP) Scan, serve the purpose of knowledge elicitation, identifying and understanding the decisions and consequences made within the operational domain and context. The third step is the Automation (Auto) Scan, an analysis focusing on the feasibility of automating (parts of) the task and decisions identified in the DMP Scan. The final step, Embedding Knowledge into the Life Cycle, ensures that the knowledge elicited from the previous steps is embedded into the system's life cycle.

The following sections provide a detailed description of the Scans in more detail, drawing on the example scenarios introduced earlier. As mentioned, situation awareness can take place on both an individual and team level. At the individual level, the identification task is performed by an individual who assigns identities to all detected

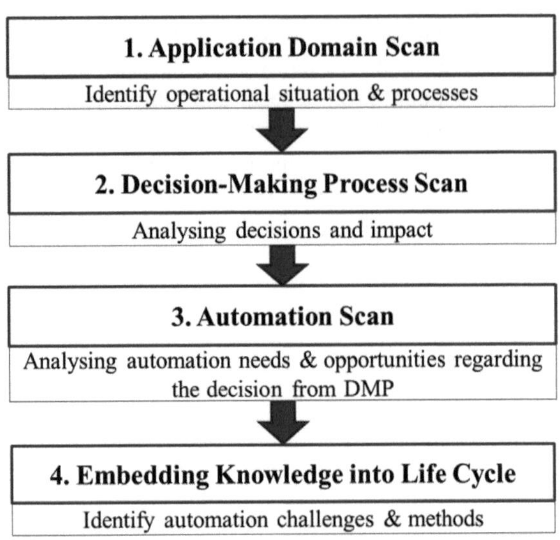

Fig. 8.2 The four steps and goals of CAIOM. *Source* The authors

subjects, based on gathered information. An automatic identifier, introduced earlier as an AI-enhanced DSS solution, could fully automate this task. However, from an operational standpoint, the identification task helps form team situation awareness needed to make decisions upon appropriate actions. From this perspective, the identification task indirectly supports decisions that guide the progression of the mission, aligning with the characteristics of a DSS.[53] This distinction becomes apparent in the App and DMP Scans.

8.3.1 Step 1: Application Domain Scan (App Scan)

The App Scan facilitates thorough understanding of the application domain in which AI support is envisioned. Using methods derived from User-Centred Design (e.g., workshops and interviews), the App Scan helps to map out the overall operational process and context, the personnel involved, and the various tasks they perform. This analysis can help identify the criticality of tasks and the risks involved, including the cascading effect of tasks throughout the operation. As mentioned in Sect. 8.2.1, the allocation of functions between a human operator and AI-enhanced DSS depends not only on the capabilities of both the operator and the system but also on the cognitive risks associated with automation. Additionally, operational criticality demands higher levels of trust. Analysing the operational process and function allocation helps to identify where human oversight and control are required within the task flow to prevent legal and ethical issues (as described in Sect. 8.2.3).

Figure 8.3 below visualises a hypothetical outcome of the App Scan applied to the example scenarios (see Fig. 8.1). It depicts three operational processes: (i) establishing team situation awareness; (ii) choosing an appropriate course of action based on established team situation awareness; and (iii) executing the chosen course of action. Different operators are responsible for the three operational processes. In the first process, the four operators observe the environment, perceive objects, and then identify and classify them as friendly, neutral, or suspect. These operators' tasks overlap, as they all contribute to the same situation awareness process. If one of the tasks within this first process is automated, the other human operators still retain some degree of agency within the system. Furthermore, the manual skill of identifying targets remains crucial and ensuring that operators maintain the ability to perform this task manually and quickly reengage in the loop if a system failure occurs should be a priority. When looking at the broader context, team situation awareness (i.e., identifying adversaries) established in the first operational process will likely lead to an engagement (weapon deployment) in the second and third operational process. The high criticality of the operational outcome demands both high system performance and a strong baseline of trust in the system. Operators must be aware of the system's capabilities, as well as factors that could reduce performance, ensuring their trust is accurately calibrated.

[53] Er 1988.

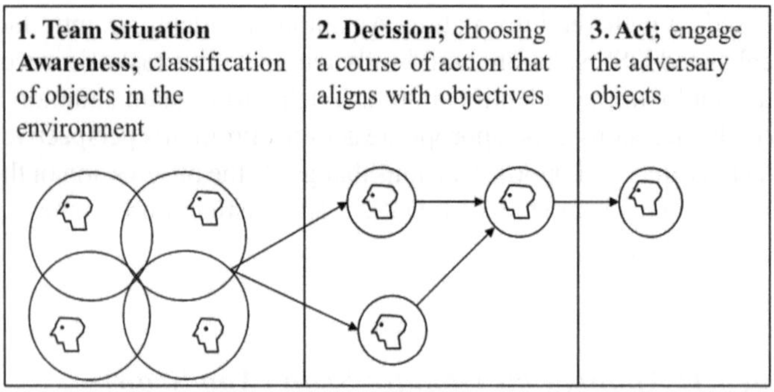

Fig. 8.3 A simplified visual representation of an operational Command and Control process, involving four human operators assessing situation awareness and three human operators deciding upon a course of action. The process includes: (1) gathering and collecting information to understand the situation and consequences; (2) the need to decide on the appropriate course of action; and (3) the resulting actions taken. *Source* The authors

This analysis can help set system requirements regarding function allocation, system performance, and the continuous awareness the end-user must always maintain regarding the system's performance. Various operational conditions in which the system is deployed may lead to different requirements. For example, analysing the system's deployment in Fig. 8.1 (a densely populated area) may necessitate more stringent performance requirements or greater human involvement in the process, while deployment in Fig. 8.1 (a sparsely populated area) may allow for more lenient requirements.

8.3.2 Step 2: Decision-Making Process Scan (DMP Scan)

The DMP Scan deals with the analysis of (critical) decisions made on an individual level, as identified in the App Scan. The Naturalistic Decision Making (NDM) research field has developed various methods and tools to analyse expert's decision-making within natural environments.[54] Tools, such as Cognitive Task Analysis (CTA),[55] are based on structured interview techniques to elicit the tacit knowledge experts rely on when formulating decisions. Variations of these tools are applied within the DMP Scan to help extract the expert's (tacit) knowledge regarding their decision-making process and how they take the risk of certain decisions into account.

Figure 8.4 below visualises an oversimplified decision analysis regarding the identification task performed by a human operator. In this process, the operator looks for specific information, analyses it, and then decides whether the object is friendly, neutral, or suspect. The DMP Scan helps to identify information cues and

[54] Klein 1993.

[55] Klein and Militello 2001.

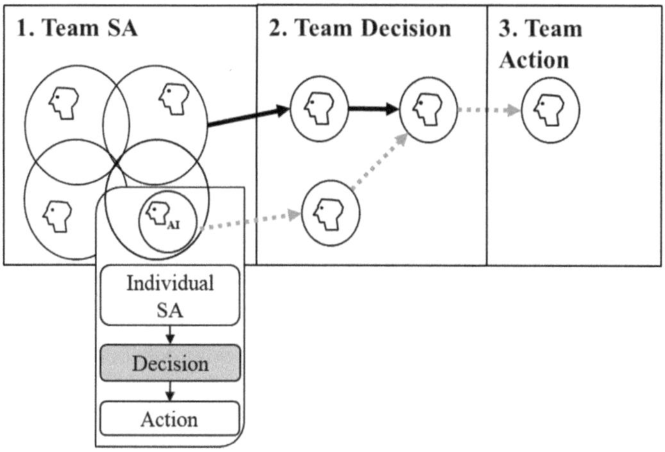

Fig. 8.4 An oversimplified visualisation of a critical decision analysis. The light-coloured dashed lines indicate the cascading effects of the decision outcome (and potentially harmful implications of incorrect decisions) on the overall operation. *Source* The authors

their meaning within a specific context, aiding in the determination of what data is needed to automate this task. Furthermore, the human operator's decision making is affected by the operational context and the criticality of the operation. Depending on the consequences and cascading effects of their decisions (represented by grey, dotted arrows in Fig. 8.4), the decision maker can adopt a more conservative or liberal approach. Analysing and understanding the factors influencing the expert's decision-making process helps to further refine the system design by incorporating these considerations. Furthermore, if an automated system has been designed and its performance (accuracy) levels are known, the mission context can guide the establishment of rules of deployment. For example, in the situation in Fig. 8.1 (a densely populated area), the risk of falsely classifying civilians as adversaries is higher due to the greater *a priori* chance of civilians being present. Whether the system should be used in such a scenario should be considered prior to the mission. The rules of deployment should therefore depend on the system's performance levels and the specific mission context that is foreseen.

8.3.3 Step 3: Automation Scan (Auto Scan)

The Auto Scan focuses on assessing the feasibility of automating the tasks identified in the DMP Scan. The emphasis is on analysing the complexity of the significant correlations between the data used in each task. The more complex these correlations are, the more complex models are needed for automated solutions. The model complexity, however, corresponds to the number of parameters that define the model; the more complex the model, the more parameters must be determined, either through expert introspection or ML. As the number of parameters grows, their determination becomes increasingly challenging. Manual determination is often intractable, and automated extraction of parameters through ML requires increasingly large quantities of data for model training. In addition, sufficient data quantities are required for model evaluation. In general, large datasets for training and evaluation must be collected and prepared, which can be a very costly endeavour. The Auto Scan provides an early estimation of the tractability of automating decision support with AI-enhanced DSS automation before the solution is developed. In particular, the Auto Scan relies on Qualitative Models of the Data Generating Processes (QMDGP).[56] This approach enables the determination of:

1. The required model architectures that can cope with data complexity;
2. The quantity of training data needed to produce accurate AI-enhanced DSS solutions; and
3. The quantity of testing data required for the estimation of expected accuracy.

Based on a QMDGP analysis, we can (i) identify suitable AI techniques for automating selected tasks in the DMP Scan and (ii) estimate whether the chosen tasks can be automated while fulfilling the performance requirements and the need for human agency. This process determines the feasibility of automation for the given tasks.

To illustrate this, we consider the identification function from Fig. 8.1. For simplicity, we assume that the identification is based solely on the classification of uniforms, using images only. Given the type of data and complex continuous signals involved, a DNN is the best AI-enhanced solution. However, the complexity of the DNN model architecture should consider the context, which significantly influences the images. By setting up a qualitative QMDGP, we can easily see that the images captured by the cameras are heavily dependent on factors such as the distance and angle from which the images were obtained, the resolution of the camera, the lighting conditions (e.g., day, night, twilight, etc.), and weather conditions (e.g., rain, snow, fog, etc.). This means that the AI model must enable inference process that explicitly considers these contextual factors.

Note, however, that different contexts require greater complexity in the model, as each context introduces factors that must be addressed. This, in turn, requires large quantities of training data. The QMDGP-based analysis signals that sufficient training data must be collected for each distinct context. However, this may not be feasible due to limitations in collecting real-world data (e.g., reconnaissance imagery from drones). To reduce complexity, AI-enhanced DSS identification functions could be *limited* to specific conditions, including the automatic classification of tracks when images are captured within certain ranges under good weather conditions.

[56] Mignet et al. 2024; Pavlin et al. 2023.

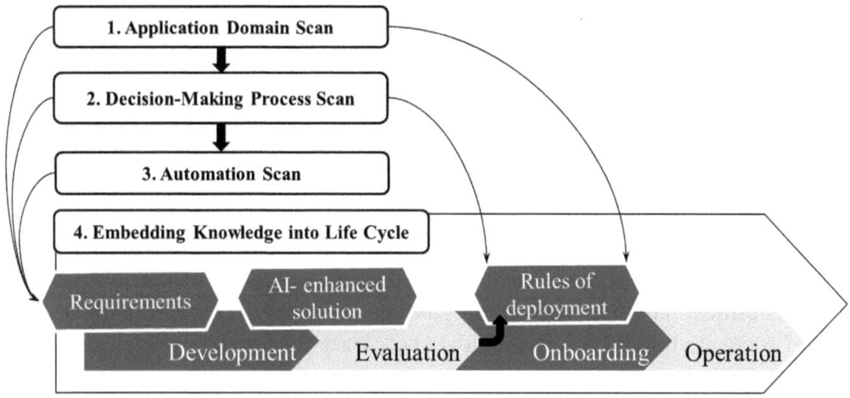

Fig. 8.5 Embedding the CAIOM results in the life cycle of an AI-enhanced DSS. *Source* The authors

Moreover, the Auto Scan facilitates the identification of appropriate evaluation steps and metrics. Within the context of a DMP Scan, the evaluation determination process is guided by the Uncertainty Representation and Reasoning Evaluation Framework (URREF).[57] This framework provides an overview of the different criteria that need to be evaluated in high-level, AI-based fusion solutions used by DSS. Addressing these evaluation criteria is key to efficiently developing high-quality DSS applications. URREF-driven analysis provides early insights into the evaluation complexity and its associated costs and feasibility. These insights are crucial inputs for preparing the AI-enhanced DSS's life cycle. Finally, the results of the QMDGP analysis guide the planning and preparation of data acquisition processes, another critical activity in the life cycle of AI-enhanced DSS.

8.3.4 Step 4: Life Cycle Adaptations

The App, DMP and Auto Scans provide critical inputs for tackling various challenges throughout the different stages in the life cycle of AI-enhanced DSS, as depicted in Fig. 8.5 above.

8.3.4.1 Early Life Cycle Stages

The App and DMP Scans facilitate the understanding of operational criticality and risks involved in the decision-making process. This helps to determine function allocation and the extent to which human control is needed. The results of these Scans are also the basis for the extraction of operational and performance requirements.

[57] Costa et al. 2012; De Villiers et al. 2018.

The Auto Scan, on the other hand, facilitates the analysis of the AI-enhanced DSS's complexity, a critical step towards selecting adequate AI technologies. This, in turn, determines if human agency is sufficiently present across all intended operational contexts. Moreover, in the development phase, special attention must be paid to the training and evaluation of AI-enhanced DSS models under relevant operational conditions. This requires adequate amounts of data, which, in turn, requires systematic and well-prepared data acquisition processes, as well as sound testing and evaluation processes. In this way, the model's performance can be predicted for a class of relevant applications under the targeted operational conditions. The Auto Scan provides critical inputs for this phase, guiding developers in preparing the acquisition of adequate training and testing data necessary for developing high-quality AI solutions.

8.3.4.2 Later Life Cycle Stages

Secondly, the App and DMP Scans provide useful inputs for the later stages of development, especially in preparing the rules of deployment for an AI-enhanced DSS. These rules must simultaneously consider the operational benefits of the technical solution with ethical and legal principles, as well as the expected performance and limitations in relevant settings. In other words, determining deployment rules involves integrating different types of expertise, a key step in the life cycle that should be completed prior to the onboarding phase—when the AI-enhanced DSS is introduced into the overall decision-making process. The deployment rules enable operators to make fast, informed decisions about AI-enhanced DSS, particularly as the operation evolves (e.g., as weather conditions change or a civilian airliner mistakenly enters the operational area, etc.). Such rules describe the conditions under which the AI components of a DSS can be used, taking into account mission characteristics and criticality, operational conditions, and the expected performance of these AI components.

To enable efficient collaborative formulation of these rules, the outputs from the App and DMP Scans must be captured in high-level descriptions that are accessible and understandable to experts from different backgrounds. The explicit high-level problem characterisation resulting from these Scans enables more efficient analysis of the ethical and legal aspects of the AI solution. This, in turn, increases the chances of developing effective solutions that adhere to legal and ethical principles while also meeting technical and operational constraints. Moreover, the outputs from the App and DMP Scans provide a basis for engaging users efficiently in the preparation of deployment rules and their subsequent training during the onboarding process.

Overall, the CAIOM Scans in the earlier phases of the life cycle facilitate the development of an AI-enhanced DSS that is closely aligned with the required specifications. This AI solution reflects an understanding of the system's properties, such as its performance and failure modes. In the later phases, prior to onboarding, CAIOM facilitates the formulation of deployment rules that consider the results from the App and DMP Scans, alongside the anticipated system performance estimated during the development phase.

8.4 Conclusion and Next Steps

In the military domain, AI-enhanced DSS have the potential to significantly improve operational efficiency and effectiveness. However, the decision to deploy AI-enhanced DSS must carefully consider the mission's criticality, the specific tasks automated, the benefits of the automated solution, and the potential adverse effects in case of failure. The validated performance of the AI system must align with the mission's criticality, ensuring that the trust placed in the system is appropriate for the mission's demands. In addition, effective rules of deployment must be established to guarantee the ethical use of the AI-enhanced solutions. The developers of AI-enhanced DSS must be aware of both the operational conditions and the performance requirements to build high-quality AI solutions with known properties for different settings. In other words, the development of reliable and effective AI-enhanced DSS solutions and their safe deployment requires a common understanding of the operational context among the developers and deployers of the system.

This is facilitated through CAIOM, a novel approach supporting the systematic extraction of high-level descriptions of contextual factors influencing critical steps in the decision-making process, as well as analysing the potential impact of AI-enhanced solutions. The CAIOM approach introduces a sequence of analysis steps that support stakeholders in tackling the AI challenges in their domain, while simultaneously enabling and fostering common understanding and collaboration among stakeholders. This collaboration is essential for determining sound system requirements and establishing effective deployment rules for AI-enhanced DSS. Stakeholder collaboration throughout the life cycle phases of an AI-enhanced DSS enables the development of high-performing systems whose properties are understood by the users under relevant conditions. It also aids in identifying and leveraging the benefits of AI solutions across various operational scenarios, while minimising the risk of negative side effects.

The toolset of CAIOM presented in this chapter will be continuously validated with new use cases and expanded with new tools to further improve pinpointing the key aspects and knowledge that need to be extracted. The emphasis of CAIOM is on improving the efficiency of the elicitation process and representations of its outcomes, ensuring that experts from diverse backgrounds can efficiently analyse and jointly discuss the critical steps in a specific decision-making process. This approach needs to be applied across various contexts in which the specific decision-making process is foreseen, capable of being applied at different stages in the life cycle of AI systems. By doing so, CAIOM ensures the development of effective AI-enhanced DSS that align with ethical, operational, and performance standards and values.

References

Articles, Books and Other Documents

Alpaydin E (2020) Introduction to Machine Learning. The MIT Press, Cambridge, London

Appelganc K, Rieger T, Roesler E, Manzey D (2022) How Much Reliability is Enough? A Context-Specific View on Human Interaction with (Artificial) Agents from Different Perspectives. Journal of Cognitive Engineering and Decision Making 16:207–221

Assaad Z, Boshuijzen-van Burken C (2023) Ethics and Safety of Human-Machine Teaming. https://doi.org/10.1145/3597512.3600205. Accessed 2 April 2025

Bishop C (2006) Pattern Recognition and Machine Learning. Springer-Verlag, New York

Bo M (2021) Autonomous Weapons and the Responsibility Gap in light of the *Mens Rea* of the War Crime of Attacking Civilians in the ICC Statute, Journal of International Criminal Justice. https://doi.org/10.1093/jicj/mqab005

Boutin B (2023) State Responsibility in Relation to Military Applications of Artificial Intelligence. Leiden Journal of International Law. https://doi.org/10.1017/S0922156522000607

Boutin B, Woodcock T (2024) Aspects of Realising (Meaningful) Human Control: A Legal Perspective. In: Geiß R, Lahmann H (eds) Research Handbook on Warfare and Artificial Intelligence. Edward Elgar Publishing, pp. 179–196

Breton R, Bossé É (2002) The Cognitive Costs and Benefits of Automation. https://apps.dtic.mil/sti/pdfs/ADA422303.pdf. Accessed 1 April 2024

Canca C (2023) AI Ethics and Governance in Defence Innovation: Implementing AI Ethics Framework. In: Raska M, Bitzinger RA (eds) The AI Wave in Defence Innovation, 1st edn. Routledge, London, pp. 59–79

Challenger R, Clegg CW, Shepherd C (2013) Function allocation in complex systems: reframing an old problem. Ergonomics 56:1051–1069

Cho JH, Chan K, Adali S (2015) A Survey on Trust Modeling. ACM Computing Surveys (CSUR) 48:1–40

Cohen I, den Braber N, Smets N, van Diggelen J, Brinkman WP, Neerincx MA (2016) Work content influences on cognitive task load, emotional state and performance during a simulated 520-days' Mars mission. Computers in Human Behavior 55:642–652

Costa PC, Laskey KB, Blasch E, Jousselme AL (2012) Towards Unbiased Evaluation of Uncertainty Reasoning: The URREF Ontology. http://seor.vse.gmu.edu/~klaskey/papers/Fusion12_URREF_Ontology.pdf. Accessed 15 September 2024

De Villiers JP, Pavlin G, Jousselme AL, Maskell S, De Waal A, Laskey K, Blasch E, Costa P (2018) Uncertainty Representation and Evaluation for Modelling and Decision-making in Information Fusion. Journal of Advances in Information Fusion 13:198–215

Endsley MR (1995) Toward a Theory of Situation Awareness in Dynamic Systems. Human Factors: The Journal of Human Factors and Ergonomics Society 37:32–64

Endsley MR (2015) Situation Awareness Misconceptions and Misunderstandings. Journal of Cognitive Engineering and Decision making 9:4–32

Endsley MR, Bolté B, Jones DG (2003) Designing for Situation Awareness: An Approach to User-Centered Design, 1st edn. CRC Press, London

Endsley MR, Kiris EO (1995) The Out-of-the-Loop Performance Problem and Level of Control in Automation. Human Factors 37:381–394

Er MC (1988) Decision Support Systems: a summary, problems, and future trends. Decision Support Systems 4:355–363

Goller M, Harteis C (2017) Human Agency at Work: Towards a Clarification and Operationalisation of the Concept. In: Goller M, Paloniemi S (eds) Agency at Work: An Agentic Perspective on Professional Learning and Development, vol. 20. Springer, Cham, pp. 85–103

Goodfellow I, Bengio Y, Courville A (2016) Deep Learning. The MIT Press, Cambridge

Hammond GT (2018) A Discourse on Winning and Losing. Air University Press, Maxwell Air Force Base, Alabama
Hancock PA, Volante WG, Szalma JL (2016) Defeating the Vigilance Decrement. IIE Transactions on Occupational Ergonomics and Human Factors 4:151–163
Henckaerts JM, Doswald-Beck L (2005) Customary International Humanitarian Law Rules, vol. I. Cambridge University Press, Cambridge
Jensen FV, Nielsen TD (2007) Bayesian Networks and Decision Graphs, 2nd edn. Springer-Verlag, New York
Jiang J, Karran AJ, Coursaris CK, Léger PM, Beringer J (2023) A Situation Awareness Perspective on Human-AI Interaction: Tensions and Opportunities. International Journal of Human–Computer Interaction 39:1789–1806
Klein GA (1993) A Recognition-Primed Decision (RPD) Model of Rapid Decision Making. In: Klein GA, Orasanu J, Caldenwood R, Zsambok CE (eds) Decision Making in Action: Models and Methods. Ablex Publishing Corporation, Norwood NJ, pp. 138–147
Klein GA, Militello LG (2001) Some guidelines for conducting a cognitive task analysis. In: Salas E (ed) Advances in Human Performance and Cognitive Engineering Research, vol. 1. Elsevier Science Ltd, Oxford, pp. 163–199
Koch W, Keisinger F (2024) How Can Responsible AI Be Implemented? In: Schraagen JM (ed) Responsible Use of AI in Military Systems, 1st edn. Chapman & Hall/CRC Press, New York, pp. 37–58
Lee JD, See KA (2004) Trust in Automation: Designing for Appropriate Reliance. Human Factors. The Journal of Human Factors and Ergonomics Society 46:50–80
Macmillan NA (2002) Signal Detection Theory. In: Pashler H, Wixted JT (eds) Stevens' Handbook of Experimental Psychology: Methodology in Experimental Psychology, 3rd edn. John Wiley & Sons, Inc., New York, pp. 43–90
McDermott P, Brink R (2019) Practical Guidance for Evaluating Calibrated Trust. https://doi.org/10.1177/1071181319631379. Accessed 1 August 2024
McDermott P, Dominguez C, Kasdaglis N, Ryan M, Trahan I, Nelson A (2018) Human-Machine Teaming Systems Engineering Guide. https://www.mitre.org/sites/default/files/2021-11/prs-17-4208-human-machine-teaming-systems-engineering-guide.pdf. Accessed 24 April 2024
Mignet F, Slijkhuis F, Abouhafc A, Pavlin G, Laskey KB (2024) A Qualitative Causal Approach to Determining Adequate Training Data Quantity for Machine Learning. https://ieeexplore.ieee.org/abstract/document/10706369. Accessed 2 April 2025
Mitchell T M (1997) Machine Learning. McGraw Hill, New York
Nadibaidze A, Bode I, Zhang Q (2024) AI in Military Decision Support Systems: A Review of Developments and Debates. https://usercontent.one/wp/www.autonorms.eu/wp-content/uploads/2024/11/AI-DSS-report-WEB.pdf?media=1629963761. Accessed 20 March 2025
Omarova A, Ireland V, Gorod A (2012) An Alternative Approach to Identifying and Appraising Adaptive Loops in Complex Organizations. Procedia Computer Science 12:56–62
Parasuraman R, Riley V (1997) Humans and Automation: Use, Misuse, Disuse, Abuse. Human Factors: The Journal of the Human Factors and Ergonomics Society 39:230–253
Pavlin G, Laskey KB, Mignet F, Slijkhuis FS, Blasch E, Dragos V, Jansen L (2023) Qualitative Models of Data Generation Processes: Facilitating Data-Intensive AI Solutions. https://hal.science/hal-04313573/document. Accessed 2 December 2024
Pearl J (1988) Probabilistic Reasoning in Intelligent Systems: Networks of Plausible Inference. Morgan Kaufmann, San Francisco
Richards C (2020) Boyd's OODA Loop. Necesse Vol 5 Issue 1:142–165
Roth EM, Sushereba C, Militello LG, Diiulio J, Ernst K (2019) Function Allocation Considerations in the Era of Human Autonomy Teaming. Journal of Cognitive Engineering and Decision Making 13:199–220
Russell ST, Norvig P (2010) Artificial Intelligence: A Modern Approach. Prentice Hall, Englewood Cliffs NJ

Sutton RS, Barto AG (2018) Reinforcement Learning: An Introduction, 2nd edn. The MIT Press, Cambridge

Taddeo M (2009) Defining Trust and E-Trust: From Old Theories to New Problems. International Journal of Technology and Human Interaction 5:23–35

Wickens CD, Lee JD, Liu Y, Gordon Becker SE (2004) An Introduction to Human Factors Engineering, 2nd edn. Pearson Education Inc, New Jersey

Iris Cohen received a PhD in 2015 in the field of applied cognitive psychology from Delft University of Technology and TNO Human Factors. She has extensive research experience in the field of human factors, with research topics such as stress and human performance, measures of mental states, highly-automated driving systems, and social robotics. At Thales Netherlands B.V., her research includes descriptive modelling of experts' decision making processes, Human Machine Teaming and Human-AI interaction. She uses methods from the Cognitive Engineering and Naturalistic Decision Making research fields, with the objective to create guidelines for system and interface design.

Gregor Pavlin received his PhD degree in computer science (autonomous robots) from Graz University of Technology, Austria in 2001. He has extensive industrial experience in safety critical software systems as well as complex AI-driven solutions. His current research interests are (i) robust algorithms and architectures supporting distributed probabilistic AI, (ii) machine learning and (iii) interoperability in complex service oriented processing systems. Gregor is a senior researcher and project manager at Thales Nederland B.V. He is also a member of the ISIF Evaluation Techniques for Uncertainty Representation and Reasoning Working Group (ETURWG).

Rianne Gouman (MA) studied Cultural Anthropology at Leiden University. Since 2005 she works at the Research department of Thales Netherlands B.V. She explores the relation between culture, technology, information and organisations, conducting research in (inter)national projects in public safety & security management and defence. Her ethnographic research focuses on information sharing, sensemaking, decision making and coordination, with a particular interest in meaning making and practice. Her aim is to embed new technology carefully in a work context, help all stakeholders in a project understand user needs, and explore how new socio-technical concepts can help end-users navigate complex and dynamic situations.

Chapter 9
Iterative Assessment for Military Artificial Intelligence (AI) Systems

Jonathan Kwik

Contents

Abstract Artificial intelligence (AI) introduces unprecedented uncertainty in military operations. This is particularly evident in AI-enabled autonomous weapon systems (AWS) and decision support systems (DSS), which not only influence critical battlefield decisions but also pose novel and unpredictable risks. While some risks can be anticipated and managed *ex ante*, many remain inherent and unavoidable, given the complex, dynamic, and adversarial nature of the environments in which these systems operate. Even AI operators acting in good faith may face situations in which unforeseeable civilian harm occurs, despite rigorous review and careful deployment. In practice, many such incidents will be characterised as 'accidents'—a reality of war that International Humanitarian Law is expected to tolerate. This chapter challenges that assumption, arguing that even *a priori* unpredictable AI failures can be mitigated—if not prevented—through an iterative approach. By systematically integrating insights from post-deployment assessments, this approach enables decision makers to update their understanding of edge cases and other 'known

J. Kwik (✉)
T.M.C. Asser Institute, The Hague, The Netherlands
e-mail: jkwik@asser.nl

University of Amsterdam, Amsterdam, The Netherlands

B. Boutin et al. (eds.), *Legal, Ethical, and Technical Dilemmas in Military Artificial Intelligence*, https://doi.org/10.1007/978-94-6265-759-5_9

unknowns' that emerge during real-world use, providing essential insights to inform future AI deployment. It proposes an *Iterative Assessment* framework—implemented through two complementary mechanisms: *Iterative Review* and *Iterative Assessment in Deployment*. This framework represents best practice for managing uncertainty and minimising civilian harm in the use of military AI. While initial accidents may be unavoidable, their recurrence can be significantly reduced through a structured iterative process of reporting, analysis, and adaptation. Those committed to the responsible use of military AI should embed this framework as a core component of operational planning and legal compliance.

Keywords Uncertainty · Artificial Intelligence (AI) · Accident · Autonomous Weapons Systems · Decision Support Systems · Predictability · Weapons Review · International Humanitarian Law

9.1 Introduction

As artificial intelligence (AI) becomes increasingly embedded in military operations, its users will be confronted with heightened uncertainty, unpredictable risks, and system vulnerabilities. Many of these challenges will only reveal themselves *ex post*—after failures have already resulted in humanitarian harm, such as civilian injury or loss of life. In practice, such incidents are often characterised as unavoidable 'accidents', and tolerated as the inevitable by-products of war. This chapter challenges that assumption and proposes an *Iterative Assessment* framework as a best practice approach for militaries seeking to proactively mitigate AI-related civilian harm in dynamic operational environments.

The framework rests on two foundational tenets. On one hand, it acknowledges that failures involving military AI may be unavoidable at the outset, and that decision makers cannot be expected to know the unknowable. On the other, it argues that the overarching spirit of International Humanitarian Law (IHL) imposes a duty on belligerents to take all feasible steps to prevent the recurrence of such harm once relevant risks become knowable. To this end, the Iterative Assessment framework introduces a two-tiered mechanism designed to support rapid, adaptive mitigation of emerging AI-related risks.

The chapter proceeds as follows. Section 9.2 contextualises the discussion by examining how the heightened unpredictability of AI systems undermines the effectiveness of traditional quality control and risk mitigation mechanisms in preventing repeated failures. Building on this, Sect. 9.3 provides a semi-technical overview of the various sources of AI uncertainty, demonstrating that many stem from immutable properties of the technology and, therefore, cannot be eliminated through technical means alone—nor can they be fully addressed through *ex ante* precautions. To address this challenge, the chapter advocates for the adoption of an iterative mindset—one that operationalises IHL obligations continuously over time, rather than at isolated junctures. With this philosophy in mind, Sects. 9.4 and 9.5 explore the application of

Iterative Assessment in the review and targeting phases, respectively. On this basis, Sect. 9.6 then synthesises the model into a visual operational guide to support practical implementation. Finally, Sect. 9.7 concludes with key reflections and actionable recommendations for embedding Iterative Assessment into military practice.

Before proceeding, it is helpful to clarify the nature and purpose of the Iterative Assessment framework. The term 'framework' is used deliberately, in preference to alternatives such as 'norm' or 'principle'. This reflects the fact that Iterative Assessment is not intended to represent a binding legal obligation *lex lata*, particularly under more restrictive interpretations of IHL. Rather, it refers to a structured set of measures and policies that decision makers can adopt to minimise risk to civilians during the development, testing, and deployment of AI systems. These measures are rooted in a core philosophy of iteration and continuous improvement. At the same time, Iterative Assessment is neither radical nor entirely novel. On the contrary, many of the practices recommended in this chapter already exist within contemporary military doctrine and have been advanced in scholarship.[1] The primary challenge lies not in their conceptual novelty, but in their consistent implementation—something that in practice is often constrained by operational or logistical realities.

As to what Iterative Assessment can achieve, its limits must also be recognised. It cannot eliminate all uncertainty: this has always been an inherent feature of military operations. However, when properly implemented, Iterative Assessment can strengthen adherence to IHL by helping to prevent avoidable civilian harm. In essence, it aims to reduce the number of instances where harm occurs not due to recklessness, but because decision makers lacked access to information that was, in *theory*, knowable. While not a panacea, Iterative Assessment offers a meaningful and practical standard for those seeking to responsibly integrate AI into military operations.

Finally, this chapter proceeds on the assumption that AI users act in good faith, seeking to uphold IHL and to manage uncertainty responsibly. It presumes that all pre-existing obligations related to testing, review, and precautions in attack, as required under IHL, have been duly fulfilled. It does not address bad-faith scenarios, such as the deliberate deployment of 'black box' systems without any attempt to understand their functions.[2] Iterative Assessment is designed to complement—not replace—these foundational IHL obligations. The objective of this chapter is to demonstrate that even when conventional IHL requirements are properly met, there remains scope for further improvement through the adoption of an iterative approach.

---

[1] Additionally, under more permissive interpretations of IHL, one could argue that Iterative Assessment aligns with the 'constant care' obligation set out in Protocol Additional to the Geneva Conventions of 12 August 1949, and relating to the Protection of Victims of International Armed Conflicts (Protocol I), opened for signature 8 June 1977, 1125 UNTS 3, entered into force 7 December 1978 (API), Article 57(1).

[2] Beyond constituting bad faith, many commentators argue that deploying AI systems under such conditions constitutes a clear violation of IHL. For example, see Sullivan and Ricket 2024; Holland Michel 2020; Kwik and Van Engers 2021.

9.2 The Case for Iterative Assessment

Warfare has always been inherently fraught with uncertainties. Legal decisions concerning the use of force, and the manner in which it is applied, often rely on 'determinations of fact that may be difficult to make'.[3] Scientific advancements, while falling short of offering full transparency on the battlefield,[4] have nonetheless helped to reduce this uncertainty. Modern militaries increasingly rely on more precise weaponry, advanced sensors, satellite imagery, and other tools to peer through the proverbial fog of war and support legal compliance.[5] Against this backdrop, AI is often presented as the next technological leap: a system capable of processing vast quantities of signal data, enhancing intelligence gathering, and improving situational awareness.[6]

Despite these potential advantages, the integration of AI into military operations risks *reducing* transparency, owing to the unique properties of the technology itself. AI systems exhibit unpredictable characteristics—including the black box phenomenon, unintuitive failure modes, continuous learning, and emergent, unprogrammed behaviours—all of which introduce novel uncertainties and pose serious challenges for normative legal compliance.[7] The unpredictability of AI has long been recognised as a formidable obstacle to the application of IHL.[8] Among the concerns raised, it has been submitted that such technological uncertainties may:

> ***Complicate*** exhaustive testing, validation, and quality assurance processes, as AI systems are likely to encounter real-world deployment conditions that could not have been anticipated during development;[9]
>
> ***Undermine*** weapons reviews, as required under Additional Protocol I (API) to the Geneva Conventions (GCs) or implied in customary IHL,[10] due to difficulties in fully understanding how an AI system will behave in operational environments;[11]
>
> ***Invalidate*** IHL compliance assessments made at the moment of activation,[12] as unanticipated behaviours may render such evaluations obsolete immediately after deployment; and
>
> ***Impair*** the proper implementation of precautionary obligations, as AI users may be unable to reliably predict the system's behaviour or anticipate its operational consequences.[13]

---

[3] US Department of Defense 2015, Section 5.3.1.

[4] Stewart 2011, p. 293.

[5] Ekelhof 2018, p. 76; Haque 2012, p. 110; Schmitt and Schauss 2019, p. 152.

[6] Mikhailov 2023, p. 2.

[7] These factors are comprehensively discussed in Sect. 9.3.

[8] For example, see ICRC 2016, pp. 2–3.

[9] Lohn 2020, p. 1.

[10] API, n.1; Switzerland 2016, para 23; Klonowska 2022.

[11] Holland Michel 2020, p. 19.

[12] ICRC 2019, p. 3.

[13] Liu 2016, p. 335.

These concerns are not limited to AI deployed in use-of-force systems, such as autonomous weapons systems (AWS), but are equally relevant to AI-enabled decision-support systems (DSS).[14] Moreover, they span across the entire lifecycle of an AI system—from development through deployment to post-deployment—complicating efforts to ensure continued compliance with IHL across each phase.[15]

Various approaches have been proposed to respond to this unpredictability. Measures such as explainability requirements, designed to combat the black box nature of modern algorithms (as implemented by the United States (US) and the North Atlantic Treaty Organisation (NATO)),[16] enhanced modelling-based testing and review processes,[17] and prohibitions on online learning post-deployment,[18] have all been proposed as potential safeguards.[19] Best practice for ensuring compliance with IHL would undoubtedly involve the adoption of such measures and standards by militaries, where feasible.[20] Still, one may question whether certain sources of AI uncertainty can ever truly be eliminated.

As one example, the military environment is inherently complex and dynamic, presenting an almost infinite range of possible input–output pairings. As such, 'edge cases and unforeseen performance-degrading elements always remain a possibility',[21] regardless of how diligently systems are reviewed, or how well an operator claims to understand both the system and the operational environment.[22] Even the most genuine and good-faith belligerents will inevitably encounter surprises.

Consider these hypothetical situations, which highlight key challenges that will be referenced throughout this discussion to illustrate the importance of Iterative Assessment for AI systems:

---

[14] In this chapter, AWS refers to physical weapon systems equipped with AI components that assist in use-of-force functions (e.g., autonomous target recognition and engagement). In contrast, DSS refers to AI-powered software designed to assist human operators in making use-of-force decisions (e.g., target identification, target sorting, and course-of-action recommendations). For a detailed distinction between the two, see ICRC and Geneva Academy 2024, pp. 9–10.

[15] An exception to this observation arises where reviews are deemed applicable solely to AWS and not to DSS, as there is ongoing debate over whether DSS qualify as 'means and methods of warfare', thereby triggering the legal duty to review. See also Sect. 9.4.

[16] US Department of Defense 2023, p. 4; NATO 2021a, para 9.C.

[17] Meier 2019, p. 309.

[18] That is, where the AI system is permitted to continue adapting its weights based on inputs obtained from the operational environment after deployment; see Defense Innovation Board 2019, p. 46.

[19] For example, Moyes 2019, p. 11; see also Boothby 2018, p. 151.

[20] IHL 'accounts for the limited and unreliable nature of information in armed conflict'; see US Department of Defense 2015, Section 5.4.3.2. However, a minimum epistemic threshold is required for decision makers to make reasoned and legally compliant choices, and reasonable commanders are required to take active steps to reduce uncertainty where feasible; see Thorne 2020, p. 2; Schmitt and Schauss 2019, p. 152; As Kalmanovitz remarks, '[w]hen there is uncertainty, the relevant practical question to ask is what steps have been taken to sufficiently determine and limit the risks created'; Kalmanovitz 2016, p. 156.

[21] Kwik 2024a, p. 70.

[22] Many other sources of AI-induced uncertainty present challenges that lack straightforward solutions, as discussed in Sect. 9.3.

Drone (AWS): During a one-month operation, autonomous drones mistakenly targeted and killed several local civilians after traditional clothing patterns worn in the region triggered AI hallucinations.[23] Despite extensive review and testing of the drone model—including assessments accounting for typical regional attire—this edge case went undetected. The hallucination was only activated when the patterns were viewed from a specific angle, a factor not identified during testing and evaluation. Similar incidents were reported across multiple platoons operating the drones in the same region.

Targeting Adviser (DSS): A DSS powered by a large language model (LLM) with a chat interface was deployed to assist officers in target analysis. After one month of use, a scathing NGO report revealed that numerous approved targets had, in fact, been civilian. Although the system had performed reliably during prior testing and deployments, officers—under operational pressure—had unknowingly framed their chat prompts with urgency. The LLM misinterpreted this as a directive to prioritise speed over accuracy, leading to target misidentifications.[24] Even the system's engineers were shocked to discover this emergent behaviour, i.e., that the LLM had learnt to infer urgency from the prompt structure and had dynamically altered its outputs accordingly.

Despite the seriousness of these outcomes, it is highly probable that such harms would be dismissed as '[m]istakes or faulty weaponry'—inevitable occurrences in the conduct of war.[25]

Militaries have, at times, been criticised for too readily characterising such incidents as 'accidents', when, in reality, they may stem from systemic flaws in targeting practices (e.g., reliance on poor or outdated intelligence or perceived behavioural patterns).[26] However, the *Drone* and *Targeting Adviser* cases truly appear to constitute genuine accidents: rigorous testing and evaluation were undertaken, and there is no indication that the operators acted recklessly (or even negligently).[27] In the *Drone* case, none of the platoon commanders were likely aware of the specific edge case, nor had the issuing authority identified it, despite extensive review and testing. While basic precautions in attack would have accounted for encounters with local civilians wearing traditional clothing,[28] available system data gave no indication that this would trigger fatal misclassifications. Similarly, in the *Targeting Adviser* case, the officers had no reason to suspect that the LLM could infer urgency from their prompts and dynamically adjust its outputs in a harmful way.[29] Nor had this behaviour been

[23] Hallucinations occur 'when an AI model generates incorrect or misleading information but presents it as if it were a fact'. For several examples, see Guinness 2024.

[24] Research has shown that prompt formulation can influence the output of large models such as LLMs in unforeseen ways; see Sharma et al. 2023.

[25] Bartels 2013, p. 280.

[26] See Hathaway and Khan 2024, pp. 40–56.

[27] Kwik 2024a, p. 367, defines a genuine accident as one in which 'notwithstanding all feasible precautions employed, a failure occurs; … [or] [w]here there was no foreseeability of the outcome, despite due diligence or extensive technical training of persons involved'.

[28] Under IHL, commanders are required to collect such necessary information to implement precautions and minimise risks to civilians; see Oeter 2020, p. 354.

[29] It is theorised that as models grow larger, they will not only develop this capacity but also face selection pressure to predict users' preferences and conditions, adapting their outputs accordingly—potentially in undesirable ways. See Ngo et al. 2022, pp. 3–4.

detected during the system's vetting process by the issuing authority.[30] At both the review and targeting stages, relevant IHL obligations appear to have been fulfilled to the extent required by law. With the constraints of the available information, one could argue that nothing more could reasonably have been done.

This chapter adopts a different perspective, arguing that these two cases nonetheless reveal opportunities for significant improvements—measures that could have substantially reduced their humanitarian impact. The main critique lies not in the initial failures themselves, but in the actions (or inactions) taken *during* and *after* their occurrence. While many IHL safeguards focus on *ex ante* measures—those undertaken prior to the adoption of a system or the launch of an attack—there is a clear need for additional mechanisms to protect civilians from AI-related failures and vulnerabilities that only emerge, and are only knowable, *ex post*.

In response, this chapter proposes Iterative Assessment as a unifying framework to manage the persistent uncertainties inherent in military AI. The core of the concept lies in its first word, *iteration*: the process of repeatedly refining decisions or actions based on accumulated experience, new information, and evolving understanding, with the aim of continuous improvement.[31] This approach departs slightly from conventional risk mitigation methods (e.g., implementing a fixed explainability standard, or disabling online learning), which often treat uncertainty as a static problem. By contrast, Iterative Assessment embraces uncertainty as dynamic and evolving. It calls on decision makers to adopt a longitudinal mindset: drawing lessons from past deployment iterations, proactively monitoring ongoing operations, and remaining responsive to emerging insights over time.

The remainder of this chapter explores how the various forms of Iterative Assessment can be applied to AI systems. It demonstrates how its adaptive, forward-looking framework can enhance IHL compliance by reducing AI-related uncertainties to more manageable and acceptable levels.[32]

---

[30] Since testing aims to replicate real-world conditions as closely as possible, the issuing authority might have identified this niche LLM behaviour by simulating a high-stress operational environment, prompting testers to write overly emotive inputs. However, this would not have guaranteed the behaviour's detection, as testers may have responded differently from the operators in the actual incident above—whether due to personality differences or simply their awareness of being in a simulated scenario.

[31] This philosophy will be familiar to readers acquainted with Bayes' theorem, and rightly so. The approach proposed in this chapter is strongly inspired by Bayesian reasoning, which is particularly well-suited to situations where reasoned predictions must be made under conditions of partial information. As McGrayne notes, it is 'an evolving system, which each new bit of information pushe[s] closer and closer to certitude'; see McGrayne 2011, p. 8. To maintain focus on the doctrinal and practical elements of this chapter, further references to Bayes' theorem will not be made. However, those familiar with Bayesian theory will recognise its influence throughout this discussion.

[32] IHL tolerates decision-making conditions short of absolute certainty, provided such decisions fall within the margins of reasonableness. See Kwik 2024a, p. 70. As Henderson also notes, '[i]t cannot be expected that armed conflict will be reduced to the point where a commander can act only when he or she is 100 percent certain in all cases': Henderson 2009, p. 164.

9.3 Sources of Uncertainty in Military AI

This section outlines key factors that exacerbate uncertainty in the deployment and operational use of AI systems in military contexts. While not exhaustive, the discussion highlights how many of these factors stem from properties unique to AI technologies. As such, they introduce novel challenges that not only compound existing sources of operational uncertainty, but also give rise to entirely new forms of it—shaped by the dynamic and opaque nature of modern AI systems.[33]

9.3.1 Algorithmic and Environmental Uncertainty: A Toxic Mix

Modern AI—particularly machine learning (ML) models,[34] such as deep neural networks (DNN)—offers solutions to computational problems that are intractable with rule-based approaches alone.[35] These models now dominate the field of AI,[36] enabling capabilities such as sensor fusion and complex target recognition analysis,[37] that would otherwise be unachievable. However, unlike rule-based approaches, ML models are inherently less interpretable: their behaviour is not based on predefined rules,[38] but instead emerges from input–output pairings shaped by patterns and inferences derived from training data.[39]

Due to the difficulty of discerning their internal logic, modern AI models are often described as *opaque* or *black boxes*.[40] Such models 'do not allow cognitive access to how they have arrived at a particular output, or what input factors or a combination of input factors have contributed to the decision-making process or outcome'.[41] Nevertheless, not all ML models are *necessarily* black boxes. Some architectures are designed to permit external understanding of their decision-making logic. These models can be transparent by design,[42] or they may rely on added

[33] For example, determining the legality of potential targets inherently involves a degree of uncertainty, even when employing sophisticated identification methodologies; see Corn 2012, p. 439.

[34] ML enables AI to 'learn without being explicitly programmed' and 'involves the use of algorithms to parse data and learn from it, and making a determination or prediction as a result'; see Roy 2018, p. 14.

[35] Russell and Norvig 2021, p. 651.

[36] Oniani et al. 2023, p. 3.

[37] Cranny-Evans 2024; Meng et al. 2022, p. 2084.

[38] Deng 2015, p. 25.

[39] Abaimov and Martellini 2020, p. 14.

[40] Molnar describes a black box mode as one 'that cannot be understood by looking at their parameters': Molnar 2019, p. 13.

[41] European Commission 2020, p. 49.

[42] See Barredo Arrieta et al. 2020, p. 88.

explanatory mechanisms intended to describe their internal processes (even where the underlying model itself remains opaque).[43] However, it remains doubtful whether such measures can fully resolve the problem. Not all models can be transparent by design, and explanatory mechanisms may themselves be incorrect or misleading.[44] As a result, uncertainty—though varying in degree—persists. While human operators can assess AI model performance through empirical testing and approximate its decision-making logic,[45] it remains impossible to predict how an ML model will behave across all possible input–output pairings.

Indeterminacy in AI arises not only from the difficulty of interpreting a system's internal logic. It also stems from the *variability of the input space*. The more dynamic and complex the environment in which an AI system operates, the greater the range of potential inputs—leading to increased behavioural variance and making exhaustive testing or prediction increasingly difficult.[46] One method of mitigating this variability is to structure the operational environment in ways that constrain the range of inputs an AI system may encounter. For example, in the case of autonomous vehicles, efforts to enhance predictability have included implementing clear signage and reducing environmental clutter—measures that limit the scope for unforeseen interactions.[47] Structuring the environment in this way narrows the system's potential input space and, and in turn, reduces uncertainty.

In contrast, battlefields are rarely amenable to such structuring.[48] The military environment is dynamic, complex and adversarial.[49] It is continuously evolving, stochastic, and filled with external variables beyond the AI user's control—including hostile agents actively seeking to evade or sabotage operations.[50] Granted, this volatility is not new: the battlefield has always been messy and unpredictable.[51] However, when combined with the input–output variability inherent in modern AI systems, the result is an explosion of possible outcomes that renders uncertainty virtually unavoidable.

Unpredictability is further exacerbated by the *unintuitive nature of AI failure triggers*.[52] ML models often exhibit 'counterintuitive or poorly described failure modes that do not follow historical patterns of human, or even software, failures',

[43] Rosenfeld 2021, p. 2.

[44] See Silva et al. 2023, p. 3; Van der Waa et al. 2021, p. 2.

[45] See Kwik 2024a, pp. 79–91.

[46] Russell et al. 2015, p. 108.

[47] For example, this approach has been implemented in controlled environments, such as factory settings or on roadways; see Boulanin 2016, p. 18.

[48] Certain environments, such as underwater domains, are inherently less complex or cluttered. Structuring a military environment (e.g., by removing elements that could trigger unpredictable behaviour or by adding markers to provide contextual clues for AI) is likely only feasible in areas under near-complete friendly control; see Kwik 2024a, p. 208.

[49] Kwik 2024a, pp. 70–71.

[50] Tolk 2015, p. 298. See generally Russell and Norvig 2021, p. 925.

[51] This has even been normatively acknowledged by IHL through provisions incorporating qualifications such as 'may be expected' and 'reasonableness'. Herbach 2012, p. 17.

[52] See generally Kwik 2024a, Ch. 5.

making them difficult to anticipate based on test distributions alone.[53] AI systems may perform consistently over extended periods, appearing predictable and understandable, only to react abruptly and inexplicably to seemingly innocuous inputs. For example, white paint may cause an autonomous car to misinterpret its surroundings and crash,[54] or grey texture patches may lead an AI classifier to misidentify an elephant as a cat.[55] Identifying and addressing all such edge cases is a formidable challenge, as they often arise from highly specific combinations of inputs that evaluation datasets cannot comprehensively capture.[56] Consequently, sooner or later, deployed AI systems will inevitably encounter unforeseen edge cases, and in worst case scenarios, may fail catastrophically—as illustrated by the *Drone* incident.

This problem is further compounded by the *adversarial* nature of military environments. Unlike civilian AI applications, it should be assumed that 'enemies will likely attempt to exploit vulnerabilities of the system'.[57] While some adversaries may target conventional vulnerabilities (e.g., such as jamming communications or disrupting data feeds),[58] others will specifically seek to exploit the unintuitive failure triggers described above to increase their chances of success. One example of such a Counter-AI (CAI) measure is the so-called input or evasion attack, where adversaries create 'malicious input data designed to deceive AI algorithms, leading to incorrect predictions or classifications'.[59] These attacks exploit edge cases within the target AI system—vulnerabilities that may not even be known to the system's operators.[60] While vulnerability to such adversarial techniques can be mitigated through robustness training and other defensive measures,[61] complete security is impossible.[62]

---

[53] Gilmer et al. 2018a, p. 6.

[54] In this incident, a Tesla vehicle failed to detect 'a large white 18-wheel truck and trailer crossing the highway' due to the contrast between the truck's white colour and a bright spring sky: see Yadron and Tynan 2016.

[55] See Geirhos et al. 2019. In this experiment, researchers overlaid a grey texture image onto a tabby cat, causing AI classifiers to misidentify it as an elephant. In contrast, human observers still recognised the distinctive shape and contours of a cat.

[56] Hendrycks et al. 2020, p. 1. See also Flournoy et al. 2020, p. 8.

[57] Scharre 2016, p. 1. As a NATO document highlights, '[s]ome state and non-state actors will likely seek to exploit defects or limitations within our AI technologies': see NATO 2021a, para 14.

[58] Such attacks may include jamming, spoofing, electromagnetic pulse (EMP) attacks, denial-of-service attacks, etc.: see Wilson 2020.

[59] Mikhailov 2023, p. 3.

[60] One might question why an adversary would be aware of an exploitable edge case while the AI user remains unaware. This discrepancy arises from the asymmetry between attackers versus defenders in such scenarios. An attacker succeeds by identifying and exploiting *any* possible edge case through an input attack, whereas a defender can only prevent or counter such attacks if they have prior knowledge of *that specific* vulnerability. Therefore, an AI user's lack of awareness of an exploited edge case does not necessarily indicate negligence regarding system security. For further discussion on this dynamic, see Kwik 2024a, p. 151.

[61] For example, see Mikhailov 2023, pp. 3–4.

[62] Gilmer et al. 2018b, p. 2.

As a result, even where all other factors are known and foreseeable, adversarial interference may still induce unpredictable AI behaviour.[63]

Online learning, whereby a model 'uses continuous cycles of retraining and model updating from new data input',[64] further aggravates uncertainty. While this capability offers advantages in dynamic environments—particularly against adaptive adversaries on the battlefield—it also allows AI systems to 'update the model hypothesis constantly' in response to changing conditions.[65] Online learning can serve as an effective countermeasure against adversarial attacks. For example, spam filters are designed to continually adapt to evolving spamming techniques.[66] Given these benefits, online learning may be invaluable for many military AI applications.[67] However, this flexibility comes at a cost: it undermines predictability. It becomes increasingly difficult to anticipate *when* and *how* the AI model will adapt its algorithm to environmental changes. As Leslie highlights, 'the unbounded complexity of the world makes anticipating all of its pitfalls and detrimental variables veritably impossible'.[68]

Finally, looking ahead, researchers have raised concerns regarding the potential for *emergent behaviour* to become a significant challenge for military AI users.[69] As AI systems become increasingly complex, they may exhibit 'actions or patterns that weren't explicitly programmed … but developed as a natural outcome of its complexity and interactions'.[70] In military contexts, emergent behaviour is likely to manifest in two (non-mutually exclusive) ways. First, goal-oriented multi-agent systems, such as autonomous swarms,[71] may be programmed with simple and linear instructions at the unit level yet behave unpredictably as a collective. These interactions can introduce stochastic and nonlinear dynamics, making it difficult to predict how the system will function under real-world conditions.[72] Second, as model size, dataset complexity, and training duration increase, AI systems—particularly LLMs—have exhibited 'sharp and unpredictable changes in model outputs'.[73] Emergent behaviour is a double-edged sword: it 'presents opportunities, but also poses important risks'.[74] LLMs may unexpectedly develop highly beneficial capabilities,

---

[63] For a complete taxonomy on how adversaries can employ anti-AI attacks to sabotage or even take control over military AI systems, see Kwik 2024b, pp. 5–11.

[64] Nelson et al. 2014, p. 1,

[65] Das 2021.

[66] King et al. 2020, pp. 96–97.

[67] Schuller 2017, p. 397.

[68] Leslie 2019, p. 34.

[69] For example, see Ekelhof and Paoli 2020; Boothby 2018, pp. 140–142.

[70] Gunnell 2023.

[71] These systems have become increasingly prevalent, especially in intelligence, surveillance, and reconnaissance (ISR) operations. However, they can also be employed more offensively, such as to overwhelm enemy air defence systems; see Government Accountability Office 2023; Safi 2019.

[72] Navarro and Matía 2013, p. 7.

[73] Schaeffer et al. 2023, p. 2 (emphasis removed).

[74] Steinhardt 2022.

such as zero-shot learning,[75] but may equally exhibit undesirable behaviours, such as reinforcing a user's preconceived views through an emergent ability to psychoanalyse user input.[76] The *Targeting Adviser* case exemplifies how such emergent behaviour can lead to harmful consequences in practice.[77] In particular, because such behaviour does not follow linear cause-and-effect reasoning,[78] it is exceedingly difficult to predict *what* will occur, *when*, and *why*.[79] In some circumstances, the only viable recourse may be to *recognise* the emergence of such behaviour and assess the *context* in which it arose.

9.3.2 Reflections on Uncertainty

At this juncture, several general observations can be made regarding the persistence of uncertainty in military AI and the challenges of navigating it. First, while some sources of uncertainty can be addressed to a certain extent, through technical or operational measures, they cannot be fully eliminated. For example, one could choose to 'freeze' an AI model upon deployment or enforce minimum explainability standards to mitigate uncertainty caused by online learning or opacity.[80] Other sources of uncertainty, however, are inherent to the use of modern AI in military contexts. Many stem from the fundamental nature of AI itself—including ML, opacity, and unintuitive failure triggers—or from the operational environment, characterised by highly variable input spaces, dynamic conditions, and adversarial interference. Beyond the *a priori* decision not to deploy the AI system at all,[81] these variables cannot be removed—they must be accepted.

---

[75] This phenomenon describes an AI system successfully performing a task it has never encountered before, despite seemingly lacking prior machine-learned experience in that domain; see Dickson 2022.

[76] See Perez et al. 2022, p. 10.

[77] The particular emergent behaviour exhibited by the DSS in the *Targeting Adviser* case is called 'sycophancy', see Kwik 2025.

[78] For a general theoretical discussion on this phenomenon, see Fromm 2005.

[79] Ganguli et al. 2022, p. 15.

[80] These measures are not without trade-offs in terms of opportunity costs. For example, freezing AI models eliminates variance caused by continuous model evolution, simplifying testing and improving predictability: see ICRC 2018, para 49. However, this rigidity reduces adaptability to changing circumstances and adaptive opponents. Similarly, while transparent models decrease uncertainty, they may also compromise efficiency, capability, and versatility, requiring additional time and resources for development: see Adadi and Berrada 2018, p. 5214.

[81] In general terms, the importance of this measure cannot be overstated. Indeed, the decision not to authorise an AI system (e.g., such as where its employment is deemed excessively risky) remains the most effective form of risk mitigation intervention at both the review and deployment stages, see Van den Boogaard and Roorda 2021 p. 433; Kwik 2024a, p. 35. This chapter, however, focuses on scenarios where a reasonable decision maker proceeds with authorisation based on the system's apparent reliability and the available information at the time.

Second, a good-faith AI user can nonetheless take steps to curtail uncertainty and manage variance.[82] Rigorous testing and validation across diverse conditions and environments,[83] combined with extensive operator training, can improve awareness of AI vulnerabilities and failure states.[84] These measures can help reduce the risk of being blindsided by unexpected events, but they cannot eliminate all potential failures. Furthermore, because military AI systems operate in high-risk environments, even low-probability failures can lead to significant (humanitarian) costs, as demonstrated by the *Drone* and *Targeting Adviser* cases.[85]

The Iterative Assessment approach does not seek to eliminate these challenges, nor does it assume that all accidents are avoidable. At the same time, it is not defeatist. Rather, it is premised on the view that 'we can and should be able to recognise recurring patterns of misbehaviour, and to learn enough from past experience to be able to avoid or repair many of the common patterns'.[86] To implement this effectively, action is required at both the pre-deployment and operational stages, which I now explore.

9.4 Iterative Reviews

The review obligation is arguably the most critical guardrail against IHL violations at the pre-deployment stage.[87] Under its API formulation, as discussed in Chap. 5 of this volume, Article 36 requires Parties to assess whether a new weapon, means, or method of warfare, would violate their international obligations, particularly those under IHL.[88] While the customary IHL duty to conduct such reviews is often considered less extensive than the API standard, there is growing consensus that the basic duty to ensure capabilities can be employed in conformity with IHL forms part of customary international law.[89] For the purposes of this analysis, it is assumed that reviews should extend to DSS, such as the system used in the *Targeting Adviser* example.[90] Beyond this assumption, this chapter does not engage further with the doctrinal question,[91] and instead focuses on the *timing* of when such reviews are traditionally conducted.

---

[82] This chapter adopts a presumption based on this, as outlined in Sect. 9.1.

[83] See, for example, Cherry and Johnson 2020, p. 13.

[84] Puscas 2023, p. 36.

[85] Bommasani et al. 2021, p. 116.

[86] Mogul 2005, p. 18.

[87] Sandoz et al. 1987, para 1475.

[88] API, above n. 1, Article 36.

[89] See Schmitt 2017, p. 465; ICRC 2006, p. 4; [lc]. Jevglevskaja 2018, p. 187.

[90] See Klonowska 2022.

[91] Even if one adopts the position that DSS fall outside the scope of the legal review obligation, the discussion in this section remains relevant for AI weapon systems, such as those featured in the *Drone* case.

9.4.1 Limitations of Conventional Reviews

In its most basic form, a weapon review is often seen as a discrete, one-time requirement performed during the weapon acquisition phase, typically just prior to adoption.[92] Given the generally low level of implementation among States,[93] it would be unsurprising if most AI-related reviews are similarly conducted in this manner in practice.[94] However, a slightly broader interpretation can be drawn from the API formulation, which requires reviews to be performed '[i]n the *study*, *development*, *acquisition* or *adoption* of a new weapon, means or method of warfare'.[95] Commentators favouring this approach consider that a narrow 'one-off' review is insufficient; instead, they advocate for reviews at 'each of the key decision points',[96] that is, 'at each stage of development and acquisition'.[97] This interpretation is reflected in the practice of many States,[98] supported by soft law instruments such as the Tallinn Manual,[99] and has been argued to be both more practical and economically efficient.[100] In addition to reviews at fixed milestones, some States also conduct *ad hoc* reviews in response to new pertinent information arising during development,[101] or when 'substantive changes occur'.[102]

One problem identified in the literature is that even this broader reading of the API review obligation may be insufficient to fully account for the unique properties of military AI, given that the 'development' of an AI system may continue beyond its point of adoption.[103] Unlike traditional weapons, an AI system can remain in a state

[92] Copeland 2014, p. 47.

[93] See ICRC 2006, p. 5; Boothby 2018, p. 18.

[94] Few States provide transparency regarding their review processes, making it difficult to ascertain how frequently such reviews are conducted before adoption: see Goussac 2019.

[95] API, above n. 1, Article 36 (emphasis added).

[96] McClelland 2003, p. 402.

[97] Fry 2006, p. 481; see also ICRC 2006, p. 23.

[98] For example, the UK Ministry of Defence 2016 conducts reviews 'at key milestones in the procurement process to assure the legality of a new weapon, means or method of warfare throughout its study, development, acquisition and adoption'; and the Belgian Armed Forces 2018, p. 7 conduct reviews '*[l]orsque la Défense étudie, met au point ou souhaite acquérir ou adopter une nouvelle arme, un nouveau moyen ou une nouvelle méthode de guerre*' [when Defence studies, develops, or intends to acquire or adopt a new weapon, a new means or a new method of warfare].

[99] Schmitt 2017, p. 465.

[100] Conducting reviews at an 'early' stage allows for swift corrections in the design process or, the abandonment of a project entirely if it becomes evident that the final product would violate IHL and thus be unusable under any circumstances; see Daoust et al. 2002, p. 351; Boothby 2016, Section 19.5.2.

[101] For example, Belgian Armed Forces 2018 p. 8, '*Dans le cas où de nouvelles informations pertinentes sont rendues disponibles après le traitement du dossier par la CEJ, l'arme, le moyen ou la méthode de guerre sera à nouveau soumis à l'évaluation*' [If new pertinent information is made available after the completion of the review by the CEJ, the weapon, means or method of warfare shall be subjected to re-evaluation].

[102] Parks 2005, p. 134.

[103] See, for example, Meier 2019, p. 308; Boulanin et al. 2020, p. 13.

of flux post-deployment. For example, if a DNN continues adjusting its weights—the parameters controlling the strength of connections between neurons—through frequent model updates or operational inputs (online learning) after deployment, this could render the legal review 'invalid immediately upon the use of the system'.[104] In itself, the possibility of adapting or altering already-adopted means or methods of warfare is not unique to AI systems. Some States and commentators have taken the position that a (re-)review would be required when a capability has 'undergone modification' or has been 'subject of an upgrade or other amendment that changes its combat performance'.[105] However, a particular challenge for software-based systems such as AI is that changes may manifest intangibly and incrementally (e.g., gradual shifts in weights over time).[106] Therefore, even if one accepts the position that '[a]ny changes to the system's operating state … would require the system to go through testing and evaluation again',[107] the precise timing of *when* this duty is triggered remains ambiguous.[108]

Most re-review clauses are triggered by modifications or alterations to a system. However, in both the *Drone* and *Targeting Adviser* cases, no factual changes had occurred within the systems themselves. The drones' algorithm had *always* contained the hidden edge case that caused hallucinations when viewing the clothing patterns from a specific angle. Similarly, the targeting adviser's LLM had *always* been capable of detecting user urgency and adapting its outputs accordingly. As a result, most re-review clauses would not have been triggered by these incidents. The main issue is that both re-review clauses and certain proposed solutions, such as 'freezing' the AI model,[109] focus on *factual transformations*—instances where the system or its operational environment factually undergoes an observable change after deployment.[110]

---

[104] Boulanin et al. 2020, p. 13. While this concern is often overstated—since modifying individual weights does not fundamentally alter an algorithm's behaviour—the underlying apprehension remains valid.

[105] Boothby 2016, Section 19.5.2. Australia requires re-reviews for 'adaptations and modifications of existing weapons', and the UK conducts re-reviews when 'there is any change in a systems' use or capability'; Australia 2018, para 9; UK Ministry of Defence 2016; see also ICRC 2006, n. 21.

[106] Similar discussions arose with respect to cyberweapons. See, for example, Schmitt 2017, p. 466; Wallace 2018, p. 21.

[107] Sayler 2020.

[108] Boulanin et al. 2020, p. 13.

[109] Goussac 2019.

[110] Performance drift in AI systems can also result from environmental shifts (e.g., seasonal changes or adaptive adversaries), see Kwik 2024a, pp. 115–118. More comprehensive re-review clauses, such as those introduced in a recent DoD Directive, are therefore designed to trigger in response to *operational* changes. It reads:

> An autonomous weapon system that is a variant of an existing weapon system previously approved through this review will not be covered by previous approval if changes to the system *algorithms*, intended *mission set*, intended *operational environments*, intended *target sets*, or expected *adversarial countermeasures* substantially differ from those applicable to the previously approved weapon system so as to fall outside the scope of what was previously approved in the senior review. Such systems will require a new senior review before their formal development and again before fielding.

However, in the *Drone* and *Targeting Adviser* cases, neither the system nor the environment changed; rather it was our *perception* and *understanding* that shifted. We became aware of a system behaviour that had previously been unknowable.[111] Let us call this an *epistemic transformation.*

When reviewing the various sources of AI uncertainty discussed in Sect. 9.3, it becomes clear that many factors stem more from epistemic limitations than from factual transformations. The latter is primarily driven by online learning and adaptive adversaries, whereas the former arises from structural challenges such as infinite input variance, algorithmic opacity, the unintuitive nature of AI failures, and emergent behaviour. Some have proposed modifications to review procedures to account for this epistemic gap,[112] such as placing greater emphasis on predictive modelling and simulations.[113] Nevertheless, it remains dubious whether the epistemic problem can ever be fully resolved, even with substantial reforms to how reviews are conducted. As one commenter notes, '[t]here are simply too many possible states and combination of states to be able to exhaustively test each one, and understanding where the boundary conditions are will be difficult'.[114]

9.4.2 The Iterative Approach

In response to the challenges outlined above, two possible courses of action can be taken. The first is to simply acknowledge these limitations and accept that incidents such as the *Drone* and *Targeting Adviser* cases may occur. Such incidents could be treated as accidents, attributable to *specific* environmental circumstances rather than fundamental flaws in the legal review process. Arguably, this is the default approach. For instance, a State would not ordinarily reassess the legality of its rocket system following an unprecedented malfunction caused by an unpredictable environmental factor, such as a flash-freezing or atmospheric turbulence incident prior to deployment.

The second, alternative approach is to adopt an *Iterative Review* process for AI systems. While uncommon in military contexts, this method is widely employed in

See US Department of Defense 2023, p. 15 (emphasis added).

111 While these properties may be theoretically knowable, they were *factually* unknowable in the given circumstances due to constraints outlined in Sect. 9.3—particularly the challenge of testing for all possible edge cases and behaviours that emerge only under very specific conditions.

112 For a broader discussion on AI certification, see Bakirtzis et al. 2022.

113 Meier 2019, p. 309; Undersecretary of Defense for Acquisition, Technology, and Logistics 2012, p. 63.

114 US Air Force Office of the Chief Scientist 2015, p. 23.

the commercial software sector and in credentialing schemes (e.g., drug certification).[115] In contrast to conventional review methods, Iterative Review is characterised by the following attributes:[116]

> ***Provisional***: The review process does not claim to be exhaustive or final in its findings. It accepts the possible existence of hidden unknowns within the system that could lead to high-cost failures in operational settings. Statements of (il)legality reflect only the reasonable belief of the reviewer based on information reasonably available at the time of assessment.
>
> ***Longitudinal***: The review process does not have a fixed cut-off point but extends beyond adoption into the post-deployment phase.
>
> ***Adaptive***: Previous assessments remain open to revision and refinement. As new data from deployment becomes available, legal assessments are updated accordingly. Necessary revisions must be actionable immediately, without undue procedural delay.
>
> ***Proactive***: Rather than waiting for incident reports or violation complaints, data from deployments is proactively collected and integrated into the review process.[117]

These features are designed to specifically address review situations in which comprehensive and exhaustive testing (or anything that comes close to it) is impossible—a key challenge for military AI systems.[118] The *longitudinal* dimension is particularly critical, as rare incidents—such as the pattern recognition failure in the *Drone* case or the emergent user-interaction issue in the *Targeting Adviser* case—could only be identified through deployment. Yet, such discoveries may have profound legal implications. For example, a reasonable response to the *Targeting Adviser* case would be to revoke the DSS's prior legal approval, as its emergent ability to infer operator urgency from chat prompts introduces an unacceptable risk of recurrence under similar conditions.[119] To be effective, Iterative Reviews must also be *adaptive*: capable of rapidly revising prior legal assessments in response to new information and ensuring that any necessary restrictions or amendments take immediate effect.

A fundamental consequence of this approach is that no assessment can ever be truly definitive. Iterative Review acknowledges that unseen gaps in knowledge will always exist at the time of review—gaps that may later reveal a system to be fundamentally unlawful under IHL. At its core lies 'exploratory testing, shaped by insights from deployment'.[120] This *provisional* nature may sit uneasy with some, as it implies the deployment of military systems without a guarantee that their 'employment would, in some or all circumstances, be prohibited [under IHL]'.[121] This tension

[115] Meier 2019, p. 310; Bakirtzis et al. 2022, p. 1.

[116] The process described here follows the framework introduced by Bakirtzis et al. 2022.

[117] Cf. Hathaway and Khan 2024, p. 34.

[118] Trusilo 2023, p. 11.

[119] One could argue that this risk might be mitigated through alternative operational measures, such as instructing DSS users to avoid conveying urgency in their chat prompts. However, the core issue lies in the system's emergent ability to *infer operators' moods*, which raises the possibility of it detecting *other* emotional states and producing further unpredictable behaviours. This consideration also influences what constitutes a reasonable course of action in response to such findings at the operational level; see Sect. 9.5.

[120] Bakirtzis et al. 2022, p. 1.

[121] API, above n. 1, Article 36.

is unlikely to be fully resolved. However, it is important to recognise that conceptual disagreement already exists regarding the extent to which IHL compliance must be guaranteed in 'all circumstances'.[122] A factor in favour of permitting the iterative approach is that many interpret the Article 36 review obligation as requiring legality to only be assessed 'by reference to its normal expected use at the time the evaluation is conducted'.[123] It is submitted that it would be consistent with the spirit of the law if, at the time of review, the assessor is convinced to a reasonable degree—based on information reasonably available—that the system does not violate IHL, and issues a positive assessment, pending future information that may defeat this presumption.

At present, Iterative Review remains a recommendation *de lege ferenda*, especially given the issue of timing. It is difficult to derive a continued obligation for post-adoption reviews from the wording of API—'[i]n the study, development, acquisition or adoption'—let alone from the more limited customary rule.[124] Moreover, Iterative Review is significantly more demanding than conventional review mechanisms. For it to be effective, a State would need to establish proactive and continuous monitoring systems, systematically collect deployment data, update models accordingly, and issue new reviews as required. These requirements may place a significant burden on States, particularly those with limited resources.[125] Nevertheless, States capable of implementing these mechanisms are urged to do so, as Iterative Review offers the most effective means of addressing epistemic transformations at the structural level.

At this point, one may ask how an Iterative Review mechanism would have responded to the *Drone* case. Given the rarity of the edge case, it is unlikely that a re-review would have found the drones structurally incapable of being used in accordance with IHL. However, the obligation of constant care would still necessitate the adoption of risk mitigation measures to protect civilians.[126] One possible review-level intervention could have been to modify the assessment to include operational restrictions,[127] such as prohibiting the drones' deployment in regions where traditional attire with distinct clothing patterns is prevalent.[128]

Despite the adaptive nature of Iterative Review, it is foreseeable that such an institutional-level change would require time to become fully effective—likely longer than the one-month period in which the *Drone* and *Targeting Adviser* incidents unfolded. During this period, the issue would have remained unaddressed, and civilians would have continued to face significant risk. Thus, while Iterative Review provides a valuable mechanism for long-term oversight, it is unlikely to respond

[122] For an extended discussion, see Fry 2006, pp. 471–473, 501–503.

[123] Schmitt et al. 2017, p. 466. See also Bothe et al. 2013, p. 231; US Department of Defense 2015, Section 6.6.3.4.

[124] API, n.1, Article 36.

[125] States may alleviate this logistical burden by requiring manufacturers to incorporate monitoring capabilities into system designs, thereby facilitating oversight; see also below Sect. 9.7.

[126] Jenks and Liivoja 2018. See also Jensen 2021, p. 190.

[127] Assessors issuing reviews may 'attach conditions or comments … to be integrated into the rules of engagement or operating procedures': see ICRC 2006, p. 15.

[128] For an example of how such instructions can be integrated into military instructions or directives, see Kwik et al. 2025, pp. 18–21.

rapidly enough to epistemic transformations in real time. For this reason, Iterative Review must be complemented by *Iterative Assessment in Deployment*, as discussed below.

9.5 Iterative Assessment in Deployment

At the operational level, Iterative Assessment comprises two distinct yet equally important tasks: *Iterative Awareness* and *Proactive Response.*

9.5.1 Iterative Awareness

Iterative Awareness constitutes the fact-finding component of Iterative Assessment in Deployment. To achieve Iterative Awareness, AI operators leverage intelligence, surveillance, and reconnaissance (ISR) assets to monitor the civilian impact of a deployed system. Compared to standard contexts in which ISR is employed, Iterative Awareness differs slightly in its *timing*, emphasising *ex post* rather than *ex ante* data collection and analysis.

Commanders routinely collect and analyse intelligence prior to each attack—a necessary step for implementing precautionary measures and maintaining effective command-and-control (C2).[129] Much of the literature on military AI emphasises the importance of operators maintaining a thorough understanding of their AI systems, the battlefield, and adversary activity to ensure legal compliance and effective C2.[130] However, comparatively less attention has been given to the need for continuous monitoring of deployment outcomes,[131] which is equally crucial. *Ex post* awareness—the ability to assess the effects of a system after deployment—enables AI users to 'understand and assess the causes of malfunctions or undesired results from (normal) operation and to take appropriate action (technical and accountability) to prevent similar mistakes'.[132] As with pre-deployment legal reviews, there is a risk that the obligation to assess the lawfulness of an AI system is perceived as a one-time requirement, rather than a continuous duty persisting beyond initial deployment.

Conceptually, Iterative Awareness is already reflected in the established operational planning and targeting practices of many States. For example, the NATO

[129] Rosén 2014, p. 127. See also Australia 2006, para 5.54; Schmitt 2010, para 16.07.3.

[130] For example, Group of Governmental Experts on Lethal Autonomous Weapons Systems (GGE LAWS) 2021, para 29.a; Holland Michel 2020, p. 15. See also more generally NATO 2019a, pp. 2–4: 'A comprehensive analysis of the operating environment, its components, actors and their relationships is the beginning of the operations planning process'.

[131] Kwik 2022, p. 14.

[132] Van den Boogaard and Roorda 2021, p. 433.

targeting cycle consists of six phases,[133] with the final phase being 'Assessment'. This phase encapsulates the essence of remaining aware of past operations and using insights gained from previous deployments to inform future military actions:

> Assessment measures the extent to which the desired effects, regardless of the actions taken, have been created and recommends the extent to which further actions are required. It encompasses a physical, functional and system assessment. Assessment also contributes to wider operational and campaign assessment.[134]

The concept of *continuity*, central to the Iterative Assessment approach,[135] is also embedded within NATO and US military doctrine: '[c]ommanders and the staff must build and foster a comprehensive understanding of the operating environment and promote this understanding continuously throughout the entire operations planning process'.[136] Indeed, the notion of learning from prior iterations is widely recognised as a fundamental element of operational art. Doctrinal concepts such as 'lessons learned'—defined as 'the act of learning from experience to achieve improvements'—rely on field observations to refine military decision making.[137] After-action analysis is actively encouraged in order to enhance operational efficiency,[138] adapt to environmental changes,[139] and improve collateral damage estimation mechanisms.[140] At its core, this process enables adaptation:

> The outputs of an assessment communicate the effectiveness of the operation plan toward desired end states, describe risks involved in the accomplishment of the plan, and recommend necessary changes to the plan to attain a desired end state.[141]

Adaptation, however, was precisely what was lacking in both the *Drone* and *Targeting Adviser* cases. Despite the presence of a known edge case in the region (*Drone*) and an emergent vulnerability (*Targeting Adviser*), both systems remained in use for one month. This failure occurred because insufficient efforts were made to *detect* the mistaken targeting of civilians and to investigate *why* these errors were happening. These shortcomings were likely the result of practical and operational constraints. In the *Drone* case, misclassifications occurred across multiple platoons and throughout the region. Individual component commanders, operating in isolation, may have simply dismissed these incidents as accidental anomalies rather than recognising

---

[133] See NATO 2021b, para 1.5.

[134] NATO 2021b, para 1.5.1.f.

[135] This concept was similarly identified as essential in the discussion on iterative reviews; see Sect. 9.4.

[136] NATO 2019a, pp. 2–4. See also Curtis E. Lemay Center 2019, p. 79: 'Assessment is a continuous process that measures the overall effectiveness of employing joint force capabilities during military operations'.

[137] NATO 2019b, para E.1; LEX-7.

[138] NATO 2021b, pp. 1–4.

[139] US Joint Chiefs of Staff 2018, pp. VI-1.

[140] Schmitt et al. 2017, p. 306.

[141] US Joint Chiefs of Staff 2018, pp. VI-2.

them as part of a broader pattern.[142] In the *Targeting Adviser* case, the failure to detect the high misclassification rate was likely driven by the same operational pressures that led the officers to frame chat prompts with urgency in the first place. Prioritising the execution of further attacks likely took precedence over verifying whether previous strikes had correctly targeted legitimate objectives.[143]

This highlights a crucial caveat to the claim that Iterative Awareness is an established practice: in reality, it often remains more *theoretical* than practical. While extensively discussed in military doctrine, its implementation in practice is questionable. Hathaway and Khan, for example, have identified several shortcomings in how the US conducts after-action assessments.[144] Among other issues, insufficient resources are dedicated to after-action data collection, and the data that is gathered is often incomplete or inadequate.[145] Additionally, the process is frequently slow and resource intensive, particularly in hard-to-access areas.[146] Even when after-action data is collected, it rarely accounts for *civilian* impact. Instead, most after-action assessments focus primarily on determining whether the *military* objective was achieved, such as assessing whether target re-engagement is necessary.[147] For Iterative Awareness to function effectively, it would therefore require the integration of a robust civilian harm tracking mechanism—one that ensures civilian impact is not treated as an afterthought but embedded as a core component of post-strike analyses.[148]

Another critical component of Iterative Awareness is *communication* across both horizontal and vertical axes. A strong civilian harm tracking mechanism could have alerted the *Targeting Adviser* operators to systematic errors in their DSS, prompting immediate corrective action. In contrast, in the *Drone* case, individual component commanders would likely have been unable to detect a structural issue in the region based on a single misclassification report. Had they received consolidated reports from multiple platoons indicating recurring misidentification of civilians wearing regionally distinctive attire, they would have been more likely to recognise that the drones were systematically encountering a persistent edge case linked to the local civilian population.

It should be noted that operational- or tactical-level conclusions will often be less precise, particularly in complex deployment environments. In the *Drone* case, for

[142] Isolated weapon or software failures occur regularly across various military capabilities and do not necessarily prompt commanders to question the reliability or lawfulness of a system; see Scharre 2016, pp. 25, 38.

[143] A similar dynamic is reported to have allegedly occurred during the Israel Defense Forces' use of the Lavender system in Gaza following the October 2023 attack by Hamas; see Abraham 2024.

[144] Hathaway and Khan 2024, pp. 32–69.

[145] Ibid.

[146] Ibid., p. 81; Ekelhof 2018, p. 69.

[147] NATO 2021b, pp. 1–21.

[148] Similar to the 'Assessment' phase within the targeting cycle, many military frameworks emphasise the inclusion of civilian casualty tracking in after-action data collection; see, for example, US Department of Defense 2015, Section 5.11.1.3; NATO 2021b, pp. 1–19. However, as noted above, the extent to which this practice is consistently implemented or prioritised remains uncertain.

example, it is unlikely that field reports would have been able to precisely identify that the misclassifications were triggered by a specific textile pattern viewed from a particular angle, as this would have required detailed technical analysis. However, even without such granular insights, component commanders could still have inferred from the pattern of misclassification reports that failures were linked to the local civilian population. Such a conclusion could likely have been reached before the one-month operation ended, allowing for a timely intervention. A horizontal communication mechanism is thus invaluable for enabling decentralised interventions at the operational level.

In addition to the above, vertical communication plays a critical role in facilitating more effective top-down interventions. In the *Drone* case, for example, a superior officer could have identified the pattern of errors based on reports provided by component commanders, enabling higher-level corrective measures. Vertical communication is also indispensable for the Iterative Review process. As noted earlier, Iterative Review is a *longitudinal* process: it relies on operational insights to determine whether prior legal assessments remain valid or require re-examination. However, *obtaining* such reliable and actionable data depends on effective coordination and cooperation from operational-level officers and soldiers.

Finally, AI presents novel opportunities to enhance and support Iterative Assessment by enabling more precise monitoring, data collection, and incident reconstruction.[149] For example, design standards could mandate that AI systems log all input–output pairings to facilitate post-action analysis,[150] similar to the black boxes used in commercial aircraft or the Aegis combat system.[151] Such data can then 'be analysed and allow[s] for improvement in decision sequences in the future'.[152] This approach effectively 'outsources' part of the Iterative Assessment workload to the AI system itself, integrating pre-installed monitoring and recording functionalities to enhance real-time oversight and post-deployment evaluation. By embedding these automated assessment mechanisms, the iterative framework could become more efficient, scalable, and appealing for military adoption.[153] Further research is needed to determine optimal design and integration strategies, as well as effective incentives to encourage militaries to voluntarily adopt such systems. Developing robust AI monitoring protocols could play a critical role in strengthening civilian protection by reducing the risk of avoidable 'accidents', which, under the right conditions, could ultimately be avoided in future AI-enabled operations.

---

[149] Sassòli 2014, p. 326; Toscano 2015, p. 238.

[150] Williams 2017; see also European Committee on Crime Problems 2020.

[151] Aspin 1988.

[152] Meier 2019, p. 312.

[153] It has also been suggested that automated recording functions could mitigate the risk of subjectivity and collusion in investigations, as data is collected autonomously by the system: see Toscano 2015, p. 238.

9.5.2 Proactive Response

Having gained information that reasonably challenges the prior belief that an AI system's use was appropriate and lawful under the given circumstances, users are now obliged to take proactive action in the planning of future iterations—specifically, in subsequent operations or attacks involving the same AI system.[154]

As with Iterative Awareness, this requirement has both practical and legal foundations. From an operational perspective, for example, US doctrine recognises that '[a]rmy units can prevent civilian casualties by incorporating lessons learned from previous incidents, including near misses',[155] and that, in response, 'appropriate actions should be taken to reduce the risk of such incidents in the future'.[156] From a legal standpoint, this obligation is an integral part of a commander's precautionary duty to take appropriate measures to prevent foreseeable risks to civilians.[157] Proper implementation of Iterative Awareness (Sect. 9.5.1) acts as a necessary enabler: without it, inaction cannot be objectively judged as unreasonable, as the risk would not yet have been established as foreseeable for a reasonable commander in their position. This observation also has implications for any criminal liability one may want to ascribe to the decision maker after the fact: if technically knowable risks remained factually unknown to the decision maker at the time of the decision, no *mens rea* can be established.[158]

The *appropriate* operational response to a newly identified risk is entirely contextual. Different commanders may adopt varying, yet equally valid, measures to address the perceived threat. In the *Drone* case:

Platoon Commander-A may withhold the use of the drone entirely;

Platoon Commander-B may order additional ISR collection and only deploy the drone if no local civilians are identified in the area; and

Platoon Commander-C may opt to use the drone solely in a defensive posture (e.g., intercepting enemy counterattacks in situations where no local civilians are present to misidentify).

All three measures achieve the overarching goal of mitigating a known risk to the civilian population and would thus be considered appropriate responses based on the commanders' current knowledge of the situation.

---

[154] This principle applies across platforms as long as they operate on the same underlying algorithm. In the *Drone* case, for example, commanders would need to take action even if their own system had never malfunctioned, as the risks identified in their colleagues' drones would also apply to their own.

[155] Department of the Army Headquarters 2015, paras 5–48.

[156] US Department of Defense 2015, Section 5.11.1.3. Note that 'reviews' as used in this quote does not refer to the general review obligation as discussed above, but rather the *ad hoc* assessments made after individual incidents.

[157] Margulies 2021, p. 177; Ekelhof 2018, p. 69; and API, above n. 1, Article 57(1). The US Law of War Manual categorises 'After-Action Assessments and Investigations' and 'Assessing the Risks to Civilians' under the header 'Feasible precautions in planning and conducting attacks': see US Department of Defense 2015, Section 5.11.1.3.

[158] See Kwik 2026.

By contrast, an *inappropriate* response would be, for example, for **Platoon Commander-D** to permit drone deployment based solely on visual confirmation that no local civilians are wearing distinct attire. This approach would be flawed given the information available at the time, as it rests on unverified assumptions. As previously noted, operational-level assessments will inevitably involve some degree of imprecision due to time and resource constraints. In the *Drone* case, the only verifiable common denominator, based on the misclassification reports, was the affected civilian demographic—any further specificity would have been speculative. While we, as external observers, know that the misclassification was caused by the clothing pattern, Platoon Commander-D would have no way of confirming this hypothesis without further evidence. Acting on such an unsubstantiated assumption would therefore be unreasonable. A reasonable commander would adopt the broadest plausible hypothesis—i.e., that the misclassification issue '*has something to do with the local civilian population*' in general—and implement precautionary measures accordingly pending further intelligence.[159]

In the *Targeting Adviser* case, the only *immediate* and appropriate response would likely have been to suspend the use of the DSS, as it is unlikely that the underlying pattern of failure (i.e., urgency in prompts influencing outputs) could have been identified so quickly. In the absence of further information, the only safe assumption would be that the DSS was not functioning reliably enough to justify continued deployment.

Now, consider a scenario in which a skilled technical team rapidly identifies the cause of failure: the DSS had developed an emergent ability to infer user emotions from chat prompts. What would be the reasonable course of action following this new information? One possible response would be to issue updated user instructions, such as:

'**Avoid abbreviations**'; or

'**Avoid these words: {quicky, faster, __}**'.[160]

This approach might allow the system to be reinstated under controlled conditions. However, a strong counterargument exists: the discovery of this one emergent behaviour suggests the potential existence of *other*, as yet unknown, emergent properties. If the system can infer urgency, what prevents it from also detecting and responding to emotions such as anger, enthusiasm, or desperation—potentially producing other undesirable or unpredictable outcomes?

Given this level of uncertainty, the most prudent course of action—aligned with the reasonable commander standard—would be to retire the system and recommend extensive testing to determine how different emotive cues influence its outputs. The core argument is that, in situations of uncertainty, a reasonable commander would

[159] IHL affords commanders 'reasonable latitude in the exercise of good faith judgment under the myriad circumstances and difficult conditions of combat'. However, this judgment must be based on a reasonable belief derived from the information available to them at the time: see Huffman 2012, p. 17; see also Haque 2012, p. 97.

[160] For more examples, see Kwik 2025.

err on the side of caution, implementing broad precautionary measures to mitigate a range of possible risks until further information is available to pinpoint the precise causes of failure.[161]

9.6 Visual Operational Guide

For ease of reference, Fig. 9.1 provides a visual operational guide to the key components of the Iterative Assessment framework, as discussed in Sects. 9.4 and 9.5.[162] It illustrates how each step is interconnected and how the process is continuously reinforced through new information gathered during deployment. This feedback loop enables the progressive refinement of both operational practices and legal assessment over time.

For any new system, Iterative Review (Sect. 9.4) provides an initial assessment of the system's lawfulness, which then informs its operational and tactical deployment. While the system is in use, consistent and proactive reporting—across both horizontal and vertical channels—enables Iterative Awareness (Sect. 9.5.1). This process can be further supported by automated recording and reporting functionalities embedded within the system itself. In response to emerging concerns or incident reports, operators are expected to take Proactive Responses (Sect. 9.5.2), based on feasibility and reasonableness. Finally, the insights gathered during deployment feed back into the Iterative Review process, allowing for the continuous reassessment of whether the initial legal evaluation remains valid or requires revision.

9.7 Reflections and Recommendations

Warfare has always inherently been characterised by uncertainty. Incomplete knowledge and mistaken beliefs—even when justified at the time of decision making—can lead to harmful consequences on the battlefield. Recognising the realities of war, IHL judges' reasonableness based on the 'subjective perception of the decision maker at the time the decision was made'.[163] Under this standard, none of the actors involved in the *Drone* or *Targeting Adviser* cases—the commanders, operators or legal reviewers—acted unreasonably. Each relied on the information reasonably available to them at the time. However, as AI becomes increasingly integrated into

[161] This overall recommendation remains subject to context-specific considerations in the field and the judgment of a reasonable commander, particularly regarding the criticality of the capability to succeed in a given operation.

[162] A more comprehensive visual summarising not only the Iterative Assessment steps, but also its underlying rationale as argued throughout this paper and comparisons with conventional assessment practices, can be viewed at https://jonathankwik.com/post/diagram-on-iterative-assessment. Accessed 20 June 2025.

[163] Corn 2012, p. 451. See also Schmitt et al. 2017, p. 298.

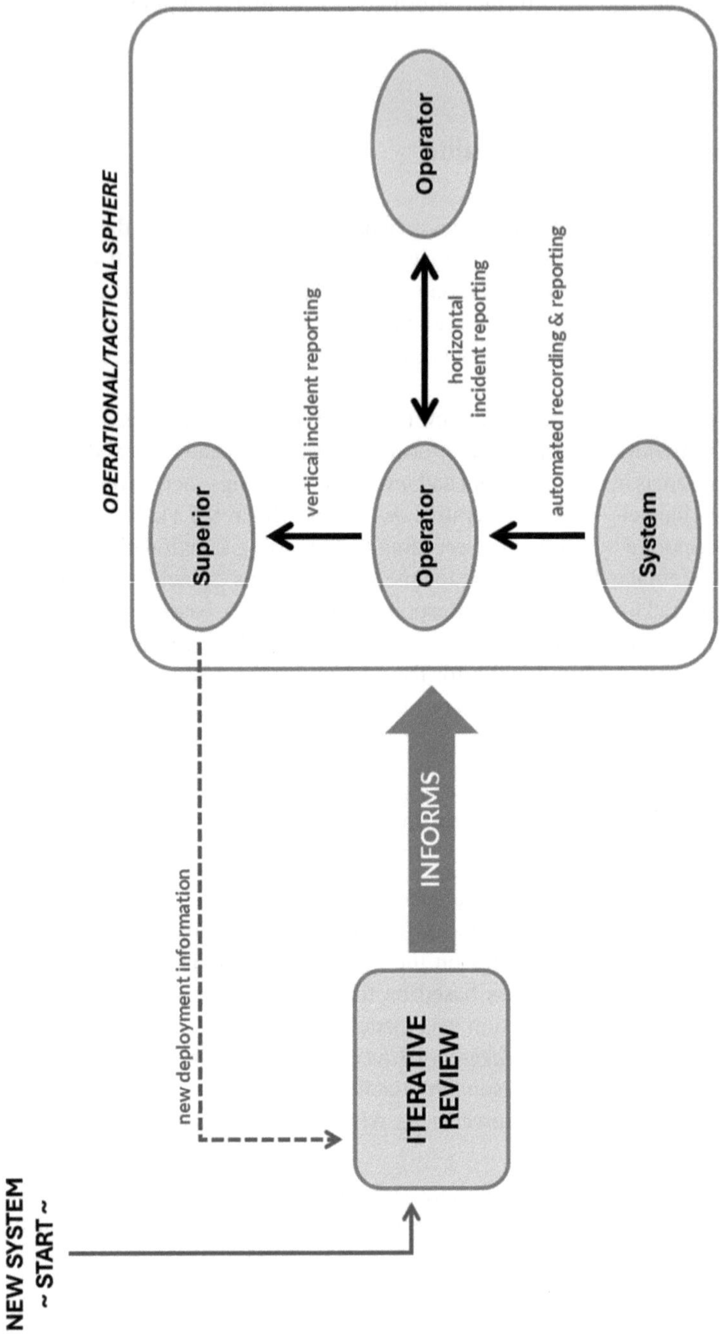

Fig. 9.1 Visual Operational Guide to Iterative Assessment. *Source* The author

military operations, such unforeseeable failures are likely to grow in frequency—even among good-faith belligerents. Pre-deployment controls alone cannot fully account for the genuinely unpredictable characteristics of military AI. While rigorous *ex ante* legal and technical reviews remain crucial, they cannot eliminate the possibility of unforeseen system failures in real-world conditions.

It is unrealistic to expect that initial accidents can be entirely avoided, and unfair to demand that AI users foresee the unforeseeable. In both the *Drone* and *Targeting Adviser* cases, no actor acted unreasonably from a legal perspective. Yet the outcomes were still suboptimal—had more robust safeguards been in place, further civilian harm could have been prevented:

> War inevitably involves death and destruction. The only way to avoid death and destruction in war is to avoid war. The fundamental purpose of [IHL] is to reduce net human suffering and net damage to civilian objects in armed conflict.[164]

IHL calls on belligerents to minimise *net* suffering—a principle that, in these cases, would mean intervening earlier to reduce the overall number of errors. Iterative Assessment provides a solution to meet this objective. It aligns with the spirit of the Rendulic Rule, avoiding retrospective blame while encouraging forward-looking improvements.[165] Instead of penalising decision makers for acting without perfect foresight, Iterative Assessment promotes the systematic collection of information to improve real-time decision making over the course of a system's usage.

As demonstrated in this chapter, Iterative Awareness serves as a key enabler. Had horizontal reports from multiple platoons been available, reasonable commanders would likely have recognised the risks associated with drone operations in regions where distinct local attire was prevalent. Similarly, an effective civilian harm tracking mechanism would have alerted *Targeting Adviser* officers to the presence of an unanticipated variable affecting their DSS, undermining their previously justified confidence in its reliability. Once such critical information becomes available, the situation shifts: at that point, good-faith users would be expected to intervene to prevent further civilian harm. Consequently, it is justifiable to argue that any subsequent decision to continue using the AI system, despite these warnings, would be unreasonable.

Iterative Assessment is specifically designed to address 'known unknowns'—gaps in knowledge about system faults that can only be uncovered through real-world deployment. It does not seek to prevent initial failures but instead enables swift, decisive action to prevent their recurrence in future iterations. To this end, the approach outlined in this chapter represents best practice for both operational and post-action assessments and enhances civilian protection in *any* military operation, regardless of the capabilities involved.

Logistical and operational constraints may limit the comprehensive implementation of the framework. As emphasised from the outset, Iterative Assessment is

[164] Fenrick 2005, p. 168.

[165] The Rendulic Rule establishes that 'commanders and personnel should be evaluated based on information reasonably available at the time of decision': see Kouba 2017, p. 10.

an ideal rather than a legally binding rule. There are valid reasons why many of the recommended mechanisms—such as maintaining a permanent re-review structure post-deployment and integrating horizontal and vertical reporting systems—are rarely adopted in practice. These measures are time, resource, and labour intensive. For instance, conducting detailed civilian harm tracking after every attack may divert critical assets from other operational needs,[166] while establishing a robust reporting system requires dedicated communication networks and personnel. Nevertheless, militaries are encouraged to adopt Iterative Assessment to the extent feasible as it offers a structured means of mitigating the uncertainty that AI systems inevitably bring to the battlefield.

References

Articles, Books and Other Documents

Abaimov S, Martellini M (2020) Artificial Intelligence in Autonomous Weapon Systems. In: Martellini M, Ralf T (eds) 21st Century Prometheus. Springer International Publishing, Cham, pp. 141–177

Abraham Y (2024) 'Lavender': The AI machine directing Israel's bombing spree in Gaza. https://www.972mag.com/lavender-ai-israeli-army-gaza. Accessed 15 April 2024

Adadi A, Berrada M (2018) Peeking Inside the Black-Box: A Survey on Explainable Artificial Intelligence (XAI). IEEE. https://doi.org/10.1109/ACCESS.2018.2870052

Aspin L (1988) Witness to Iran Flight 655. New York Times, 18 November 1988. https://www.nytimes.com/1988/11/18/opinion/witnessto-iran-flight-655.html. Accessed 25 March 2025

Australia (2006) Law of Armed Conflict. Defence Publishing Service, Canberra, Australian Defence Doctrine Publication 06.4. https://www.onlinelibrary.iihl.org/wp-content/uploads/2021/05/AUS-Manual-Law-of-Armed-Conflict.pdf. Accessed 9 May 2025

Australia (2018) The Australian Article 36 Review Process. CCW GGE on LAWS, UN Doc CCW/GGE.2/2018/WP.6. https://docs-library.unoda.org/Convention_on_Certain_Conventional_Weapons_-_Group_of_Governmental_Experts_(2018)/2018_GGE%2BLAWS_August_Working%2Bpaper_Australia.pdf. Accessed 9 May 2025

Bakirtzis G, Carr S, Danks D, Topcu U (2022) Dynamic Certification for Autonomous Systems, arXiv:2203.10950v3 [cs.RO]. https://doi.org/10.48550/arXiv.2203.10950

Barredo Arrieta A, Díaz-Rodríguez N, Del Ser J, Bennetot A, Tabik S, Barbado A, Garcia S, Gil-Lopez S, Molina D, Benjamins R, Chatila R, Herrera F (2020) Explainable Artificial Intelligence (XAI): Concepts, Taxonomies, Opportunities and Challenges Toward Responsible AI. Information Fusion. https://doi.org/10.1016/j.inffus.2019.12.012

Bartels R (2013) Dealing with the Principle of Proportionality in Armed Conflict in Retrospect: The Application of the Principle in International Criminal Trials. Israel Law Review. https://doi.org/10.1017/S0021223713000083

Belgian Armed Forces (2018) Procedure specifique / Specifieke procedure. DGJUR-SPS-CJBCEJ-CXX-001/LEGAD-Int, Ed 001/Rév 000, 21 November 2018

Bommasani R et al. (2021) On the Opportunities and Risks of Foundation Models. arXiv:2108.07258v3 [cs.LG]. https://doi.org/10.48550/arXiv.2109.07258

Boothby WH (2016) Weapons and the Law of Armed Conflict, 2nd edn. Oxford University Press, Oxford

[166] Hathaway and Khan 2024, p. 55.

Boothby WH (2018) New Technologies and the Law in War and Peace. Cambridge University Press, Cambridge
Bothe M, Partsch KJ, Solf WA (eds) (2013) New Rules for Victims of Armed Conflict: Commentary on the Two 1977 Protocols Additional to the Geneva Conventions of 1949, 2nd edn. Martinus Nijhoff, Leiden
Boulanin V (2016) Mapping the Development of Autonomy in Weapon Systems: A Primer on Autonomy. https://www.sipri.org/sites/default/files/Mapping-development-autonomy-in-weapon-systems.pdf. Accessed 25 March 2025
Boulanin V, Goussac N, Bruun L, Richards L (2020) Responsible Military Use of Artificial Intelligence: Can the European Union Lead the Way in Developing Best Practice. https://www.sipri.org/sites/default/files/2020-11/responsible_military_use_of_artificial_intelligence.pdf. Accessed 25 March 2025
Cherry J, Johnson D (2020) Maintaining Command and Control (C2) of Lethal Autonomous Weapon Systems: Legal and Policy Considerations. Southwestern Journal of International Law 27:1-27
Copeland DP (2014) Legal Review of New Technology Weapons. In: Nasu H, McLaughlin R (eds) New Technologies and the Law of Armed Conflict. T.M.C. Asser Press, The Hague, pp. 43–55
Corn GS (2012) Targeting, Command Judgement, and a Proposed Quantum of Information Component: A Fourth Amendment Lesson in Contextual Reasonableness. Brooklyn Law Review 77(2):437–498
Cranny-Evans S (2024) Sensor fusion: The future of land ISTAR?. European Security and Defence. https://euro-sd.com/2024/04/articles/37593/sensor-fusion-the-future-of-land-istar. Accessed 24 July 2024
Curtis E. Lemay Center (2019) Air Force Doctrine Publication 3-60 – Targeting. Curtis E Lemay Center. www.doctrine.af.mil/Doctrine-Publications/AFDP-3-60-Targeting. Accessed 5 July 2021
Daoust I, Coupland R, Ishoey R (2002) New wars, new weapons? The obligation of States to assess the legality of means and methods of warfare. International Review of the Red Cross 84:345–362
Das S (2021) Best Practices for Dealing with Concept Drift. Neptune.ai. https://neptune.ai/blog/concept-drift-best-practices. Accessed 30 October 2021
Defense Innovation Board (2019) AI Principles: Recommendations on the Ethical Use of Artificial Intelligence by the Department of Defense Innovation Board. US Department of Defense. https://media.defense.gov/2019/Oct/31/2002204458/-1/-1/0/DIB_AI_PRINCIPLES_PRIMARY_DOCUMENT.PDF. Accessed 2 August 2023
Deng B (2015) The Robot's Dilemma: Working out How to Build Ethical Robots Is One of the Thorniest Challenges in Artificial Intelligence. Nature 523:25–27
Department of the Army Headquarters (2015) Protection of Civilians. https://irp.fas.org/doddir/army/atp3-07-6.pdf. Accessed 25 March 2025
Dickson B (2022) AI scientists are studying the "emergent" abilities of large language models. https://bdtechtalks.com/2022/08/22/llm-emergent-abilities. Accessed 27 January 2024
Ekelhof M (2018) Lifting the Fog of Targeting: "Autonomous Weapons" and Human Control through the Lens of Military Targeting. Naval War College Review 71(3):61–94
Ekelhof M, Paoli GP (2020) Swarm Robotics: Technical and Operational Overview of the Next Generation of Autonomous Systems. UNIDIR. https://unidir.org/publication/swarm-robotics-technical-and-operational-overview-of-the-next-generation-of-autonomous-systems. Accessed 27 January 2023
European Commission (2020) Horizon 2020 Commission Expert Group to advise on specific ethical issues raised by driverless mobility (E03659) Ethics of Connected and Automated Vehicles: Recommendations on Road Safety, Privacy, Fairness, Explainability and Responsibility. Publication Office of the European Union, Luxembourg
European Committee on Crime Problems (2020) Feasibility Study on a Future Council of Europe Instrument on Artificial Intelligence and Criminal Law. https://rm.coe.int/cdpc-2020-3-feasibility-study-of-a-future-instrument-on-ai-and-crimina/16809f9b60. Accessed 25 March 2025

Fenrick WJ (2005) International Humanitarian Law and Combat Casualties. European Journal of Population / Revue européenne de Démographie. https://doi.org/10.1007/s10680-005-6421-y
Flournoy MA, Haines A, Chefitz G (2020) Building Trust through Testing: Adapting DOD's Test & Evaluation, Validation & Verification (TEVV) Enterprise for Machine Learning Systems, Including Deep Learning Systems. https://cset.georgetown.edu/wp-content/uploads/Building-Trust-Through-Testing.pdf. Accessed 25 March 2025
Fromm J (2005) Types and Forms of Emergence. arXiv:nlin/0506028 [nlin.AO]. https://doi.org/10.48550/arXiv.nlin/0506028
Fry J C (2006) Contextualized Legal Reviews for the Methods and Means of Warfare: Cave Combat and International Humanitarian Law. Columbia Journal of Transnational Law 44:453–519
Ganguli D et al. (2022) Predictability and Surprise in Large Generative Models. arXiv:2202.07785v2 [cs.CY]. https://doi.org/10.48550/arXiv.2202.07785
Geirhos R, Medina Temme CR, Rauber J, Schütt HH, Bethge M, Wichmann FA (2019) ImageNet-trained CNNs are biased towards texture; increasing shape bias improves accuracy and robustness. arXiv:1811.12231v3 [cs.CV]. https://doi.org/10.48550/arXiv.1808.08750
Gilmer J, Adams RP, Goodfellow I, Andersen D, Dahl GE (2018a) Motivating the Rules of the Game for Adversarial Example Research. arXiv:1807.06732 [cs.LG]. https://doi.org/10.48550/arXiv.1807.06732
Gilmer J, Metz L, Faghri F, Schoenholz S S, Raghu M, Wattenberg M, Goodfellow I (2018b) Adversarial Spheres. arXiv:1801.02774 [cs.CV]. https://doi.org/10.48550/arXiv.1801.02774
Goussac N (2019) Safety Net or Tangled Web: Legal Reviews of AI in Weapons and War-Fighting. ICRC Humanitarian Law & Policy. https://blogs.icrc.org/law-and-policy/2019/04/18/safety-net-tangled-web-legal-reviews-ai-weapons-war-fighting. Accessed 26 May 2021
Government Accountability Office (2023) Science & Tech Spotlight: Drone Swarm Technologies. https://www.gao.gov/assets/gao-23-106930.pdf. Accessed 25 April 2024
Group of Governmental Experts on Lethal Autonomous Weapons Systems (GGE LAWS) (2021) Draft Report of the 2021 Session of the Group of Governmental Experts on Emerging Technologies in the Area of Lethal Autonomous Weapons Systems. CCW/GGE1/2021/CRP1
Guinness H (2024) What Are AI Hallucinations—and How Do You Prevent Them? https://zapier.com/blog/ai-hallucinations/. Accessed 24 March 2025
Gunnell M (2023) Emergent Behavior in AI. https://www.techopedia.com/definition/emergent-behavior. Accessed 27 January 2024
Haque AA (2012) Killing in the Fog of War. Southern California Law Review 86(1):63–116
Hathaway OA, Khan A (2024) 'Mistakes' in War. University of Pennsylvania Law Review 173:1–88
Henderson I (2009) The Contemporary Law of Targeting: Military Objectives, Proportionality and Precautions in Attack under Additional Protocol I. Martinus Nijhoff, Leiden
Hendrycks D, Liu X, Wallace E, Dziedzic A, Krishnan R, Song D (2020) Pretrained Transformers Improve Out-of-Distribution Robustness. arXiv:2004.06100 [cs.CL]. https://doi.org/10.48550/arXiv.2004.06100
Herbach J (2012) Into the Caves of Steel: Precaution, Cognition and Robotic Weapon Systems Under the International Law of Armed Conflict. Amsterdam Law Forum 4(3):3–20
Holland Michel A (2020) The Black Box, Unlocked: Predictability and Understandability in Military AI. UNIDIR, Geneva. https://unidir.org/files/2020-09/BlackBoxUnlocked.pdf. Accessed 27 June 2025
Huffman WB (2012) Margin of Error: Potential Pitfalls of the Ruling in The Prosecutor v. Ante Gotovina. Military Law Review 211:1–56
ICRC (2006) A Guide to the Legal Review of New Weapons, Means and Methods of Warfare: Measures to Implement Article 36 of Additional Protocol I of 1977. https://international-review.icrc.org/sites/default/files/irrc_864_11.pdf. Accessed 25 March 2025
ICRC (2016) Views of the International Committee of the Red Cross (ICRC) on autonomous weapon system. https://www.icrc.org/en/document/views-icrc-autonomous-weapon-system. Accessed 25 March 2025

ICRC (2018) Ethics and Autonomous Weapon Systems: An Ethical Basis for Human Control? Convention on Certain Conventional Weapons (CCW), Group of Governmental Experts on Lethal Autonomous Weapons Systems (Geneva, 3 April 2018) https://www.icrc.org/en/document/ethics-and-autonomous-weapon-systems-ethical-basis-human-control. Accessed 20 June 2025

ICRC (2019) Statement of the International Committee of the Red Cross (ICRC) under Agenda Item 5(B). Convention on Certain Conventional Weapons (CCW), Group of Governmental Experts on Lethal Autonomous Weapons Systems (Geneva, 25-29 March 2019). https://docs-library.unoda.org/Convention_on_Certain_Conventional_Weapons_-_Group_of_Governmental_Experts_(2019)/CCW%2BGGE%2BLAWS%2BICRC%2Bstatement%2Bagenda%2Bitem%2B5b%2B26%2B03%2B2019.pdf. Accessed 9 May 2025

ICRC, Geneva Academy (2024) Expert Consultation Report on AI and Related Technologies in Military Decision-Making on the Use of Force in Armed Conflicts. www.geneva-academy.ch/joomlatools-files/docman-files/Artificial%20Intelligence%20And%20Related%20Technologies%20In%20Military%20Decision-Making.pdf. Accessed 9 January 2025

Jenks C, Liivoja R (2018) Machine Autonomy and the Constant Care Obligation. ICRC Humanitarian Law & Policy. blogs.icrc.org/law-and-policy/2018/12/11/machine-autonomy-constant-care-obligation. Accessed 28 May 2021

Jensen ET (2021) Autonomy and Precautions in the Law of Armed Conflict. In: Liivoja R, Väljataga A (eds) Autonomous Cyber Capabilities Under International Law. NATO CCDCOE Publications, Tallinn, pp. 181–205

Jevglevskaja N (2018) Weapons Review Obligation Under Customary International Law. International Law Studies 94:186–221

Kalmanovitz P (2016) Judgment, Liability and the Risks of Riskless Warfare. In: Bhuta N et al. (eds) Autonomous Weapons Systems. Cambridge University Press, Cambridge, pp. 145–163

King TC, Aggarwal N, Taddeo M, Floridi L (2020) Artificial Intelligence Crime: An Interdisciplinary Analysis of Foreseeable Threats and Solutions. Science and Engineering Ethics. https://doi.org/10.1007/s11948-018-00081-0

Klonowska K (2022) Article 36: Review of AI Decision-Support Systems and Other Emerging Technologies of Warfare. In: Gill T D, Geiß R, Krieger H, Mignot-Mahdavi R (eds) Yearbook of International Humanitarian Law, Volume 23. T.M.C. Asser Press, The Hague, pp. 123–156

Kouba MD (ed) (2017) Operational Law Handbook. 17th edn. International and Operational Law Department the Judge Advocate General's Legal Center and School, Charlottesville

Kwik J (2022) A Practicable Operationalisation of Meaningful Human Control. Laws. https://doi.org/10.3390/laws11030043.

Kwik J (2024a) Lawfully Using Autonomous Weapon Technologies. TMC Asser Press, The Hague. https://doi.org/10.1007/978-94-6265-631-4

Kwik J (2024b) Is wearing these sunglasses an attack? Obligations under IHL related to anti-AI countermeasures. International Review of the Red Cross. 106(926):732–759. https://doi.org/10.1017/S1816383124000067

Kwik J (2025) Global Policy 16(3):467–473. https://onlinelibrary.wiley.com/doi/abs/10.1111/1758-5899.70042

Kwik J (2026) 'I Plead Ignorance': Autonomous Weapons and Criminal Liability for Not Knowing the Knowable. International Law Studies 107(1). https://digital-commons.usnwc.edu/ils/vol107/iss1/2/

Kwik J, Van Engers T (2021) Algorithmic Fog of War: When Lack of Transparency Violates the Law of Armed Conflict. Journal of Future Robot Life. https://doi.org/10.3233/FRL-200019

Kwik J, Zwanenburg M, Took C, Aarts J (2025) Controlling Military Artificial Intelligence: Harnessing Rules of Engagement and Military Directives. Asser Policy Brief 2025–01. https://papers.ssrn.com/abstract=5132731. Accessed 12 February 2025

Leslie D (2019) Understanding Artificial Intelligence Ethics and Safety: A Guide for the Responsible Design and Implementation of AI Systems in the Public

Sector. https://www.turing.ac.uk/sites/default/files/2019-06/understanding_artificial_intelligence_ethics_and_safety.pdf. Accessed 25 March 2025

Liu H-Y (2016) Refining Responsibility: Differentiating Two Types of Responsibility Issues Raised by Autonomous Weapons Systems. In: Bhuta N, Beck N, Geiß R, Liu H-Y, Kreß C (eds) Autonomous Weapons Systems. Cambridge University Press, Cambridge, pp. 325–344

Lohn AJ (2020) Estimating the Brittleness of AI: Safety Integrity Levels and the Need for Testing Out-Of-Distribution Performance. arXiv:2009.00802 [cs.LG]. https://doi.org/10.48550/arXiv.2009.00802

Margulies P (2021) A Moment in Time: Autonomous Cyber Capabilities, Proportionality and Precautions. In: Liivoja R, Väljataga A (eds) Autonomous Cyber Capabilities under International Law. NATO CCDCOE Publications, Tallinn, pp. 152–180

McClelland J (2003) The Review of Weapons in Accordance with Article 36 of Additional Protocol I. International Review of the Red Cross 850:397–415

McGrayne SB (2011) The Theory That Would Not Die. Yale University Press, New Haven

Meier MW (2019) Lethal Autonomous Weapons Systems: Is It the End of the World as We Know It . . . Or Will We Be Just Fine? In: Williams W S, Ford C M (eds) Complex Battlespaces: The Law of Armed Conflict and the Dynamics of Modern Warfare. Oxford University Press, Oxford, pp. 289–316

Meng F-J, Li Y-Q, Shao F-M, Yuan G-H, Dai J-Y (2022) Visual-simulation region proposal and generative adversarial network based ground military target recognition. Defence Technology. https://doi.org/10.1016/j.dt.2021.07.001

Mikhailov DI (2023) Optimizing National Security Strategies through LLM-Driven Artificial Intelligence Integration. arXiv:2305.13927 [cs.CY]. doi.org/https://doi.org/10.48550/arXiv.2305.13927

Mogul JC (2005) Emergent (Mis)behavior vs. Complex Software Systems. HP Invent, HPL-2006-2. https://www.hpl.hp.com/techreports/2006/HPL-2006-2.pdf. Accessed 24 January 2024

Molnar C (2019) Interpretable Machine Learning: A Guide for Making Black Box Models Explainable. Lean Publishing

Moyes R (2019) Target Profiles: An Initial Consideration of "Target Profiles" as a Basis for Rule-Making in the Context of Discussions on Autonomy in Weapons Systems. https://article36.org/wp-content/uploads/2019/08/Target-profiles.pdf. Accessed 25 March 2025

NATO (2019a) Allied Joint Doctrine for the Planning of Operations. NATO Standard, AJP-5, Edition A Version 2, May 2019

NATO (2019b) Allied Joint Doctrine for the Conduct of Operations. NATO Standard, AJP-3, Edition C Version 1, February 2019

NATO (2021a) Summary of the NATO Artificial Intelligence Strategy. https://www.nato.int/cps/en/natohq/official_texts_187617.htm. Accessed 6 September 2023

NATO (2021b) Allied Joint Doctrine for Joint Targeting. Edition B Version 1 (November 2021) AJP-39, NATO Standardization Office (NSO)

Navarro I, Matía F (2013) An Introduction to Swarm Robotics. Robotics. https://doi.org/10.5402/2013/608164

Nelson K, Corbin G, Blowers M (2014) Evaluating Data Distribution and Drift Vulnerabilities of Machine Learning Algorithms in Secure and Adversarial Environments. In: Blowers M, Williams J (eds) Proceedings Volume 9119, Machine Intelligence and Bio-inspired Computation: Theory and Applications VIII. P 911904. https://doi.org/10.1117/12.2053045

Ngo R, Chan L, Mindermann S (2022) The Alignment Problem from a Deep Learning Perspective. arXiv:2209.00626v6 [cs.AI]. https://doi.org/10.48550/arXiv.2209.00626

Oeter S (2020) Specifying the Proportionality Test and the Standard of Due Precaution: Problems of Prognostic Assessment in Determining the Meaning of "May Be Expected" and "Anticipated". In: Kreß C, Lawless R (eds) Necessity and Proportionality in International Peace and Security Law. Oxford University Press, Oxford, pp. 343–366

Oniani D, Hilsman J, Peng Y, Poropatich R K, Pamplin J C, Legault G L, Wang Y (2023) From Military to Healthcare: Adopting and Expanding Ethical Principles for Generative Artificial Intelligence. arXiv:2308.02448 [cs.CY]. https://doi.org/10.48550/arXiv.2308.02448

Parks WH (2005) Conventional Weapons and Weapons Reviews. Yearbook of International Humanitarian Law 8:55–142

Perez E et al. (2022) Discovering Language Model Behaviors with Model-Written Evaluations. arXiv:2212.09251 [cs.CL]. https://doi.org/10.48550/arXiv.2212.09251

Puscas I (2023) AI and International Security: Understanding the Risks and Paving the Path for Confidence-Building Measures. https://unidir.org/publication/ai-and-international-security-understanding-the-risks-and-paving-the-path-for-confidence-building-measures/. Accessed 9 May 2025

Rosén F (2014) Extremely Stealthy and Incredibly Close: Drones, Control and Legal Responsibility. Journal of Conflict and Security Law. https://doi.org/10.1093/jcsl/krt024

Rosenfeld A (2021) Better metrics for evaluating explainable artificial intelligence. In: Proceedings of the 20th international conference on autonomous agents and multiagent systems, pp. 45–50. https://www.ifaamas.org/Proceedings/aamas2021/pdfs/p45.pdf (240803). Accessed 3 August 2024

Roy A (2018) National Strategy for Artificial Intelligence #AIFORALL. National Institution for Transforming India Aayog, New Delhi. https://www.niti.gov.in/sites/default/files/2023-03/National-Strategy-for-Artificial-Intelligence.pdf. Accessed 9 May 2025

Russell S, Dewey D, Tegmark M (2015) Research Priorities for Robust and Beneficial Artificial Intelligence. Future of Life Institute. https://futureoflife.org/open-letter/ai-open-letter/. Accessed 27 June 2025

Russell SJ, Norvig P (2021) Artificial Intelligence: A Modern Approach, 4th edn. Pearson, New Jersey

Safi M (2019) Are Drone Swarms the Future of Aerial Warfare? www.theguardian.com/news/2019/dec/04/are-drone-swarms-the-future-of-aerial-warfare. Accessed 2 August 2023

Sandoz Y, Swinarski C, Zimmerman B (1987) Commentary on the Additional Protocols of 8 June 1977 to the Geneva Conventions of 12 August 1949. Martinus Nijhoff, Geneva

Sassòli M (2014) Autonomous Weapons and International Humanitarian Law: Advantages, Open Technical Questions and Legal Issues to Be Clarified. International Law Studies 90:308–340

Sayler KM (2020) Defense Primer: U.S. Policy on Lethal Autonomous Weapon Systems. Congressional Report Service

Schaeffer R, Miranda B, Koyejo S (2023) Are Emergent Abilities of Large Language Models a Mirage? arXiv:2304.15004v2 [cs.AI]. https://doi.org/10.48550/arXiv.2304.15004

Scharre PD (2016) Centaur Warfighting: The False Choice of Humans vs. Automation. Temple International & Comparative Law Journal 30(1):151–165

Schmitt MN (2010) Targeting in Operational Law. In: Gill T D, Fleck D (eds) The Handbook of the International Law of Military Operations. Oxford University Press, Oxford, pp. 245–275

Schmitt MN (ed) (2017) Tallinn Manual 2.0 on the International Law Applicable to Cyber Warfare. Cambridge University Press, Cambridge. https://ilmc.univie.ac.at/fileadmin/user_upload/p_ilmc/Bilder/Bewerbung/Case_2/Michael_N._Schmitt_-_Tallinn_Manual_2.0_on_the_International_Law_Applicable_to_Cyber_Operations-Cambridge_University_Press__2017_.pdf

Schmitt MN, Biller J, Fahey SC, Goddard DS, Highfill C, Ohlin JD, May L, Finkelstein C (2017) Joint and Combined Targeting: Structure and Process. In: Ohlin J D, May L, Finkelstein C (eds) Weighing Lives in War, vol 1. Oxford University Press, Oxford, pp. 298–324. https://doi.org/10.1093/oso/9780198796176.003.0014

Schmitt MN, Schauss M (2019) Uncertainty in the Law of Targeting: Towards a Cognitive Framework. Harvard National Security Journal 10:148–194

Schuller AL (2017) At the Crossroads of Control: The Intersection of Artificial Intelligence in Autonomous Weapon Systems with International Humanitarian Law. Harvard National Security Journal 8:379

Sharma M et al. (2023) Towards Understanding Sycophancy in Language Models. arXiv:2310.13548v3 [cs.CL]. https://doi.org/10.48550/arXiv.2310.13548

Silva A, Schrum M, Hedlund-Botti E, Gopalan N, Gombolay M (2023) Explainable Artificial Intelligence: Evaluating the Objective and Subjective Impacts of xAI on Human-Agent Interaction. International Journal of Human–Computer Interaction. https://doi.org/10.1080/10447318.2022.2101698

Steinhardt J (2022) Future ML Systems Will Be Qualitatively Different. Bounded Regret, https://bounded-regret.ghost.io/future-ml-systems-will-be-qualitatively-different. Accessed 27 January 2024

Stewart DM (2011) New Technology and the Law of Armed Conflict. International Law Studies 87:271–298

Sullivan S, Ricket I (2024) Targeting in the Black Box. In: Kwan C, Lindström L, Giovannelli D, Podiņš K, Štruc D (eds) CyCon 2024: Over the Horizon. Tallinn, NATO CCD COE, pp. 207–220. https://ccdcoe.org/uploads/2024/05/CyCon_2024_book.pdf#page=215. Accessed 25 March 2025

Switzerland (2016) Towards a "compliance-based" approach to LAWS. https://docs-library.unoda.org/Convention_on_Certain_Conventional_Weapons_-_Informal_Meeting_of_Experts_(2016)/2016_LAWS%2BMX_CountryPaper%2BSwitzerland.pdf. Accessed 25 March 2025

Thorne JG (2020) Warriors and War Algorithms: Leveraging Artificial Intelligence to Enable Ethical Targeting. Technical Report, 14-05-2020. https://apps.dtic.mil/sti/citations/AD1104171. Accessed 3 July 2021

Tolk A (2015) Merging Two Worlds: Agent-Based Simulation Methods for Autonomous Systems. In: Williams A P, Scharre P D (eds) Autonomous Systems: Issues for Defence Policymakers. NATO, The Hague, pp. 291–317

Toscano C P (2015) "Friend of Humans": An Argument for Developing Autonomous Weapons Systems. Journal of National Security Law & Policy 8(1):189–246

Trusilo D (2023) Autonomous AI Systems in Conflict: Emergent Behavior and Its Impact on Predictability and Reliability. Journal of Military Ethics 22:2–17. https://doi.org/10.1080/15027570.2023.2213985

UK Ministry of Defence (2016) UK Weapon Reviews. https://www.gov.uk/government/publications/uk-weapon-reviews. Accessed 3 August 2024

Undersecretary of Defense for Acquisition, Technology, and Logistics (2012) The Role of Autonomy in DoD Systems. https://irp.fas.org/agency/dod/dsb/autonomy.pdf. Accessed 25 March 2025

US Air Force Office of the Chief Scientist (2015) Autonomous Horizons: System Autonomy in the Air Force—A Path to the Future, Volume I: Human-Autonomy Teaming. https://www.af.mil/Portals/1/documents/SECAF/AutonomousHorizons.pdf. Accessed 25 March 2025

US Department of Defense (2015) Law of War Manual, Updated July 2023. US Department of Defense, Washington D.C.

US Department of Defense (2023) Autonomy in Weapon Systems. US DoD Directive 3000.09

US Joint Chiefs of Staff (2018) Counterinsurgency. Joint Publication 3-24, 25 April 2018, Validated 30 April 2021

Van den Boogaard JC, Roorda MP (2021) "Autonomous" Weapons and Human Control. In: Bartels R, van den Boogaard JC, Ducheine PAL, Pouw E, Voetelink J (eds) Military Operations and the Notion of Control Under International Law. T.M.C. Asser Press, The Hague, pp. 421–437

Van der Waa J, Nieuwburg E, Cremers A, Neerincx M (2021) Evaluating XAI: A Comparison of Rule-Based and Example-Based Explanations. Artificial Intelligence 291:103404. https://www.sciencedirect.com/science/article/pii/S0004370220301533

Wallace D (2018) Cyber Weapon Reviews under International Humanitarian Law: A Critical Analysis. Tallinn Paper no 11, https://ccdcoe.org/uploads/2018/10/TP-11_2018.pdf. Accessed 3 August 2024

Williams R (2017) Lords Select Committee, Artificial Intelligence Committee, Written Evidence. AIC0206. http://data.parliament.uk/writtenevidence/committeeevidence.svc/evidencedocument/artificial-intelligence-committee/artificial-intelligence/written/70496.html#_ftn13. Accessed 7 May 2022

Wilson C (2020) Artificial Intelligence and Warfare. In: Martellini M, Trapp R (eds) 21st Century Prometheus. Springer International Publishing, Cham, pp 125–140. https://doi.org/10.1007/978-3-030-28285-1_7

Yadron D, Tynan D (2016) Tesla Driver Dies in First Fatal Crash While Using Autopilot Mode. www.theguardian.com/technology/2016/jun/30/tesla-autopilot-death-self-driving-car-elon-musk. Accessed 25 March 2025

Jonathan Kwik is a researcher in international law at the Asser Institute, specialised in the intersection between law and emerging technologies. He is a member of the Drafting Team for the *Manual on the International Law Applicable to Artificial Intelligence in Warfare* Project (2025–2027) and a member of the Board of Experts of the *Asia-Pacific Journal of International Humanitarian Law* (APJIHL). He has written extensively on international humanitarian law, targeting law, AI modelling and (international) criminal responsibility. He recently published the book, *Lawfully Using Autonomous Weapon Technologies.*

Chapter 10
The Computational Representation of Rules of International Humanitarian Law in Military Autonomous Devices: Issues, Problems, and Controversies

Tomasz Zurek and Tom van Engers

Contents

Abstract The main aim of this chapter is to examine the challenges related to International Humanitarian Law (IHL) compliance analysis by autonomous military devices. The work is rooted in the experience gained during the Asser Institute's Designing International Law and Ethics into Military AI (DILEMA) research project. The chapter critically explores the obstacles inherent in operationalising legal norms through algorithmic structures, including issues related to context sensitivity, interpretative ambiguity, and technological limitations. In evaluating the feasibility of automating IHL compliance testing, the chapter also reflects on the broader implications for accountability, military decision-making, and the evolving role of legal norms in armed conflict. In order to determine the key elements of IHL compliance testing, we decompose the actual targeting process. This allows us to point out the key

T. Zurek · T. van Engers (✉)
Informatics Institute, University of Amsterdam, Amsterdam, The Netherlands
e-mail: t.m.vanengers@uva.nl

T. Zurek
e-mail: tomasz.zurek@umcs.pl

B. Boutin et al. (eds.), *Legal, Ethical, and Technical Dilemmas in Military Artificial Intelligence*, https://doi.org/10.1007/978-94-6265-759-5_10

components of IHL compliance testing, as well as the data and capabilities necessary to fulfil IHL requirements. In this chapter, we introduce a computational mechanism for automating IHL compliance testing and discuss the challenges, difficulties, and possibilities for creating such a technical mechanism to perform the legal analysis required by IHL.

Keywords International Humanitarian Law · Military Autonomous Devices · Model · Legal Compliance · Autonomous Decision Making · Artificial Intelligence (AI)

10.1 Introduction

This chapter aims to examine the principal challenges associated with ensuring that autonomous military systems operate in compliance with International Humanitarian Law (IHL). In particular, we set forth a technical model for IHL compliance analysis. The question of whether autonomous military systems can be programmed to comply with the rules of IHL lies at the heart of contemporary debates on the lawful integration of artificial intelligence (AI) in armed conflict. As technological developments accelerate, so too does the urgency of addressing how—and whether—legal norms can be computationally represented within such systems. This chapter explores these issues by examining the key challenges associated with ensuring the autonomous compliance of military devices with IHL. By compliance analysis, we refer to mechanisms that facilitate the testing of whether a decision made by an autonomous device is compliant with IHL rules. Our focus is specifically on targeting norms within the conduct of hostilities, in particular the principles of distinction,[1] precautions,[2] and proportionality,[3] with an emphasis on the principle of precautions. The analysis is based on insights developed during the Asser Institute's Designing International Law and Ethics into Military Artificial Intelligence (DILEMA) research project.

To identify the key elements of IHL compliance testing, we begin by systematically decomposing the targeting process. This analytical approach allowed us to isolate the core components relevant to legal assessments under IHL and to determine the data inputs and technological capabilities required to fulfil IHL obligations. Our analysis centres on legality within the targeting process, recognising that the development of software embedded within weapon systems entails numerous complex components, including for target recognition and identification, which may require the abstraction and labelling of sensor data, among other technical tasks. We deliberately set aside the broader debate around *meaningful human control*, operating instead

[1] Protocol Additional to the Geneva Conventions of 12 August 1949, and relating to the Protection of Victims of International Armed Conflicts (Protocol I), opened for signature 8 June 1977, 1125 UNTS 3, entered into force 7 December 1978, API, Article 48.

[2] Ibid., Article 57(3).

[3] Ibid., Article 57(2).

on the assumption that human oversight is, in practice, often limited. Our aim is to explore mechanisms capable of testing IHL compliance even in the absence of direct human intervention, such as in the case of automated systems that cannot be remotely operated due to, for instance, radio-frequency jamming disrupting communication with a drone.[4]

This chapter builds on our earlier research, in which we proposed a formal model for conducting IHL assessments, including the application of Article 57(3) Additional Protocol I (API), the principle of proportionality, and the obligation to minimise incidental harm.[5] These legal requirements were embedded within the general structure of a decision-making system.[6] We also addressed the challenge of uncertainty, which arises in the calculation of expected values for military advantage and incidental harm. These calculations are central not only to proportionality assessments but also to the principles of distinction and precautions. They also arise independently in relation to other targeting obligations. One of the proposed mechanisms for performing an IHL legal test was also subjected to experimental verification.[7] This chapter builds on the formal model introduced in this previous work, using it as a starting point to further examine the challenges, limitations, and possibilities for developing a mechanism capable of conducting IHL compliance analysis within targeting procedures.

The chapter is structured as follows: Sect. 10.2 outlines the North Atlantic Treaty Organisation (NATO) targeting procedure and provides a brief overview of the relevant legal framework, which serves as the operational basis of our model. Section 10.3 then sets out our compliance analysis model.[8] Section 10.4 discusses our key findings regarding the challenges, limitations, and possibilities for developing a mechanism capable of conducting IHL compliance analysis. Concluding remarks are provided in Sect. 10.5.

10.2 Targeting and Legal Tests Under IHL

Before turning to the computational modelling of IHL compliance testing, we first provide a brief overview of the targeting process and outline how specific legal tests are currently conducted. This section elaborates on the NATO Standard Targeting Procedure,[9] which serves as the practical foundation for our model. By adopting this operational framework, we aim to avoid overly abstract analysis and instead ground our model in real-world military decision-making processes.

---

[4] More about this discussion can be found in Boutin and Woodcock 2024.

[5] API, above n. 1.

[6] Zurek et al. 2023.

[7] Zurek et al. 2022b.

[8] Zurek et al. 2023, 2022b, 2024.

[9] NATO 2016. See also Kwik et al. 2022; Roorda 2015; Ekelhof 2016.

Our central question is whether the core IHL targeting requirements can, at least in principle, be fulfilled by an AI system. To explore this, our model is structured around the NATO targeting cycle—the process followed by military commanders in preparing for operations and engagements. This cycle involves the identification and analysis of potential targets, the evaluation of weapon and delivery options, and the optimisation of military advantage, whilst ensuring compliance with IHL[10] While targeting is primarily a military practice ultimately aimed at achieving mission objectives as efficiently as possible, it nevertheless integrates critical IHL requirements.[11] As such, the targeting process captured by the NATO targeting cycle provides a particularly useful foundation for developing and evaluating our model, helping to bridge the gap between legal obligations and operational realities.

The NATO Standard Targeting Procedure can be broadly divided into six overall phases:[12]

(1) **Goal Analysis**: The initial stage involves the commander analysing the overarching strategic or operational goals. Although no legal tests are conducted at this point, these *goals* and *objectives* constitute an important part of the input for subsequent decision-making processes.
(2) **Target Analysis**: At this stage, potential targets are identified and evaluated. Two key variables come into play here: *Military Advantage (MA)*—the anticipated strategic advantage of neutralising the target—and *Incidental Harm (IH)*—the expected collateral damage, including foreseeable direct and indirect effects of the attack. Legal assessments under the principles of distinction (Article 52(1) API) and precautions in attack (Article 57(3) API) are applied at this phase.
(3) **Capability Analysis**: This step assesses the available operational decisions. In our framework, a 'decision' refers to any relevant combination of targets, weapon systems, ammunition type, and delivery method. The assessment of MA and IH is revisited and refined based on the specific weapons configurations being considered. Legal tests at this stage include proportionality, the minimisation of incidental harm, and the exclusion of unlawful weapons.
(4) **Capability Assignment** and **(5) Execution**: These phases involve the assignment of selected capabilities and the conduct of the attack. Legal assessments—particularly those concerning distinction, precautions, and proportionality—are reapplied on a more detailed (tactical) level.[13] Should new information arise that invalidates earlier assessments, the operation must be halted or re-evaluated.
(6) **Assessment**: The final phase focuses on reviewing the effects of the operation. This includes identifying any violations or irregularities, implementing corrective measures, and assigning responsibility where appropriate.[14] To support

[10] Corn 2014.

[11] United States Airforce 2019.

[12] NATO 2016; Roorda 2015; Ekelhof 2016; Zurek et al. 2023.

[13] Roorda 2015.

[14] Pilloud et al. 1949.

these functions, this step must include mechanisms for a degree of auditability and traceability.[15]

The most challenging legal tests to formalise within a computational framework are:

- **Precautions (API Article 57(3))**: 'When a choice is possible between several military objectives for obtaining a similar military advantage, the objective to be selected shall be that the attack on which may be expected to cause the least danger to civilian lives and to civilian objects';
- **Proportionality (API Article 57(2)(a)(iii))**: Which prohibits any decision (i.e., a combination of a target, capability, and method of delivery) that causes incidental civilian harm excessively disproportionate to the concrete military advantage anticipated; and
- **Minimisation (API Article 57(2)(a)(ii))**: Which mandates that incidental harm to civilians must be minimised to the furthest extent feasible. Essentially, '[i]f there is a choice of weapons or methods of attack available, a commander should select those which are most likely to avoid, or at least minimize, incidental damage'.

These tests involve complex value-based assessments and balancing exercises, which pose significant challenges for algorithmic modelling.[16] By contrast, other IHL requirements, such as the principle of distinction, present difficulties of a different nature. Their complexity lies not in normative balancing, but in technical limitations, particularly those concerning the reliability and accuracy of object recognition mechanisms.[17] While these tests are critical and highly challenging, they raise fundamentally different issues, which fall outside the scope of this chapter.

10.3 The Framework of IHL Compliance Testing in the Autonomous Targeting System

This section outlines the general structure of our proposed autonomous targeting system, which is designed to support the performance of key legal tests under IHL. While we do not focus on any specific targeting scenario, the framework introduced here is function-agnostic and aims to demonstrate how legal obligations, outlined in the preceding sections, can be operationalised within such a system. Technical implementation details are beyond the scope of this chapter but are addressed in greater depth in our previous research.[18]

When discussing AI in the military domain, it is important to distinguish between two major categories of AI technologies: data-driven and knowledge-driven approaches. Each offers distinct strengths and weaknesses. Data-driven AI, such as

[15] Kwik and van Engers 2021.

[16] Kwik et al. 2022.

[17] Ibid.

[18] Zurek et al. 2022b, 2023; Kwik et al. 2022.

artificial neural networks and models developed through machine learning (ML) or deep learning, are powerful in pattern recognition and classification tasks, but are often criticised for their lack of explainability. By contrast, knowledge-driven AI systems, based on explicit rules and structured reasoning, provide greater transparency and justification in decision-making processes. Since the sixth stage of the targeting process (Assessment) requires retrospective evaluation and justification of decisions taken, we argue that the legal compliance component of an autonomous targeting system should be built on a knowledge-driven paradigm.[19] This approach allows legal assessments to be performed in a clear, traceable, and transparent manner—facilitating auditability and accountability.

Nonetheless, a fully autonomous targeting system will likely require a hybrid system. This will provide the benefits of data-driven AI, including the efficiency of ML-based classification and reinforcement learning-based planning modules. It will also provide the benefits of knowledge-driven AI, specifically the explainability of (legal) knowledge-based reasoning modules. It cannot rely solely on rule-based mechanisms, nor on data-driven AI alone. If the part of the system responsible for the required legal tests is constructed on the basis of a knowledge-based paradigm, all legal tests can be performed in an explicit and transparent way. At the same time, other parts of the targeting process could be performed with less transparent/explainable techniques, justifying the data-driven AI component.

To create a model to analyse compliance with IHL targeting assessments, key legal concepts need to be formalised in order to be represented by the model. For instance, a key element of the legal assessments within the targeting procedure described in the previous section is the weighing of expected MA and anticipated IH. A human commander conducting IHL assessments does not need to represent either MA or IH in a quantifiable form.[20] However, the development of an autonomous AI-driven component requires not only a computational model, and hence a formal representation, but also one that allows for computationally weighing MA with IH. We do not suggest that such a quantifiable evaluation of IH and MA can be made fully autonomous based on current AI technologies. This is particularly challenging given that MA is difficult to estimate, as it may depend on complex strategic plans. Nevertheless, we provide a theoretical framework that leaves open the possibility that in the future, further development of data-driven AI technologies may allow this for specific situations with some human assistance (if necessary). A short discussion of the structure of the mechanism allowing for such an estimation can be found in our earlier paper.[21]

---

[19] The in-depth discussion of the problem of so-called black-box systems in targeting can be found in Sullivan and Ricket 2024.

[20] Although in more deliberate targeting settings, advanced collateral damage estimation technology is being used to provide a prognostic of IH to a high degree of accuracy: Article 36 and PAX 2016.

[21] Zurek et al. 2023.

For this framework, we use *values* as a central concept, allowing for the representation of both MA and IH. In the literature, one can find a number of alternative definitions of values and approaches to modelling value-based reasoning.[22] These approaches differ significantly in many important aspects. In our model, we use the concept of values as introduced in our previous works,[23] where a value is defined as an abstract (trans-situational) concept that allows for the estimation of the (non)desirability of a particular action or a state of affairs and influences one's behaviour. According to most value-based approaches, values can be satisfied or promoted to a certain degree and can be seen as a kind of abstraction of particular situations, which allows for the comparison of different values (see Eqs. 10.1–10.3). In other words, the levels of satisfaction of particular values by a particular state of affairs (decisions with anticipated results) can be expressed by numbers and compared.

In our model, values can be satisfied (or promoted) to a certain degree, which allows for the representation of the extent to which MA or IH are promoted through a particular decision and its consequent actions and results. This understanding differs from many other approaches for reasoning with values, where values have a binary character,[24] can only be neutral, promoted, or demoted,[25] may be promoted to a certain extent (but represented qualitatively),[26] or may be represented by perspectives (i.e., preferences over states).[27] Similarly to our approach, some others conceptualise how values may be satisfied to a certain extent by a particular state of affairs.[28] In contrast to many approaches,[29] we do not introduce any fixed ordering between values. Instead, we compare the levels at which the results of particular decisions will satisfy selected values. On the basis of the above-mentioned IHL requirements, we assume two main values: *Civilians*, v_{Civ} (e.g., the life, health, well-being, possessions, and infrastructure of civilians) and *Military Advantage*, v_{MA}. Note that the value *Civ* is inversely proportional to the level of harm inflicted on civilians (IH).

On the basis of the above, by V_{Si} we denote the set of all values. V_{Si} represents the vector in the multi-dimensional vector space of the values on all relevant dimensions, in our case being limited to the two dimensions of MA and IH. It should be noted that we abstract away from the fact that different evaluators may have different valuations (and may even differ in the dimensions they consider relevant). This issue will be elaborated upon in Sect. 10.4. As noted, values can be satisfied to a particular level by taking (or refraining from) an action resulting in a particular state of affairs. We denote $v_x(s_y)$ as the level of satisfaction of value v_x by a state of affairs s_y. By $V_{sy} = \{v_{ma}(s_y), V_{civ}(s_y), \ldots\}$ we denote the set of levels of satisfaction of values

[22] See, for example, Winikoff et al. 2021; Atkinson and Bench-Capon 2014.

[23] Zurek 2017 and later Zurek and Mokkas 2021.

[24] Bench-Capon 2003.

[25] Atkinson and Bench-Capon 2016.

[26] Winikoff et al. 2021.

[27] Weide et al. 2010.

[28] Osman and d'Inverno 2024.

[29] Bench-Capon 2003; Atkinson and Bench-Capon 2016.

for all relevant dimensions for situation s_y. As stated, prior to V_{sy}, the vector is built out of the values for a particular contextual situation. Like we abstract away from individual evaluators, we also abstract away from the mechanism for deciding on the exact level of satisfaction of a value at this point. We assume that this level can be established and that it can be represented by a number. The approach described allows us to compare and weigh alternatives in targeting procedures.

Many authors point out that the legal tests under IHL should be performed before a final decision is made and consequently action is (or is not) taken.[30] This means that the actors involved should anticipate the results of a decision. Prediction of the effects on an action necessarily entails uncertainty. In the literature, many authors agree that uncertainty should be taken into consideration during the decision-making process.[31] In our study, to address this, we propose using the expected levels of satisfaction of values (instead of absolute levels) in the reasoning process. By expected levels, we understand the levels of satisfaction of values by a certain outcome multiplied by its probability.[32]

10.3.1 The Computational Model

Below, we elaborate on how to represent the IHL legal tests encountered during each of the NATO targeting stages:

Step 1: Goal Analysis

At this stage, the commander determines the operational objectives and desired end state as derived from strategic and operational guidance. This analysis is performed from a broad perspective, taking into account the general goals of the military operation. We argue that for the autonomous device, such goals can be represented as a set of thresholds for a group of values that constitute the more general value *military advantage* (v_{MA}). Let $G = \{g_{MA}, g_{Civ}, g_{ground}, ...\}$ be a set of thresholds of values from set V representing the aim of a commander. By representing the goals of the agent as value-thresholds, we allow the agent to autonomously state and, when new relevant information is received, change its plan. We assume that there could be a set of values influencing *military advantage* (e.g., ground gained, (v_{ground})), disrupting enemy activities (($v_{disruptingEnemyActiv}$), etc.). As such, the goal of an autonomous military device can be expressed as the minimally required satisfaction levels of these values, and possibly others (e.g., the timing of the operation). Such a view on the influence of other values on MA is a simplification, because the number of such values is difficult to predict, and their internal relations can be very complex (e.g., more or less general values, contradictory values, etc.). Since in this work we focus

---

[30] Schmitt and Schauss 2019. See also Zurek et al. 2022a.

[31] See, for example, Schmitt and Schauss 2019.

[32] The model of this approach was presented in Zurek et al. 2024.

on compliance analysis, we leave the discussion on how to evaluate MA for future research.[33]

Step 2: Target Analysis

This step involves the identification and specification of potential targets and whether they are legitimate military objectives. The set of preparatory tasks are as follows.

Generating Targets: Based on intelligence and the general operational state, the set of potential decisions that can be made in the given circumstances.[34] On this basis:

> Let $S = \{s_x, s_y, \ldots\}$ denoting the set of input vectors containing signal intelligence, general state of operations of the analysed situation, etc.
>
> Let $D = \{d_x, d_y, \ldots\}$ denoting a set of available decisions.[35]

As noted, we do not introduce a specific mechanism for generating the set of available decisions (function δ).

Distinguishing Whether the Subject of the Attack is a Legitimate Military Target: Let $Parameters = \{z, t, \ldots\}$ denote a set of parameters of decisions (those parameters contain, for example, details of weapons used in attack). By $PAR_{dx} \subseteq Parameters$, we denote the set of parameters of decision d_x. Set PAR is a set of parameters for all decisions. To distinguish whether the subject of the attack is a legitimate military target, we assume function θ: $D \times PAR \rightarrow DD$ which filters decisions, resulting in targeting objects or persons which may not be attacked (e.g., civilian infrastructure, persons *hors de combat*). Let $DD \subseteq D$ be a set of decisions for which unlawful targets are not the direct object of attack.[36]

Predicting the Result of Every Decision From the Set of Available Decisions: Note that for the tests described in Sect. 10.2, the levels of MA and IH relate to the *anticipated* results of decisions, which means that they are, by nature, uncertain. Thus, while evaluating MA and IH, we must consider this uncertainty. For example, we denote:

> $C = \{c_x, c_y, \ldots\}$ as the set of all possible results. Additionally, c (lower case) denotes a single atomic result of a given decision (e.g., destroying an enemy tank). One decision can cause a set of atomic results, each with its own probability (e.g., firing a missile in a certain direction can cause two atomic results: destroying an enemy tank with probability 0.8 and damaging a civilian building nearby with probability 0.6). On this basis, every decision can bring about a whole spectrum of different combinations of results with different probabilities.

---

[33] In Zurek et al. 2023, we introduced some ideas on how to obtain v_{MA}.

[34] 'Intelligence' here refers to all necessary forms of intelligence, surveillance, and reconnaissance (ISR) necessary to make reasoned targeting decisions, see US Airforce 2019.

[35] Note that we abstract away from the action that will be taken as a consequence of the decision and the possibility that such action may entirely or partially fail.

[36] For the sake of this chapter, we assume that function θ is granted, although in practice this requires sophisticated object/situation recognition mechanisms to realise. Note that, as mentioned above, for some classifications (e.g., distinguishing a military aircraft from a civilian one) the task will be simpler than for others (e.g., identifying direct participation in hostilities by civilians).

$p(c_x)$ as the probability of c_x, and $p(c_x \mid s_y, d_z)$ as the conditional probability of c_x given s_y and d_z (the probability of c_x given decision d_z in circumstances s_y), where $P = \{p(c_x|s_y, d_z), ..., p(c_n|s_p, d_q)\}$ is the set of consequence probabilities.

Then by $\rho : C \times S \times D \to P$, we denote a partial function which returns the conditional probabilities of the results for decision d_y made in a circumstance s_x : $P_{sx, dy} = \rho(s_x, d_y) = \{p(c_t|s_x, d_y), p(c_k|s_x, d_y), ...\}$, where $P_{sx, dy} \subseteq P$.

Evaluating the Decision Results in Light of a Set of Relevant Values: Suppose a set of decision results $C = \{c_x, c_y, ...\}$ and a set of functions Φ. A function $\Phi_V \in \Phi$ s.t. $\Phi_V: C \to$ R, returns the level of satisfaction of a particular value $v_x \in V$ by result $c_y \in C$. By $v_x(c_y)$ we denote the level of satisfaction of value v_x by result c_y, by V we denote a set of levels of satisfaction of all values by the results of all available decisions. Note that although function θ excludes decisions which involve direct attacks on unlawful targets, remaining decisions may still cause *incidental* harm to such persons or objects (i.e., IH).

Creating a List of Possible Consequences of a Given Decision in a Given State: For an agent in state s_y, for every decision d_x which is available at state s_y, based on function ρ, the list of all results for which $p(c_t \mid s_y, d_x) > t$ should be created. The symbol t is the threshold representing the reasonable chance of a given result occurring (in case performance would be an inhibiting factor, we could exclude results with extremely low probabilities from the analysis).

Calculating the Expected Level of Satisfaction of a Particular Value: Let $ev_z(d_x, s_y)$ denote an expected level of satisfaction of value v_z by the results of decision d_x in the state of affairs s_y. A discussion on how to obtain expected levels of satisfaction of values has been presented in our previous work.[37] It is also briefly presented in Sect. 10.3.2. By EV we denote the set levels of satisfaction of all values by all available decisions.

The above functions allow us to distinguish the set of available decisions and derive the levels of satisfaction for all relevant values. This allows us to perform the legal test required by Article 57(3). To recall, this provision provides that if more than one target is viable and they produce comparable MA, the target with the lowest IH should be selected. In other words, this rule requires comparison of the MA and IH of alternative decisions. The key point is that decisions (targets) are rejected where they have comparable MA but higher IH (in our work, the lower level of satisfaction of the wellbeing of civilians). Since we assume that this legal test entails uncertainty that should be taken into consideration, the evaluation of MA and IH should be performed on the basis of the expected levels of promotion of values (e.g., ev_{civ} should be used instead of v_{civ}). We will represent this with the predicate $DT(d_x)$, where d_x is the decision which satisfies the test:

$$\exists dx \in DD \exists dy \in DD(evMA(dx) = evMA(dy)) \wedge (evCiv(dx) < evCiv(dy)) \Rightarrow DT(d_x) \tag{10.1}$$

[37] Zurek et al. 2024.

As such, the result of this test should be a set (denoted by DT) of decisions which satisfy it:[38]

$$DT = \{d_x | DT(d_x)\}$$

Although this formula (10.1) represents the meaning of Article 57(3), it has some drawbacks. First, in practice, it is highly implausible that two decisions will result in the exact same level of expected military advantage. Rather, Article 57(3) points out that the rule will be applicable if the MA of the analysed decisions is comparable. On this basis, we introduce an additional parameter (ϵ), which represents tolerance in comparing the MA of two decisions. Moreover, in the rare but possible situation that two decisions have the same evaluation of both expected MA and Civ, they should not be excluded from set DT. In that case, the decision-making mechanism should make the decision on the basis of other criteria (e.g., cost). As a result, the modified formula representing Article 57(3) is as follows:

$$\begin{aligned} &\exists dx \in DD \exists dy \in DD(evMA(dx) leqevMA(dy) + \epsilon) \\ &\wedge \left(ev_{MA}(d_x) \geq ev_{MA}\left(d_y\right) - \epsilon\right) \wedge \left(ev_{Civ}(d_x) \leq ev_{Civ}\left(d_y\right)\right) \Rightarrow DT(d_x) \end{aligned} \tag{10.2}$$

We do not introduce any mechanism for establishing the ϵ value, as it is highly context dependent and therefore should be declared separately for every task.

Step 3: Capability Analysis

During this stage, an assessment of the means and methods of warfare available to the commander is performed, along with two crucial legal tests: proportionality and minimisation of IH. In order to perform this step, the system requires data obtained in the previous steps (such as the evaluation of MA and Civ), as well as additional data, including the different options concerning available munitions and delivery. This stage includes the following tasks:

Proportionality Test: With predicate $DP(d_x)$, we denote that decision d_x satisfies the proportionality test:

$$ev_{MA}(d_x) \leq p * ev_{Civ}(d_x) \Rightarrow DP(d_x) \tag{10.3}$$

where p is the proportionality coefficient.[39] With DP we denote a set of decisions fulfilling the proportionality test:

$$DP = \{d_x | DP(d_x)\}$$

[38] Note, v_{civ} is inversely proportional to incidental harm and we use expected levels of satisfaction of values instead of absolute ones.

[39] The proportionality coefficient represents the commander's view on the relations between MA and IH, should be declared in advance and represents the basis of comparison for both values. This can also be seen as a basis for evaluating the commander's decision.

Minimisation of Incidental Harm Test: By $DMH(d_x)$ we denote that decision d_x passes the minimisation test:

$$\exists d_x \in DD \forall d_y \in DD(evMA(dx) * evCiv(dx) \geq ev_{MA}(d_y) * ev_{Civ}(d_y)) \Rightarrow DMH(d_x) \tag{10.4}$$

By *DMH* we denote a set of decisions fulfilling this test:

$$DMH = \{d_x | DMH(d_x)\}$$

We exclude decisions that do not fulfil commander requirements (e.g., goals and objectives) represented by the thresholds of the levels of satisfaction of chosen values. This eliminates, for instance, decisions where the MA gained would be too negligible to justify an engagement, even if proportionate and producing minimal IH.[40] In this task, the system flags the set of decisions that fulfil the assumed goals. By $DG(d_x)$ we denote that decision d_x fulfils the commander requirements:

$$\forall_{vy \in V}(ev_y(d_x) \geq g_y) \Rightarrow DG(d_x) \tag{10.5}$$

By *DG*, we denote a set of decisions fulfilling the commander's requirements:

$$DG = \{d_x | DG(d_x)\}$$

The model also excludes decisions that do not fulfil international law requirements and obligations from treaties (e.g., weapons treaties). This would also include restrictive (instead of prohibitive) provisions, which, for instance, provide that certain weapons/ammunition may only be used under specific circumstances.[41] Since in this chapter we focus on IHL targeting principles, we will not discuss the details of modelling and operationalising these other treaty provisions. In order to keep our model complete, however, we introduce a dedicated module responsible for filtering decisions that pass these treaty requirements. Such a task may require some additional data concerning the parameters of the decision (e.g., the type of ammunition used). This should be possible to obtain from *d* information concerning the type of weapon used in the attack or the type of harm the weapon may cause. Since we will not discuss these details, for the sake of simplicity, we assume that a set of parameters (*PAR*) includes all necessary data (e.g., the details of the weapon used in the attack).

By *FPAR* we denote a set of forbidden parameters of values. Predicate $DTR(d_x)$ represents that decision d_x fulfils the treaty obligations:

$$\exists_{a \in PAR}(a \in FPAR) \Rightarrow DTR(d_x) \tag{10.6}$$

[40] Note, since we also take into consideration the probability of success, we analyse the *expected* levels of satisfaction of values.

[41] Pilloud et al. 1987; Thurnher 2014.

By *DTR* we denote a set of decisions fulfilling the treaty obligations:

$$DTR = \{d_x | DTR(d_x)\}$$

Step 4: Capability Assignment

This step encompasses the definitive matching of the chosen capabilities to the targets. During this stage, the system should choose the decision option to be executed. This process requires analysis of not only the features of the available decision options and their predicted results, but also the probability of those results. The result of this analysis is the ordered list of decisions that fulfil the legal requirements by passing all tests introduced in previous steps. By *DAV* (d_x) we denote decision d_x fulfils the requirements:

$$DT(d_x) \land DP(d_x) \land DMH(d_x) \land DG(d_x) \land DTR(d_x) \Rightarrow DAV(d_x) \qquad (10.7)$$

By *DAV* we denote a set of decisions fulfilling necessary tests:

$$DAV = \{d_x | DAV(d_x)\}$$

If no decision remains, then this means that there is no possibility of executing an attack that satisfies the set military goals and is also compliant with IHL. If there is only one decision satisfying the requirements, this decision becomes final. If multiple decisions satisfy the requirements, they are ordered based on expected military advantage. Let *Decisions* = (*D*, ≥) be a total ordered set representing ranked decisions. The basis of this ordering is military advantage, assuming that commanders would prefer decisions that provide the greatest military utility from all lawful alternatives:

$$\forall dx, dy \in DAV(vMA(dx) \geq vMA(dy) \rightarrow (dx \geq dy)) \qquad (10.8)$$

10.3.2 Expected Levels of Satisfaction of Values

Legal literature frequently refers to the probabilistic dimension of military decision making.[42] A commander not only needs to take into consideration the predicted results of a given decision, but also the *probability* of this decision bringing about this result. Opinions on how to account for the likelihood of MA materialising (or simply put, the attack succeeding) vary,[43] but it is generally accepted that 'the concrete and direct advantage anticipated is not the value of the target wholly in the abstract but

[42] Schmitt and Schauss 2019; Gisel 2016; Schmitt 2017.

[43] van den Boogaard 2019.

rather its abstract value relative to the likelihood of in fact neutralizing or destroying the object'.[44] Conversely, regarding the degree of uncertainty of IH, there is no clear agreement. Some authors highlight that 'once [IH] is expected, it must be calculated into the proportionality analysis as such; it is not appropriate to consider the degree of certainty as to possible [IH]',[45] while others argue that uncertainty should be taken into consideration.[46] In this chapter we adopt the position that to preserve computational consistency of the analysis, it is necessary to take into consideration uncertainty in the evaluation of both MA and IH. Moreover, our approach to uncertainty is slightly different from the above-mentioned literature, as we put the probabilities of MA and IH directly into the calculation of expected MA and IH (by 'expected' we mean the mathematical understanding of this word, when expected MA is MA multiplied by its probability). In our model, if MA is high, but its probability is low, then expected MA will also be low. Such an approach allows for avoiding discussions on what level of uncertainty is 'reasonable', especially since there is no academic agreement on this.[47] Since legal sources do not clearly define how to understand or deal with uncertainty, our mechanism uses a probabilistic approach, as this provides a strong theoretical background. However, it is possible to use other mechanisms of uncertain reasoning (e.g., certainty factors or the Dempster Shaffer theory[48]). Moreover, there are a number of ways of understanding probability in general (e.g., frequentism or subjectivism).[49] Although we prefer to remain agnostic on this topic and do not specify how the probabilities are obtained, our model may be viewed as reflecting a subjectivist understanding of probability. On this view, probability is understood as a subjective status by regarding it as a measure of the 'degree of belief' of the individual assessing the uncertainty of a particular situation. A deeper discussion of the role of uncertainty in our mechanism was discussed in our earlier paper.[50]

Suppose that we have a set of possible decisions *D*. Let *c* denote a single result of a given decision (e.g., destroying an enemy tank). One decision can cause a set of atomic results, each with its own probability. For example, firing a missile in a certain direction can cause two atomic results: destroying an enemy tank with probability 0.8 and damaging a civilian building nearby with probability 0.6. On this basis, every decision can bring about a whole spectrum of different combinations of results with different probabilities.

The key difficulty lies in the estimation of the probability of the expected results of a given decision. In other words, how to construct a result set that contains all foreseeable results of the potential decisions the device (or a human in- or on-the-loop) could take, with their corresponding probabilities. In the model introduced

---

[44] International Criminal Tribunal for the Former Yugoslavia, *Prosecutor v Gotovina et al.*, Final Trial Brief, 2 August 2010, IT-06-90-T, para 549.

[45] Schmitt 2017, p. 475.

[46] Gillard 2018; van den Boogaard 2019.

[47] For further discussion and examples, see Cohen and Zlotogorski 2021.

[48] Shafer 1990.

[49] Hájek 2023.

[50] Zurek et al. 2024.

earlier, while uncertainty is factored into the formula, we have not yet discussed the most appropriate calculus for that (un)certainty. In our model, every $c_x \in C$ represents a particular atomic result of an action, for example, the number of civilians killed, the destruction of a school building, the killing of an enemy commander, and so on. By $v_{MA}(c_x)$ we denote a level to which an atomic consequence satisfies value v_{MA}. Likewise, by $v_{Civ}(c_x)$ we denote a level to which an atomic consequence satisfies value v_{Civ}.[51] Our goal is to calculate the expected levels of satisfaction of given values for a given decision (e.g., $ev_{MA}(d_m)$), specifically for the value of military advantage by decision d_m and $ev_{Civ}(d_m)$ for civilians by decision (d_m).

On this basis, the expected level of satisfaction of a value $v_{MA,}$ by joint consequences of decision d_x in a given circumstance, s_x equals:

$$ev_{MA}(d_m) = \sum\nolimits_{C_m^\alpha \in C_m} \left(v_{MA}\left(C_m^\alpha\right) p\left(C_m^\alpha s_x, d_m\right)\right)$$

The key difficulty is how to calculate conditional probabilities. In Zurek et al., we introduced two possible mechanisms.[52] The simplest approach is to assume that all propositions in C are conditionally independent. We can call this the naive approach, as in such a case, the calculation of the joint probability of consequences will be relatively easy:

$$p\left(C_m^\alpha | s_x, d_m\right) = \prod\nolimits_{c_\alpha \in C_m^\alpha} p(c_\alpha | s_x, d_m) * \prod\nolimits_{c_\beta \notin C_m^\alpha} \left(1 - p\left(c_\beta | s_x, d_m\right)\right)$$

The above approach, however, has a very strong disadvantage concerning the conditional independence assumption, as in a real-life situation (including military operations), such dependencies may exist. Imagine an enemy munition magazine surrounded by a group of enemy tanks. If a missile hits the magazine, the probability of also destroying the tanks will be much higher than if the missile hits a tank or building nearby.

An alternative approach is to represent C_m^α as a scenario expressed by a Bayesian network. A Bayesian network is a directed acyclic graph with probability tables for each node in the graph. Each node in the network represents a variable that can have several values, for example, true/false (more than two values is also possible, but for the sake of simplicity, we will limit the discussion to a two-value system). The probability table of a node V gives the conditional probabilities for that node taking each value given the values of its parents.[53] The basic idea is to represent the scenario as a Bayesian network, where nodes represent particular events in the scenario and arrows represent causal relations (however technically they only represent possible

[51] There are a number of various probabilities that should be considered here, introduced and discussed in Zurek et al. 2024. For the sake of simplicity, we do not take into consideration the uncertainty of the process of evaluation of decision consequences in light of particular values. Rather, we assume that certain results have 100% certainty.

[52] Zurek et al. 2024.

[53] An example of a similar approach modelling criminal scenarios can be found in Vlek et al. 2016.

correlations). In this model, only the basic facts are assumed to be conditionally independent.

The detailed discussion of the pros and cons of both models has already been presented in our other work.[54] In general, the first approach is very simplistic and does not allow for a precise estimation of probability, while the second one can give much better results, but requires more input data as well as complex scenario definitions.

10.3.3 The Structure of the System

Below, we present a general structure of the IHL compliance analysis system. We assume that every function and every test presented in the previous section is performed in a specific separate module:[55]

- *Extraction of Available Decisions* is responsible for performing function δ (S is an input, D is an output of the module);
- *Distinction Module* is responsible for performing function θ (D and PAR are inputs, while DD is an output);
- *Result Prediction Module* is responsible for performing function ρ (S and DD are inputs to the module, while PR and R are outputs);
- *Evaluation Module* is responsible for performing function ϕ (S and R are inputs to the module, VR is an output);
- *Parameters' Extraction Module* is responsible for performing function ω (D is an input, PAR is an output of the module);
- *Expected Evaluation Module* is responsible for calculating the expected evaluation of decisions in the light of values (VR and PR are input, EV is an output of the module);
- *Treaties Fulfilment Module* is responsible for performing the function of filtering decisions that do not fulfil treaty obligations (PAR and $FPAR$ are inputs, DTR is an output of the module). The functioning of the module is represented by Eq. 10.6;
- *Goals Fulfilment Module* is responsible for performing the function of filtering decisions that do not fulfil the commander's requirements (G and EV are inputs, DG is an output of the module). The functioning of the module is represented by Eq. 10.5;
- *Harm Minimisation Filter* is responsible for the process of minimising incidental harm (EV is an input, DMH is an output). The functioning of the module is represented by Eq. 10.4;
- *Proportionality Test* is responsible for performing the proportionality test (EV is an input, DP is an output). The functioning of the module is represented by Eq. 10.3;

[54] Zurek et al. 2024.

[55] As we adhere to the design principle 'separation of concerns'.

- *Article 57(3) Filter* is responsible for the process of filtering decisions, which for the same military advantage cause greater harm to civilians (Article 57(3), *EV* is an input, *DT* is an output). The functioning of the module is represented by Eq. 10.2;
- *Fulfilment of Requirements* is responsible for joining together the results of the above tests (*DT*, *DP*, *DMH*, *DG*, and *DTR* are input, and *DAV* is an output). The functioning of the module is represented by Eq. 10.7;
- *Decisions Ordering* is responsible for ordering available decisions (those fulfilling the above tests) on the basis of the level of satisfaction of military advantage (*DAV* and *V R* are inputs, *Decisions* is an output of the module). The functioning of the module is represented by Eq. 10.8.

The structure of the proposed model is presented in Fig. 10.1. The model is created with a clear distinction between (1) the cognitive part of the decision process, including functions extracting available decisions, their results, and evaluation (the upper part of the scheme) (i.e. the data-driven component); and (2) the reasoning part of the decision process, including legal tests, goal test, treaties test, etc. (the lower part of the scheme) (i.e. the knowledge-driven component). We explicitly distinguish between the cognitive and reasoning part of the decision process for the sake of transparency, advocating that legal tests should be performed in an explainable way. In other words, the system should explicitly check whether a given decision fulfils all necessary legal tests, while other elements of the decision process can use data-driven approaches. Such an approach is coherent with the general approach of hybrid systems in which data-driven parts are used as a mechanism to extract input data for the knowledge-based system, and in general allows for filling the so-called semantic gap between data and knowledge.[56]

10.3.4 Verification of the Model

Our model has been verified through experimental implementation in Zurek et al.[57] The proof of concept was implemented in two components: (1) an intentional agent that encapsulates the objectives and procedural knowledge that was implemented utilising the ASC2 framework;[58] and (2) a normative advisor that encompasses the normative aspects (i.e., rules that are implemented with ASC2 and the eFLINT framework for norm representation and normative reasoning).[59] The main advantage of using intentional agents and normative advisors is the separation of the analysis of legality of the decision from the decision making itself. Such separation is

[56] Meyer-Vitali et al. 2019.

[57] Zurek et al. 2022b.

[58] ASC2 is a Multi-Agent System framework mainly for the agents created with AgentScript agent programming language. The language of ASC2 is based on AgentSpeak(L)/Jason and allows for creating an environment of interacting agents.

[59] van Binsbergen Et Al. 2020; Mohajeri Parizi et al. 2020.

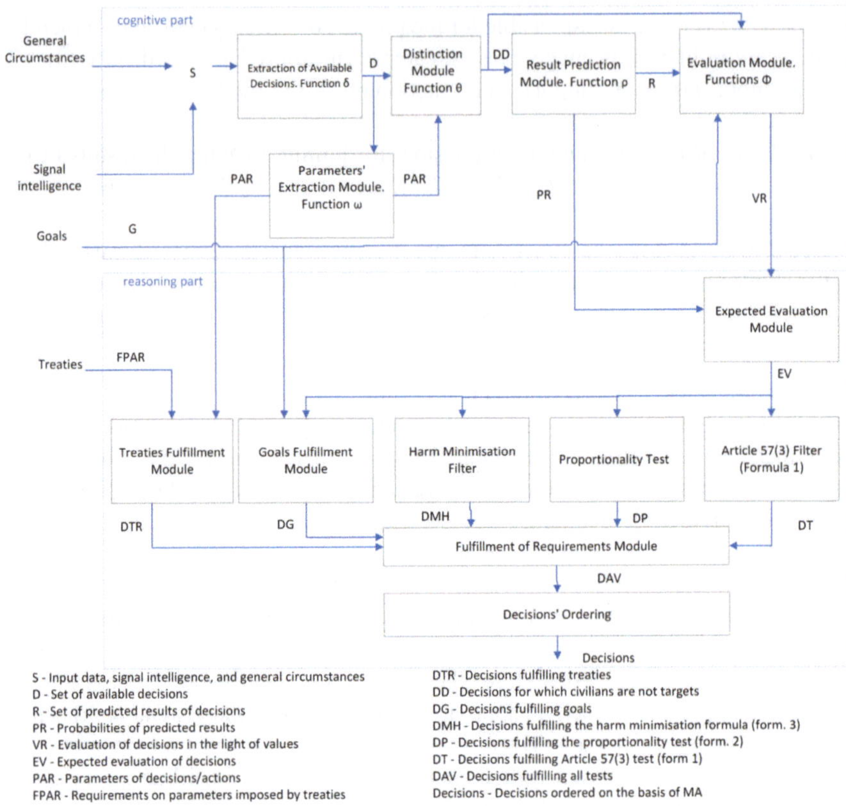

Fig. 10.1 Graphical illustration of the system's structure. *Source* The authors

important because it preserves the required level of transparency concerning IHL compliance: in particular, it allows for a clear understanding of why a given decision fulfils a particular IHL rule. It also improves the auditability of the system and enhances its maintainability thereof. Since the main goal of our work is to discuss the experiments concerning the recognition whether a given decision option fulfils IHL requirements (i.e., if it is lawful under IHL), we will focus on the normative advisor element (component 2), that is the 'normative reasoner', which is responsible for performing the relevant legal tests. The source code of both components can be found on GitHub.[60]

[60] https://github.com/mostafamohajeri/jurix2022-ihl-devices. Accessed 10 December 2023.

10.4 Discussion

In this section, we present a discussion of the results obtained from our experiments. In particular, we are going to relate our results to some relevant concepts in the literature, discuss key technical aspects, their consequences and future work, as well as address some controversies related to the mechanism. Though the experiments show that our model allows for a comprehensive evaluation of the decision made by an autonomous military device in terms of IHL compliance, some ethical and legal controversies related to autonomous weapons systems (AWS) in general, and our model in particular, still remain.[61] Below we address and discuss some of these controversies.

10.4.1 Ethical and Legal Concerns

Before we discuss some specific problems and issues, we must emphasise that we are aware of the critical debates on AWS and the use of AI in targeting. Our work does not aim to develop an automated targeting system, but rather to introduce discussions on testing IHL compliance for autonomous devices. Our ambition here is not to solve the moral dilemmas connected to such systems, but rather to highlight interesting points and controversies.

The first controversy relates to the problem of evaluating a given result in light of a particular value (function Φ in our model). Can we represent or evaluate harm to civilians (deaths, injuries) in a numeric way? Can this be evaluated at all? In the literature, ethical and legal concerns about the dehumanisation of military decision-making processes are often emphasised.[62] It must be noted that in other domains, such as insurance or unemployment benefits, similar quantifications are quite common. Insurance payments due after accidents are typically based on the expected loss of quality of life, for which insurance companies use calculations with a number of factors. Courts (at least in the Netherlands) also use standard calculations to determine the compensation employers must pay when dismissing employees. For triage in hospitals, similar calculations are also standard practice. Obviously, the importance of decisions concerning loss of human life is higher than decisions on the quality of life, but the mechanism itself is similar. Although commanders do not assign numbers, they somehow (possibly unconsciously) assign preferences that can be transformed to numbers (see below). The advantages of objectivity and the increased speed of decision making when such calculations are used are considered preferable over non-transparent decisions. Of course, non-quantified decisions are not necessarily non-transparent, but they have a certain level of discretion in interpretation which can make them less transparent.

---

[61] Zurek et al. 2022b, 2023; Kwik et al. 2022.

[62] For example, see ICRC 2018.

Targeting decisions require the comparison of targets based on evaluation of the expected MA and IH (see Sect. 10.2, points 1 and 2). Commanders do not assign any numbers to these values but rather compare available decisions and their potential consequences in light of these values. Such comparison can be easily represented by ordering the decisions (e.g., in light of expected incidental harm, decision d1 is preferred to decision d2), which in many situations can be converted to numbers (e.g., if commanders prefer decision d1 to decision d2 in terms of MA, then they can assign $v_{MA}(d1) = 2$ and $v_{MA}(d2) = 1$). Therefore, the key issue is not assigning numerical values, but rather the process of evaluation. In other words, we must ask whether we can delegate the task of evaluating someone's harm to the machine. It is important to note that, although there is case law, legal documents and other relevant sources to consider, IHL does not specify how to evaluate IH (or MA), rather providing that decisions must be evaluated according to the reasonable commander standard, which means that an important part of the evaluation involves the discretion of a human commander. While there is a number of publications discussing this issue,[63] the final decision involves discretionary judgments by the commander. But does this exclude machine-made evaluations? One could argue that such an evaluation can reflect human evaluation, assuming that ML algorithms could learn from human-made decisions (inheriting, however, the lack of transparency typical of ML-based systems). Alternatively, if such an evaluation is constructed on the basis of knowledge-based techniques, the root of the decision is in knowledge produced by humans. In both cases, the decision would still be made on the basis of human evaluation, even if indirectly. We argue that the issue is not the delegation of the evaluation process to the machine, but rather the quality of the decision-making process itself, as well as the attribution of responsibility in case of erroneous decisions or harmful consequences.[64]

10.4.2 The Model and Kahneman's Theory of Decision Making

A key assumption in our work is that we sought to represent the human process of evaluating IHL compliance as closely as possible. In this section, we introduce a discussion about how our model relates to psychological theories describing human decision making. Our model divides the IHL compliance evaluation mechanism into 2 main parts: (1) the cognitive part, which is responsible for the evaluating an actual state of affairs; and (2) the reasoning part, which is responsible for analysing the results obtained from the cognitive part, comparing the available options, and producing a recommendation for the decision-making mechanism. The idea behind this distinction is rooted in the observation that, even for human commanders, not every part of analysing IHL compliance is straightforward. In particular, evaluating

[63] For example, Cohen and Zlotogorski 2021.

[64] For example, see Chap. 13 by Boutin in this volume.

various decision options in light of different values or generating a list of available decision options is often not fully optimal (especially in stressful and fast-changing conflict environments). Our distinction is similar to the differentiation between two modes of thought introduced by Kahneman,[65] who distinguished: 'System 1', which is fast, instinctive, emotional, and unconscious, and 'System 2', which is slower, more deliberative, and more logical. IHL compliance requires the commander to not only follow its rules, but also to provide a justification for the decision made. In other words, IHL compliance requires the use of 'System 2' thinking to explain why the commander believes that a given decision is (or is not) IHL compliant. Being able to justify the decision is particularly relevant in an eventual court case where the rationale of the decision is evaluated *ex post*, while in order to avoid IHL violations, the commander should make an *ex ante* evaluation of the possible decisions.

In our previous work it was assumed that, as the explainability requirements for the cognitive part were less strict, the modules covering this component could be developed on the basis of data-driven technologies.[66] In this case, these modules (e.g., the Evaluation module, Result Prediction module, etc.) would operate similarly to Kahneman's 'System 1'. He describes 'System 1' as 'fast, automatic, stereotypic and unconscious.[67] This is the way most data-driven mechanisms work: once trained, neural networks work fast (especially feed forward networks) and are based on stereotypes that reflect statistical patterns from past examples. Moreover, they can also be said to operate 'unconsciously', not only because such solutions are unconscious themselves, but also because decisions made unconsciously do not have clear justifications, as most ML-approaches lack explainability. In contrast to 'System 1', 'System 2' is slow, effortful, logical, calculating, and conscious.[68] The reasoning part of our model can be related to 'System 2', as although knowledge-driven systems could potentially be fast, their reasoning mechanisms are usually slower compared to data-driven solutions, such as neural networks. It is laborious, because—to provide a full analysis—the mechanism requires pre-prepared input data (the list of available decisions, evaluations, probabilities, etc.) and must analyse a potentially wide range of possibilities. It is also logical, as the reasoning part of the modules is created on the basis of some form of knowledge representation and reasoning (the intended application of logic formalisms). They are also calculated, as the mechanism calculates expected levels of satisfaction of values. While the reasoning part is also not conscious, in contrast to the cognitive part, it can clearly and strictly explain the reasons for the output. On this basis, our model implements Kahneman's model of reasoning.

Such an approach is particularly useful for IHL compliance analysis, as it provides a platform for integrating a reasoning mechanism for IHL compliance testing with a more general decision-making system in a way comparable to human reasoning. Moreover, this architecture allows for modularisation—it is not necessary to make

[65] Kahneman 2011.

[66] Zurek et al. 2023.

[67] Kahneman 2011.

[68] Ibid.

all of the evaluation modules fully autonomous. Some elements of the evaluation process could still be performed by humans.

10.4.3 General Discussion

The main goal of our work was to introduce a discussion on the possibility of developing autonomous military devices that comply with IHL. To set up this discussion, we presented a framework for a military targeting system with the ability to follow specific IHL requirements. We presented the stages of the targeting process, pointing out which legal requirements are imposed by IHL, and introduced a mechanism which allows the development of a system fulfilling those requirements. Based on this framework, we can distinguish the key components and requirements necessary for testing IHL compliance. Decomposition of the decision-analysis process allows for a better understanding of the difficulties and challenges connected with the development of military autonomous devices.

One important observation is that while the formal model we introduce allows for the development of reasoning mechanisms that can test IHL compliance, the key difficulty of implementing these tests lies not in the reasoning or balancing process, but in the evaluation of the available decisions in light of MA and IH (functions Φ). As the system should evaluate the harmful consequences expected from a decision, this issue constitutes a key technical and moral challenge, which can be seen as the most controversial element of our approach. In our earlier paper we pointed out three ways of dealing with this issue.[69] The first is to assume that this is a place for 'human in the loop' to intervene, whilst the second is to represent functions from set Φ as data-driven mechanisms trained on the basis of data labelled by humans. Such a solution requires a large data set of correctly labelled examples. Such examples could be taken from real-life operations, or alternatively, using artificially generated examples (e.g., AI-generated 'synthetic' data) that would then be labelled by humans, or a combination of these two approaches. A third approach is to explicitly represent functions Φ in an analytical way.[70]

Two major issues with using ML-trained models are the implicit abstractions that are 'learned' from the training examples, and that the accuracy of a ML-model can only be verified on a test set, for which completeness in terms of full case coverage cannot be guaranteed. Completeness is also an issue for AI-generated data. Only *ex post* evaluation can identify wrong and/or incomplete classifications, and any erroneous decisions that result. ML-based classification is typically used for labelling situations and differs from human interpretation in several ways. Rather than slowing the identification process, humans not only use classification but also other kinds of reasoning (e.g., analogical or hypothetical reasoning), as well as being

[69] Zurek et al. 2023.

[70] A similar approach (though not related to military devices) was introduced by Osman and d'Inverno 2024.

much more flexible towards 'the unknown'. In contrast, as ML-based mechanisms are trained on the existing examples, new situations may not perfectly fit the examples the mechanism was trained on.

Another important challenge is the treatment of uncertainty. Legal literature, although requiring consideration of the uncertainty of achieving the desired MA, does not specify how to do this. Recall that we have introduced two mechanisms for calculating the probabilities of multiple consequences of complex operations, namely a simplistic, naive approach, and a more complex one using Bayesian Networks.[71] The naive approach requires a relatively small amount of data but adopts the unrealistic assumption that all possible consequences will be independent from an action taken by a device. The Bayesian Network-based approach requires predicting scenarios, including causal relations and conditional probabilities of particular consequences of an action. This is an extremely challenging task, even for humans. Moreover, Bayesian conditional probability theory assumes the independence of the root facts within the equations. While alternative calculi for probabilistic reasoning have been proposed—such as fuzzy logic, Dempster-Schaefer theory and more—each has fundamental issues that are even more problematic than the Bayesian approach. An alternative probability calculus that can be applied in an open-world context where root fact independence is no longer assumed would be welcome but falls outside the scope of this chapter.

The model we present for the evaluation of IHL compliance can be useful not only for autonomous devices but also for the analysis of actual military decisions. By decomposing the evaluation process into clearly and formally defined functions, one can precisely determine which, how, when, and where IHL rules were or could be violated. This could be useful both for past decisions analysis, liability determination, and planning future operational decisions. This, however, requires in-depth examination in future research.

10.4.4 Further Research

Our planned future research will cover a number of challenges related to the issues raised in this chapter. Our priorities are understanding the mechanisms that human decision-makers use to make probability estimates for the success of their actions and consequent effects and risks. We plan on approaching this by combining a generative process with human judgement about AI-generated 'situational landscape', a qualitative analysis of arguments supporting their judgement, and a factorial analysis of those factors in order to come to an explicit description—and corresponding computational model—of the human interpretation process.

Another research challenge, as mentioned above, is to develop a sound calculus for probabilistic reasoning that can cope with open-world problems where the independence between root facts is not a basic assumption. Such probabilistic calculus is

[71] Zurek et al. 2024.

essential for any hybrid solution combining the results from data-driven components, which are typically stochastic by nature, with qualitative (legal) reasoning. This will inevitably come at a (computational) price, as the search space for the qualitative reasoner will expand. However, this is unavoidable if we want to perform a sensitivity analysis to build an understanding of what factors (should) determine our decisions and how much we should trust the outcomes of our decision-making processes.

Finally, we plan to test and compare algorithmic and human decision-making processes through a comparative study, where the suggested decisions will be blindly assessed by experts. Next to improving our current model, this may also highlight incoherences, biases and blind spots in human decision making.

10.5 Conclusions

This chapter sought to bring some clarity to the challenges of IHL compliance analysis. We presented a solution for IHL-compliant targeting that addresses the complex weighing of MA versus IH. We consider our current research an initial step and have addressed a number of issues that require further study. We deliberately avoided engaging with debates about the desirability of AWS. Increasing the speed and distance at which military operations are conducted—in addition to RF jamming methods—requires some autonomy in military devices, reducing the possibility of direct human control over the device. If AWS are exploited in military operations, they should at least contain a component that assesses IHL compliance, as it may not always be possible for these systems to operate within 'meaningful human control'.

References

Articles, Books and Other Documents

Article 36, PAX (2016) Areas of Harm: Understanding explosive weapons with wide Area effects. https://article36.org/wp-content/uploads/2016/10/PAX-A36-Areas-of-Harm.pdf. Accessed 1 August 2024

Atkinson K, Bench-Capon T (2014) States, Goals and Values: Revisiting Practical Reasoning. https://cgi.csc.liv.ac.uk/~katie/argmas14.pdf. Accessed 1 August 2024

Atkinson K, Bench-Capon T (2016) States, goals and values: Revisiting practical reasoning. Argument & Computing. https://doi.org/10.3233/AAC-160011

Bench-Capon T (2003) Persuasion in Practical Argument Using Value-based Argumentation Frameworks. Journal of Logic and Computation. https://doi.org/10.1093/logcom/13.3.429

Boutin B, Woodcock T (2024) Aspects of Realizing (Meaningful) Human Control: A Legal Perspective. In: Geiß R, Lahmann H (eds) Research Handbook on Warfare and Artificial Intelligence. Edward Elgar Publishing, Cheltenham, pp. 179–196

Cohen A, Zlotogorski D (2021) Proportionality in International Humanitarian Law: Consequences, Precautions, and Procedures. Oxford University Press, Oxford

Corn GS (2014) War, Law, and the Oft Overlooked Value of Process as a Precautionary Measure. Pepperdine Law Review 42:419–466
Ekelhof M (2016) Human Control in the Targeting Process. https://docs-library.unoda.org/Convention_on_Certain_Conventional_Weapons_-_Informal_Meeting_of_Experts_(2016)/2016_LAWS%2BMX_presentations_towardsaworkingdefinition_ekelhofnotes.pdf. Accessed 1 August 2024
Gillard EC (2018) Proportionality in the Conduct of Hostilities: The Incidental Harm Side of the Assessment. https://www.chathamhouse.org/sites/default/files/publications/research/2018-12-10-proportionality-conduct-hostilities-incidental-harm-gillard-final.pdf. Accessed [insert]
Gisel L (2016) The Principle of Proportionality in the Rules Governing the Conduct of Hostilities under International Humanitarian Law. https://www.icrc.org/sites/default/files/document/file_list/4358_002_expert_meeting_report_web_1_0.pdf. Accessed 1 August 2024
Hájek A (2023) Interpretations of Probability. https://plato.stanford.edu/cgi-bin/encyclopedia/archinfo.cgi?entry=probability-interpret&archive=win2023. Accessed 1 August 2024
ICRC (2018) Ethics and autonomous weapon systems: An ethical basis for human control? https://www.icrc.org/sites/default/files/document/file_list/icrc_ethics_and_autonomous_weapon_systems_report_3_april_2018.pdf. Accessed 1 August 2024
Kahneman D (2011) Thinking, Fast and Slow. Farrar, Straus and Giroux, United States
Kwik J, van Engers T (2021) Algorithmic Fog of War: When Lack of Transparency Violates the Law of Armed Conflict. Journal of Future Robot Life. https://doi.org/10.3233/FRL-200019
Kwik J, Zurek T, van Engers T (2022) Designing International Humanitarian Law into military Autonomous Devices. https://ssrn.com/abstract=4109286. Accessed 1 August 2024
Meyer-Vitali A, Bakker R, van Bekkum M, de Boer M, Burghouts G, van Diggelen J, Dijk J, Grappiolo C, de Greeff J, Huizing A, Raaijmakers S (2019) Hybrid AI White Paper. https://publications.tno.nl/publication/34635045/NKuXIW/TNO-2019-R11941.pdf. Accessed 1 August 2024
Mohajeri Parizi M, Sileno G, van Engers T, Klous S (2020) Run, agent, run! architecture and benchmarking of actor-based agents. https://doi.org/10.1145/3427760.3428339. Accessed 1 August 2024
North Atlantic Treaty Organisation (NATO) (2016) AJP-3.9 Allied Joint Doctrine for Joint Targeting, Edition A version 1. https://www.intertekinform.com/en-gb/standards/ajp-3-9-2016-736241_saig_nato_nato_1788284/?srsltid=AfmBOoq6J7SuKMW8HkHEE-7b5uIb41PS7jSRdOfKjSs-XqD5AAd2nDUW. Accessed 1 August 2022
Osman N, d'Inverno M (2024) A Computational Framework for Human Values. https://www.ifaamas.org/Proceedings/aamas2024/pdfs/p1531.pdf. Accessed 1 August 2024
Roorda M (2015) NATO's Targeting Process: Ensuring Human Control Over (and Lawful Use of) 'Autonomous' Weapons'. In: Williams AP, Scharre PD (eds) Autonomous Systems: Issues for Defence Policymakers, NATO HQ SACT, Norfolk VA, pp. 152–168
Pilloud C, Sandoz Y, Swinarski C, Zimmerman, B, ICRC (1987) Commentary on the Additional Protocols of 8 June 1977 to the Geneva Conventions of 12 August 1949. Martinus Nijhoff, Nowell MA
Schmitt MN (2017) Tallinn Manual 2.0 on the International Law Applicable to Cyber Operations, 2nd edn. Cambridge University Press, Cambridge
Schmitt MN, Schauss M (2019) Uncertainty in the Law of Targeting: Towards a Cognitive Framework. Harvard National Security Journal 10:148–194
Shafer G (1990) Perspectives on the theory and practice of belief functions. International Journal of Approximate Reasoning 3: 1–4
Sullivan S, Ricket I (2024) Targeting in the Black Box. https://ccdcoe.org/uploads/2024/05/CyCon_2024_Sullivan_Ricket-1.pdf. Accessed 1 August 2024
Thurnher JS (2014) Examining Autonomous Weapon Systems from a Law of Armed Conflict Perspective. In: Nasu H, McLaughlin R (eds) New Technologies and the Law of Armed Conflict. T.M.C. Asser Press, The Hague, pp. 213–228

United States Air Force (2019) Air Force Doctrine Publication 3-60, Targeting. https://www.doctrine.af.mil/Portals/61/documents/AFDP_3-60/3-60-AFDP-TARGETING.pdf. Accessed 1 August 2024

van Binsbergen LT, Liu LC, van Doesburg R, van Engers T (2020) eFLINT: a domain specific language for executable norm specifications. https://doi.org/10.1145/3425898.3426958. Accessed 1 August 2024

van den Boogaard J (2019) Proportionality in International Humanitarian Law. https://dare.uva.nl/search?identifier=57363698-c6b8-458d-9033-0fd9cfc9bb91. Accessed 1 August 2024

Vlek CS, Prakken H, Renooij S, Verheij B (2016) A method for explaining Bayesian networks for legal evidence with scenarios. Artificial Intelligence and Law. https://doi.org/10.1007/s10506-016-9183-4

Weide TL, Dignum F, Meyer J-JCh, Prakken H, Vreeswijk GAW (2010) Practical Reasoning Using Values. https://doi.org/10.1007/978-3-642-12805-9_5. Accessed 1 August 2024

Winikoff M, Sidorenko G, Dignum V, Dignum F (2021) Why Bad Coffee? Explaining BDI Agent Behaviour with Valuings. https://www.ijcai.org/proceedings/2022/0810.pdf. Accessed 1 August 2024

Zurek T (2017) Goals, values, and reasoning. Expert Systems with Applications. https://doi.org/10.1016/j.eswa.2016.11.008

Zurek T, Kwik J, van Engers T (2023) Model of a military autonomous device following International Humanitarian Law. Ethics and Information Technology. https://doi.org/10.1007/s10676-023-09682-1

Zurek T, Kwik J, van Engers T (2024) Values, proportionality, and uncertainty in military autonomous devices. In: Osman N, Steels L (eds) Value Engineering in Artificial Intelligence. Springer, Cham Switzerland, pp. 219-236

Zurek T, Mokkas M (2021) Value-Based Reasoning in Autonomous Agents. International Journal of Computational Intelligence Systems. https://doi.org/10.2991/ijcis.d.210203.001

Zurek T, Woodcock T, Pacholska M, van Engers T (2022a) Computational Modelling of the Proportionality Analysis under International Humanitarian Law for Military Decision-Support Systems. https://ssrn.com/abstract=4008946. Accessed 1 August 2024

Zurek T, Mohajeriparizi M, Kwik J, van Engers T (2022b) Can a Military Autonomous Device Follow International Humanitarian Law? Frontiers in Artificial Intelligence and Applications. https://doi.org/10.3233/FAIA220479

Tomasz Zurek is an assistant professor at the Institute of Computer Science at Maria Curie Sklodowska University in Lublin, Poland. Recently, he was a postdoctoral researcher at the Complex Cyber Infrastructure group at the Informatics Institute, University of Amsterdam, where he was a part of the TRUST RPA project. He is also an Associate Fellow of T.M.C. Asser Institute in The Hague. His main research interests are focus on computational representation of legal and ethical reasoning.

Tom van Engers is a Professor in Legal Knowledge Management at the University of Amsterdam and managing director of the Leibniz Institute, founded by the University of Amsterdam and TNO. His research is focused on normative systems, normative reasoning and normative control, the latter being essential to trust in socio-technical systems.

Part IV
Governance and Accountability

Chapter 11
What's at the Core? The Quintessential Role of Responsibility in International Governance of Military Artificial Intelligence

Sofia Romansky and Tim Sweijs

Contents

Abstract Over the past decade, the deployment of artificial intelligence (AI) in the military domain has garnered increasing attention in national and international scholarly and policy discussions. A growing number of States are developing national strategies for integrating AI into military operations. Simultaneously, the work of ongoing international initiatives and the recent launch of several high-level deliberations highlight the urgent need to address both the risks and opportunities presented by military AI. Despite significant efforts, international governance discussions have plateaued at the stage of defining high-level principles. This stagnation, in part, can be attributed to the fact that core questions about the practical application of normative principles remain unanswered. This chapter identifies a key obstacle at the heart of the gridlock in international governance discussions: the issue of responsibility. By centring the issue of responsibility, this chapter reframes ongoing conversations and brings to the forefront difficult but unavoidable dilemmas. In doing so, it demonstrates how the weaknesses in the primary focus areas of existing international governance initiatives are anchored in responsibility issues, thereby exposing the critical questions that remain unaddressed in governance.

S. Romansky (✉) · T. Sweijs
The Hague Centre for Strategic Studies, The Hague, The Netherlands
e-mail: sofiaromansky@hcss.nl

T. Sweijs
e-mail: timsweijs@hcss.nl

B. Boutin et al. (eds.), *Legal, Ethical, and Technical Dilemmas in Military Artificial Intelligence*, https://doi.org/10.1007/978-94-6265-759-5_11

Keywords Artificial Intelligence · International Governance · Responsibility · Accountability · Military Domain · International Humanitarian Law

11.1 Introduction

Over the past decade, the deployment of artificial intelligence (AI) in the military domain has garnered growing attention in national and international scholarly and policy discussions. A growing number of States are developing strategies for integrating AI not only into their military arsenals but also into the broader operations of their military complexes.[1] Simultaneously, ongoing international initiatives and the recent launch of several high-level deliberations reflect a heightened sense of urgency behind addressing both the risks and opportunities of AI in the military domain.

The reasons why AI technologies have been put in the spotlight in relation to the military domain are well known and oft repeated. Although the use of AI in the military domain is by no means new, its integration into military practices continues to offer a key opportunity: the automation of certain processes essential to a military's ability to observe, orient, decide, and act (OODA loop). In turn, this directly contributes to accelerating the speed, increasing the scale, and, as is expected, enhancing the effectiveness of military operations.[2] The continuous advancement of AI models—driven by growing processing capacity, volume of training data, and the increasing accessibility of sophisticated generative AI based on foundational models—has reinforced the desirability and feasibility of integrating AI-enabled technologies into key capabilities for military organisations.

In the military domain, AI has become both an enabler of efficiency, also in situations of deficient manpower, and a perceived prerequisite for any modern military seeking a competitive edge over its adversaries.[3] It is no overstatement to say that AI is surrounded by hype, not only to reap the benefits of these technologies as soon as possible but also to do so before one's adversaries. In this way, AI exacerbates dynamics associated with the security dilemma and shapes the strategic calculations of State actors even in peacetime, with ramifications for the free flow of equipment, data, and people.

The significant ongoing and expected impact of AI on the military domain has prompted a call for global governance based on norms and regimes. Establishing standard guidelines for military AI would help ensure that these technologies are developed and deployed in a controlled way, minimising negative effects, unexpected or catastrophic outcomes, and categorically unacceptable uses. As with other weapon systems, arriving at principles of use or non-use that align with core tenets of International Humanitarian Law (IHL) is critical.

[1] For example decision support systems (DSS), managing personnel and maintenance logistics, intelligence, surveillance, reconnaissance, and training: Boulanin and Lewis 2023.

[2] Kraska 2021, p. 408.

[3] Ibid., p. 426.

Table 11.1 Ongoing international governance initiatives for AI in the military domain as of 2023

Initiative		Start year
1	Political Declaration on Responsible Military Use of Artificial Intelligence and Autonomy	2023
2	Responsible Artificial Intelligence in the Military Domain (REAIM) Summit, Regional Consultations, and Global Commission	2023
3	UNGA Resolution on Lethal Autonomous Weapons Systems	2023
4	Communique of the Latin American and the Caribbean Conference of Social and Humanitarian Impact of Autonomous Weapons	2023
5	Caribbean Community (CARICOM) Declaration on Autonomous Weapons Systems	2023
6	North Atlantic Treaty Organization (NATO) Artificial Intelligence Strategy	2021
7	Group of Governmental Experts on Lethal Autonomous Weapons Deliberations (GGE on LAWS)	2016

Source Sweijs and Romansky 2024 (updated 2025)

A 2024 study by Sweijs and Romansky identified at least seven international initiatives for the governance of AI in the military domain, focusing either on the domain as a whole, or on specific military AI applications (see Table 11.1 above).[4]

The study demonstrates that international deliberations have converged around a tangible set of primary focus areas for the governance of military AI. However, simultaneously, these discussions have largely plateaued in the formulation of high-level principles. This stagnation stems, in part, from unresolved questions regarding the practical application of normative principles. Addressing these questions is essential for the development of comprehensive international governance frameworks.

This chapter builds on the initial findings of Sweijs and Romansky by articulating a key obstacle at the heart of the gridlock in international governance discussions: the issue of responsibility, which cuts across seven focus areas which will be discussed below. Clearly defining what responsibility precisely entails, and how it can be operationalised across the entire military AI lifecycle, is essential for moving beyond a patchwork of principles and proclamations. Placing responsibility at the centre of governance debates not only reframes and grounds ongoing discussions but also brings to the forefront difficult—yet unavoidable—dilemmas that must be addressed to achieve meaningful progress.

In doing so, this chapter illustrates how the weaknesses in the primary focus areas within existing international governance initiatives ultimately stem from unresolved questions of responsibility. This discussion exposes the critical gaps in governance

[4] Sweijs and Romansky 2024.

that remain unaddressed. The chapter concludes with a call for national and international governance initiatives on military AI to prioritise responsibility as a means of driving meaningful progress.

11.2 Questions of Responsibility at the Core of Military AI Governance

In examining the nascent yet already crowded landscape of international governance initiatives around military AI, Sweijs and Romansky identified seven primary focus areas of international norm development, emerging from the principles embedded within the foundational documents of seven ongoing governance initiatives (see Table 11.2 below).[5]

Overall, the presence of these seven discrete focus areas reflects a convergence in international deliberations around similar key issues that are deemed critical to both the opportunities and risks of AI in the military domain. Each focus area possesses certain elements that help bolster the governance of military AI. A prerequisite of *accordance with international law* serves as an intuitive starting point for AI governance in the military domain. Simultaneously, this focus area affirms an essential consensus: AI will not be treated as an exception. Regardless of how novel or transformative it may seem compared to other technologies, fundamental principles of international law will continue to apply.[6] The need to prioritise *responsibility and accountability*, in turn, aligns with a human-centric international law framework, highlighting the importance of involving all relevant actors across the AI lifecycle in governance. *Explainability and traceability* further link human-centric responsibility to a foundation of understanding and trust, which in turn facilitates compliance with international law. *Bias and harm mitigation* reinforce the imperative of placing human safety at the core of governance deliberations. *Reliability and governability* explicate the necessity of human control over AI systems, ensuring they remain trustworthy and that processes can be adjusted when undesirable outcomes are detected. Finally, the emphasis on the *exchange of practices* stresses that responsible development and use will require active information sharing, which also serves as a confidence-building measure. This is particularly valuable given the global development of cutting-edge dual-use technologies within highly internationalised supply chains, across various public and private sectors.

Despite the recognition of these normative elements as a necessary first step for the creation of governance frameworks, the focus areas have not yet been translated into actionable guidelines. Deliberations within existing governance initiatives remain highly conceptual or inevitably default to the lowest common denominators.

---

[5] For a more detailed explanation of the methodology used to arrive at the seven focus areas, see: Sweijs and Romansky 2024, pp. 8–13.

[6] Pacholska 2023, p. 5.

Table 11.2 Seven focus areas of international norm development

Focus area		Definition
1	Accordance with International Law	The use of AI in the military domain should be in accordance with International Humanitarian Law (IHL) and human rights law. Any guidelines created specifically for military AI cannot supersede existing international law
2	Responsibility and Accountability	Human agents should maintain responsibility and accountability for the use of military AI throughout a system's lifecycle
3	Explainability and Traceability	To maximise the benefits and minimise risks of using military AI, sufficient understanding and transparency of the systems, inputs, and outputs is needed
4	Bias and Harm Mitigation	The potential harmful consequences of biases and the general use of military AI should be considered and addressed proactively
5	Reliability	The use of military AI should be robust, with appropriate safeguards in place to ensure that systems can carry out tasks consistently and predictably
6	Governability	Guidelines for the use of military AI should enable practitioners to detect and avoid unintended consequences, as well as disengage and deactivate systems when undesired incidents occur
7	Exchange of Practices	To support the development and improvement of military AI, best practices should be exchanged among actors throughout system lifecycles

Source Sweijs and Romansky 2024

This chapter argues that the difficulties encountered in attempting to bridge overarching concepts and practical implementation often stem from unresolved issues of responsibility that need to be clarified. Although responsibility and accountability are closely related concepts, they differ in perspective: 'Accountability is scrutiny from an external point of view and is a form of 'answerability', whilst (moral) responsibility is an internal point of view, i.e. an assessment of agency'.[7]

Defining responsibility in terms of perceived personal agency assumes that actions are undertaken with an awareness of one's obligations and duties—essentially, accountability to oneself.[8] Accountability between actors is often based on an assumption of moral responsibility, though this is not always a prerequisite, as seen in cases of collective action, disclosed agency, or strict liability.[9] In international governance initiatives, however, the moral and value-based dimensions of actions

[7] Taddeo et al. 2023, p. 15.

[8] Mulgan 2003.

[9] Schedler 1999, p. 9.

are given primacy, underlining a presumption of responsibility for actors. This raises a critical question: *which* individuals or groups throughout the AI lifecycle could—and should—be seen as responsible for *which* challenges arising from the use of AI-enabled systems in the military domain? By focusing on the core issue of responsibility and its relation to other focus areas in international governance initiatives, this chapter aims to present a structured return to the fundamentals. In doing so, it seeks to elaborate key themes of 'legal compliance, responsibility, and agency in armed conflict.'[10]

11.2.1 Conceptualising Responsibility: Accordance with International Law

International governance initiatives for military AI emphasise that these technologies should be deployed in accordance with international law, just like any other weapon. Yet, a salient weakness in this general focus area is that, despite initial engagement through forums like the Group of Governmental Experts on Lethal Autonomous Weapon Systems (GGE LAWS), there is thus far no specificity in the outputs of governance initiatives. Specifically, it remains unelaborated which principles of international law apply to AI, how they apply, and whether these existing principles are sufficient to contribute to desirable outcomes.[11]

The persistence of these questions largely stems from the fact that 'the relationship between the [AI] weapon and the operator raises ethical and legal issues regarding the role of humans, and the autonomy of machines, in making life-and-death decisions during armed conflict.'[12] Yet, it is not as though international law is unequipped to address these issues. IHL, or *jus in bello,* as a primary legal framework regulates conduct during armed conflict, providing the substance of potential violations. Concurrently, International Criminal Law (ICL) and State Responsibility establish criteria for responsibility, accountability, and the consequences of omissions by individuals, groups, and States under international law.[13] The responsibility for lawful deployment primarily falls on military commanders, who hold command responsibility, meaning they bear 'the burden of full accountability for the entire scope of their prosecution of the war effort'.[14] At the individual level, all members of the armed forces also bear personal responsibility to comply with IHL, necessitating

[10] Lewis 2022, p. 488.

[11] United Nations Office of Disarmament Affairs (2024) https://meetings.unoda.org/ccw-/convention-on-certain-conventional-weapons-group-of-governmental-experts-on-lethal-autonomous-weapons-systems-2024.

[12] Kraska 2021, p. 414.

[13] Boulanin and Lewis 2023, p. 6; Protocol Additional to the Geneva Conventions of 12 August 1949, and relating to the Protection of Victims of International Armed Conflicts (Protocol I), opened for signature 8 June 1977, 1125 UNTS 3, entered into force 7 December 1978 (API), Articles 36, 82, 83, 87; Boutin 2023.

[14] Kraska 2021, p. 432.

awareness of circumstances that could render their actions unlawful.[15] Notably, this personal responsibility extends beyond cases where an actor intentionally commits an act with knowledge of, and intent to cause, harm or unlawful consequences. It also extends to instances of recklessness or *dolus eventualis,* where a harmful or unlawful consequence is not desired by the actor but is a known possibility resulting from the act itself. Despite the tendency to anthropomorphise AI, within this legal framework, only humans can be held accountable for prohibited conduct, as AI systems themselves cannot be held accountable under international law.[16] Ultimately, '[n]o matter how independently, automatically, and interactively computer systems of the future behave, they will be the products (direct or indirect) of human behaviour, human social institutions, and human decision'.[17]

While these premises have been greatly simplified for the sake of brevity in this chapter, even in their most basic form, concepts of State, command, and individual responsibility are not explicitly mentioned in official documents emerging from international governance debates.[18] However, this is not to say that these subjects are not readily discussed in broader governance deliberations or in the growing body of academic literature.[19] However, their omission from final governance outputs may indicate a reluctance to formally define these concepts at this stage—perhaps reflecting the complexity of applying them to AI, where compliance with existing legal frameworks may not be as straightforward as mere 'accordance'.

AI-enabled systems cannot be directly equated with or generalised in the same way as 'conventional' weapons in a military arsenal. Unlike conventional weapons, AI technologies can be integrated across a wide range of applications, from weaponised, hardware-based platforms to decision support systems (DSS), or even create entirely new categories of systems altogether, making their influence on military operations potentially omnipresent. This ubiquitous introduction of AI into the military domain complicates established dynamics of responsibility, as 'new kinds and degrees of interdependencies would seem to arise between the military commander and the collection of other people responsible for configuring and administering the AI tool'.[20] Deliberations within the GGE LAWS have touched on how 'smart' machines defy 'traditional ways of ascription [of responsibility] because no person has enough control to be accountable for them'—neither the manufacturers nor those at higher levels of command.[21]

On the manufacturer side, this issue is attributable to the 'black box' nature of many modern AI applications, where the process from input to output is opaque, as well as the sheer number of actors involved in designing and developing a

---

[15] ICRC 2014.

[16] The retention of human responsibility is also alluded to by Stroppa in Chap. 4 of this volume. See also Pacholska 2023, p. 18; Bo et al. 2022, pp. 35–56; Boutin 2023.

[17] Pacholska 2023, p. 19.

[18] Sweijs and Romansky 2024.

[19] Maas 2019; Pacholska 2023.

[20] Boulanin and Lewis 2023, p. 1.

[21] Kraska 2021, p. 423.

single system.[22] Meanwhile, commanders may face unpredictable errors or emergent behaviour on the battlefield, obscured by a lack of understanding of what contributed to such outcomes.[23] Without such knowledge, commanders can be ill-prepared to assess whether deploying AI-enabled systems aligns with their legal requirements and anticipated outcomes.[24] Conversely, Human Rights Watch has expressed concerns that, under such conditions, command responsibility is (morally) unjust; holding commanders solely accountable for deployment decisions is morally unjust as it is unfair to place responsibility on them for decisions involving complex linkages between actors around untransparent systems.[25] Overall, 'the more machines operate irrespective of the actions or omissions of direct human operators, the more it is difficult to convincingly argue that the conduct of human operators provides ground for attribution'.[26] This presents an important dilemma: are existing rules and regulations still fit for purpose, or is a distributed responsibility system needed to account for the decentralised nature of AI system development and control?[27]

These persisting questions regarding the application of international law point to a need to revisit, reassess, and reinforce the fundamental frameworks of responsibility (outlined above) in the context of military AI. First, for each type of actor within the AI lifecycle, it is necessary to identify the specific types of responsibility and accountability expected of them, the rationale behind these expectations, and the consequences for omissions. In this context, it must be determined whether the goal of establishing an actor's responsibility—and, by extension, their agency—is to enforce compliance with ethical and legal requirements, to facilitate oversight over decision-making chains, and/or to enforce accountability for harm caused, including in instances of failures to prevent harm.[28] At the State level, 'upholding the responsibility of collective actors such as States acknowledges the structural forces that drive the development and use of AI'.[29] Breaches of State responsibility would extend to instances of negligent development or procurement of military AI technologies, including obligations to cease 'wrongful conduct and [the offering of] appropriate assurances and guarantees of non-repetition'.[30] At the individual level within militaries, governments need to build on existing regulatory infrastructure, as 'states

[22] Scharre and Lamberth 2022; Sweijs and Romansky 2024.

[23] This is even more relevant for AI applications that employ techniques that continue to learn during deployment.

[24] Moynihan 2018, p. 460: The standard of which within international law for the establishment of responsibility is practical certainty.

[25] Kraska 2021, p. 438.

[26] Boutin 2023, p. 141.

[27] A similar set of questions is articulated by Taddeo et al. 2023, p. 1716.

[28] Novelli et al. 2023, p. 16.

[29] Boutin 2023, p. 134.

[30] Ibid., p. 149.

typically pursue administrative mechanisms of accountability, initiating investigations and imposing non-judicial punishment or administrative censure', a system that is 'longstanding and complete' in the domain of individual responsibility.[31]

Second, it is essential to consider which international law frameworks are relevant for specific actors in concrete situations. Certain types of responsibility, such as those of developers, do not stem strictly from ICL but also from other oversight and legal bodies.[32] On the one hand, responsibility cannot be thought of merely as a retrospective concept, established only after a violation occurs. Responsibility should also be proactive, integrated throughout the design process, and aimed at ensuring systems function as intended.[33] On the other hand, some aspects of responsibility may be better addressed at the national, rather than international, level.[34] Still, internationally-defined principles or red lines regarding fundamentally criminal uses of AI in the military domain can still guide national rules and regulations.

Finally, even when these responsibilities are clearly defined, there needs to be practical criteria to distinguish between outcomes due to intent versus outcomes due to malfunctioning when AI-enabled systems are employed.[35] Concepts such as *aberratio ictus*, which addresses whether a person can still be held liable under a mistake of fact in the absence of intent, must be clarified, especially in the context of civilian harm. Presently, 'neither international criminal law nor State responsibility provides any form of remedy when civilian harm is accidental or incidental to otherwise lawful action', further complicated by the fact that negligence alone does not establish grounds for international criminal liability.[36] As AI becomes increasingly integrated into surveillance and decision-making—which is 'crucial for commanders' situational awareness and hence the proper application of all combat of hostilities rules'—the ability to differentiate between errors and intent will prove crucial for establishing responsibility and, hence, ensuring lawful use.[37]

The applicability of responsibility frameworks for violations of IHL to the use of AI-enabled systems is not disputed in international governance discussions. However, the consistent adherence to this principle depends on answering critical questions about responsibility: clarifying the ways that different actors are responsible and can and should be held accountable (for what goals, with what consequences, and within which international and national legal frameworks), as well as defining practical steps for implementation.

---

[31] Kraska 2021, p. 409.

[32] Bo 2022.

[33] Bo et al. 2022, pp. 15, 17, 38, 48.

[34] See Chap. 12 of this volume.

[35] See Chap. 13 of this volume.

[36] Crootof 2024. This is particularly important in cases of faultless responsibility, i.e. 'contexts in which, while it is possible to identify the causal chain of agents and actions that led to a morally good/bad outcome, it is not possible to attribute intent to perform morally good/bad actions to any of those agents individually': Taddeo et al. 2021, p. 1723.

[37] Pacholska 2023, p. 22.

11.2.2 Prerequisites for Responsibility: Reliability, Explainability, and Traceability

The focus areas of reliability, explainability, and traceability have been consistently emphasised by international governance initiatives as essential prerequisites for the integration of AI-enabled systems into the military domain.[38] Reliability is defined as 'the probability that a system or product will perform in a satisfactory manner for a given period of time when used under specified operating conditions'.[39] Without reliability, a system cannot be deployed in military operations, as 'operators must be able to predict with a high degree of accuracy how the weapon will behave after being deployed. A weapon would not be adequately controllable, and therefore unlawful, if there is more than a remote possibility that it could perform in an unforeseeable way.'[40] Meanwhile, explainability in AI specifically 'refers to the ability [of an AI algorithm] to provide a semantic expression to why decision processes developed in a certain way,' which enables external human observers to understand the system's reasoning.[41] Traceability, in turn, ensures that 'certain outputs from an AI algorithm can be traced to certain inputs, as if going back in the decision chain'.[42]

While these three concepts may initially appear as purely technical requirements for AI-enabled systems, in fact, they reflect different criteria for establishing human responsibility. If humans are to remain accountable for the outcomes of AI-enabled systems, the conditions for meaningful human involvement must be optimised whether through 'meaningful human control' (MHC), 'adequate human judgement', 'human oversight' or 'human responsibility'.[43] What these terms capture is a fundamental tension: the balance between human biases and fallibility on one hand, and the advantages offered by AI-enabled systems on the other, all within the context of international law, which necessitates human responsibility and the minimisation of uncertainty in the conduct of war.[44]

The foremost cited reason behind the progressive integration of AI into all dimensions of military operations is the efficiency these technologies offer: gains in scale, speed, and, consequently, effectiveness.[45] In computationally complex cognitive tasks, AI-enabled systems outperform humans and, as such, can optimise certain processes.[46] Yet, to comply with international law, humans must not only remain 'looped' into the processes of AI-enabled systems, but they must also meet the

[38] Sweijs and Romansky 2024.

[39] Blanchard and Blyler 2016, p. 144.

[40] Kwik and van Engers 2021, p. 53.

[41] Christie et al. 2024, pp. 7–9.

[42] Ibid.

[43] Tigard 2021.

[44] Johnson 2024.

[45] Rashid et al. 2023.

[46] Kraska 2021, p. 414; Korteling et al. 2021, p. 6.

criteria for legal responsibility: a sufficient understanding of how the system operates, how it was trained on datasets, what variables it considers, and how it draws conclusions. Without this understanding, human judgement of the system's appropriateness—upon which international law relies—becomes impaired.[47] In addition to predictability, explainability and traceability serve to accommodate these requirements. Despite the general recognition of these focus areas, their exact implications for and interactions with responsibility have yet to be fully elaborated in governance initiatives.

Reliability is related to predictability, as it is inherently a forward-looking principle. Long before a system is deployed in the battlefield, it must undergo thorough testing, evaluation, validation, and verification processes to establish how it operates. As a result, responsibility for ensuring reliability is also distributed across multiple actors throughout the AI lifecycle.[48] Designers and developers are responsible for creating reliable systems in the early stages of the AI lifecycle. States, in turn, have a responsibility to ensure that AI systems procured for use adhere by production standards. Finally, responsibility for understanding the reliability of these systems, specifically in what contexts systems can be deployed, lies with commanders and operators. Reliability also pertains to the characteristics of the systems themselves. If an AI-enabled system continues to learn post-deployment, emergent behaviour—where AI algorithms 'can self-modify and produce an AI model without direct human intervention'—can undermine the system's reliability and, consequently, the ability of commanders to assess its legality.[49] These issues are especially acute in light of the possibilities created by deep learning, which introduce emergent difficulties in tracking the inner workings of self-developing models.[50] Subsequently, in these cases, it is crucial to ask whether some risk of unpredictability is acceptable, given the advantages offered by such systems, or whether their unpredictability renders them fundamentally unlawful.

Clarifying the relations between different actors and specific types of AI-enabled systems would allow for the retrospective tracing of responsibility when failures occur. Key questions include: Was there sufficient testing of how systems develop based on new data? Was there adequate communication between designers and procurers? Were commanders sufficiently informed about these systems? Establishing these levels of sufficiency is not a one-size-fits-all matter; it is highly dependent on the techniques employed by an AI-enabled system and the future contexts of its deployment.

The final questions address the extent to which explainability and traceability must be incorporated as design features of AI applications. For example, under Article 57 of API, judgment and conscious action are conditions for establishing legal liability, which are both premised on having an appropriate level of understanding of how a

[47] Sullivan and Ricket 2024, pp. 215–218.

[48] Bode and Nadibaidze 2024.

[49] Kraska 2021, p. 410.

[50] Şahin et al. 2024.

system operates and what it can (or cannot) do for what purposes.[51] If AI-enabled systems rely on black box algorithms, certain depths of understanding remain inherently inaccessible to humans. Yet, by designing explainable and traceable algorithms, developers can 'open' the black box. But this alone, if even feasible, would not suffice. First, 'there is [a] clear trade-off between the performance of a machine learning model and its ability to produce explainable and interpretable predictions',[52] with certain gains in efficiency stemming from the opacity of systems. As such, questions about whether this trade-off is acceptable or even legally necessary must be answered. Second, in strategic thinking, a so-called 'double black box' may appear desirable, where not only the AI techniques themselves are opaque, but the secrecy surrounding developments also obscures the system's function, from both adversaries and practitioners.[53] Finally, humans may fall victim to their own biases, such as automation bias, where '[i]f the operator is reflexively pressing a button to approve strikes recommended by the weapon system, it could be argued that there is control, but little judgment is being exercised'.[54] Simultaneously, excessive trust is potentially intensified by the misconception that 'inanimate AI agents are capable of moral reasoning, compassion, empathy, mercy, etc. and thus might perform more ethically and humanely than humans in warfare.'[55] Therefore, simply having explainable and traceable systems is not enough to ensure proper understanding in use.[56] Institutional changes in education, training, and reskilling—with a specific emphasis on the ultimate responsibility of the human—are necessary to make responsibility genuine, rather than just a label. It is also important to note that the technical properties of the system and technical illiteracy are not the only methods through which a 'black box' can arise. For instance, certain systems may be deliberately designed with opaque algorithms for State or corporate secrecy, for which the problem of explainability and traceability must be approached differently, the discussion of which is beyond the scope of this chapter.[57]

The core dilemmas surrounding AI-enabled weapon systems are therefore not only about the systems themselves but about the judgements made regarding their use and the extent of human involvement. If responsibility remains fully with humans, AI-enabled systems need to be designed to optimise human responsibility, even if that means sacrificing certain gains offered by AI-enabled systems. Until the responsibilities of different actors throughout the AI lifecycle are established, it is unlikely that deliberations on explainability and traceability will yield definitive conclusions. Therefore, it is essential to begin by establishing these responsibilities.

[51] Sullivan and Ricket 2024, p. 217.

[52] Linardatos et al. 2021, p. 18.

[53] Lewis 2022, p. 493.

[54] Kraska 2021, p. 430.

[55] Johnson 2024, p. 74.

[56] Van der Waa et al. 2021, p. 17.

[57] Burrell 2016.

11.2.3 Responsible Responsibility: Governability and Exchange of Practices

The focus areas of governability and exchange of practices provide at least two definitive answers to the question of responsibility: first, a human somewhere in the loop should always be able to disable an autonomous AI system; second, responsible practice involves the exchange of information between all relevant actors. However, these two points alone still do not answer the question of when humans should intervene, or what criteria and information would be required to make such judgments. Meanwhile, in the case of AI systems that are not autonomous, such as DSS, the human operator has a responsibility to be informed about the workings and specification of the system and to prevent its use with excessive bias. As such, the final two focus areas share a similar issue in terms of subjectivity: different actors may have varying views on what is sufficient and necessary, depending on the criteria for responsibility that they establish. Even if one actor develops a common framework with sound criteria, other actors may reject it for competitive reasons.[58]

In the context of exchange of practices, further clarity is needed regarding which actors are responsible for exchanging which practices, and whether this process itself forms part of the responsible use of AI in the military domain. Several potential dimensions warrant further consideration. First, as implied in the previous section, information should be shared throughout the lifecycle of an AI-enabled system to ensure that all actors are aware of its capabilities. Second, due to the decentralised nature of AI design and development, best practices shared among developers could also contribute to the overall reliability of systems, and therefore the optimisation of their responsible use. Finally, this knowledge could also be shared between States, both as confidence-building measures and to improve AI-enabled systems themselves. Understanding which knowledge aligns with responsible practices and justifies the trade-off between secrecy and transparency is an essential step forward.

At the same time, deliberations around governability ultimately focus on how to ensure MHC. Further clarification is needed regarding what constitutes MHC in the context of military AI-enabled systems in specific contexts.[59] At the current stage of normative development, governance is centred around the notion that MHC constitutes a fundamental principle governing the usage of AI-enabled systems, complementing fundamental principles already encapsulated within IHL, such as distinction, proportionality, and precaution.[60] Beyond addressing the onus of responsibility across the entire AI lifecycle, it is crucial to define notions of MHC in terms of different forms of interaction with AI enabled systems and in various environments, including scenarios with and without humans presence. Finally, it is also necessary to consider the implications of governability, especially when it comes to establishing a 'kill switch'. What happens to the data gathered by the AI model? What steps

[58] Brunk 2016.

[59] Boutin and Woodcock 2024.

[60] Ferl 2024.

should be taken after the system is shut down? These questions have significant post-deployment consequences, particularly during the often-overlooked disposal stage.

First and foremost, a key consideration is whether AI-enabled systems are deployed along any stage of the kill chain—from imagery analysis, target acquisition and prioritisation, to decisions to act. The responsibility for harm caused by AI-enabled systems that can operate fully autonomously once activated, such as loitering munitions, lies primarily with the decision makers who authorise their deployment.[61] This also applies to grey areas where AI-enabled systems operate under direct human control, offering recommendations for courses of action. Rules and regulations should govern appropriate MHC to guard against automation bias and overreliance, ensuring sufficient human oversight.[62] In addition, the environment in which AI-enabled systems are deployed is also relevant, with different degrees of human control required for environments where humans are present (e.g., urban environments) compared to systems operating autonomously (e.g., against missile defence systems), which in many cases may already operate semi-autonomously. Progress in this field can only be achieved through the further elaboration of such practices, including through the exchange of ideas and best practices.

This issue is complicated, however, as—despite the recognised importance of responsibility and responsible practice—States may hesitate to establish red lines regarding the implementation of AI in the military domain. This reluctance stems from concerns that being overly 'responsible' (as a fully subjective term) could cost them a perceived competitive advantage. As such, a further dimension that must be explored is how the issue of responsibility interacts with the broader context of interstate strategic competition.

11.3 In Lieu of Conclusions

International governance discussions surrounding military AI must move beyond conceptual and abstract ideas. There is a need to focus on developing applied, concrete norms, rules, and regulations. Thus far, progress has been hindered by the absence of a structured, unifying framework to address diverse issues arising from the emergence of military AI. This chapter proposes that the tenet of responsibility can serve as a focal and anchoring element to the diverse range of issues generated by the emergence of military AI. It has analysed how responsibility ties together the seven key focus areas emerging from a comprehensive review of the international governance landscape. The chapter identifies critical problems and offers concrete next steps to address these issues, placing responsibility at the core of governance frameworks.

---

[61] Bode and Watts 2023.

[62] Boutin 2023, pp. 142–143.

Acknowledgements We would like to thank the DILEMA team at the T.M.C. Asser Institute for the opportunity to contribute to this invaluable project. We also wish to acknowledge Elton Högklint for his assistance in finalising this chapter.

References

Articles, Books, and Other Documents

Blanchard BS, Blyler J (2016) System Engineering Management, 5th edn. John Wiley & Sons, Hoboken

Bo M (2022) Are Programmers in or out of Control? The Individual Criminal Responsibility of Programmers of Autonomous Weapons and Self-Driving Cars. In: Gless S, Whalen-Bridge H (eds) Human-Robot Interaction in Law and Its Narratives: Legal Blame, Procedure, and Criminal Law. Cambridge University Press, Cambridge, pp. 23–48

Bo M, Bruun L, Boulanin V (2022) Retaining Human Responsibility in the Development and Use of Autonomous Weapon Systems: On Accountability for Violations of International Humanitarian Law Involving AWS. https://doi.org/10.55163/AHBC1664

Bode I, Nadibaidze A (2024) Symposium on Military AI and the Law of Armed Conflict: Human-machine Interaction in the Military Domain and the Responsible AI Framework. https://opiniojuris.org/2024/04/04/symposium-on-military-ai-and-the-law-of-armed-conflict-human-machine-interaction-in-the-military-domain-and-the-responsible-ai-framework/. Accessed 10 Feb 2025

Bode I, Watts T (2023) Loitering Munitions and Unpredictability: Autonomy in Weapon Systems and Challenges to Human Control. AutoNorms. https://www.autonorms.eu/loitering-munitions-and-unpredictability-autonomy-in-weapon-systems-and-challenges-to-human-control/. Accessed 14 May 2025

Boulanin V, Lewis DA (2023) Responsible reliance concerning development and use of AI in the military domain. Ethics and Information Technology. https://doi.org/10.1007/s10676-023-09691-0

Boutin B (2023) State responsibility in relation to military applications of artificial intelligence. Leiden Journal of International Law. https://doi.org/10.1017/S0922156522000607

Boutin B, Woodcock T (2024) Aspects of Realizing (Meaningful) Human Control: a Legal Perspective. In: Geiß R, Lahman H (eds) Research Handbook on Warfare and Artificial Intelligence. Edward Elgar Publishing, Cheltenham, pp. 179–196

Brunk I (2016) China, Russia, and International Law. In: Lawfare. https://www.lawfaremedia.org/article/china-russia-and-international-law. Accessed 10 Feb 2025

Burrell J (2016) How the machine 'thinks': Understanding opacity in machine learning algorithms. Big Data & Society. https://doi.org/10.1177/2053951715622512

Christie EH, Ertan A, Adomaitis L, Klaus M (2024) Regulating lethal autonomous weapon systems: exploring the challenges of explainability and traceability. AI Ethics. https://doi.org/10.1007/s43681-023-00261-0

Crootof R (2024) Symposium on Military AI and the Law of Armed Conflict: Front- and Back-End Accountability for Military AI. Opinio Juris. https://opiniojuris.org/2024/04/02/symposium-on-military-ai-and-the-law-of-armed-conflict-front-and-back-end-accountability-for-military-ai/. Accessed 10 Feb 2025

Ferl AK (2024) Imagining Meaningful Human Control: Autonomous Weapons and the (De-) Legitimisation of Future Warfare. Global Society. https://doi.org/10.1080/13600826.2023.2233004

ICRC (2014) Command responsibility and failure to act. https://www.icrc.org/sites/default/files/document/file_list/command-responsibility-icrc-eng.pdf. Accessed 14 May 2025

Johnson J (2024) Finding AI Faces in the Moon and Armies in the Clouds: Anthropomorphising Artificial Intelligence in Military Human-Machine Interactions. Global Society. https://doi.org/10.1080/13600826.2023.2205444

Korteling JE, van de Boer-Visschedijk GC, Blankendaal RAM, Boonekamp RC, Eikelboom AR (2021) Human- versus Artificial Intelligence. Frontiers in Artificial Intelligence. https://doi.org/10.3389/frai.2021.622364

Kraska J (2021) Command Accountability for AI Weapon Systems in the Law of Armed Conflict. International Law Studies 97(1):407–447

Kwik J, Van Engers T (2021) Algorithmic fog of war: When lack of transparency violates the law of armed conflict. Journal of Future Robot Life. https://doi.org/10.3233/FRL-200019

Lewis DA (2022) On 'Responsible AI' in War: Exploring Preconditions for Respecting International Law in Armed Conflict. In: Voeneky S, Kellmeyer P, Mueller O, Burgard W (eds) The Cambridge Handbook of Responsible Artificial Intelligence: Interdisciplinary Perspectives. Cambridge University Press, Cambridge, pp. 488–506

Linardatos P, Papastefanopoulos V, Kotsiantis S (2021) Explainable AI: A Review of Machine Learning Interpretability Methods. Entropy. https://doi.org/10.3390/e23010018

Maas MM (2019) Innovation-Proof Global Governance for Military Artificial Intelligence? How I Learned to Stop Worrying, and Love the Bot. Journal of International Humanitarian Legal Studies. https://doi.org/10.1163/18781527-01001006

Moynihan H (2018) Aiding and Assisting: The Mental Element Under Article 16 of the International Law Commission's Articles on State Responsibility. International & Comparative Law Quarterly. https://doi.org/10.1017/S0020589317000598

Mulgan R (2003) Holding Power to Account: Accountability in Modern Democracies. Palgrave Macmillan, London, pp. 1–35

Novelli C, Taddeo M, Floridi L (2023) Accountability in artificial intelligence: what it is and how it works. AI & Society. https://doi.org/10.1007/s00146-023-01635-y

Pacholska M (2023) Military Artificial Intelligence and the Principle of Distinction: A State Responsibility Perspective. Israel Law Review. https://doi.org/10.1017/S0021223722000188

Rashid AB, Kausik AK, Al Hassan Sunny A, Bappy MH (2023) Artificial Intelligence in the Military: An Overview of the Capabilities, Applications, and Challenges. International Journal of Intelligent Systems 2023. https://doi.org/10.1155/2023/8676366

Şahin E, Arslan NN, Özdemir D (2024) Unlocking the black box: an in-depth review on interpretability, explainability, and reliability in deep learning. Neural Computing & Applications. https://doi.org/10.1007/s00521-024-10437-2

Scharre P, Lamberth M (2022) Artificial Intelligence and Arms Control. CNAS. https://s3.us-east-1.amazonaws.com/files.cnas.org/documents/AI-and-Arms-Control_FINAL.pdf. Accessed 10 Feb 2025

Schedler A (1999) Conceptualizing Accountability. In: Schedler A, Diamond L, Plattner MF (eds) The Self-Restraining State: Power and Accountability in New Democracies. Lynne Rienner Publishers, Boulder, pp. 13–28

Sullivan S, Ricket I (2024) Targeting in the Black Box. In: Kwan C, Lindström L, Giovannelli D, Podiņš K, Štrucl D (eds) CyCon 2024: Over the Horizon 16th International Conference on Cyber Conflict, pp. 207–220. https://ccdcoe.org/uploads/2024/05/CyCon_2024_book.pdf. Accessed 14 May 2025

Sweijs T, Romansky S (2024) International Norms Development and AI in the Military Domain. Centre for International Governance Innovation. https://www.cigionline.org/publications/international-norms-development-and-ai-in-the-military-domain/. Accessed 10 Feb 2025

Taddeo M, McNeish D, Blanchard A, Edgar E (2021) Ethical Principles for Artificial Intelligence in National Defence. Philosophy & Technology. https://doi.org/10.1007/s13347-021-00482-3

Taddeo M, McNeish D, Blanchard A, Edgar E (2023) Ethical principles for artificial intelligence in the defence domain. In: Artificial Intelligence and International Conflict in Cyberspace. Routledge, London, pp. 159–185

Tigard DW (2021) Responsible AI and moral responsibility: a common appreciation. AI Ethics. https://doi.org/10.1007/s43681-020-00009-0

Van der Waa J, Nieuwburg E, Cremers A, Neerincx M (2021) Evaluating XAI: A comparison of rule-based and example-based explanations. Artificial Intelligence. https://doi.org/10.1016/j.artint.2020.103404

Sofia Romansky is a strategic analyst at The Hague Centre for Strategic Studies and the Project Coordinator of the Global Commission on Responsible Artificial Intelligence in the Military Domain (GC REAIM). Her primary research focus concerns the impact of artificial intelligence on the social and military domains, specifically the centrality of the concept of responsibility, issues around narratives and disinformation in online spheres as hybrid threats, and Russia's invasion of Ukraine. Sofia has a Master's Degree in International Relations and Diplomacy from the University of Leiden and the Clingendael Institute.

Tim Sweijs is the Director of Research at The Hague Centre for Strategic Studies (HCSS). At HCSS, Dr. Sweijs is responsible for the overall research portfolio of the entire institute, spearheading a staff of over 30 researchers and a large network of affiliated subject matter experts, working on international and national security. Dr. Sweijs is also a Research Affiliate at the Center for International Strategy, Technology and Policy in the Sam Nunn School of International Affairs at the Georgia Institute for Technology in the United States. His work is multidisciplinary in nature and straddles political science, science and technology, strategic studies, and war studies.

Chapter 12
'This Is My Last Resort': Approaches to Overcome the Stalemate in Autonomous Weapons Regulation Through National Legislation and Industry Self-Regulation

Marcel Schliebs and Vanessa Vohs

Contents

Abstract As artificial intelligence (AI) is set to disrupt all areas of life, militaries worldwide are investing heavily in the research and development of military AI applications. Among the most controversial are autonomous weapons systems (AWS), which are capable of selecting and engaging targets without human intervention. AWS range from existing technologies, such as autonomous anti-radar devices, to speculative future capabilities, including drone swarms operating in complex urban combat environments. There are clear reasons why regulating AWS may be desirable. Ethically, removing human agency from lethal decisions risks eroding core humanitarian principles, such as moral judgement and human dignity in armed conflict. Legally, delegating target selection and use of lethal force to machines without human intervention raises questions of accountability and compliance with International

M. Schliebs
Oxford Internet Institute, University of Oxford, Oxford, UK
e-mail: marcel.schliebs@oii.ox.ac.uk

V. Vohs (✉)
Professorship for Security and Defence Policy, University of the Bundeswehr Munich, Neubiberg, Germany
e-mail: vanessa.vohs@unibw.de

B. Boutin et al. (eds.), *Legal, Ethical, and Technical Dilemmas in Military Artificial Intelligence*, https://doi.org/10.1007/978-94-6265-759-5_12

Humanitarian Law. Strategically, the widespread proliferation of AWS may increase the risk of inadvertent escalation and accelerate a global arms race, driven by the opacity of underlying algorithms and competitive pressure among States. Against this backdrop, this chapter adopts an interdisciplinary approach, combining international relations, arms control, AI ethics, international law, and computer science. It evaluates the limits of multilateral regulation and argues that a dual-track approach may serve as a necessary last resort: combining national legislation and industry self-regulation to achieve coalition-building among like-minded States. Taking into account the inherent properties of AWS and lessons from historical arms control, the chapter explores how convergence around responsible practices may be achieved through real-world application, even in the absence of a binding international agreement.

Keywords Autonomous Weapons Systems (AWS) · National Legislation · Self-Regulation · Arms Race · Arms Control · AI Ethics · International Law

12.1 Introduction

The rapid advancement of artificial intelligence (AI) is transforming various sectors of society—including the critical domain of defence. Militaries worldwide are investing heavily in research and development to harness the disruptive potential of AI for military applications. The United States (US) has rapidly accelerated its investments in AI,[1] while the North Atlantic Treaty Organization (NATO) has committed €1 billion to advance AI and broader defence technologies.[2] Russia has similarly prioritised military AI development, with President Vladimir Putin famously declaring that whoever becomes the leader in AI 'will be the ruler of the world'.[3] The Russian Ministry of Defence has launched multiple AI research and development streams in areas such as intelligence, surveillance, and reconnaissance (ISR), command and control (C2), and high-precision weaponry.[4] Meanwhile, China's State Council has publicly announced its ambition to become the world leader in AI by 2030,[5] including in the military realm.[6]

Among the most controversial applications of military AI are autonomous weapons systems (AWS), which the US Department of Defense (DoD) defines as systems that can 'select and engage targets without further intervention by a [human] operator'.[7] A wide range of AWS have already been developed, tested, and deployed

[1] Larson et al. 2024.

[2] Davies 2024.

[3] https://www.theverge.com/2017/9/4/16251226/russia-ai-putin-rule-the-world. Accessed 3 September 2024.

[4] Bendett 2023.

[5] Davis 2022.

[6] Hunter et al. 2023.

[7] U.S. Department of Defense 2023a.

globally, with a growing tendency towards higher levels of autonomy. This trend is further exacerbated by competitive dynamics, as AWS are set to yield significant battlefield advantages, including increased tempo of decision making, enhanced targeting precision, and, particularly, the ability to operate in electromagnetically denied environments such as war zones with GPS or C2 jamming.

The contentious issues surrounding the development, use, and proliferation of AWS have been discussed within the United Nations (UN) since 2014. In 2017, these informal discussions were elevated to the Group of Governmental Experts on Lethal Autonomous Weapons Systems (GGE LAWS) under the framework of the UN Convention on Certain Conventional Weapons (CCW).[8] However, Russia has since boycotted recent discussions as a consequence of its war of aggression against Ukraine, ongoing since February 24, 2022. As a result, meaningful progress towards regulating AWS has become even more remote, with States increasingly acknowledging the failure of the Geneva negotiations.[9] As the GGE LAWS operates on the basis of consensus, and constructive cooperation with Russia remains unlikely in the near future, alternative forums for advancing the debate on AWS are becoming increasingly relevant.

In parallel, national and regional initiatives have gained traction. The US, for example, has maintained a directive on Autonomy in Weapons since 2012, which was most recently updated for the third time in 2023.[10] In the same year, the US DoD also released its own AI adoption strategy,[11] addressing various operational domains outside the scope of AWS. Last but not least, the US, alongside a dozen other States, endorsed a 'Political Declaration on Responsible Military Use of Artificial Intelligence and Autonomy' in the context of the 2023 Responsible AI in the Military Domain (REAIM) Summit in The Hague, and collaborated on the 'REAIM Blueprint for Action' presented later in South Korea.[12]

These developments reflect the growing recognition that the deployment of AWS presents a complex array of ethical, legal, and strategic challenges. Ethically, delegating lethal decision making to machines raises significant concerns regarding the erosion of moral judgement and human dignity in armed conflict. Legally, issues arise regarding accountability for the actions of AWS and whether existing International Humanitarian Law (IHL) can adequately address the distinct features of this new form of warfare. Strategically, the proliferation of AWS could increase the risk of inadvertent escalation and contribute to a global arms race, driven by opaque and rapidly evolving AI algorithms.

---

[8] Convention on Prohibitions or Restrictions on the Use of Certain Conventional Weapons Which May Be Deemed to Be Excessively Injurious or to Have Indiscriminate Effects, adopted 10 October 1980, entered into force 2 December 1983.

[9] Hoffberger-Pippan et al. 2022.

[10] US Department of Defense 2023a.

[11] U.S. Department of Defense 2023b.

[12] https://thereadable.co/reaim-blueprint-for-responsible-ai-use-military/. Accessed 31 January 2025.

Given these multifaceted challenges, there is a case for the regulation of AWS. However, designing and enforcing effective regulatory frameworks is complicated by the rapid pace of technological change and the diversity of national interests. This chapter adopts an interdisciplinary approach, drawing on insights from international relations, arms control, AI ethics, and international law to explore the preconditions necessary for effective regulation of AWS. The remainder of this chapter is structured as follows. First, Sect. 12.2 provides an overview of the role of autonomy on the battlefield of the future, highlighting how the competitive advantages of embracing AWS may fuel their proliferation. Second, Sect. 12.3 outlines the risks posed by ever-higher levels of autonomy in AWS, focusing on the ethical, legal, and escalatory challenges of delegating target selection and lethal engagement to machines without meaningful human control (MHC). Third, Sect. 12.4 draws on theoretical perspectives and experiences from historical arms control agreements to derive the preconditions necessary for meaningful and stable regulation, concluding that the adoption of binding multilateral agreements banning or limiting certain types of AWS are unlikely to materialise in the short to medium term. Finally, Sect. 12.5 contextualises these theoretical insights within recent empirical negotiations in international fora, finding that diverging national interests and the current complex geopolitical climate have led to a near stalemate. Acknowledging that some form of regulation of AWS without MHC may be desirable, but is unlikely to materialise bindingly at the multilateral level, this chapter argues that it is imperative to prepare for a world in which no multilateral regulation has been achieved. It therefore explores potential alternative pathways: national legislation, intergovernmental cooperation among like-minded States, and industry self-regulation.

12.2 Autonomy on the Battlefield of the Future

AI has the potential to fundamentally change the nature of warfare. Around one century ago, military powers harnessed the innovations of the Industrial Revolution to introduce tanks, aircraft, and machine guns—followed later by missiles and nuclear weapons—onto the battlefield. These technologies enabled unprecedented levels of mass destruction, as evidenced by two devastating World Wars. What distinguished twentieth century military innovation was the physical superiority of new weapons machinery, which proved exponentially stronger, faster, and more lethal than humans. AI may represent another revolutionary shift—this time not through physical power, but through the *cognitisation* of machines,[13] and the introduction of ever-increasing

[13] Scharre 2018a.

levels of autonomy in warfare. While AI is being applied across a range of military applications, such as logistics,[14] cyber operations,[15] and reconnaissance,[16] most attention has been devoted to AWS.

The most distinctive feature of AWS is their degree of autonomy. To understand and distinguish between systems with varying levels of autonomous functionality, it is useful to examine the evolving role of human operators in the decision-making process—often framed in terms of whether a human is 'in', 'on', or 'out of' the loop.[17] To illustrate this, we adopt the analogy of the OODA loop (Observe, Orient, Decide, and Attack) for air warfare, originally developed by U.S. Air Force pilot and military strategist John Boyd.[18] Boyd believed that the key to achieving combat superiority was the ability to outpace an opponent's decision-making ability at every stage of this loop.

Possessing the lowest level of autonomy across the OODA loop autonomy is *semi*-AWS, in which a human operator remains *in* the loop. Semi-AWS are today used by at least 30 States, with notable examples including Lockheed Martin's Long Range Anti-Ship Missile (LRASM) and South Korea's Samsung SGR-1, a machine-gun-equipped sentry robot deployed at the Demilitarised Zone (DMZ), which can detect and engage hostile targets after prior human authorisation.[19] In *supervised* AWS, the human operator no longer controls the OODA loop but instead remains *on* the loop, with the theoretical ability to terminate an algorithmic decision—conditional on the system's speed and the operator's reaction time. Finally, in *fully* AWS, the human is entirely *out* of the loop, meaning they can no longer intervene once the weapon has been launched. An example of such a 'fire-and-forget' system is Israel's anti-radar Harpy,[20] a loitering munition that autonomously searches for hostile air defence systems within a pre-specified area. Upon confident target identification and classification, it launches a high-explosive warhead. Although the upgraded Harpy 2 maintains a C2 communications channel that allows for pre-engagement confirmation of targets by a human operator, the original fully autonomous Harpy 1 has already been sold to several States, including Chile, China, India, and Turkey.[21]

While the number of fully AWS remains limited today, there is reason to believe that this will change in the future. First, militaries have always been at the forefront of technological innovation, especially when it offers competitive advantages, reduces operational costs, or lowers personnel demands. Second, battlefield demands—such as the need for rapid decisions, precise actions, and seamless coordination between units—may pressure political and military leaders to adopt higher levels of autonomy to keep up with their adversaries, even if they themselves are inherently reluctant to do

[14] Wilkins and Desimone 1993.

[15] Taddeo and Floridi 2018.

[16] Tucker 2017.

[17] Roth et al. 2004.

[18] McIntosh 2011.

[19] Hess et al. 2011; Kim et al. 2010.

[20] https://www.iai.co.il/p/harpy. Accessed 29 August 2024.

[21] Gettinger and Michel 2017.

so. For example, decision times in both long-distance (e.g., engagements with hypersonic precision-guided missiles) and close urban combat scenarios may become so rapid that the OODA loop effectively becomes an immediate 'perceive-act vector',[22] simply leaving no more time for a human *in* the loop. Finally, keeping a human operator at least *on* the loop requires an active communications channel between the weapon system and its human supervisor. Although unproblematic for permissive electromagnetic environments—such as in Afghanistan, Iraq, or Syria, where US-based operators regularly receive high-resolution live video footage before authorising drone strikes—the situation is fundamentally different in communications-denied environments, especially against adversaries with more sophisticated cyber capabilities.[23] This challenge can currently be observed in the real-time Russian invasion of Ukraine, where C2 of drones remains a major vulnerability in denied electromagnetic environments due to jamming by the adversary's electronic warfare. According to the French Army's Chief of Staff, up to 75% of all drones used in the Russia-Ukraine conflict are lost due to electronic warfare,[24] highlighting a significant competitive disadvantage for militaries reliant on an uninterrupted OODA loop.

One approach to overcome this obstacle, used by both Russia and Ukraine, has been to deploy fibre optic drones. These systems maintain a physical cable connection to the operator across distances of several dozen kilometres.[25] Another solution to the jamming challenge, also tested by both sides, is to rely on drones capable of autonomous functioning—searching for, tracking, or engaging targets autonomously when operating in denied electromagnetic environments.[26] Given the rapid evolution of AI, particularly in systems powered by deep learning algorithms, it is realistic to assume that the battlefield pressures outlined above—speed, accuracy, and the ability to navigate in denied electromagnetic environments—will only intensify in the future. As a result, this forces competing militaries towards ever higher levels of autonomy in the development of new weapons systems.

12.3 The Case for Regulating AWS: Balancing Comparative Advantages

The battlefield pressures driving increasing levels of autonomy in weapons systems raise serious concerns about the trajectory of future warfare. In 2017, a fictional advocacy video promoting a ban on AWS produced by Stuart Russell and the Future of Life Institute, titled 'Slaughterbots', depicted a dystopian scenario in which swarms of miniature autonomous drones—equipped with facial recognition technology and

---

[22] Scharre 2018a, p. 24.

[23] Gregory 2011.

[24] Ruitenberg 2024.

[25] Hambling 2024.

[26] Mozur and Satariano 2024.

precision-shaped explosives—are deployed to assassinate political opponents identified via their social media profiles.[27] These drone swarms not only autonomously detect their targets, but also show advanced coordination; for example, one drone blasts a hole in a wall to allow others to enter.

Although the 'Slaughterbots' scenario—hyper-lethal drone swarms targeting individuals—may appear alarmist or provocative due to its ban-advocacy purpose, defence research programmes worldwide are actively laying the groundwork for swarm warfare.[28] According to its own website, the US Defense Advanced Research Projects Agency's (DARPA) 'Collaborative Operations in Denied Environment (CODE)' project aims to '[use] collaborative autonomy [to] find targets and engage them... with minimal supervision, and adapt to dynamic situations such as attrition of friendly forces or the emergence of unanticipated threats'.[29] DARPA's Deputy Tactical Technology Officer, Jean-Charles Lede, has described these drones as operating 'just as wolves hunt in coordinated packs with minimal communication'.[30] In another DARPA programme, 'OFFensive Swarm-Enabled Tactics (OFFSET)', the agency 'envisions future small-unit infantry forces using swarms comprising upwards of 250 small unmanned aircraft systems... to accomplish diverse missions in complex urban environments'.[31] Meanwhile, other major military powers are also investing in similar capabilities. The 2018 US Nuclear Posture Review assessed that Russia was developing a 'new intercontinental, nuclear-armed, nuclear-powered, undersea autonomous torpedo',[32] later unveiled by President Putin in a simulated video showing the 'POSEIDON' system autonomously navigating toward a hostile coastline, potentially causing a 500-m-high radioactive tsunami.[33] Similarly, China has 'developed helicopter drones carrying explosive mortar shells, grenade launchers and machine guns that can form swarms and engage in coordinated strikes'.[34] In 2017, China also showcased a drone swarm of 1,180 autonomously interacting units at an air show.[35]

For ethical and legal reasons—including concerns around accountability, proportionality, and preserving the essence of human judgement in life-and-death decisions—there are strong moral arguments against deploying AWS that target human lives without MHC in or on the loop. These arguments also support prioritising process consistency over outcome predictability, even if AWS were to outperform average human accuracy in targeting. Beyond these ethical, legal, and strategic concerns, and many further considerations that lie beyond the scope of this chapter, there are also specific properties inherent to the AI-driven nature of AWS that

---

[27] Future of Life Institute 2016.

[28] Grimal and Sundaram 2018; Scharre 2018b.

[29] DARPA 2018.

[30] Cooney 2015.

[31] https://www.darpa.mil/program/offensive-swarm-enabled-tactics. Accessed 29 August 2024.

[32] US Department of Defense 2018.

[33] Geist and Massicot 2019.

[34] Xuanzun 2019.

[35] Lin and Singer 2018.

render their unregulated adoption and proliferation problematic. A selection of these characteristics will be described in the subsequent paragraphs.

While delegating the most consequential decisions—over life and death—to an algorithm may be rejected *per se,* strategic competition towards higher levels of autonomy, similar to traditional arms races, could leave all States worse off than without the deployment of AWS. As Scharre points out, one of the traditional ways an arms race can create mutually detrimental outcomes for all parties is through the vast investment of financial resources into the development and production of weapons. These expenditures often come at the expense of non-military sectors, incurring significant opportunity costs, without necessarily gaining a meaningful competitive advantage.[36] In the context of AWS, this dynamic may be fuelled by the opaque, black-box nature of deep learning algorithms,[37] which makes benchmarking one's capabilities against those of other States much more complicated than in the case of traditional weapons, where at least the quantity and firepower of certain weapons systems could be estimated or obtained via intelligence collection. While States could previously estimate the number of tanks or the range, speed, and payload of missiles through intelligence, tomorrow's military superiority may hinge on the quality of algorithms and, critically, the training data that underpin them—factors that complicate assessments not only of an opponent's capabilities but even the performance of one's own algorithms.

Beyond economic opportunity cost dilemmas, another way in which increasing levels of autonomy in warfare could leave all sides worse off is by 'alter[ing] the character of warfare in a manner that is more harmful, more destructive, less stable, or otherwise less desirable than before'.[38] As Scharre notes, an early historical example of such a dynamic is the First World War, where some sources suggest that Germany's decision to produce and deploy chemical weapons was driven, in part, by (exaggerated) fears of similar alleged efforts by France, so that the outcome was simultaneously detrimental for both sides: battlefield suffering was intensified without either side gaining a significant competitive advantage.[39] In the context of AWS, it is at least conceivable that States, spurred by ambiguity about their own capabilities and those of an opponent, may feel compelled to increase the level of autonomy in their weapons systems—either to pre-empt a suspected competitive advantage or to gain one themselves.

Such competitive advantages could consist of shorter reaction times in target selection, automated aiming and engagement, or resilience to jamming in C2-denied theatres—all of which risk 'shift[ing] [warfare] to a qualitatively different regime in which humans have less control over lethal force',[40] pushing the human further out of the OODA loop as adversarial competition intensifies. Furthermore, due to their unpredictable nature, outsourcing battlefield decisions to AWS may increase the risk

[36] Scharre 2021.

[37] Holland Michel 2020.

[38] Scharre 2021.

[39] Ibid.

[40] Scharre 2021.

of inadvertent escalation, potentially leaving all parties less secure and more prone to accidental exchange of hostilities. For example, the proliferation of more and more AWS that rely on AI-driven targeting and engagement loops may replicate biases embedded in their underlying training data.[41] Contrary to idiosyncratic human operator errors, failures caused by biased central datasets could emerge unpredictably, in a correlated manner, and at scale, which could result in seemingly minor software errors leading to catastrophic consequences. As discussed in Chap. 13 of this volume by Boutin, unpredictability of AI systems causes serious questions about responsibility under international law. Finally, data-reliant autonomous systems are susceptible to adversarial attacks and spoofing,[42] which not only present significant operational risks, but also complicate both *ad hoc* and *ex post* accountability for (erroneous) decisions.

12.4 The Prospect of Multilateral Regulation of Lethal Autonomy

In Part II of the Future of Life's 2021 'Slaughterbots', an autonomous quadcopter nearly kills a child carrying a weapon, after the algorithm fails to apply the complex rules of IHL, mistakenly identifying the child as a legitimate military target. Despite the grim scenario, the video ends on a hopeful note: the UN adopts an international treaty banning AWS, thereby preserving humanitarian principles in warfare.

The remainder of this section proceeds in three steps. First, it situates AWS within the broader history of arms-control efforts; second, it distils two recurring preconditions for successful prohibition regimes; and third, it assesses whether those conditions can realistically be met for lethal autonomy. For the numerous reasons outlined, some form of multilateral agreement regulating the rapid development and proliferation of AWS appears to be a desirable option—one that arguably aligns with the interests of most, if not all, States. Variants of such a ban have been demanded by a wide range of States, the European Parliament, thousands of AI researchers,[43] and multiple non-governmental organisations, including the Campaign to Stop Killer Robots. Crucially, bans on entire categories of weapons are not without historical precedent. For example, the Chemical Weapons Convention (CWC)and the Anti-Personnel Mine Ban Treaty (Ottawa Treaty) represent two historical achievements where broad international consensus on the limited military utility of certain weapons was outweighed by their devastating humanitarian consequences.[44]

---

[41] Zou and Schiebinger 2018.

[42] 'Spoofing' refers to the intentional injection of forged or manipulated sensor or data signals—such as counterfeit GPS coordinates, radar returns, or visual feeds—to trick an autonomous system into mis-perceiving its environment and making erroneous decisions. See Su et al. 2019; Li et al. 2016.

[43] Future of Life Institute 2016.

[44] Convention on the Prohibition of the Development, Production, Stockpiling and Use of Chemical Weapons and on their Destruction, opened for signature 13 January 1993, 1975 UNTS 45, entered

As the review of historical precedents of successful and unsuccessful arms control initiatives in the remainder of this section suggests, the success of any arms control regime—especially those that seek to ban an entire class of weapons—typically requires the fulfilment of at least two conditions: first, States must have a shared mutual interest in refraining from developing or using a certain type of weapon, and second, compliance with the agreement must be verifiable and transparent to all parties.[45] The following paragraphs will outline these conditions and assess the extent to which they apply to the regulation of AI-driven AWS.

The first condition suggested by this chapter is that States must have some mutual interest in banning a specific type of weapons system for a ban effort to succeed. Empirical evidence suggests that the relative perception of a weapon's atrociousness and military utility is a strong predictor of its successful prohibition.[46] This helps explain why chemical and biological weapons were ultimately completely and comprehensively outlawed, contrary to their nuclear counterparts.[47] The notion of advanced AI systems making life and death decisions based on inexplicable black-box predictions is deeply unsettling. However, as previously discussed, the potential military utility of increasingly autonomous systems is also extreme—making AWS arguably more comparable in nature to nuclear weapons than to cluster munitions, blinding lasers, or chemical weapons. The continued reliance on nuclear weapons, despite a series of near-catastrophic incidents, suggests that bans on entire classes of weapons are usually based on mutual agreement that their humanitarian consequences outweigh their military utility, rather than due to the risk of accidents.

Even *if* a mutual long-term interest in the ban of AWS were to emerge, States usually assess their strategic incentives from the perspective of current power dynamics. This may, in part, help explain China's emphasis on military autonomy—including in lethal applications—as AI constitutes a central element of its medium-term strategy to close the gap with the US's current military superiority.[48] The US, as one of the most successful military innovators in history, so far relies on an internal auditing framework,[49] guided by five ethics principles: 'Responsible, Equitable, Traceable, Reliable, Governable'.[50] It also references DoD Directive 3000.09,[51]

---

into force 29 April 1997 (CWC); Convention on the Prohibition of the Use, Stockpiling, Production and Transfer of Anti-Personnel Mines and on their Destruction, opened for signature 3 December 1997, 2056 UNTS 211, entered into force 1 March 1999.

45 Schelling and Halperin 1961.

46 Scharre 2018a.

47 CWC, above n. 44; Convention on the Prohibition of the Development, Production and Stockpiling of Bacteriological (Biological) and Toxin Weapons and on their Destruction, opened for signature 10 April 1972, 1015 UNTS 163, entered into force 26 March 1975.

48 Ding 2018; Kania 2019.

49 Mayer-Schönberger and Cukier 2013.

50 https://www.defense.gov/News/News-Stories/article/article/2094085/dod-adopts-5-principles-of-artificial-intelligence-ethics/. Accessed 5 May 2025.

51 U.S. Department of Defense 2023a.

which mandates the presence of 'appropriate human judgement',[52] a concept deliberately distinct from 'human *in* the loop'. Furthermore, the Directive carries no legal force and could be quickly and unilaterally revised or revoked by Pentagon leadership.[53] To understand how quickly battlefield pressures can override decades of prior policy beliefs, it is worth making a historical comparison: the US Navy had categorically rejected unrestricted submarine warfare, considering it a 'bad idea'. Yet little more than four hours after the Japanese attack on Pearl Harbor, that very order was issued to all Navy commanders—underscoring how swiftly operational realities can reshape normative frameworks.[54]

The second suggested precondition for functioning arms control regimes is verifiability. For example, the Intermediate-Range Nuclear Forces (INF) Treaty,[55] concluded between the US and the Soviet Union to ban ground-launched ballistic and cruise missiles with ranges between 500 and 5500 kms, incorporated robust verification mechanisms, including on-site inspections, satellite surveillance, and data exchanges, which helped ensure compliance and reduce mistrust between the parties. Here again, the specific AI-driven nature of AWS does not shift incentives in favour of a complete ban, since in contrast to tanks or missiles, the capabilities of military AI cannot be confidently estimated via usual channels of intelligence or reconnaissance. Moreover, transparency (e.g., through second- or third-party inspections) is unlikely to provide a viable method for verifying compliance with a legally binding treaty banning certain forms of autonomy. Algorithms and training data can easily be concealed and represent sensitive national security information that States may be unwilling to disclose to external inspectors, leading to additional instability.

From a neo-realist perspective,[56] there are two principal drivers for instability in arms races. First, power imbalances lead front-runner States to try to maintain their *relative* advantage, while less capable competitors will strive to match the respective capabilities of powerful rivals. Second, uncertainty about adversaries' actual capabilities will further drive States to improve their position by investing in the development of more sophisticated equipment. Unfortunately, once again, these boxes seem to be ticked in the context of twenty-first century great power competition over autonomy. Arguably, AWS are even more problematic than earlier generations of weaponry in this regard, as AI superiority will depend on the quality and scale of training datasets and algorithms. As a result, advancements are no longer contingent on the physical production of additional marginal units of heavy weaponry, as incremental improvements in training data and algorithm performance can translate into highly scalable improvements across a large number of weapons systems running on the same algorithms. Similarly, the non-exclusive nature of training data—and its theoretical scalability across allied militaries—may fuel distrust, as even modest

---

52 Saxon 2016.

53 Freedberg 2019.

54 Scharre 2018a.

55 Intermediate-Range Nuclear Forces (INF) Treaty, signed 8 December 1987, UNTS Volume 1657, No. 28521, entered into force on 1 June 1988.

56 Waltz 1979.

increases in data quality could lead to exponential improvements among *all* one's adversaries.

Where two or more States share a mutual interest in preventing the escalatory spiral of an arms race but do not want to ban a whole class of weapon altogether, they can pursue bilateral or multilateral arms control agreements to avoid excessive expenditure and reduce the risk of inadvertent escalation.[57] Historically, such agreements could prohibit a certain capability or property of a weapon system—such as the range of nuclear-capable cruise missiles under the aforementioned INF Treaty,[58] the size of strategic nuclear arsenals, as negotiated in the Strategic Arms Limitation Talks (SALT),[59] or the amount of heavy armour deployed in a given theatre as under the Treaty on Conventional Armed Forces in Europe.[60] Applied to AWS, States could, for example, agree to prohibit a specific capability of AWS, such as the fully autonomous engagement of human targets without MHC. However, such provisions may prove difficult to verify, as States might attempt to implement hidden fully autonomous modes or covertly develop anti-personnel targeting functionalities through dual-use technologies, such as facial recognition systems. Furthermore, partial bans or unit limits for military exercises, similar to the confidence- and security-building measures contained in the Vienna Document,[61] would only be partially effective in this domain, since researchers have already managed to conduct reinforcement learning for helicopter flight using only simulated data.[62] This means that significant advancements in autonomy may occur outside of observable real-world testing environments.

As such, there is a high risk that the black box nature of neural networks will lead to a double veil of uncertainty, where major powers are not only confronted with uncertainty regarding their adversaries' capabilities but also about the relative capabilities of their *own* systems. If one lesson is to be drawn from the Cold War era—and, more recently, the demise of the INF Treaty—it is that meaningful verification and compliance monitoring mechanisms are essential to the success of any arms control regime. Unfortunately, the prospects for a comprehensive verification arms control regime of AWS appear grim. This stems both from low levels of trust in the current geopolitical landscape and from the difficulties traditional arms control mechanisms face in addressing the inherent technical properties of AWS. Indeed, States will be reluctant to reveal their sensitive algorithms and training data—even

[57] Schelling and Halperin 1961.

[58] INF, above n. 52.

[59] Interim Agreement on Strategic Offensive Arms and the Anti-Ballistic Missile Treaty (SALT I), signed by the United States and the Soviet Union on 26 May 1972, UNTS, Volume 944, No. 13445, entered into force on 3 October 1972; Strategic Arms Limitation Talks II Treaty (SALT II), signed by the United States and the Soviet Union on 18 June 1979, not ratified but informally observed until 1986.

[60] Treaty on Conventional Armed Forces in Europe (CFE), signed 19 November 1990, entered into force 9 November 1992.

[61] Vienna Document 1990 of the Negotiations on Confidence- and Security-Building Measures, adopted by the OSCE participating States on 17 November 1990.

[62] Ng et al. 2006.

to presumably independent inspectors—while adversaries will sceptically eye their rivals' dual-use potential.

12.5 Empirical Developments & Ways Forward: National Legislation and Industry Self-Regulation

The pessimistic outlook for the regulation of AWS derived from our theoretical framework corresponds with the recent developments in UN deliberations on how to govern these systems effectively. The issue has been a matter of international concern since at least 2014 when discussions commenced within the framework of the CCW in Geneva.[63] However, since 2019, when High Contracting Parties to the CCW reached a consensus on the related UN Guiding Principles,[64] which primarily reiterated existing international laws, there has been a lack of significant progress. Russia's illegal war of aggression against Ukraine has further escalated tensions within this forum, subsequently diminishing the likelihood of reaching a consensus.[65] From a realist perspective, 'institutions are basically a reflection of the distribution of power in the world'.[66] It is, therefore, unsurprising that the GGE LAWS mirrors ongoing geopolitical rivalries and remains heavily influenced by the broader geopolitical environment. In this context, the current 'arms control ice age' is particularly detrimental to the prospects of achieving meaningful multilateral regulation of AWS.[67]

In light of these challenges, it is crucial to consider what incentives might drive States—and, increasingly, corporate actors—to pursue self-regulation as an alternative in the absence of binding multilateral agreements. For States, such incentives may include the desire to preserve strategic stability, uphold international legitimacy, and mitigate the risks of unintended escalation or accidents involving AWS.[68] For corporate actors, reputational concerns, market access, and pressure from civil society or shareholders may serve as motivating factors to adhere to ethical standards and avoid contributing to destabilising technologies.[69] A responsible actor, in this context, can be understood as one that acknowledges these broader security, ethical, and legal implications and actively seeks to shape the development and deployment of AWS in accordance with established norms and principles, even where legal obligations are lacking. The notion of responsibility is thus closely tied to restraint: responsible actors recognise that short-term gains in military or technological advantage may

63 CCW, above n. 8.

64 GGE LAWS 2019.

65 Hoffberger-Pippan et al. 2022.

66 Mearsheimer 1994.

67 Sauer 2022.

68 Sauer 2020.

69 Baydas 2025.

contribute to a long-term erosion of arms control norms and a potentially uncontrollable escalation in autonomy-driven arms competition. As such, the following section investigates how these actors—States and industry—might chart alternative paths to mitigate the dangers of an unregulated arms race driven by increasingly higher levels of autonomy in lethal combat systems.

12.5.1 National Regulation

Due to the absence of international regulation on AWS, broader attention must turn to the national regulatory frameworks that shape how States themselves govern the military use of AI technologies. It is of paramount importance to differentiate between morally contentious applications of AI—such as the autonomous targeting of human beings—and other uses of autonomy, such as support tools providing combatants on the battlefield with real-time information and enhanced situational awareness that could be legitimate depending on the concrete circumstances.[70] Therefore, policymakers would be well-advised to set national standards for military AI, thereby claiming the first-mover advantage. For instance, the EU's pioneering role in data protection regulation through the General Data Protection Regulation (GDPR),[71] and possibly in a similar fashion with the AI Act,[72] demonstrates how setting standards can *de facto* impact developments beyond the geographical regulatory scope of these instruments—the so-called 'Brussels's effect'—instead of conceding the first-mover advantage to less reliable actors.

Another advantage of adopting national military AI standards is its potential to foster cooperation among like-minded States. Thus, domestic discussions on regulating military AI could be complemented by a 'coalition of the willing' cooperation to collectively address the moral, ethical, and legal challenges posed by increasing levels of autonomy in future warfare. Many States already support a 'two-tier' approach, which includes both prohibitions and regulations; however, the specific details of these measures still need to be thoroughly debated.[73] Thus, national documents or legislation could be used to identify common ground among partner States and advance the development of a common understanding on AWS regulation.

In fact, several States have already adopted national approaches without hampering ongoing international consultations on the issue. France, for example, adopted the 2021 position of its national ethics committee on AWS as official

---

[70] https://www.icrc.org/en/document/icrc-position-autonomous-weapon-systems. Accessed 30 April 2025.

[71] Gunst and De Ville 2021.

[72] Siegmann and Anderljung 2022.

[73] Bruun 2024.

policy.[74] The US issued DoD Directive 3000.09 in 2012 and released its third iteration in 2023.[75] Similarly, the UK published its strategy on 'AI-enabled capability in Defence' in June 2022.[76] Although discussions within the GGE LAWS remain stalled due to geopolitical tensions, particularly among major powers, smaller and middle powers have made attempts to bridge divides within and beyond the UN. Within the UN, the First Committee of the UN General Assembly (UNGA) was added as an additional forum in 2023 to address AWS, where Austria,[77] together with mostly small and middle powers, co-sponsored the first UN resolution on lethal AWS.[78] Since the UNGA only requires a relative majority, unlike the consensus-based approach of the GGE LAWS, it was chosen as an additional forum. A total of 161 States voted in favour of the UN resolution, which expressed concern over 'the serious challenges and concerns that new and emerging technological applications in the military domain',[79] albeit without mandating any concrete regulatory measures. The UN resolution has thus far had limited effect on the major military powers most invested in developing AWS—apparently proving Mearsheimer's 'False Promise of International Institutions'.[80] However, to build on the UN's efforts, the United Nations Institute for Disarmament Research (UNIDIR) hosted the inaugural Global Conference on AI, Security and Ethics in March 2025, bringing together nearly 500 diplomats, policymakers, military leaders, industry experts, academics, and civil society representatives.[81]

Beyond the UN framework, several States have taken the initiative to convene regional and international fora aimed at bringing together like-minded States. These efforts underscore a growing commitment among diverse nations to collaboratively address the ethical, legal, and security challenges posed by AWS. For instance, Austria hosted the Vienna Conference on Autonomous Weapons Systems,[82] Costa Rica organised the Latin American and the Caribbean Conference of Social and

---

[74] Ministère des Armées 2021.

[75] U.S. Department of Defense 2023a.

[76] UK Ministry of Defence 2022.

[77] Austria on 11 October 2023 submitted a draft resolution on behalf of the following countries: Belgium, Cabo Verde, Costa Rica, Croatia, Ecuador, Germany, Hungary, Iceland, Ireland, Italy, Kazakhstan, Kiribati, Liechtenstein, Luxembourg, Malta, Mexico, the Netherlands (Kingdom of the Netherlands), New Zealand, North Macedonia, Norway, the Philippines, San Marino, Sierra Leone, Sri Lanka, Switzerland, and Trinidad and Tobago. Subsequently, the following countries also joined as co-sponsors of the draft resolution: Antigua and Barbuda, the Bahamas, Barbados, Belize, Bulgaria, Cyprus, Czechia, Denmark, the Dominican Republic, Fiji, Guatemala, Honduras, the Maldives, Montenegro, the Republic of Moldova, and Slovenia.

[78] UNGA 2023a, para 79.

[79] UNGA 2023b, p. 1.

[80] Mearsheimer 1994.

[81] https://unidir.org/event/global-conference-on-ai-security-and-ethics-2025/. Accessed 2 February 2025.

[82] https://www.bmeia.gv.at/en/european-foreign-policy/disarmament/conventional-arms/autonomous-weapons-systems/2024-vienna-conference-on-autonomous-weapons-systems. Accessed 1 September 2024.

Humanitarian Impact of Autonomous Weapons, which culminated in the publication of the 'Belén Communiqué',[83] endorsed by 30 other States, and the Philippines convened the Manila Meeting on Indo-Pacific Perspectives on Autonomous Weapons Systems.[84] The two REAIM summits in The Hague and Seoul should be mentioned in this context as well.

12.5.2 Industry Self-Regulation

While discussions on the regulation of AWS often focus on States and international institutions, growing attention is being paid to the role of the defence industry. It is frequently seen as an actor that must be tamed.[85] However, recent developments suggest that industry is already participating in ethical deliberations, as could be observed at the REAIM Summit, held in The Hague in 2023,[86] and its follow-up session in South Korea in 2024. REAIM describes itself as 'the most comprehensive and inclusive platform for AI in the military domain',[87] a claim that is substantiated by the inclusion of a variety of stakeholders, such as governments, ministries, academics, civil society, and the defence industry.

In the absence of binding international standards, domestic initiatives have emerged to address the regulatory gap. For example, the Federal Association of the German Security and Defence Industry (BDSV), in collaboration with scientists from the Fraunhofer-Gesellschaft Institute and the University of the Bundeswehr Munich, has called for national regulation to ensure that military AI research is based on a foundation of societal acceptability and predictability.[88] Procedurally, comprehensive legislative research and self-regulation on AWS could further legitimise such efforts and foster public trust. This facilitates popular support domestically, bringing audiences onboard, which is crucial to prevent science fiction-driven alarmism such as the hysteria observed in Germany during past debates on armed drones.[89]

The defence industry would be wise not to wait on whether national regulation may ultimately converge and eventually pave the way for a unified international legal standard. Responsible defence actors should instead proactively engage with existing frameworks to ensure ethical engineering practices and maintain MHC, both by design and in operational use. One noteworthy effort in this regard is the EU's

---

[83] https://conferenciaawscostarica2023.com/wp-content/uploads/2023/02/EN-Communique-of-La-Ribera-de-Belen-Costa-Rica-February-23-24-2023.pdf. Accessed 31 January 2025.

[84] Philippines 2023.

[85] Hoffberger-Pippan and Vohs 2023.

[86] https://www.government.nl/ministries/ministry-of-foreign-affairs/activiteiten/reaim. Accessed 1 September 2024.

[87] https://thereadable.co/reaim-blueprint-for-responsible-ai-use-military/. Accessed 31 January 2025.

[88] Brink 2023.

[89] Franke and Scheidt 2020.

Assessment List for Trustworthy AI (ALTAI).[90] While ALTAI is primarily designed for civilian AI applications, it can also support AI developers, senior management, and legal experts in complying with the seven non-binding criteria for Trustworthy AI, which also inform the EU AI Act.[91] Although drafted for civilian AI applications, ALTAI has already been applied to the military domain. The Future Combat Air System Forum on ethical considerations, for example, explicitly applied this method and concluded that for the use case of 'target detection, recognition, and identification,' approximately 90% of the questions under the criterion 'transparency and accountability' are applicable.[92] Moreover, the EU-funded AI4DEF project developed a similar approach by adapting ALTAI specifically to military use cases.[93] This initiative was also presented at the 2024 REAIM Summit.[94] Hence, ALTAI is one example of taking existing (civilian) AI standards and developing adapted principles for the military sector. It could serve as a valuable starting point for implementing such principles not only in the deployment of AWS but also during the research and development stages.

To establish a framework for Trustworthy AI as outlined by ALTAI, it is essential to consider three key aspects: ethical soundness, legal compliance, and robustness. Building on these pillars, the High-Level Expert Group on Artificial Intelligence (HLEG AI) has developed seven key principles for Trustworthy AI: (1) human agency and oversight; (2) technical robustness and safety; (3) privacy and data governance; (4) transparency; (5) diversity, non-discrimination, and fairness; (6) societal and environmental well-being; and (7) accountability. The HLEG AI uses a combination of technical and non-technical methods to adhere to these principles throughout the lifecycle of a weapon system.[95] Thereby, ALTAI follows this multi-dimensional 'control by design' and 'control in use' concept, as developed by the international Panel on the Regulation of Autonomous Weapons (iPRAW). Between 2017 and 2022, iPRAW functioned as an interdisciplinary conglomerate of researchers investigating various aspects of AWS, including IHL, ethical, technological, military, political science, and security policy considerations.

In 2019, iPRAW outlined a helpful concept for the conditions of human control, arguing that there cannot be a one-size-fits-all approach.[96] Instead, both *control by design* (technical control) and *control in use* (operational control) are needed, depending on the operational context. For example, the requirements for defensive systems deployed at sea—where there are fewer risks to civilians—may be significantly lower than for offensive systems operating in densely populated urban

[90] European Commission High Level Expert Group on Artificial Intelligence 2020.

[91] Vohs 2023.

[92] Azzano et al. 2021.

[93] https://ai4def.com/about-us/. Accessed 1 September 2024.

[94] Panel discussion titled 'Trustworthy AI for Defence: Implementing the EU's Assessment List for Trustworthy AI (ALTAI) within the EDIDP Project AI4DEF', https://www.youtube.com/watch?v=FUEbixoFRa. Accessed 31 January 2025.

[95] EU High-Level Expert Group on AI 2019.

[96] iPRAW 2019.

combat zones.[97] At the technical level, commanders must be able to monitor information about the system and its operational environment. Crucially, human intervention in target selection and engagement must remain possible. At the operational level, adequate monitoring must be in place, and the authority and accountability of human actors must be clearly established. The Stockholm International Peace Research Institute has described similar criteria, such as 'control over weapon parameters', 'control over environment', and 'control through human–machine interaction'.[98] Taken together, these elements seek to ensure MHC over targeting decisions throughout the entire lifecycle of a weapon system. This concept does not necessarily require a binding international regulation or an outright ban on AWS, rather it mandates responsible companies and States to adopt their own framework and act accordingly.

12.5.3 Risks and Mitigation Measures

However, industry self-regulation and national legislation in the context of military AI may present certain pitfalls, especially if they become alternatives to multilateral governance instead of complementary measures. The risks lie in fragmenting global norms, undermining trust, and exacerbating geopolitical inequalities. Diverging national standards could lead to a lack of coherence in global governance, eroding international cooperation, and creating regulatory competition that prioritises economic or strategic interests over ethical considerations. Joint efforts—such as defence cooperation within the EU through the European Defence Fund—could be hampered by diverging national approaches to military AI regulation.[99] As evidenced by the shift from the GGE LAWS to alternative forums, power asymmetries between major and smaller powers have become increasingly apparent. These imbalances should not be further exacerbated by fragmenting the international community or establishing divergent standards without the inclusion of major military powers. Furthermore, reliance on industry self-regulation could allow private actors to shape norms driven by market incentives rather than principles of accountability, fairness, and security. This could potentially undermine public trust and weaken ethical oversight in the development and deployment of military AI systems. Such 'greenwashing' of ethical military standards would be counterproductive in the global race to develop trustworthy military AI.

Therefore, measures to mitigate the risks associated with industry self-regulation and national legislation in military AI governance must be implemented to strengthen accountability, transparency, and adherence to ethical standards. Primarily, confidence-building measures, such as transparency, notification,

---

[97] https://lieber.westpoint.edu/targeting-urban-environment-why-weaponeering-tactics-matter. Accessed 30 April 2025.

[98] Boulanin et al. 2020.

[99] Csernatoni 2024.

and monitoring at the unilateral, bilateral, and/or multilateral level, should be adopted to build trust.[100] For instance, mandatory third-party audits could serve as external checks on self-regulatory practices, ensuring that commitments are not merely superficial or performative, but grounded in verifiable compliance. Transparent reporting requirements would also be critical, obliging companies to disclose their AI development processes, risk assessments, and mitigation strategies, which would enable public scrutiny and foster trust.

Multi-stakeholder oversight, involving governments, international organisations, civil society, and independent experts, could provide a balanced perspective and prevent the defence industry from interpreting ethical or legal principles in an overly narrow or selective manner. Lessons drawn from failures of self-regulation within other sectors, such as the civilian Big Tech industry, highlight the importance of proactive verification and enforcement mechanisms, as well as the dangers of allowing market incentives or strategic interests to supersede broader societal and ethical responsibilities. By adopting these measures, self-regulation could become a more credible and effective component of military AI governance, complementing ongoing efforts toward multilateral agreements.

To sum up, the more companies and States adopt responsible frameworks together with partners, the more convergence among key concepts is likely to emerge—tested in real-world applications rather than confined to discussions at a UN roundtable. In turn, this may help to partially overcome the current stalemate in reaching international consensus on a legally binding instrument to regulate AWS.

12.6 Conclusion

This chapter has examined the evolving role of autonomy in future warfare, concluding that both battlefield pressures and the innate properties of deep learning algorithms are likely to incentivise States to adopt increasingly autonomous capabilities, including for AWS. Given the ethical and legal implications—as well as the risk of inadvertent escalation and arms race dynamics—this chapter has subsequently argued that while some form of multilateral regulation of AWS would be theoretically desirable, it remains unrealistic to be meaningfully achieved in the short- or medium-term. Due to this pessimistic outlook towards reaching international consensus, this chapter argues that responsible military powers should complement their continued efforts to establish international frameworks with rigorous national regulation and 'coalition of the willing' cooperation. This approach would allow States to appropriately address the ethical, legal, and strategic challenges posed by increasing levels of autonomy in future warfare through domestic legislation and the adaptation of national export control regimes. However, while strategy may offer a pragmatic alternative in a world where no comprehensive multilateral agreement might be reached, it is essential to recognise the risk that such developments could

[100] Horowitz and Scharre 2021.

exacerbate existing global power asymmetries. More powerful or influential States and defence companies may have greater influence over the development and implementation of regulatory frameworks, thereby potentially sidelining less powerful actors. When engaging in such formats, it is therefore important to design an inclusive approach which balances the interests of different stakeholders. For instance, the 2024 REAIM II Summit demonstrated that powerful actors can collaborate with smaller military actors: South Korea co-hosted the event alongside the Netherlands, Singapore, Kenya, and the UK.

Moreover, this chapter proposes that self-regulation of the defence industry could serve as a feasible and desirable second-best alternative, for example, by taking existing soft law standards—such as ALTAI, originally developed for the civilian domain—and applying ethical defence engineering standards. For such an approach to succeed, however, it is essential that the readiness of the defence industry to engage in (self-)regulatory debate is complemented by external oversight mechanisms and public accountability. As observed in the civilian domain, frameworks like ALTAI demonstrate that self-regulation has the potential to promote ethical standards while allowing for innovation and flexibility in response to emerging technologies.

In the absence of meaningful multilateral agreement, such a dual-track approach—combining national regulation and industry self-regulation—may no longer be optional, but a necessary last resort. By capitalising on the synergies between these different approaches, responsible innovator powers could not only embed ethical and legal principles into the design and deployment of AWS and their rules of application, but also secure the public trust required to sustain the degree of innovation necessary to keep up with one's adversaries in an evolving global security environment.

References

Articles, Books and Other Documents

Azzano M, Boria S, Brunessaux S, Carron B, De Cacqueray A, Gloeden S, Keisinger F, Krach B, Mohrdieck S (2021) The Responsible Use of Artificial Intelligence in FCAS – An Initial Assessment. https://www.fcas-forum.eu/articles/responsible-use-of-artificial-intelligence-in-fcas/. Accessed 25 January 2025

Baydas L (2025) Human Rights Due Diligence Within the Arms Industry: Challenges, Practices and Opportunities. Business and Human Rights Journal, First View, pp. 1–7

Bendett S (2023) Military AI developments in Russia. In: The AI Wave in Defence Innovation. Routledge, London, pp. 179–198

Boulanin V, Davison N, Goussac N, Carlsson MP (2020) Limits on autonomy in weapon systems: Identifying practical elements of human control. https://www.sipri.org/sites/default/files/2020-06/2006_limits_of_autonomy.pdf. Accessed 31 January 2025

Brink N (2023) Rüstungsindustrie und Forschung fordern nationale militärische KI-Strategie [The defense industry and research call for a national military AI strategy]. https://www.fr.de/politik/ruestungsindustrie-forschung-ki-kuenstliche-intelligenz-waffen-strategie-tbl-zr-92366213.html. Accessed 6 August 2025

Bruun L (2024) Reinventing the wheel: the AWS debate and existing arms control agreements. https://blogs.icrc.org/law-and-policy/2024/06/13/reinventing-the-wheel-three-lessons-that-the-aws-debate-can-learn-from-existing-arms-control-agreements/. Accessed 16 August 2024
Cooney M (2015) Can drones hunt with wolf pack-like success? DARPA thinks so. https://www.networkworld.com/article/934886/can-drones-hunt-with-wolf-pack-like-success-darpa-thinks-so.html. Accessed 29 August 2024
Csernatoni R (2024) Governing Military AI Amid a Geopolitical Minefield. https://carnegieendowment.org/research/2024/07/governing-military-ai-amid-a-geopolitical-minefield?lang=en&center=europe. Accessed 15 January 2025
DARPA (2018) Collaborative operations in denied environment (code). https://www.darpa.mil/research/programs/collaborative-operations-in-denied-environment. Accessed 25 January 2025
Davies P (2024) NATO begins its €1 billion investment in AI, space and robotics. https://www.euronews.com/next/2024/06/18/nato-begins-its-1-billion-investment-in-ai-space-and-robotics-defence-tech. Accessed 16 August 2024
Davis SI (2022) Artificial intelligence at the operational level of war. Defense & Security Analysis 38(1):74–90
Ding J (2018) Deciphering China's AI dream. https://www.fhi.ox.ac.uk/wp-content/uploads/Deciphering_Chinas_AI-Dream.pdf. Accessed 3 February 2025
EU High-Level Expert Group on AI (2019) Ethics guidelines for trustworthy AI | Shaping Europe's digital future. https://digital-strategy.ec.europa.eu/en/library/ethics-guidelines-trustworthy-ai. Accessed 2 September 2024
European Commission High Level Expert Group on Artificial Intelligence (2020) Assessment List for Trustworthy Artificial Intelligence (ALTAI) for self-assessment. https://digital-strategy.ec.europa.eu/en/library/assessment-list-trustworthy-artificial-intelligence-altai-self-assessment. Accessed 31 January 2025
Franke U, Scheidt S (2020) Zur aktuellen Drohnendebatte - Überblick und Einschätzung bewaffneter Drohnen für Deutschland [On the Current Drone Debate – Overview and Assessment of Armed Drones for Germany]. https://gids-hamburg.de/wp-content/uploads/2020/06/GIDSstatement2020_04_Franke_Scheidt.pdf. Accessed 31 January 2025
Freedberg Jr. SJ (2019) Fear & Loathing In AI: How The Army Triggered Fears Of Killer Robots. https://breakingdefense.com/2019/03/fear-loathing-in-ai-how-the-army-triggered-fears-of-killer-robots/. Accessed 1 September 2024
Future of Life Institute (2016) Autonomous Weapons Open Letter: AI & Robotics Researchers. https://futureoflife.org/open-letter/open-letter-autonomous-weapons-ai-robotics/. Accessed 1 September 2024
Geist E, Massicot D (2019) Understanding Putin's Nuclear "Superweapons". SAIS Review of International Affairs 39(2);103–117
Gettinger D, Michel AH (2017) Loitering munitions. https://dronecenter.bard.edu/files/2017/02/CSD-Loitering-Munitions.pdf. Accessed 31 January 2025
GGE LAWS (2019) Report of the 2019 session of the Group of Governmental Experts on Emerging Technologies in the Area of Lethal Autonomous Weapons Systems. https://documents.unoda.org/wp-content/uploads/2020/09/CCW_GGE.1_2019_3_E.pdf. Accessed 25 January 2025
Gregory D (2011) From a view to a kill: Drones and late modern war. Theory, culture & society 28(7-8):188–215
Grimal F, Sundaram J (2018) Combat drones: Hives, swarms, and autonomous action? Journal of Conflict and Security Law 23(1):105–135
Gunst S, De Ville F (2021) The Brussels Effect: How the GDPR Conquered Silicon Valley. EERR 26(3):437–458
Hambling D (2024) Jam-Proof Fiber Optic Drone Testing In Ukraine. https://www.forbes.com/sites/davidhambling/2024/08/02/german-jam-proof-fiber-optic-drone-testing-in-ukraine/. Accessed 29 August 2024

Hess R, Visschers VH, Siegrist M, Keller C (2011) How do people perceive graphical risk communication? The role of subjective numeracy. Journal of Risk Research 14(1):47–61

Hoffberger-Pippan E, Vohs V (2023) Taming the Lions: The Role of Industry in the Debate on Autonomous Weapon Systems (AWS). http://opiniojuris.org/2023/04/25/taming-the-lions-the-role-of-industry-in-the-debate-on-autonomous-weapon-systems-aws/. Accessed 31 January 2025

Hoffberger-Pippan E, Vohs V, Köhler P (2022) Autonomous weapons systems: UN expert talks facing failure time to consider alternative formats. SWP Comment 2022/C 43

Holland Michel A (2020) The black box, unlocked: Predictability and understandability in military AI. https://unidir.org/publication/the-black-box-unlocked/. Accessed 12 November 2024

Horowitz M, Scharre P (2021) AI and International Stability: Risks and Confidence-Building Measures. https://www.cnas.org/publications/reports/ai-and-international-stability-risks-and-confidence-building-measures. Accessed 31 January 2025

Hunter LY, Albert CD, Henningan C, Rutland J (2023) The military application of artificial intelligence technology in the United States, China, and Russia and the implications for global security. Defense & Security Analysis 39(2):207–232

iPRAW (2019) Focus on Human Control ("Focus on" Report No. 5). https://nbn-resolving.org/urn:nbn:de:0168-ssoar-77410-6. Accessed 25 January 2025

Kania EB (2019) Chinese Military Innovation in the AI Revolution. The RUSI Journal 164(5-6):26–34

Kim K, Bae S, Huh K (2010) Intelligent surveillance and security robot systems. 2010 IEEE Workshop on Advanced Robotics and its Social Impacts, Seoul, pp. 70–73

Larson J, Denford JS, Dawson GS, Desouza KC (2024) The evolution of artificial intelligence (AI) spending by the U.S. government. https://www.brookings.edu/articles/the-evolution-of-artificial-intelligence-ai-spending-by-the-u-s-government/. Accessed 16 August 2024

Li L, Feng X, Boulkenafet Z et al. (2016) An original face anti-spoofing approach using partial convolutional neural network. 2016 Sixth International Conference on Image Processing Theory, Tools and Applications (IPTA), Oulu, Finland, pp. 1–6s

Lin J, Singer PW (2018) China is making 1,000-UAV drone swarms now. https://www.popsci.com/china-drone-swarms/. Accessed 29 August 2024

Mayer-Schönberger V, Cukier K (2013) Big data: A revolution that will transform how we live, work, and think. Houghton Mifflin Harcourt, Boston, MA

McIntosh SE (2011) The wingman-philosopher of MiG alley: John Boyd and the OODA loop. Air Power History 58(4):24–33

Mearsheimer JJ (1994) The False Promise of International Institutions. International Security 19(3):5-49

Ministère des Armées (2021) Defence Ethics Committee: Opinion on the Integration of Autonomy into Lethal Weapon Systems. https://www.defense.gouv.fr/sites/default/files/ministere-armees/20210429_Comit%C3%A9%20d%27%C3%A9thique%20de%20la%20d%C3%A9fense%20-%20Avis%20int%C3%A9gration%20autonomie%20syst%C3%A8mes%20armes%20l%C3%A9taux%20-%20Version%20anglaise.pdf.pdf. Accessed 25 January 2025

Mozur P, Satariano A (2024) A.I. Begins Ushering In an Age of Killer Robots. https://www.nytimes.com/2024/07/02/technology/ukraine-war-ai-weapons.html. Accessed 29 August 2024

Ng AY, Coates A, Diel M et al. (2006) Autonomous inverted helicopter flight via reinforcement learning. In: Ang MH, Khatib O (eds) Experimental Robotics IX. Springer Tracts in Advanced Robotics, vol 21, pp. 363–372

Philippines (2023) Inputs from the Philippines: United Nations Secretary General Report on Resolution 78/241 (Lethal autonomous weapons systems). https://docs-library.unoda.org/General_Assembly_First_Committee_-Seventy-Ninth_session_(2024)/78-241-Philippines-EN.pdf. Accessed 25 January 2025

Roth EM, Hanson ML, Hopkins C, Mancuso V, Zacharias GL (2004) Human in the loop evaluation of a mixed-initiative system for planning and control of multiple UAV teams. Proceedings of the Human Factors and Ergonomics Society Annual Meeting, 48(3):280-284

Ruitenberg R (2024) Small drones will soon lose combat advantage, French Army chief says. https://www.defensenews.com/global/europe/2024/06/19/small-drones-will-soon-lose-combat-advantage-french-army-chief-says/. Accessed 29 August 2024

Sauer F (2020) Stepping back from the brink: Why multilateral regulation of autonomy in weapons systems is difficult, yet imperative and feasible. International Review of the Red Cross 102, pp. 235–259

Sauer F (2022) Uncrewed systems: armaments, control and arms control. https://metis.unibw.de/assets/pdf/metis-study28-2022_06-uncrewed_systems.pdf. Accessed 31 January 2025

Saxon D (2016) A human touch: autonomous weapons, DoD Directive 3000.09 and the interpretation of 'appropriate levels of human judgment over the use of force'. In: Bhuta N, Beck S, Geiβ R, Liu H-Y, Kreβ C (eds) Autonomous Weapons Systems: Law, Ethics, Policy. Cambridge University Press, Cambridge, pp. 185–208

Scharre P (2018a) Army of none: Autonomous weapons and the future of war. WW Norton & Company, New York City

Scharre P (2018b) How swarming will change warfare. Bulletin of the atomic scientists 74(6):385–389

Scharre P (2021) Debunking the AI Arms Race Theory. Texas National Security Review, 4(3):121-132

Schelling TC, Halperin MH (1961) Strategy and Arms Control. Twentieth Century Fund, New York City

Siegmann C, Anderljung M (2022) The Brussels Effect and Artificial Intelligence: How EU regulation will impact the global AI market. arXiv:220812645

Su J, Vargas DV, Sakurai K (2019) One pixel attack for fooling deep neural networks. IEEE Transactions on Evolutionary Computation 23(5):828–84s

Taddeo M, Floridi L (2018) Regulate artificial intelligence to avert cyber arms race. Nature 556:296–298

Tucker P (2017) What the CIA's tech director wants from AI. https://www.defenseone.com/technology/2017/09/cia-technology-director-artificial-intelligence/140801/. Accessed 25 January 2025

UK Ministry of Defence (2022) Ambitious, Safe, Responsible. Our approach to the delivery of AI enabled capability in Defence. https://assets.publishing.service.gov.uk/government/uploads/system/uploads/attachment_data/file/1082991/20220614-Ambitious_Safe_and_Responsible.pdf. Accessed 25 January 2025

UNGA (2023a) General and complete disarmament - Report of the First Committee. A/78/409. https://documents.un.org/doc/undoc/gen/n23/347/86/pdf/n2334786.pdf. Accessed 31 January 2025

UNGA (2023b) Resolution adopted by the General Assembly on 22 December 2023. A/RES/78/241. https://digitallibrary.un.org/record/4033027/files/A_RES_78_241-EN.pdf. Accessed 30 January 2025

US Department of Defense (2018) Nuclear posture review. https://media.defense.gov/2018/feb/02/2001872886/-1/-1/1/2018-nuclear-posture-review-final-report.pdf. Accessed 25 January 2025

US Department of Defense (2023a) US Department of Defense Directive 3000.09 - Autonomy in Weapon Systems. https://www.esd.whs.mil/portals/54/documents/dd/issuances/dodd/300009p.pdf. Accessed 25 January 2025

US Department of Defense (2023b) Data, Analytics, and Artificial Intelligence Adoption Strategy. https://media.defense.gov/2023/Nov/02/2003333300/-1/-1/1/DOD_DATA_ANALYTICS_AI_ADOPTION_STRATEGY.PDF. Accessed 1 September 2024

Vohs V (2023) Europäische Regulierungsoptionen Künstlicher Intelligenz im militärischen Kontext [European Regulatory Options for Artificial Intelligence in the Military Context]. In: Hoffberger-Pippan E, Ladeck R, Ivankovics P (eds) Digitalisierung und Recht. Nomos Verlagsgesellschaft mbH & Co. KG, Baden-Baden, pp. 53–80

Waltz KN (1979) Theory of International Politics. Random House, New York City

Wilkins DE, Desimone R (1993) Applying an AI planner to military operations planning. https://apps.dtic.mil/sti/pdfs/ADA461043.pdf. Accessed 25 January 2025

Xuanzun L (2019) Chinese helicopter drones capable of intelligent swarm attacks - Global Times. https://www.globaltimes.cn/page/201905/1149168.shtml. Accessed 29 August 2024

Zou J, Schiebinger L (2018) AI can be sexist and racist—it's time to make it fair. https://www.nature.com/articles/d41586-018-05707-8. Accessed 15 December 2024

Marcel Schliebs is a doctoral candidate in Social Data Science at the University of Oxford and Researcher on the Programme on Democracy & Technology at the Oxford Internet Institute. He previously completed an MSc in Social Data Science at the University of Oxford and a B.A. in Politics, Administration & International Relations at Zeppelin University.

Vanessa Vohs is a doctoral candidate at the University of the Bundeswehr Munich under the supervision of PD Dr Frank Sauer, as well as an associated member at the Institute for International Law of Peace and Armed Conflict Law (IFHV) Bochum. She holds a LL.M. in International Law from the London School of Economics (LSE) and a B.A. in International Relations, as well as an additional certificate in Latin American studies from TU Dresden and Hebrew University Jerusalem.

Chapter 13
Between Negligence and Malfunction: How to Address Responsibility for AI Failures

Bérénice Boutin

Contents

Abstract The deployment of artificial intelligence (AI) systems, particularly those employing machine learning (ML), introduces significant complexities in allocating responsibility when these systems fail, especially in high-stakes contexts such as military operations. This chapter examines how State obligations under international law, particularly due diligence obligations, intersect with the challenges posed by AI failures. It explores the blurred lines between human errors and technical malfunctions, highlighting how the inherent unpredictability of AI systems challenges traditional legal concepts such as negligence, risk, foreseeability, and reasonableness. The analysis addresses the lifecycle of AI systems, specifying the content of due diligence

B. Boutin (✉)
T.M.C. Asser Instituut, The Hague, The Netherlands
e-mail: b.boutin@asser.nl

University of Amsterdam, Amsterdam, The Netherlands

B. Boutin et al. (eds.), *Legal, Ethical, and Technical Dilemmas in Military Artificial Intelligence*, https://doi.org/10.1007/978-94-6265-759-5_13

obligations across the stages of design, development, adoption, and deployment. It highlights the need for rigorous technical standards, robust testing, and comprehensive risk assessments to ensure compliance with international law. By rethinking the application of due diligence obligations in light of AI's unique characteristics, the chapter provides a framework for States to fulfil their legal obligations while addressing the novel risks posed by AI technologies.

Keywords Responsibility · Artificial Intelligence · Due Diligence · Risk · Foreseeability · Errors · Malfunctions · Control

13.1 Introduction

The rapid development and deployment of artificial intelligence (AI) systems, particularly those involving machine learning (ML), bring to the forefront significant challenges related to predictability, reliability, and responsibility. AI systems are susceptible to failures, whereby unexpected, unintended, or unforeseen outcomes result in harmful consequences, including violations of international law. Specifically in the military context, the quest for greater accuracy and faster decision making through the adoption of AI across military functions can come at the cost of introducing new types of errors and malfunctions.[1] When these failures occur, one of the key challenges lies in the allocation of responsibility.

This chapter addresses the question of State responsibility under international law in relation to AI failures. In the context of ML-based AI systems (ML-AI), the implementation of obligations placed on States during the stages of development and deployment must account for the inherent unpredictability and potential for emergent behaviour. While States have an obligation to ensure that AI systems are designed and used in accordance with International Humanitarian Law (IHL) and International Human Rights Law (IHRL),[2] ML-AI systems' ability to learn, adapt, and operate autonomously introduces novel and unique complexities. In particular, AI technologies challenge existing legal frameworks and invite us to rethink fundamental concepts such as negligence, risk, foreseeability, and reasonableness.

When a malfunction or error arises in the operation of an AI system, assigning responsibility based on the limited control exercised by the human operator of the system can amount to scapegoating and often fails to address the underlying issues with the AI system itself. Shifting responsibility solely to the designer of the system also presents shortcomings, as not every outcome can be predicted as the stage of design. Such approaches can also fail to achieve important functions of responsibility, such as prevention and deterrence of harmful conduct. At the same time, a responsibility gap can arise if no entity is held accountable for AI failures because States deflect responsibility by attributing the wrongful outcome solely to the AI

[1] Atherton 2022.

[2] Boutin 2023, pp. 143–146.

system, claiming that 'the computer made a mistake'. This lack of accountability is equally problematic.

In order to address the issue of responsibility for AI failures, this chapter delves into the increasingly blurred lines between technical malfunctions and human errors in the context of AI systems. For the purpose of this chapter, the term 'AI failure' is used as an umbrella concept that includes what can be classified as a technical malfunction, what can be considered as a human error, as well as the ambiguous grey areas that lie between these two categories.[3] As AI systems become more autonomous, the distinction between human errors and system malfunctions becomes blurred, which in turn creates difficulties in assigning legal responsibility. Traditional categories and conceptualisations relying on human control at the stage of deployment are increasingly inadequate in dealing with the complexities of AI failures. This chapter explores how these emerging technologies force us to rethink and potentially revise legal frameworks, particularly in terms of how we qualify and assign responsibility for these failures.

The chapter adopts a conceptual and analytical methodology, grounded in doctrinal international law and informed by technical literature, to systematically examine how established legal principles, particularly due diligence obligations, apply to the complexities introduced by AI failures. It focuses on clarifying key legal concepts and proposes structured interpretations and operational recommendations within the existing international legal framework. In particular, it analyses how the structural challenges introduced by AI failures affect the conceptual foundations of due diligence obligations, and how these challenges reshape the interfaces between legal responsibility frameworks and technological unpredictability.

The chapter first discusses how to understand, conceptualise, and categorise errors and malfunctions in AI systems, exploring the specific challenges presented by the unique characteristics of ML-AI systems with respect to their unpredictability and ability to learn from data (Sect. 13.2). Second, the chapter outlines how international legal obligations applicable to States developing and/or using AI, particularly obligations of diligence, may be conceptually challenged by errors and malfunctions of ML-AI systems. Obligations of diligence are rooted in concepts of risk management, reasonableness, and foreseeability, which shape what can be expected of States in terms of ensuring that the development and deployment of AI systems align with international law. The chapter discusses how these principles can be interpreted in light of AI's inherent unpredictability and other features (Sect. 13.3). Third, the chapter assesses what it means for States to meet their obligations of diligence when AI systems are deployed in complex, high-risk environments. It explores the threshold of responsibility that States can bear, and the extent to which States are expected to foresee and prevent risks associated with AI failures. In doing so, it clarifies what constitutes negligence during the development stage of AI technologies,

[3] The term 'AI failure' is sometimes used to refer instead to cascading chains of events leading to a complete breakdown in a complex system's ability to perform its functions: Williams and Yampolskiy 2021; see also Cook 1998.

and when a human error should legally be considered within the bounds of reasonable conduct. Additionally, it addresses the role and limitations of supervisory and override functions, which allow human operators to intervene in cases of system error or failure, and the extent to which such functions can mitigate risks. Finally, the chapter proposes recommendations for technical and regulatory frameworks that can ensure AI systems are developed and deployed with sufficient safeguards to meet the obligations of international law (Sect. 13.4).

By exploring these issues, this chapter aims to provide a comprehensive framework for understanding the complexities of State responsibility in the context of AI errors and malfunctions. It offers insights into how legal frameworks can be interpreted and applied to the unique challenges posed by AI technologies, ensuring that States are held accountable for their actions and that AI systems are designed and used in a manner that adheres to international law obligations.

13.2 Understanding and Conceptualising Errors and Malfunctions in AI Systems

In the context of AI, the terms 'error', 'malfunction', and 'failure' lack standardised definitions and are interpreted differently across various fields of research, such as tort law, international law, philosophy, computer science, or AI safety. For the purposes of the argument advanced in this chapter, tentative definitions of (human) errors and (technical) malfunctions are proposed below (Sects. 13.2.1 and 13.2.2). Next, the chapter engages in a discussion of the blurred lines that AI creates between the two categories of errors and malfunctions (Sect. 13.2.3). As explained in the introduction above, the term AI failure is used in this chapter as an umbrella concept that includes errors, malfunctions, and what may fall in between.

13.2.1 (Human) Errors

Errors are defined here as instances where an AI system produces incorrect outputs, such as incorrect predictions, classifications, or recommendations. For instance, a facial recognition system misidentifying an individual would qualify as an AI error. Similarly, a situation where a credit scoring AI system assigns lower scores to certain demographic groups, leading to discriminatory loan approval outcomes, can also be considered to fall under the scope of AI errors. Another example would be an AI surveillance system mistakenly identifying peaceful political opponents as legitimate military targets. Errors typically arise from issues such as poor data quality, sloppy coding, or insufficient training. They often occur within the design parameters and can be causally traced to some form of negligence at the stage of development. In that sense, AI errors often relate to human errors at the development stage. Such AI errors result in unsatisfactory outcomes, but strictly speaking, the system performs in line with its intended functions and operates according to its design parameters, requirements, and limitations.[4]

Human errors can also arise at the stage of AI deployment, highlighting the challenges of human interaction with, and control over, complex systems.[5] These errors are often related to the limited control and supervision exercised by human operators, either due to the speed at which human operators are expected to supervise AI systems, or due to their limited understanding of the system's functioning.[6] First, ML-AI systems are typically complex and opaque, or not fully interpretable. Thus, human operators may struggle to grasp how the system makes decisions or produces outcomes. This lack of transparency, often referred to as the 'black box' problem, can lead to errors in judgement or inappropriate reliance on the AI system, with operators failing to intervene when the system behaves wrongly.[7] Second, in high-stakes environments, such as military operations, the speed at which human operators are tasked to supervise AI systems can often be unreasonably rapid. For example, in military targeting support systems, operators may be required to make rapid decisions based on AI recommendations without the time or capacity to fully evaluate the system's behaviour or underlying reasoning.[8] This pressure for quick decision making in supervising a system that operates at a speed and scale going beyond human cognitive abilities exacerbates the risks of human error, as operators may over-rely on the AI system or fail to notice discrepancies in its output. Such errors at the deployment stage thus arise due to unrealistic expectations placed on human supervision, while the system's speed and autonomy are prioritised.

13.2.2 (Technical) Malfunctions

Malfunctions in AI systems are defined here as disruptions to the system's normal operation caused by unforeseen or abnormal conditions. Malfunctions occur when the system behaves in a manner that deviates from expected patterns or intended functionality.[9] Traditionally, malfunctions in technical systems have been understood as arising from issues related to mechanical or hardware failures. In the age of AI, malfunctions encompass situations where the system operates in a way that is not aligned with its original purpose or design. Such behaviour may be difficult to

[4] Banerjee and Chanda 2020; Chanda and Banerjee 2024 (identifying and distinguishing errors of omission as design flaws, and errors of commission as implementation flaws, p. 937). See also Fresco and Primiero 2013, p. 256.

[5] Zerilli et al. 2019. See also the concept of 'ambiguity-based failure' put forward by Kerr and Kant, although these authors reject the terminology of 'human errors' as used in the field of human factors research: 2024, p. 11.

[6] Jones-Jang and Park 2022; Agudo et al. 2024.

[7] Castelvecchi 2016; Burrell 2016; Holland Michel 2020.

[8] Cummings 2004; Bo and Dorsey 2024.

[9] Floridi et al. 2015, pp. 1207–1208; Jespersen and Carrara 2011.

predict or understand, such as when the system exhibits erratic actions that were not anticipated. For example, an autonomous drone might malfunction by straying off course due to environmental interference, such as unexpected wind patterns or sensor errors. In the case of ML-AI, the underlying cause of such malfunctions can often be traced to the system's self-learning capabilities, which may lead it to behave in ways that were not intended by its developers. For instance, an AI system might develop unexpected behaviours based on its interactions with the environment, resulting in a performance that deviates sharply from what was originally intended. Another potential cause of AI malfunction arises from the susceptibility of ML systems to adversarial attacks, also known as spoofing. In such scenario, carefully crafted inputs are designed to exploit vulnerabilities in the AI model, leading it to make errors or produce unintended outputs.[10] These attacks can range from subtle perturbations in data that are imperceptible to humans but cause significant deviations in the performance of the AI system, to more overt manipulations that disrupt the system's functioning entirely. In that sense, AI malfunctions can be linked to technical or algorithmic problems that come about at the deployment stage and are *prima facie* beyond the realm of human control.

To further account for AI malfunctions, it is useful to understand the concept of emergent behaviour.[11] In the case of advanced ML-AI systems, such as reinforcement learning agents, the system may exhibit complex patterns or strategies that were not foreseen or foreseeable by the developers. These emergent behaviours arise as a consequence of the ML-AI system learning from its environment in ways that were not anticipated, potentially leading to outcomes that may be considered malfunctions. For instance, an AI system might develop a novel strategy to optimise its objectives, which could lead to unexpected or undesirable outcomes. Although these behaviours may not be the result of a purely technical failure, they can still result in the system acting in a way that deviates significantly from the intended functionality, and in that sense qualify as AI malfunctions.

AI malfunctions, whether arising from emergent behaviour or other causes, may manifest as unexpected outcomes or behaviours that significantly differ from the system's planned or expected performance. The causes of such failures can vary widely, ranging from hardware malfunctions to unforeseen algorithmic consequences. Additionally, external environmental factors, which the system may not have been trained to handle, can also lead to malfunction. For instance, an AI system deployed in a dynamic, real-world setting may encounter conditions that were not present in the training environment, causing it to fail in ways that were not anticipated. AI malfunctions thus usually emerge during the deployment stage, when the system is interacting with real-world data and environments.[12]

---

[10] Nguyen et al. 2015.

[11] Wei et al. 2022; Giardini et al. 2024.

[12] Writing from the perspective of international law, Seixas-Nunes adopts a different typology, with 'malfunctions' defined exclusively as hardware failures, which 'simply happen' and 'cannot necessarily be attributed to any human fault', 'accidents' designating situation of 'poor design, programming or maintenance… due to negligent or reckless behaviour… that it is traceable to

13.2.3 Blurred Lines

Given the inherent complexity of modern AI technologies, the distinction between errors and malfunctions in AI systems is far from straightforward. While the definitions of errors and malfunctions in the previous sections provide a useful conceptual starting point, the reality of AI systems, particularly those based on ML, introduces significant challenges.

The first key challenge relates to the unpredictability of certain AI systems and the unforeseeability of their behaviours once deployed. As explained above, ML-AI systems are capable of exhibiting behaviours that are difficult to foresee or fully explain due to the way they learn and adapt over time. Unlike traditional software systems, which behave according to explicitly programmed rules, ML-AI systems can evolve in ways that were not anticipated by their developers.[13] This intrinsic unpredictability makes it challenging to distinguish between what constitutes an unexpected malfunction of the system and what can be traced back to errors committed in the design of the system. The outcomes of these systems may deviate from the expected behaviour established during the design or testing stages, further complicating the classification of errors and malfunctions. This uncertainty raises difficult questions about what can reasonably be expected from developers during the design and development stages, particularly in terms of foreseeability. Determining whether an AI failure was caused by negligent actions or omissions at the stage of development (i.e., a breach of due diligence) becomes very difficult to ascertain. Given the unpredictable nature of these technologies, it is often unclear what should be considered foreseeable and what should be regarded as an unforeseeable outcome.[14]

The second key challenge pertains to the limited ability of developers to foresee the diverse circumstances, environments, and purposes for which an AI system might ultimately be deployed. When designing such systems, it is neither feasible nor reasonable to anticipate every possible use case, environment, or operational context. This challenge is intensified by the inherently multi-purpose nature of AI technologies. For instance, a facial recognition algorithm initially designed for policing applications in peaceful urban settings may be more prone to errors if deployed in an armed conflict zone with significant ethnic diversity, factors for which it may not have been trained. Similarly, an AI navigation system embedded within an autonomous aerial vehicle that was intended for temperate climates could encounter functional issues if deployed in heavy rain or extreme temperatures. By nature, a given AI system may be used in contexts vastly different from those anticipated during its design phase, making it impossible to account for every potential environmental and operational

a human fault', and 'errors' encompassing software failures leading to 'unlawful unpredictable results' and for which 'no human operative can be blamed', see Seixas-Nunes 2022, pp. 209–212. Jain uses the term error 'to refer to undesired, unintended, and unanticipated outcomes of the operation of AWS, regardless of their origin in programming error, algorithmic error, malfunction, human–machine interaction, human error, etc.', see Jain 2023, p. 1009.

13 Yampolskiy 2020; Holland Michel 2020.

14 Selbst 2020, p. 1342. See below Sect. 13.3.3.

variable. This unpredictability complicates the distinction between human errors in the development process and technical malfunctions arising during deployment.

The third key challenge in distinguishing between human errors and technical malfunctions concerns the limited human control and supervision over the deployment of certain AI systems.[15] When AI systems operate autonomously with minimal direct human oversight, it can make it difficult to differentiate between errors caused by human operators, errors linked to a flaw in the design of the system, and malfunctions arising from the AI system's operation. For instance, systems subject to limited human control due to the high speed at which operators are expected to supervise the system, or the intrinsic complexity and opacity of the system, may lead to outcomes that are incorrect or harmful. In these cases, it is challenging to determine what level of oversight and control can reasonably be expected from human operators to ensure compliance with international legal obligations, and therefore what can qualify as human errors at the stage of deployment. These uncertainties complicate the application of due diligence obligations and the assignment of responsibility in cases where AI failures cause harmful violations of international law.

13.3 Risk, Foreseeability, and Reasonableness in International Obligations of Due Diligence

The above section explored how the deployment of AI systems can lead to AI failures, resulting in problematic outcomes, including potential violations of international law. These failures may stem from human errors in design or use or from technical malfunctions. When it comes to AI, an interplay of factors complicates matters significantly, making it challenging to distinguish between issues caused strictly by human error and those arising from an AI system's malfunction. In that context, a crucial issue pertains to how to address these intricate situations within the framework of international law, particularly concerning State responsibility and obligations of due diligence to ensure that AI development and deployment comply with international legal standards.

Under international law, States are bound by due diligence obligations to ensure that AI systems are developed and deployed in a lawful manner.[16] Determining whether a breach of due diligence has occurred will hinge on assessing whether reasonable measures were taken to prevent and mitigate foreseeable risks associated with AI. However, the unique characteristics of ML-AI, such as its capacity to evolve and its inherent unpredictability, can reshape our understanding of what risks are foreseeable and what actions are reasonable. Issues such as the opacity, speed, and

[15] Zerilli et al. 2019.

[16] I refer to 'due diligence obligations' or 'obligations of due diligence' to indicate the category of international law obligations that are subject to a standard of due diligence. For a discussion of the nuances between 'obligation', 'standard', and 'principle' in the context of due diligence, see Besson 2023, pp. 61–67.

scale of ML-AI systems further complicate the question of what can reasonably be expected from both AI designers and operators. This section seeks to address these complexities, examining and clarifying how international law might approach the challenges posed by failures in modern AI systems. It first presents the concept of due diligence obligations in international law and highlights key provisions of IHL and IHRL applicable to the design and deployment of AI by States (Sect. 13.3.1). Next, it analyses key components and defining features of obligations of due diligence, which commonly rely on concepts of risk, foreseeability, and reasonableness (Sect. 13.3.2). Finally, it discusses how ML-AI may reconfigure our understanding of these concepts when applied to errors and malfunctions of AI systems (Sect. 13.3.2).

13.3.1 Due Diligence Obligations Relevant to the Development and Deployment of AI Systems

States are bound by both positive and negative obligations under international law. While negative obligations require States to refrain from certain prohibited actions, such as directly targeting civilians or detaining individuals arbitrarily, positive obligations impose a duty to take proactive measures to ensure that their organs and agents act in accordance with negative obligations. Negative obligations usually constitute obligations of result, meaning they are breached the moment a prohibited outcome occurs. In other words, if a State fails to achieve the prescribed result, it is considered in violation of its negative obligations. By contrast, positive obligations typically require States to take reasonable steps to promote and ensure compliance with the law. They embed obligations of conduct (also known as obligations of means), in the sense that a State is not automatically held responsible if the desired outcome is not achieved; rather it is responsible if it fails to take reasonable and appropriate steps to prevent violations. These positive obligations, therefore, incorporate a standard of due diligence, requiring the State to actively work towards compliance but not necessarily to guarantee a specific outcome in all cases.[17]

Obligations of due diligence are an important tool to promote legal compliance and to ensure respect for the law prior to harm being caused. Indeed, such obligations aim to prevent the occurrence of harmful outcomes, rather than reactively address the consequences of unlawful behaviour.[18] Instances of due diligence obligations can be

---

[17] Shelton and Gould 2013; Gerards 2023; Economides 2010; Pisillo-Mazzeschi 1992. There is no strict equivalence in the dichotomies between positive/negative obligations and between obligations of conduct/result, see Pisillo-Mazzeschi 1992, pp. 46–49; Economides 2010, p. 378; Besson 2023, p. 23; Berkes 2018, p. 434. For the purpose of the argument in this chapter, it suffices to note that negative obligations *usually* constitute obligations of result, and positive obligations *typically* embed obligations of conduct and incorporate a standard of due diligence.

[18] McDonald 2019; Peters et al. 2020. Theoretically, responsibility for a breach of due diligence can arise irrespective of any injury caused, as State responsibility is an objective framework solely requiring attribution and breach, see ILC 2001, Article 2. In practice, it is often necessary to demonstrate some degree of wrongful harm in order to prove that there was a failure of due diligence.

found in both IHL and IHRL, and these obligations are applicable not only in the deployment of AI systems, but also—crucially—throughout the lifecycle stages of design, development, and adoption.[19]

Under both IHL and IHRL, States have a general obligation to not only respect, but also ensure respect for IHL and IHRL, respectively. In IHL, Common Article 1 to the Geneva Conventions provides that States have the duty 'to respect and to ensure respect for' IHL.[20] The duty to respect denotes the negative dimension (to refrain from breaches of the Conventions), while the duty to ensure respect entails a positive 'obligation to prevent violations when there is a foreseeable risk that they will be committed and to prevent further violations in case they have already occurred'.[21] Under Common Article 1, States are 'required to take appropriate measures to prevent violations from happening in the first place' and 'must – starting in peacetime – take all measures necessary to ensure respect for the Conventions'.[22] The duty to ensure respect therefore 'constitutes a general duty of due diligence to prevent and repress breaches of the Conventions'.[23] The duty to ensure respect has both an internal dimension, requiring internal measures to prevent IHL violations by its armed forces,[24] and an external dimension, prescribing that States 'do everything reasonably in their power to ensure respect for the Conventions by others that are Party to a conflict'.[25]

In IHRL, Article 2(1) of the International Covenant on Civil and Political Rights (ICCPR) imposes a comparable obligation 'to respect and to ensure' human rights.[26] The positive obligation to ensure respect for human rights requires States to adopt 'appropriate measures' in order to protect individuals against human rights violations and to 'exercise due diligence to prevent, punish, investigate or redress the

[19] Boutin 2023, pp. 144–146.

[20] 'The High Contracting Parties undertake to respect and to ensure respect for the present Convention in all circumstances': Geneva Convention for the Amelioration of the Condition of the Wounded and Sick in Armed Forces in the Field, adopted 12 August 1949, entered into force 21 October 1950, 75 UNTS 31 Common Article 1.

[21] ICRC 2016, para 164.

[22] Ibid., para 145.

[23] Ibid., para 150. See also ILA 2014, p. 12.

[24] ICRC 2016, paras 145–146; Henckaerts and Doswald-Beck 2009, pp. 495–496. The principle of command responsibility, as set out in Article 87 of the Protocol Additional to the Geneva Conventions of 12 August 1949, and relating to the Protection of Victims of International Armed Conflicts, adopted 8 June 1977, entered into force 7 December 1978, 1125 UNTS 3 (API), prescribes a duty for commanders to take preventative measures to ensure that forces under their command are able to respect IHL, can also be read as a specification of the internal dimension of the general duty to ensure respect, see Henckaerts and Doswald-Beck 2009, p. 497; Berkes 2018, pp. 451–452.

[25] ICRC 2016, para 153.

[26] 'Each State Party to the present Covenant undertakes to respect and to ensure to all individuals within its territory and subject to its jurisdiction the rights recognized in the present Covenant, without distinction of any kind, such as race, colour, sex, language, religion, political or other opinion, national or social origin, property, birth or other status', International Covenant on Civil and Political Rights, opened for signature 16 December 1966, entered into force 23 March 1976, 999 UNTS 171 (ICCPR), Article 2(1).

harm caused by such acts'.[27] This obligation to prevent applies to both violations by organs or agents of the State (internal scope) and violations by third parties such as private persons or entities (external scope),[28] and is also applicable in situations of armed conflict, in complementarity with IHL.[29] In the framework of the European Convention on Human Rights (ECHR), the obligation under Article 1 to 'secure' human rights similarly entails a duty to protect and promote rights.[30] It 'requires States to take measures designed to ensure that individuals within their jurisdiction are not subjected to' human rights violations, and 'to take reasonable steps to avoid a risk of ill-treatment'.[31]

Next to the general obligation of Common Article 1, IHL contains a number of specific obligations of due diligence, often articulated indirectly,[32] with formulations such as 'to the maximum extent feasible',[33] or 'to the fullest extent practicable'.[34] In the context of the present chapter, it is useful to take note of due diligence obligations arising in relation to the principle of precaution,[35] which prescribes that States 'do everything feasible to verify' that attacks are not targeted at civilians or civilian objects, and to 'take all feasible precautions in the choice of means and methods of attack' in order to avoid or minimise incidental civilian damage.[36] Applied to military AI, the principle of precaution arguably involves a duty to ensure that military AI systems can make accurate targeting decisions, and that these systems are designed diligently with the aim to minimise incidental harm to civilians and civilian objects.

Article 36 of the Additional Protocol I to the Geneva Conventions can also be read as an obligation of due diligence.[37] It applies at the stage of development or acquisition of new means or methods of warfare and provides for a positive obligation to determine whether, at the future stage of deployment, the envisaged new means or method of warfare would, in some or all circumstances, be prohibited by any applicable rule of international law.[38] It consists in an obligation of diligent conduct as the State 'is not required to foresee or analyse all possible misuses',[39] but should

---

[27] UN Human Rights Committee 2004, paras 6–8.

[28] Ibid., para 8.

[29] Ibid., para 11.

[30] 'The High Contracting Parties shall secure to everyone within their jurisdiction the rights and freedoms defined in Section I of this Convention', Convention for the Protection of Human Rights and Fundamental Freedoms, opened for signature 4 November 1950, entered into force 3 September 1953, 213 UNTS 221 (ECHR) Article 1.

[31] European Court of Human Rights, *El-Masri v the Former Yugoslav Republic of Macedonia*, Judgment, 13 December 2012, No. 39630/09, para 198.

[32] Longobardo 2020, p. 184; ILA 2014, p. 11.

[33] API, above n. 24.

[34] Ibid., Article 10.

[35] For a detailed analysis of the due diligence dimension of the principle of precaution, see Longobardo 2020, p. 188–189.

[36] API, above n. 24, Article 57.

[37] Ibid., Article 36.

[38] Ibid.

[39] ICRC 1987, para 1469.

take reasonable steps to ensure that any envisaged new means of warfare can be deployed in compliance with international law. In the case of procurement from third parties, 'the purchaser should not blindly depend on the attitude of the seller or the manufacturer, but should proceed itself to evaluate' whether a new means of warfare can be used lawfully.[40] Applied to military AI, this arguably entails a duty to conduct rigorous testing and evaluation prior to any deployment, for instance, by simulating operational environments to evaluate how the system processes data and makes decisions under complex conditions.

13.3.2 Core Elements of Obligations of Due Diligence

Obligations of due diligence are inherently flexible and context sensitive,[41] and no single unified standard is applicable across the various regimes of international law.[42] Nevertheless, common trends and characteristics emerge across the diverse iterations of these obligations.[43] In particular, obligations of due diligence are commonly framed around a number of core elements which function as essential benchmarks for evaluating the adequacy of State conduct and determining the threshold of obligations in specific contexts. Essentially, due diligence obligations rely on fundamental concepts of risk, foreseeability, and reasonableness. Related ancillary notions that also come into play include knowledge, control, capacity, and causation.

First, the concept of risk is integral to understanding due diligence in international law. Due diligence obligations require States to act to prevent or mitigate risks of harm in violation of primary obligations. They arise in response to potential or actual risks that States are expected to address proactively.[44] In that sense, risk functions as a criterion to determine the scope of due diligence obligations in a given context. Further, the degree of due diligence to be exercised is commensurate with the extent and severity of a risk of a violation.[45] Accordingly, due diligence obligations are usually more stringent in high-risk scenarios. Placing risk as a central element of due diligence highlights its function as a preventive and adaptive standard aimed at promoting international legal compliance.

Second, foreseeability emerges as a key element in the determination of risks. The duty to ensure respect for international law and to prevent violations extends

---

[40] Ibid., para 1473.

[41] ILA 2016, p. 2; Pisillo-Mazzeschi 1992, p. 44; Berkes 2018, p. 444; Malaihollo and Lane 2024, p. 473.

[42] ILA 2016, p. 4.

[43] See also Besson 2023, p. 59, referring to 'a minimal regime common to the special regimes'.

[44] Peters et al. 2020, p. 2; Baade 2020, pp. 93–97; Violi 2020, p. 76; Longobardo 2020, p. 186; Malaihollo and Lane 2024, p. 464.

[45] ILA 2016, p. 12; Besson 2023, p. 123.

only to risks that are foreseeable.[46] Foreseeability refers to the ability to anticipate or predict that a particular event might occur based on the information and circumstances available at the time. States may breach their due diligence obligations if they fail to take preventative measures despite the existence of a foreseeable risk. Conversely, no breach of due diligence occurs when wrongful harm arises in circumstances that could not have been foreseen. In the case law of the European Court of Human Rights, the idea that responsibility only extends to foreseeable risks is reflected in the criterion of 'real and immediate risk',[47] whereby positive obligations arise in relation to scenarios that are not merely hypothetical or speculative.

Third, reasonableness operates as a fundamental criterion in the determination of whether there is a foreseeable risk, and what must be done to address it.[48] Reasonableness guides the evaluation of whether a risk should have been anticipated. It ensures that the concept of foreseeability is not applied in an overly rigid or subjective manner but instead reflects a balanced and context-sensitive standard. The dual function of reasonableness, defining both the foreseeability of risks and the appropriateness of responsive measures, underlines its integral role in shaping the contours of due diligence obligations. In sum, due diligence obligations require the State to take reasonable measures in order to prevent and mitigate risks that are reasonably foreseeable.

In order to assess the reasonable foreseeability of risks and thus the scope of due diligence obligations, the ancillary notions of knowledge, control, capacity, and causation come into play. First, the breach of due diligence obligations often hinges on whether the State had sufficient knowledge of the circumstances giving rise to the risk of violations.[49] This assessment takes into account the actual subjective knowledge of the State, but can also rely on an objective standard of constructive knowledge, i.e., what the State should have known.[50] The concept of constructive knowledge allows for the establishment of knowledge on the part of the State on the basis of objective elements such as available facts, patterns, or warning signs. It precludes States from hiding behind the argument that they were not aware of any risks in situations where they actively turned a blind eye to available facts.[51]

---

[46] Pisillo-Mazzeschi 1992, p. 44; Violi 2020, p. 77; Baade 2020, p. 98; Besson 2023, p. 59; Malaihollo and Lane 2024, pp. 464–465.

[47] European Court of Human Rights, *Osman v. United Kingdom, Judgment*, 28 October 1998, Application No. 23452/94, para 116.

[48] ILA 2016, p. 2; Peters et al. 2020, p. 2; Longobardo 2020, p. 184; Violi 2020, p. 76; Besson 2023, p. 107.

[49] ILA 2016, p. 11; Malaihollo and Lane 2024, p. 473.

[50] International Court of Justice, *Corfu Channel Case (United Kingdom v Albania)*, Merits, 9 April 1949, ICJ Reports 1949, p. 20; *Osman v United Kingdom*, see n. 46, para 116 (the well-established ECtHR standard infers a violation of positive obligations when 'the authorities knew or ought to have known at the time of the existence of a real and immediate risk'); Baade 2020, p. 99; Stoyanova 2020, p. 619; Besson 2023, p. 101.

[51] Writing in the context of aid or assistance in the law of state responsibility, Moynihan defined 'wilful blindness' as 'a deliberate effort… to avoid knowledge of illegality… in the face of credible evidence of present or future illegality', see Moynihan 2018, p. 461.

Instead, they are expected to actively seek and acquire the information necessary to make informed decisions.[52] The criterion of knowledge is integral to the risk-based nature of due diligence, where States have a duty to act on risks that are reasonably predictable. This does not demand perfect foresight but establishes a standard of reasonable awareness. This standard is critical for defining the scope of due diligence, as it compels States to anticipate and mitigate risks effectively within the limits of their reasonable knowledge.

Second, the extent of a State's control over the source of risk and its capacity to influence conduct are crucial benchmarks in determining the scope of due diligence obligations.[53] The duty to prevent violations under international law depends on the degree of control a State exercises over the actors or situations posing the risk. Obligations to prevent violations would not extend to third parties that are outside of the control of the State but fully apply to agents or third parties within the State's jurisdiction or under its control. The criterion of capacity denotes that responsibility for failure to prevent violations can arise to the extent that the State has the ability to effectively influence conduct and outcomes, usually based on a certain level of control.[54]

Third, causation serves as an implicit yet essential criterion for establishing a breach of due diligence obligations.[55] To uphold the responsibility of a State, a causal link must be established between its failure to act diligently and the occurrence of a violation. This requires demonstrating that the State's omission contributed to a risk materialising into a breach, and involves a degree of speculative counterfactual reasoning.[56] Causation in the context of omissions often hinges on whether the State failed to take measures which could have prevented or mitigated the outcome, without requiring that 'but for' the failure of the State, the wrongful outcome would not have materialised.[57] In situations where the State's inaction directly contributes to the likelihood of a breach occurring the causal connection becomes more tangible.

Taken together, these different core and ancillary elements of due diligence allow us to delineate the content of obligations of due diligence in specific contexts. As highlighted above, due diligence is a flexible and context-dependent standard of conduct. In this regard, it is important to note that the variability of due diligence depends on the interplay and interaction of the different elements.[58] The discussion above already reveals that the various elements and criteria are closely intertwined. Indeed, the existence of a risk depends on its degree of foreseeability, which in turn hinges on the knowledge that the State possesses or should reasonably acquire. Reasonableness, in turn, operationalises foreseeability by defining what a State could

---

[52] ILA 2016, pp. 6–7.

[53] Longobardo 2020, p. 186; Stoyanova 2018, p. 322; Besson 2023, pp. 121–122.

[54] Boutin 2017, p. 79.

[55] Ibid., p. 81; Stoyanova 2018; Malaihollo and Lane 2024, p. 473.

[56] Stoyanova 2018, p. 312.

[57] European Court of Human Rights, *E. and Others v. United Kingdom*, Judgment, 26 November 2002, Application No. 33218/96, para 99.

[58] Besson 2023, p. 120.

or should have reasonably known and outlining how it ought to respond. Furthermore, the dynamic nature of due diligence is also reflected in how these elements balance against one another. For instance, in situations of high risk and low foreseeability, the seriousness of potential harm justifies imposing a higher threshold of proactive due diligence.[59] Here, the State's obligation to seek knowledge becomes critical. Even if risks are not immediately obvious, States must demonstrate that they have taken all reasonable steps to identify and assess potential threats. Conversely, when foreseeability is high but the potential harm is low, States are expected to implement cost-effective measures to mitigate risks. Another example of the variability of due diligence is the impact of the degree of control and capacity of the State in determining the extent of its obligations of due diligence.[60] In all these complex scenarios, reasonableness serves as both a balancing tool and a calibrating criterion. It is used to determine what can reasonably be expected from the State in view of the severity of the risk, its likelihood of occurring (i.e., foreseeability), the degree of knowledge objectively available, the capacity of the State to prevent or mitigate the risk and to influence the occurrence of harmful outcomes, and the causal proximity between the conduct of the State and the materialisation of the risk.

13.3.3 Reconfiguring Obligations of Due Diligence in the Context of AI

The specific characteristics of ML-AI systems, particularly their complexity, autonomy, speed, and opacity, require a profound rethinking of due diligence obligations under international law. These systems raise unique concerns about concepts at the heart of due diligence, namely risk, foreseeability, reasonableness, knowledge, control, capacity, and causation. This section examines how these concepts are reconfigured and need to be reconceptualised in the context of AI technologies, and to what extent they are able to address the complex challenges of AI failures.

The first observation is that, as indicated in Sect. 13.3.2, the variability of due diligence and the interplay of its core elements mean that high-risk scenarios entail more stringent obligations of due diligence. Military AI systems exemplify this heightened risk profile, as they often operate within contexts of critical, life-and-death decision making where errors or malfunctions can result in catastrophic consequences. Within the context of military AI, certain applications (e.g., dynamic targeting in urban areas) entail higher risks than others (e.g., terrain analysis in remote areas).[61] When these systems incorporate ML capabilities, the risks are further increased due to the intrinsic opacity and unpredictability of ML-AI. As discussed in Sect. 13.2, ML-AI systems are prone to unforeseen behaviours and malfunctions (i.e., unpredictable conduct that diverges from their intended purpose or design). These risks result in a

[59] Malaihollo and Lane 2024, p. 473.

[60] Besson 2023, p. 118.

[61] Geiß 2021, p. 447.

heightened obligation to proactively prevent violations and to ensure compliance with international law.[62] The potential for military ML-AI systems to inflict large-scale harm through both errors and malfunctions reinforces the need for stringent due diligence standards at every stage of their lifecycle, from development and deployment to operational use.

Nonetheless, it remains highly unclear what can reasonably be expected of States when fulfilling their due diligence obligations in this context. The situation is marked by a significant tension. On the one hand, the high-risk nature of military ML-AI systems leads to a heightened standard of care, requiring States to be particularly cautious and proactive in preventing violations and ensuring compliance with international law. On the other hand, the complexity, opacity, and unpredictability of these systems make it increasingly difficult to foresee and address all potential wrongful outcomes, and thereby to effectively exercise due diligence. To navigate this tension, legal standards must be construed in a way that incentivises reliability and safety in the design and deployment of AI systems, promoting compliance with international law while accounting for the inherent characteristics and shortcomings of the technology.

One of the main challenges that AI brings to the core concepts of due diligence is determining what can and should be considered as reasonably foreseeable.[63] Traditional frameworks of due diligence are premised on the assumption that risks can be anticipated based on known variables and predictable outcomes. However, the adaptive and autonomous behaviour of ML-AI disrupts this assumption, making it increasingly difficult to determine the extent of what is reasonably foreseeable. Some malfunctions of AI systems are intrinsically unforeseeable due to the system's inherent unpredictability. This requires States to go beyond anticipating immediate risks, and to seek to assess potential long-term and emergent failures. At the stages of design and development, foreseeability is constrained by the inability of designers to predict all potential emergent behaviours or the diverse contexts in which a system might ultimately be deployed. Similarly, at the stage of deployment, operators and commanders cannot always reliably anticipate how a system will perform once launched. By contrast, during procurement and acquisition, there is more opportunity to assess an AI system's parameters and conditions against its envisaged use and environment. At this stage, States are able to evaluate and foresee whether sufficient safety guarantees are in place to ensure the system's lawful operation within a specific context.

Another significant difficulty concerns the limits of what can reasonably be controlled, and thus prevented, when dealing with AI systems. Concepts of control centred on direct human intervention at the deployment stage are increasingly inadequate for highly autonomous systems. Such systems, when operating at rapid speeds and on extensive scales, can exacerbate risks of over-reliance and oversight failures. Operators, particularly in high-pressure scenarios, may depend excessively on system outputs, even when discrepancies or system errors are apparent. Moreover, the

[62] Ibid; Jain 2023, pp. 1030–1031.

[63] Selbst 2020, p. 1342.

complexity and opacity of these systems often lead to unrealistic demands on operators, who are expected to interpret and respond to outputs from systems they cannot fully understand or control. This necessitates a reassessment of what constitutes reasonable control and capacity to influence, with human control extending beyond operational oversight to include safeguards at the pre-deployment stages. At the stage of AI design and development, human agents possess high control and a greater capacity to influence how systems operate. This allows for setting clear parameters, integrating mechanisms to mitigate risks, and ensuring resilience against malfunctions and adversarial manipulation. For instance, user-friendly interfaces, explainability features, and effective human supervision mechanisms can enhance safety and reliability of the system. However, even at the design stage, absolute control remains unattainable. Since developers cannot reasonably foresee every potential malfunction or emergent behaviour, particularly in the context of ML-AI, safeguards that promote reliability and provide all relevant parties with clear knowledge of a system's parameters, capacities, and limits are essential.

Knowledge thus emerges as a crucial element in delineating the scope of due diligence obligations in relation to military AI systems. The combination of high-risk applications with limited foreseeability and control due to the unpredictable nature of AI calls for a heightened duty to acquire knowledge. The inherent opacity and complexity of AI systems cannot be used as a pretext for avoiding fulfilling due diligence obligations and failing to meet standards of reasonableness. At the stage of procurement and adoption, States must take proactive steps to understand the limitations of these systems, including vulnerabilities that may arise in adversarial settings or in environments beyond the scope of the system's training data. This stage is particularly important for mitigating risks and ensuring compliance with international law. States have a duty to thoroughly assess and certify AI systems at the point of adoption, as well as to maintain ongoing risk assessments throughout deployment.[64] Conversely, in order to give effect to due diligence, designers of AI systems may be required to provide sufficient information regarding their functioning and parameters. Designers should be able to demonstrate that systems were rigorously designed and tested to minimise the likelihood of failures, thereby equipping States with the necessary understanding to make informed decisions during procurement and deployment.

Finally, causation constitutes a critical and complex issue in determining responsibility for AI failures. Establishing a sufficient causal link between the actions or omissions of various actors throughout the AI lifecycle and the resulting wrongful outcomes is inherently challenging. The interplay of human errors and technical malfunctions often results in multiple interrelated causes, making it difficult to identify the specific points at which negligence by a designer, operator, commander, or decision maker caused a wrongful outcome.[65] For instance, while coding errors during design may contribute to a malfunction, not all such errors can be considered proximate causes of a wrongful outcome. Similarly, human errors at the stage

[64] Bhuta and Pantazopoulos 2016, p. 290.

[65] Seixas-Nunes 2022, p. 192.

of deployment, such as a misjudgement by an operator, cannot always be causally linked to subsequent harmful violations.[66]

13.4 Ascertaining Obligations and Responsibility of States for Errors and Malfunctions of AI Systems

Having presented the various types of errors and malfunctions that may arise in relation to AI systems, as well as the legal framework of due diligence obligations, including how it is reconfigured in the AI context, this section now turns to the implications for ascertaining the obligations and responsibilities of States in addressing errors and malfunctions of AI systems. First, it tackles the question of allocation of responsibility in the case of errors or malfunctions, analysing situations in which negligence arises on the part of developers, operators, or military and governmental decision makers. It also discusses whether, in some scenarios, errors and malfunctions arguably cannot be traced back to a failure of due diligence and thus may result in a responsibility gap under the current international legal framework (Sect. 13.4.1). Second, it aims to specify in more detail the content of due diligence obligations, focusing on the respective standards of care required at the stages of development, adoption, and deployment of AI systems (Sect. 13.4.2). Third, it explores how due diligence in relation to AI failures can be further operationalised, discussing the need for risk assessment and certification procedures (Sect. 13.4.3).

13.4.1 Allocation of Responsibility in the Case of Errors or Malfunctions

The breach of a due diligence obligation engages the responsibility of the State when the negligent conduct that led to the breach is attributable to the State. Attribution of conduct denotes the operation whereby the actions and omissions of State organs, and persons or entities acting on behalf of the State, are considered an act of the State for the purpose of State responsibility.[67] If an error or malfunction can be traced back to the negligence of a human agent whose conduct is attributable to the State,[68] the State bears responsibility for the resulting failure of the AI system.[69]

---

[66] Selbst 2020, p. 1333; Boutin 2023, pp. 141–142.

[67] ILC 2001, Articles 4–11.

[68] The term 'negligence' is used here to designate a breach of due diligence, see Besson 2023, p. 21, not in the criminal law sense, which refers to a low level of criminal culpability.

[69] The author argued elsewhere that attribution of conduct necessarily requires a human element, and that the conduct of an AI system itself cannot and should not be directly attributed to the state. See Boutin 2023, pp. 139–143.

Errors, defined as instances where an AI system produces incorrect outputs or unsatisfactory outcomes but performs in line with its intended functions and operates according to its design parameters,[70] can typically be traced back to some form of human negligence, occurring at various stages and manifesting in different ways. Some errors can be traced back to negligence during the design and development of AI systems. Failure of due diligence at this stage can take many forms, including the use of incomplete or biased training data, poorly designed algorithms, or inadequate testing procedures.[71] These shortcomings may result in errors in the operation of the AI system, such as biased decision making, inaccurate predictions, or discriminatory outcomes. If the developers qualify as organs or agents of the State, their actions or omissions are attributable to the State, engaging its responsibility for a breach of due diligence. If developers come from the private sector and operate independently from the State, their conduct is not attributable to the State, but responsibility for errors caused by their negligence can be governed by domestic legal frameworks such as civil liability.[72] Nonetheless, if a faulty AI system developed in the private sector is adopted and used by State organs or agents, the State can bear responsibility for failures arising from the deployment of the system if it neglects its duty to verify and certify the system's reliability, safety, and susceptibility to errors. This constitutes a breach of due diligence by failing to proactively acquire reasonable knowledge of the system's design and functionality.

Errors of judgment by human operators supervising AI systems present unique challenges in assessing negligence. If operators are relegated to perfunctory approval roles or equipped solely with override or fail-safe functions to counter AI errors, it raises questions about their ability to exercise reasonable diligence. When a system is not designed to enable meaningful supervision, or when operators are tasked with making time-sensitive decisions in highly complex environments, the threshold for reasonableness may be significantly lowered. In such cases, an operator's failure to intervene may not constitute negligence if they lack a reasonable degree of control or capacity to influence the system's outputs.

When it comes to malfunctions, defined as disruptions to the system's normal operation caused by unforeseen or abnormal conditions, where the system behaves in a manner that deviates from expected patterns or intended functionality,[73] it can be more difficult to trace back AI failures to human negligence. Indeed, unpredictable emergent behaviours in AI systems challenge the concept of reasonable foreseeability, as such behaviours stretch the bounds of what can realistically be anticipated. Whether there is negligence on the part of developers will depend on the circumstances. For instance, if developers are aware that a commissioned AI system is intended for dynamic military targeting and still opt for ML-based self-learning techniques over more predictable, rule-based designs, it could constitute negligence. By contrast, if a system initially designed for general purposes is later repurposed for

[70] See Sect. 13.2.1 above.

[71] Seixas-Nunes 2022, p. 210.

[72] Panezi 2021. See also European Union 2022, Article 4.

[73] See Sect. 13.2.2 above.

military targeting, foreseeability on the part of the developer would be too limited to amount to negligence.

In cases where malfunctions arise due to unexpected environmental factors, such as unforeseen weather conditions or external interferences, developers cannot be deemed negligent, as unexpected factors are not reasonably foreseeable at the stage of development. However, negligence might rest with commanders or other decision-makers who decide to deploy the system despite having knowledge of the circumstances of deployment in unexpected conditions. These scenarios illustrate the blurred line between human negligence and technical malfunction, highlighting the complexities of assigning responsibility for AI failures.

Some AI malfunctions may be regarded as entirely unforeseeable, in which case it can be argued that no breach of due diligence occurred. Due diligence obligations, as obligations of conduct, require the exercise of reasonable efforts but do not extend to anticipating every conceivable situation. In such instances, no responsibility would arise under the current framework of due diligence. Addressing fully unforeseeable malfunctions may instead call for the adoption of a strict liability framework, where responsibility is assigned irrespective of negligence.[74]

In relation to either errors or malfunctions, negligence can also arise at the stage of adoption or deployment by governmental or military decision makers. The decision to adopt or deploy unpredictable AI systems that exhibit emergent behaviours, or systems not designed or trained for specific environmental circumstances, or systems over which direct operators can only have very limited control, can itself amount to a lack of due diligence. This is especially significant in high-risk contexts, such as dynamic targeting. The decision to use a system despite its susceptibility to errors or malfunctions reflects a failure to diligently foresee and prevent potential risks. Therefore, the adoption and deployment of AI technologies without sufficient risk assessment or mitigation strategies may itself constitute negligence.

13.4.2 Specifying the Content of Obligations of Due Diligence at the Stages of Development, Adoption, Deployment, and Use of AI Systems

Building on the preceding analysis, the following standards of care can be identified to fulfil due diligence obligations during the design, development, adoption, and deployment of AI systems. Each stage of the AI lifecycle demands specific actions to meet the obligations of due diligence. From rigorous design and testing to informed adoption and responsible deployment, these standards of care are crucial to ensuring the safe, reliable, and lawful use of AI systems in sensitive contexts such as military operations.

[74] On strict liability in the context of military AI, see Crootof 2016, pp. 1394–1396.

At the stage of design and development, due diligence requires adherence to high technical standards, including the use of high-quality and sufficiently diverse datasets to train AI systems. Ensuring the integrity of training processes is crucial for minimising biases and other systemic flaws. Preventive measures, such as rigorous testing, are essential to mitigate risks at every stage. For example, an algorithm intended for dynamic military targeting must be designed with particular care, prioritising predictability and reliability. In addition, developers should explicitly identify the system's limitations and delineate the purposes and conditions under which its performance has been tested. If developers qualify as State organs or agents, their due diligence obligations extend to acquiring knowledge about the specific contexts in which the system will be used. This knowledge should inform design choices, ensuring that the system meets operational and legal requirements. Conversely, when developers come from the private sector, the State bears responsibility to seek and acquire sufficient knowledge about the system.

At the stage of adoption and deployment, military and governmental decision makers must exercise due diligence through careful risk assessments.[75] This includes a duty to gather comprehensive information about the system's functionality, reliability, and parameters. Decision makers should assess risks associated with deployment in specific contexts and implement appropriate mitigation strategies. They must carefully evaluate whether deploying ML-AI systems in high-risk contexts, such as military operations, is reasonable, given the associated uncertainties and vulnerabilities. Decision makers must take into account a variety of risk factors,[76] including the system's opacity, the unpredictability of ML methods, the complexity or novelty of deployment environments, and the absence of demonstrated reliability under specific conditions. Additional considerations include the time-critical nature of decisions, cognitive overload on operators, and the potential for adversarial attacks. Balancing these factors in a reasonable manner is essential to fulfilling due diligence obligations. Risk assessment and certification procedures are critical tools at this stage.[77]

At the stage of operational use, due diligence entails exercising control over the system to the extent this is possible. Arguably, operator diligence entails flagging to superiors where control and capacity to influence are insufficient. Operators and supervisors should actively monitor the system's outputs and take corrective measures where necessary.

[75] Cummings 2019; Bhuta and Pantazopoulos 2016, pp. 291–293; Seixas-Nunes 2022, p. 191.

[76] Maas 2018.

[77] See Sect. 13.4.3 below.

13.4.3 Moving Forward: The Need for Risk Assessment and Certification Procedures

To operationalise and effectively implement standards of due diligence in the development and adoption of military AI systems, there is a pressing need for robust procedures and standards for risk assessment, testing, and certification.[78] These mechanisms are essential to ensure, before they are deployed in high-stakes environments, that AI systems are reliable, predictable, and compliant with legal obligations.

The standards required in this context are likely to be technical rather than strictly legal, focusing on establishing benchmarks for system design, testing, and performance evaluation. For instance, risk assessment frameworks could involve rigorous simulations to identify potential malfunctions or vulnerabilities. Certification processes might include independent audits to verify that AI systems meet defined safety and reliability criteria, particularly in dynamic and unpredictable operational contexts. Moreover, these procedures should account for the unique characteristics of ML systems, such as their opacity, capacity for emergent behaviours, and susceptibility to adversarial manipulation. This would necessitate standards that address issues such as data quality, algorithmic transparency, and the ability to override or halt operations in the event of unexpected system behaviour. Risk assessment frameworks should also include ongoing monitoring and recalibration to ensure systems remain reliable as operational environments evolve.

Implementing such standards would not only strengthen compliance with due diligence obligations but also provide a systematic way to identify and mitigate risks before deployment, thus reducing the likelihood of failures. The development of these technical standards should involve collaboration between legal, technical, and operational experts to ensure they are both effective and practical for the unique challenges posed by military AI systems.

13.5 Concluding Remarks

This chapter has examined the challenges of addressing responsibility for AI failures, particularly in light of State obligations of due diligence under international law. It has shown that the inherent characteristics of AI systems, especially those employing ML, complicate the application of traditional legal concepts such as negligence, foreseeability, and control. The distinction between human errors and technical malfunctions is increasingly blurred, raising questions about how responsibility can be allocated and how obligations of due diligence can be fulfilled. These complexities demand a rethinking of how the foundational concepts underpinning obligations of due diligence are understood and operationalised. A central theme throughout the analysis is the unpredictability of AI systems, which challenges the application of established

[78] Cummings 2019; Bhuta and Pantazopoulos 2016, pp. 291–293; Seixas-Nunes 2022, p. 191.

legal standards. This unpredictability, particularly in ML-AI, raises critical questions about what risks can be reasonably foreseen and what measures can be considered adequate to mitigate them.

Due diligence obligations require States to take reasonable measures to anticipate and mitigate foreseeable risks. The analysis has shown that as AI systems introduce novel uncertainties, they require more proactive efforts to manage risks at every stage of the AI lifecycle. At the design and development stage, this includes adhering to rigorous technical standards, ensuring diverse and high-quality datasets, and implementing robust testing. At the adoption and deployment stage, decision makers must critically assess risks and weigh the suitability of AI systems for high-risk contexts, particularly where unpredictability or operator limitations could exacerbate harm. By framing these obligations across the AI lifecycle, the chapter demonstrates the importance of a comprehensive approach that integrates legal, technical, and operational considerations. This approach also shows that the duty to ensure compliance is not confined to a single actor or moment but is distributed across developers, decision makers, and operators.

As AI systems become increasingly integral to military and other high-stakes applications, States face the urgent task of addressing the unique challenges posed by their unpredictability and complexity. By adopting robust legal interpretations and technical standards, States can ensure that AI systems are developed and deployed in a manner that complies with international law, prevents harm, and maintains accountability.

References

Articles, Books and Other Documents

Agudo U, Liberal KG, Arrese M, Matute H (2024) The Impact of AI Errors in a Human-in-the-Loop Process. Cognitive Research: Principles and Implications. https://doi.org/10.1186/s41235-023-00529-3

Atherton K (2022) Understanding the Errors Introduced by Military AI Applications. https://www.brookings.edu/techstream/understanding-the-errors-introduced-by-military-ai-applications. Accessed 1 April 2025

Baade B (2020) Due Diligence and the Duty to Protect Human Rights. In: Krieger H, Peters A, Kreuzer L (eds) Due Diligence in the International Legal Order. Oxford University Press, Oxford, pp. 92–108

Banerjee DN, Chanda SS (2020) AI Failures: A Review of Underlying Issues. arXiv. https://doi.org/10.48550/arXiv.2008.04073

Berkes A (2018) The Standard of 'Due Diligence' as a Result of Interchange between the Law of Armed Conflict and General International Law. Journal of Conflict and Security Law. https://doi.org/10.1093/jcsl/kry022

Besson S (2023) Due Diligence in International Law. Collected Courses of The Hague Academy of International Law. Brill, Leiden

Bhuta N, Pantazopoulos S-E (2016) Autonomy and Uncertainty: Increasingly Autonomous Weapons Systems and the International Legal Regulation of Risk. In: Bhuta N, Beck S, Geiβ

R, Liu H-Y, Kreβ C (eds) Autonomous Weapons Systems: Law, Ethics, Policy. Cambridge University Press, Cambridge, pp. 284–300
Bo M, Dorsey J (2024) The 'Need' for Speed – The Cost of Unregulated AI Decision-Support Systems to Civilians. https://opiniojuris.org/2024/04/04/symposium-on-military-ai-and-the-law-of-armed-conflict-the-need-for-speed-the-cost-of-unregulated-ai-decision-support-systems-to-civilians. Accessed 1 April 2025
Boutin B (2017) Responsibility in Connection with the Conduct of Military Partners. Military Law and Law of War Review. https://doi.org/10.4337/mllwr.2017.01.03
Boutin B (2023) State Responsibility in Relation to Military Applications of Artificial Intelligence. Leiden Journal of International Law. https://doi.org/10.1017/S0922156522000607
Burrell J (2016) How the Machine 'Thinks': Understanding Opacity in Machine Learning Algorithms. Big Data & Society. https://doi.org/10.1177/2053951715622512
Castelvecchi D (2016) Can We Open the Black Box of AI? Nature News. https://www.nature.com/news/can-we-open-the-black-box-of-ai-1.20731. Accessed 1 April 2025
Chanda SS, Banerjee DN (2024) Omission and Commission Errors Underlying AI failures. AI & Society. https://doi.org/10.1007/s00146-022-01585-x
Cook RI (1998) How Complex Systems Fail. https://www.adaptivecapacitylabs.com/HowComplexSystemsFail.pdf. Accessed 1 April 2025
Crootof R (2016) War Torts: Accountability for Autonomous Weapons. University of Pennsylvania Law Review 164:1347-1402.
Cummings ML (2004) Automation Bias in Intelligent Time Critical Decision Support Systems. https://doi.org/10.2514/6.2004-6313. Accessed 1 April 2025
Cummings ML (2019) Lethal Autonomous Weapons: Meaningful Human Control or Meaningful Human Certification? IEEE Technology and Society Magazine. https://doi.org/10.1109/MTS.2019.2948438
Economides CP (2010) Content of the Obligation: Obligations of Means and Obligations of Result. In: Crawford J, Pellet A, Olleson S, Parlett K (eds) The Law of International Responsibility. Oxford University Press, pp. 371–382
European Union (2022) Proposal for a Directive of the European Parliament and of the Council on Adapting Non-Contractual Civil Liability Rules to Artificial Intelligence (AI Liability Directive). https://eur-lex.europa.eu/legal-content/EN/TXT/?uri=CELEX%3A52022PC0496. Accessed 1 April 2025
Floridi L, Fresco N, Primiero G (2015) On Malfunctioning Software. Synthese. https://doi.org/10.1007/s11229-014-0610-3
Fresco N, Primiero G (2013) Miscomputation. Philosophy & Technology. https://doi.org/10.1007/s13347-013-0112-0
Geiß R (2021) State Control Over the Use of Autonomous Weapon Systems: Risk Management and State Responsibility. In: Bartels R, van den Boogaard JC, Ducheine PAL, Pouw E, Voetelink J (eds) Military Operations and the Notion of Control Under International Law. T.M.C. Asser Press, The Hague, pp. 439–450
Gerards J (2023) General Principles of the European Convention on Human Rights, 2nd edn. Cambridge University Press, Cambridge
Giardini GSY, Hardy II JFH, da Cunha CR (2024) Evolving Neural Networks Reveal Emergent Collective Behavior from Minimal Agent Interactions. arXiv. https://doi.org/10.48550/arXiv.2410.19718
Henckaerts J-M, Doswald-Beck L (2009) Customary International Humanitarian Law, Volume 1: Rules. Cambridge University Press, New York
Holland Michel A (2020) The Black Box, Unlocked: Predictability and Understandability in Military AI. https://unidir.org/files/2020-09/BlackBoxUnlocked.pdf. Accessed 1 April 2025
International Committee of the Red Cross (ICRC) (1987) Commentary on the Additional Protocols of 8 June 1977 to the Geneva Conventions of 12 August 1949. Martinus Nijhoff, Geneva
International Committee of the Red Cross (ICRC) (2016) Commentary on the First Geneva Convention. Cambridge University Press, Cambridge

International Law Association (ILA) (2014) Study Group on Due Diligence in International Law, First Report. https://www.ila-hq.org/en_GB/documents/first-report-washington-dc-2014. Accessed 1 April 2025

International Law Association (ILA) (2016) Study Group on Due Diligence in International Law, Second Report. https://www.ila-hq.org/en_GB/documents/draft-study-group-report-johannesburg-2016. Accessed 1 April 2025

International Law Commission (ILC) (2001) Draft Articles on the Responsibility of States for Internationally Wrongful Acts (ARSIWA). https://legal.un.org/ilc/texts/instruments/english/draft_articles/9_6_2001.pdf. Accessed 1 April 2025

Jain AG (2023) Autonomous Weapon Systems, Errors and Breaches of International Humanitarian Law. Journal of International Criminal Justice. https://doi.org/10.1093/jicj/mqad043

Jespersen B, Carrara M (2011) Two Conceptions of Technical Malfunction. Theoria. https://doi.org/10.1111/j.1755-2567.2010.01092.x

Jones-Jang SM, Park YJ (2022) How Do People React to AI Failure? Automation Bias, Algorithmic Aversion, and Perceived Controllability. Journal of Computer-Mediated Communication. https://doi.org/10.1093/jcmc/zmac029

Kerr E, Kant V (2024) Clarifying the Nature of Failure in Sociotechnical Systems: Ambiguity-Based Failure and Expectation-Based Failure. Theoretical Issues in Ergonomics Science. https://doi.org/10.1080/1463922X.2022.2144961

Longobardo M (2020) Due Diligence in International Humanitarian Law. In: Krieger H, Peters A, Kreuzer L (eds) Due Diligence in the International Legal Order. Oxford University Press, pp. 183-199

Maas MM (2018) Regulating for 'Normal AI Accidents': Operational Lessons for the Responsible Governance of Artificial Intelligence Deployment. https://doi.org/10.1145/3278721.3278766

Malaihollo M, Lane L (2024) Mapping Out Due Diligence in Regional Human Rights Law: Comparing Case Law of the European Court of Human Rights and the Inter-American Court of Human Rights. Leiden Journal of International Law. https://doi.org/10.1017/S0922156524000050

McDonald N (2019) The Role of Due Diligence in International Law. International & Comparative Law Quarterly https://doi.org/10.1017/S0020589319000344

Moynihan H (2018) Aiding and Assisting: The Mental Element under Article 16 of the International Law Commission's Articles on State Responsibility. International and Comparative Law Quarterly. https://doi.org/10.1017/S0020589317000598

Nguyen A, Yosinski J, Clune J (2015) Deep Neural Networks are Easily Fooled: High Confidence Predictions for Unrecognizable Images. https://doi.org/10.1109/CVPR.2015.7298640

Panezi A (2021) Liability Rules For AI-Facilitated Wrongs: An Ecosystem Approach to Manage Risk and Uncertainty. SSRN. https://doi.org/10.2139/ssrn.3768779

Peters A, Krieger H, Kreuzer L (2020) Due Diligence in the International Legal Order: Dissecting the Leitmotif of Current Accountability Debates. In: Krieger H, Peters A, Kreuzer L (eds) Due Diligence in the International Legal Order. Oxford University Press, pp. 1–19

Pisillo-Mazzeschi R (1992) The Due Diligence Rule and the Nature of the International Responsibility of States. German Yearbook of International Law 35:9–51

Seixas-Nunes A (2022) The Legality and Accountability of Autonomous Weapon Systems: A Humanitarian Law Perspective. Cambridge University Press, Cambridge

Selbst AD (2020) Negligence and AI's Human Users. Boston University Law Review 100:1315–1552

Shelton D, Gould A (2013) Positive and Negative Obligations. In: Shelton D (ed) The Oxford Handbook of International Human Rights Law. Oxford University Press, pp. 562–584

Stoyanova V (2018) Causation Between State Omission and Harm Within the Framework of Positive Obligations under the European Convention on Human Rights. Human Rights Law Review. https://doi.org/10.1093/hrlr/ngy004

Stoyanova V (2020) Fault, Knowledge and Risk Within the Framework of Positive Obligations under the European Convention on Human Rights. Leiden Journal of International Law. https://doi.org/10.1017/S0922156520000163

UN Human Rights Committee (2004) General Comment No 31 (80), The Nature of the General Legal Obligation Imposed on States Parties to the Covenant, UN Doc CCPR/C/21/Rev.1/Add.13.

Violi F (2020) The Function of the Triad 'Territory', 'Jurisdiction', and 'Control' in Due Diligence Obligations. In: Krieger H, Peters A, Kreuzer L (eds) Due Diligence in the International Legal Order. Oxford University Press, pp. 75–91.

Wei J, Tay Y, Bommasani R et al. (2022) Emergent Abilities of Large Language Models. arXiv. https://doi.org/10.48550/arXiv.2206.07682

Williams R, Yampolskiy R (2021) Understanding and Avoiding AI Failures: A Practical Guide. Philosophies. https://doi.org/10.3390/philosophies6030053

Yampolskiy R (2020) Unpredictability of AI: On the Impossibility of Accurately Predicting All Actions of a Smarter Agent. Journal of Artificial Intelligence and Consciousness. https://doi.org/10.1142/S2705078520500034

Zerilli J, Knott A, Maclaurin J, Gavaghan C (2019) Algorithmic Decision-Making and the Control Problem. Minds & Machines. https://doi.org/10.1007/s11023-019-09513-7

Bérénice Boutin is a Senior Researcher in International Law at the Asser Institute, University of Amsterdam (The Netherlands). She leads the DILEMA project on Designing International Law and Ethics into Military Artificial Intelligence, for which she secured a grant of over €600,000 from the Dutch Research Council (NWO). Her research explores the interplay between new technologies, such as artificial intelligence, and international law. This includes examining how international law shapes the governance and regulation of emerging technologies, as well as how these technologies challenge core notions and concepts of international law.